The Animation Studies Reader

The Animation Studies Reader

Edited by
Nichola Dobson,
Annabelle Honess Roe,
Amy Ratelle and Caroline Ruddell

BLOOMSBURY ACADEMIC
NEW YORK · LONDON · OXFORD · NEW DELHI · SYDNEY

BLOOMSBURY ACADEMIC
Bloomsbury Publishing Inc
1385 Broadway, New York, NY 10018, USA
50 Bedford Square London, WC1B 3DP, UK

BLOOMSBURY, BLOOMSBURY ACADEMIC and the Diana logo are
trademarks of Bloomsbury Publishing Plc

First published in the United States of America 2019

A catalog record for this book is available from the Library of Congress.

ISBN: HB: 978-1-5013-3261-6
       PB: 978-1-5013-3260-9
       ePDF: 978-1-5013-3262-3
       eBook: 978-1-5013-3263-0

Typeset by Integra Software Services Pvt. Ltd.
Printed and bound in the United States of America

To find out more about our authors and books visit www.bloomsbury.com
and sign up for our newsletters.

CONTENTS

LIST OF FIGURES

LIST OF CONTRIBUTORS

Lisa Bode is Senior Lecturer in Film and Television Studies at the University of Queensland. Her research focuses on intersections between digital animation and live-action cinema, photorealism in animation, screen performance, visual effects, posthumous stardom and cultural reception. She is the author of *Making Believe: Screen Performance and Special Effects in Popular Cinema* (Rutgers University Press, 2017) and she has published in *animation: an interdisciplinary journal*, *Cinema Journal*, and various edited collections.

Malcolm Cook is Lecturer in Film at the University of Southampton. He has published a number of chapters and articles on animation, early cinema and their intermedial relationships. His book *Early British Animation: From Page and Stage to Cinema Screens* will be published by Palgrave Macmillan in 2018. His forthcoming work includes research into the use of music in Len Lye's British films, the role of advertising in the formation of Aardman Animations and the place of singalong films in early cinema. He is currently preparing (with Kirsten Thompson) an edited collection on the relationships between animation and advertising.

Amy M. Davis is Lecturer in Film and Animation Studies at the University of Hull, where she teaches (among other things) modules on American Animation History and Disney Studies. She is the author of *Good Girls & Wicked Witches: Women in Disney's Feature Animation* (John Libbey & Co., 2006) and *Handsome Heroes & Vile Villains: Men in Disney's Feature Animation* (John Libbey & Co., 2013), as well as various papers on Disney, US animation and horror.

Rayna Denison is Senior Lecturer in Film, Television and Media Studies at the University of East Anglia, where she teaches and does research into contemporary animation and film, particularly Japanese animation and Asian film. She is the author of *Anime: A Critical Introduction* (Bloomsbury, 2015), and is the editor of *Princess Mononoke: Understanding Studio Ghibli's Monster Princess* (Bloomsbury, 2018). She is the co-editor for the Eisner Award nominated *Superheroes on World Screens* (with Rachel Mizsei-Ward, University of Mississippi Press, 2015).

Nichola Dobson is Teaching Fellow in Design and Screen Cultures at Edinburgh College of Art. Founding editor of *Animation Studies* (2006–11) and *Animation Studies 2.0* (2012–present), she has published on animation, television genre and fan fiction, including *Norman McLaren: Between the Frames* (2018) for Bloomsbury and *Historical Dictionary of Animation and Cartoons* (2009) for Scarecrow Press. She is currently working on a book on TV animation with Paul Ward for Edinburgh University Press. She is currently President of the Society for Animation Studies.

Tom Gunning is the Edwin A. and Betty L. Bergman Distinguished Service Professor in the Departments of Art History, Cinema and Media Studies, and the College at the University of Chicago. He is the author of books including *D.W. Griffith and the Origins of American Narrative Film* (University of Illinois Press) and *The Films of Fritz Lang: Allegories of Vision and Modernity* (British Film Institute). He has published over 150 articles on early cinema, film history and theory, avant-garde film, film genre, and the relation between cinema and modernism. With Andre Gaudreault he originated the influential theory of the 'Cinema of Attractions'. In 2009, he was the first film scholar to receive an Andrew A. Mellon Distinguished Achievement Award, and in 2010, he was elected to the American Academy of Arts and Sciences.

Eric Herhuth is Assistant Professor of Communication at Tulane University. His research areas include animation and film studies, aesthetics and politics, media and film theory, and modernity and globalization. He has published in the *Quarterly Review of Film and Video, Cinema Journal, animation: an interdisciplinary journal*, and *Theory & Event*, and he is the author of *Pixar and the Aesthetic Imagination: Animation, Storytelling, and Digital Culture* (University of California Press, 2017).

Christopher Holliday teaches Film Studies and Liberal Arts at King's College London specializing in film genre, international film history and contemporary digital media. He has published several book chapters and articles on digital technology and computer animation, including work in *Animation Practice, Process & Production* and *animation: an interdisciplinary journal*. He is the author of *The Computer-Animated Film: Industry, Style and Genre* (Edinburgh University Press, 2018), and co-editor of *Fantasy/Animation: Connections Between Media, Mediums and Genres* (Routledge, 2018) for Routledge's AFI Film Readers series that examines the historical, cultural and theoretical points of intersection between fantasy and animation.

Annabelle Honess Roe is Senior Lecturer in Film Studies at the University of Surrey. She is the author of *Animated Documentary* (Palgrave 2013), which was the recipient of the Society for Animation Studies' 2015 McLaren-Lambart award for best book. She is co-editor of *Vocal Projections: Voices in*

Documentary (Bloomsbury, forthcoming) and editor of *Beyond Stop Motion Film: Production, Style and Representation in Aardman Animations* (I.B. Tauris, forthcoming) and has published in journals including the *Journal of British Cinema and Television* and *animation: an interdisciplinary journal*.

Lilly Husbands has a PhD from Kings College, London and teaches contextual studies, animation theory and digital cultures at Royal College of Art, University of Arts London and Middlesex University. She has published articles and book chapters on experimental animation. She is currently co-editing a book entitled *Experimental Animation: From Analogue to Digital*, forthcoming from Routledge and is Associate Editor for the Sage journal *animation: an interdisciplinary journal*.

Alison Reiko Loader is a lapsed National Film Board of Canada animation director who specializes in digital animation, old optical technology and media installation. With fellowships from the Social Sciences and Humanities Research Council of Canada and other agencies, her PhD in Communication Studies brings together her interests in feminist media history, the moving image and scientific visual culture. She has taught studio and graduate seminars in Fine Arts at Concordia University in Montreal since 2001 and has helped mentor 3D Animation and CGI students down the street at Dawson College, as a part of their teaching team since 2010.

Mihaela Mihailova is Postdoctoral Fellow in Film Studies in the Department of English at Michigan State University. Mihaela's research interests include animation, film and media theory, early Soviet cinema, contemporary Eastern European cinema, video games and comics. She has published articles in *animation: an interdisciplinary journal, Studies in Russian and Soviet Cinema, Post Script: Essays in Film and the Humanities* and *Kino Kultura*. She has also contributed chapters to *Animating Film Theory* (ed. Karen Beckman) (co-written with John MacKay) and *Animated Landscapes: History, Form, and Function* (ed. Chris Pallant).

Van Norris has been Senior Lecturer in Film, Media and Animation History and Theory Studies at the School of Media and Performing Arts, University of Portsmouth since 2003, where he has taught on Animation history and theory, Post-Classical Hollywood cinema, British and American comedy forms and the graphic narrative form. Despite writing extensively on science fiction television, US superhero movies, comedy cinema and cinema soundtracks for various edited collections, his research has been dominated by discussions of animation formally, industrially and culturally. This ranges from contributions to *animation: an interdisciplinary journal* and *Animation Studies* and a 2014 monograph for Palgrave, *British Television Animation 1997–2010: Drawing on Comic Tradition*.

Chris Pallant, Senior Lecturer, Canterbury Christ Church University, is the author of *Demystifying Disney* (2011), *Storyboarding: A Critical History* (2015) and editor of *Animated Landscapes: History, Form and Function* (2015) and *Animation: Collected Published Writings* (2018). He is also the founding series editor of Bloomsbury's *Animation: Key Films/Filmmakers* (launching 2018). Chris has published on a range of topics, including the 'cartoonism' of Tarantino's films, performance capture technology, the animated landscape of New York, and the work of Rockstar Games. He currently serves as Vice-President for the Society for Animation Studies and is Festival Director for Canterbury Anifest.

Amy Ratelle is the editor of *Animation Studies*, the online peer-reviewed journal of the Society for Animation Studies (SAS). She received her PhD in Communication and Culture, a joint programme between Ryerson University and York University, and degrees in Film Studies from Ryerson University (BFA), and Carleton University (MA). Her monograph *Animality and Children's Literature and Film* was published by Palgrave Macmillan in 2015. Her research areas include animation, animality studies, children's literature and culture, and critical media studies. She is currently an academic administrator at the Faculty of Arts and Science at the University of Toronto.

Caroline Ruddell is Senior Lecturer in Film and Television at Brunel University London. Before this, she taught film, television and popular culture at St. Mary's University, Strawberry Hill. She specializes in film theory, representation onscreen and animation, and has published widely in these areas. Caroline is currently researching Lotte Reiniger's silhouette films and craft-based, handmade animation. She is Associate Editor for *animation: an interdisciplinary journal* and sits on various Editorial Boards.

Nicholas Sammond is Associate Professor of Cinema Studies at the University of Toronto. He is the author of *Babes in Tomorrowland: Walt Disney and the Making of the American Child, 1930–1960* (Duke University Press, 2005), and edited and contributed to *Steel Chair to the Head: The Pleasure and Pain of Professional Wrestling* (Duke University Press, 2005). Nic's most recent book is *Birth of an Industry: Blackface Minstrelsy and the Rise of American Animation* (Duke University Press, 2015). His next major project, on abjection and resistance, includes an edited volume, *The Abject Objection*, and the monograph *Fluid Resistance*, which examines abjection in Cold War vernacular media.

Paul Taberham is Senior Lecturer in Animation Studies at the Arts University Bournemouth. He received his PhD in 2013 from the University of Kent, and is the author of *Lessons in Perception: The Avant-Garde Filmmaker as Practical Psychologist* (2018). In addition, he is the co-editor of *Cognitive Media*

Theory (2014) and *The New Experimental Animation: From Analogue to Digital* (2018). Paul has appeared on radio, spoken internationally at conferences and has published articles for several edited collections and journals. He also serves as a fellow for The Society for Cognitive Studies of the Moving Image.

Victoria Grace Walden is a full-time teaching fellow in media and film studies at the University of Sussex. She has written extensively about Holocaust memory and animation, and her main research interest is film philosophy. Her forthcoming book explores how the gaps between images, media and bodies in intermedial projects about the Holocaust, including animations, encourage the spectator to engage in the production of Holocaust memory as they provoke affect and imagination during the screening.

Paul Ward is Professor of Animation Studies at the Arts University Bournemouth, UK. His research interests include animated documentary, TV animation and the relationship between animation theory, practice and pedagogy. He is the co-editor (with Caroline Ruddell) of the new book series *Palgrave Animation*. He has given invited and keynote presentations at conferences and festivals in the UK, Switzerland, Denmark, South Korea and the Netherlands, and has been a Visiting Professor at the Politecnico di Milano, Italy. His work has been translated into German, Czech, Korean, Farsi and Japanese. He was President of the Society for Animation Studies for five years from 2010 to 2014.

Aylish Wood is Professor of Animation and Film Studies at the University of Kent. She has published articles in *Screen, New Review of Film and Video, Journal of Film and Video, Games and Culture, Film Criticism* and *animation: an interdisciplinary journal*. Her books include *Technoscience in Contemporary American Film* (2002); *Digital Encounters* (2007) a cross-media study of digital technologies in cinema, games and installation art; and *Software, Animation and the Moving Image: What's in the Box* (2015), a study of intersections between software and the production of moving images, encompassing games, animations, visual effects cinema and science visualizations.

ACKNOWLEDGEMENTS

We are grateful to our contributors of new material: Lisa Bode, Malcolm Cook, Eric Herhuth, Christopher Holliday, Lilly Husbands, Mihaela Mihailova, Chris Pallant, Paul Taberham and Victoria Grace Walden who have provided us with such excellent chapters. Also, thanks to the authors of our reprint chapters, Amy M. Davis, Rayna Denison, Tom Gunning, Van Norris, Alison Reiko Loader, Nicholas Sammond, Paul Ward and Aylish Wood, for writing such seminal work. We are privileged to include all of this scholarship in our new collection and are proud to be in such fine company.

We would like to acknowledge Georgia Kennedy of Bloomsbury Press who patiently listened to us set out our vision during the Society for Animation Studies Conference in Canterbury in 2015 and who encouraged us to push forward with our plans for this book. Thanks to the team at Bloomsbury, Erin Duffy, Susan Krogulski and our Editor Katie Gallof who have provided guidance and support. Thanks also to the Society for Animation Studies, to members old and new for their friendship, scholarship and inspiration, and excellent annual conferences; we would probably not have met without them.

Last but absolutely not least we are grateful for the support from all of our colleagues, friends and particularly our families. We thank them and dedicate this book to them.

The editors are grateful to the following organizations and publications for their kind permission to allow previously published material to be re-printed here. Chapter 2 (Tom Gunning, 'The Cinema of Attractions: Early Film, Its Spectator and the Avant-Garde') was first published in *Wide Angle* 8(3–4), 1986. Chapter 3 (Aylish Wood, 'Re-Animating Space') was first published in *animation: an interdisciplinary journal* 1(2), 2006. Chapter 8 (Paul Ward, 'Some Thoughts on Theory-Practice Relationships in Animation Studies') was first published in *animation: an interdisciplinary journal* 1(2), 2006. Chapter 9 (Annabelle Honess Roe, 'Absence, Excess and Epistemological Expansion: Towards a Framework for the Study of Animated Documentary') was first published in *animation: an interdisciplinary journal* 6(3), 2011. Chapter 17 (Nicholas Sammond, 'Race, Resistance and Violence in Cartoons') is an abridged and edited version of Chapter 4 ('Race') from *Birth of an Industry: Blackface Minstrelsy and the Rise of American Animation* (Duke

University Press, 2015). Chapter 18 (Alison Loader, 'We're Asian: More Expected of Us: Representation, The Model Minority & Whiteness on *King of the Hill*') was first published in *Animation Studies* 5 (2010). Chapter 20 (Rayna Denison, 'Anime's Bodies') was first published in *Anime: A Critical Introduction* (Bloomsbury, 2015). Chapter 21 (Amy M. Davis, 'Women in Disney's Animated Features 1989–2005') is an abridged version of chapter 6 ('The Disney Films 1989–2005: The Eisner Era') from *Good Girls and Wicked Witches: Changing Representations of Women in Disney's Feature Animation, 1937–2001* (Indiana University Press, 2007). Chapter 22 (Van Norris, 'Taking an Appropriate Line: Exploring Representation of Disability within British Mainstream Animation') was first published in *Animation Studies* 3 (2008).

Introduction

Nichola Dobson, Annabelle Honess Roe, Amy Ratelle and Caroline Ruddell

Animation studies has grown exponentially in the past three decades. In that time it has evolved from a nascent sub-area of film studies that charted the history of the cartoon form, and the studios and animators who produced it, via the 'first tentative steps' (Wells 1998: 8) to a legitimate field of academic enquiry in its own right. Vibrant and diverse, contemporary animation studies reflects the multiplicity and intermediality of animation. This book has been conceived in recognition of that diversity and a desire to map out the key issues, topics and debates in the field for those studying and researching animation today. Unlike those first 'tentative steps' in the 1990s, we no longer need to defend the validity of animation or animation studies. The pejorative perception of animation as 'just' children's entertainment or funny cartoons, and therefore not worthy of intellectual enquiry, has, we hope, long been surpassed. As animation has become increasingly 'pervasive' (Buchan 2013: 1), so too has animation's cultural value been raised. The challenge now for animation studies, as a relatively young field, is to identify and articulate its key lines of enquiry.

Whereas early film studies coalesced around questions of ontology – or the material nature of film and its relationship to reality – animation studies hasn't experienced the same trajectory of coherent theoretical debate. This is undoubtedly due to animation's diversity of form, technique and materiality. Animation is as varied as the number of things you can make move incrementally in front of a real or virtual camera, from paint to pixel, and the different techniques and technologies you can use to do so, from hand cut-out silhouettes to Flash. The theoretical and conceptual questions raised by, for example, stop-motion puppet animation might be very different to those posed by abstract digital animation. Because of this, animation studies has never been drawn to the pursuit of a 'grand' theory. In addition, animation's affinity with film – the dependence on the same basic apparatus of camera, film, projector (or their digital variants) and the tripartite relationship between creator, text and viewer – has meant that animation studies has sometimes struggled to find its own identity in the shadow of film studies, its dominant sibling. However, as this book demonstrates, there are prevailing concepts and concerns that have emerged as fundamental to studying and understanding animation. These, much like animation itself, are rich and varied and as such are representative of the dynamic, ever-evolving field that is animation studies.

This book is organized into three parts that approach different areas of animation studies. The first part, 'Theory, Philosophy, Concepts', explores the theoretical and conceptual questions that underpin much of animation studies and that are concerned, variously, with the ontology of animation, its relationship to reality, and the impact it has on audiences. Part Two, 'Forms and Genres', looks at the different types of animation within the frameworks of medium, genre and audience. The final part, 'Representation', includes chapters that investigate issues of representation and identity in animation. All the parts include both previously published, seminal writing on animation and new chapters specifically written for this book. We hope that the book as a whole gives a comprehensive overview of animation studies as it currently stands and will provide an essential resource to both newcomer and expert. With its focus on animation studies, rather than the history of the animated form or the work of specific animation studios or animators, this book is designed to sit alongside the many excellent existing books on animation history by addressing the concepts and ideas that underpin the study of animation.

References

Buchan, S. (2013), *Pervasive Animation*, London: Routledge.
Wells, P. (1998), *Understanding Animation*, London: Routledge.

PART ONE

Theory, Philosophy and Concepts

Introduction

While animation has never cohered around the pursuit of a single theoretical line of enquiry or a 'grand theory', as Husbands and Ruddell explore in the opening chapter of this part, there are nonetheless several theoretical concepts and questions that have emerged as central to understanding animation. These include the fundamental 'spectacle' or appeal of animation's visuality (Gunning), its relationship with reality (Bode and Mihailova) and explorations of animation's various 'unique' capacities in comparison to live-action, in particular its construction of space (Wood) and its relationship with memory (Walden) and performance (Honess Roe). In addition, animation theory has always enjoyed a particularly close and mutually informative relationship with animation practice, as articulated in Paul Ward's chapter.

1

Approaching Animation and Animation Studies

Lilly Husbands and Caroline Ruddell

Animation encompasses an extraordinarily wide-ranging set of techniques and practices and thus constitutes an equally diverse field of study. Because of this diversity, animation presents particular challenges in terms of agreeing on a single definition, and similarly it defies a unified theoretical approach to studying it. This chapter seeks to explore these issues and to outline exactly why animation is difficult to define, and why interdisciplinary theoretical approaches to studying it are necessary. We will outline some of the main ways that we might think about animation, in terms of how (or even whether) it can be defined and what some of its unique features and expressive capacities are. In doing so, this chapter offers an introduction to some of the key theoretical building blocks of animation studies.

What is animation?

What is useful when thinking about animation is to ask oneself, and to continue to ask oneself, some fairly simple questions. For example, 'what is animation?', and 'what can it do?' 'How is it different or similar to live-action?' On the surface these are simple enough questions, but ones that also prove surprisingly elusive. Consider the first question – 'what is animation?' One way to approach this is to consider different types of animation and we could try to answer the question by listing many examples and techniques, including scratch film, lightning sketches, stop motion, 2D cel animation, 3D computer animation, motion and performance capture. But simply listing different techniques of animation does not help us to define its ontology, or its fundamental nature, beyond basic material terms – i.e. the process and material of its construction.[1] We might instead consider key studios, directors or animators, all of whom have different styles and techniques, for example the stylized realism of Disney and Pixar, the scratch films of Len Lye, the silhouette cut outs of Lotte Reiniger and the sand or ink on glass of Caroline Leaf. Again, however, simply listing those involved in creating animation does not sufficiently provide an understanding of what animation *is*.

If listing techniques, animators or studios does not provide much in the way of answers, then it might help to consider what makes animation different from live-action. First, animation is produced *frame-by-frame* or in computer-animated increments, whereas live-action cinema is filmed in real time. Secondly, animation is entirely *constructed*, whereas live-action has a 'profilmic world' that exists in front of the camera. These two key differences between live-action and animation are at the heart of attempts to define animation.

Philip Denslow, after acknowledging that there is no single definition of animation, writes that 'the reason we are examining this issue is that no matter what definition you choose, it faces challenges from new developments in the technology used to produce and distribute animation' (1997: 1). Denslow goes on to outline a number of instances where the uses of various technologies problematize a single definition of animation; Denslow's examples, where he wonders whether virtual reality or 'computer generated lifeform simulation' can be considered animation, are almost certainly accepted as examples of animated texts today (1997). Unlike Denslow, who is reluctant to settle on one definition of animation, Brian Wells has argued that one definition should be possible and once outlined should be adopted by all in the academic community. For Wells, a series of properties define animation such as movement and 'aliveness' (2011), and he also prioritizes its construction frame-by-frame. Raz Greenberg is keen to differentiate animation from film and insists they must be defined separately, arguing that animation can be defined according to the presence or absence of objects when he says 'an initial definition for the animated text is "the process of movement or change, performed by an artificially-created text-specific object"' (2011: 6). The construction of movement is key for Greenberg.

Despite Greenberg's and Wells's separate attempts to 'lock down' a definition of animation these have for the most part not been taken up. This is probably because (despite Brian Wells's frustration about such arguments) animation is extremely wide-ranging, exists across different media and genres, and is produced with so many different and continually changing technologies, that it is likely that few scholars see much value in having a one-size-fits-all definition. Nichola Dobson takes this view in her *Historical Dictionary of Animation and Cartoons*, suggesting that due to the very 'fluid nature of the form' single definitions are problematic (2009: xxxvii–xxxviii). While such definitions have not taken hold, the notion that animation is an entirely *constructed* form has become a central tenet of animation studies.

If we cannot define animation in any one meaningful way, we can consider how we recognize it visually, particularly alongside live-action. It is simple enough to distinguish between the animated and live-action components of *Who Framed Roger Rabbit* (Robert Zemeckis 1988), for example, but sometimes difficult to identify the use of animation techniques to 'doctor', alter or enhance live-action images, as is standard in contemporary mainstream commercial Hollywood cinema. An interesting example is the film *Gladiator* (Ridley Scott 2000) where a computer-generated version of Oliver Reed had to be used to finish his scenes because he died during shooting. Here, such unprecedented events during filming led to the use of animation to 'fix' the problem. In this context, the differences between animation and live-action are often, and increasingly, difficult to discern. Even in 1997, Denslow noted the 'problem': that it is increasingly difficult to tell the difference between some examples of animation and live-action, most notably with regard to compositing techniques (1997: 2). The potential confusion between what might be animated and what might be live-action has grown exponentially in the decades since Denslow's writing. Compositing techniques (the combination of animated images and live-action images into one single image) in particular complicate the *recognition* of animation. While Roger Rabbit is clearly animated and Eddie Valiant (Bob Hoskins) is clearly live-action, in a special effects–heavy superhero/action film such as *Wonder Woman* (Patty Jenkins 2017), we may not always recognize what elements of the images are traditionally shot on film, or what has been enhanced or altered through animation techniques. Darley would call this a 'hybrid medium', in a similar way to how Mark Langer refers to a 'collapse of [...] boundary' between live-action and animation (quoted in Darley 2007: 69).

In contemporary cinema this 'collapse of boundary' is often apparent. A memorable example is *The Life of Pi* (Ang Lee 2012), which depicts a tiger in the same diegetic space – a small lifeboat – as Pi; we know that a tiger was not in the same spatial field as actor Suraj Sharma on filming, and we are aware that this is a case of compositing (whether we are familiar with the term or not). Two things are likely to happen on such viewing: first that we might try to understand how such images were achieved (or if we know the techniques involved we will look for evidence of them), and secondly, this does not distract from our enjoyment of the scene because a certain 'realism' is achieved (see Mihailova in this volume). Where we may be distracted is where, for example, animation, without live-action footage, is used to depict the human; *Final Fantasy: The Spirits Within* (Hironobu Sakaguchi and Motonori Sakakibara 2001) and *Beowulf*'s (Robert Zemeckis 2007) photorealistic depiction of their characters is distracting. We are aware this it is animation but it is striving too hard to *be* live-action/photorealistic to the extent that it is unsettling to the viewer (see Sobchack 2006, and Bode in this volume).

Given the lack of consensus on a definition of animation, and the fact that in themselves definitions do not tend to be overly useful (something which most animation scholars agree on), it might be more constructive to consider some of animation's unique qualities, particularly in relation to what it has the capacity to do visually. All animation techniques share the capacity for plasticity and for depicting life and movement. Indeed, there are two unique properties that have deeply informed the study of animation and could be considered as distinctive qualities of animation: the illusion of life and metamorphosis.

Animation's unique properties: The illusion of life and metamorphosis

Esther Leslie argues that 'animation is understood to be the inputting of life, or the inputting of the illusion of life, into that which is flat or inert or a model or an image' (2014: 28). This 'illusion of life' is a feature that pervades animation studies and is often claimed as central to what animation is.[2] Animation's illusion of life comes in part from the creation of movement, because movement suggests life as opposed to the stillness of death. Movement in animation, because it is *created* frame-by-frame, is an illusion, unlike in live-action film where it is *captured* in/on camera. Indeed, movement is stressed in several authors' definitions of animation, including Norman McLaren's oft-quoted notion that 'animation is not the art of drawings that move but the art of movements that are drawn' (quoted in Furniss 1998: 5). However, the creation of movement does not always entail the illusion of life. While the illusion of life is readily apparent in animation that creates a character, such as Mickey Mouse, who appears 'alive' by virtue of his movement, it would be less apparent in abstract animated shapes that are animated to move in time to music, or an animated company logo that may well depict movement without creating any sense of 'life'. This distinction indicates what is problematic about understanding the 'illusion of life' as a central feature of animation: while it is applicable to a huge proportion of animated examples (including all character animation), it is not a property of all animation.

Because animation is completely constructed and produced incrementally, it has the capacity for depicting metamorphoses. Paul Wells defines this as 'the ability for an image to literally change into another completely different image, for example, through the evolution of the line, the shift in formations of clay, or the manipulation of objects or environments' and he notes that metamorphoses is 'unique to the animated form' (1998: 69). Aylish Wood's work on animated space (reprinted in this volume) provides a very useful example of how thinking about metamorphosis can illuminate the study of animation (2006). Wood's arguments are about particular kinds of animation, such as sand and ink on glass, that highlight the fluidity of animation particularly through the ways that space is imagined and produced in the films she analyses. For Wood, because we can see 'in between' the frames, and because we can see 'the sustained metamorphoses of resolving transitions', space becomes an expressive element in its own right (2006: 150).

Although Wood is discussing particular kinds of animation, metamorphosis is central to how we might think about animation more generally. It captures the constructed nature of animation in a very visible way; it forces us to think about frame by frame construction or creation of incremental movement as we can see the sand/ink transforming between frames. Metamorphosis also raises the question of how we might engage with such images and their transition from one thing into another; for Wood, the movement of the sand/ink is a further element of the text that the viewer might engage with.

Both metamorphoses and the illusion of life can be thought of in terms of movement, but even this can be considered problematic if applied to all animation. Many examples of animated texts tend to foreground their 'animatedness', or medium specificity, and to call attention to themselves through unconventional techniques and uses of technology. For instance, works by experimental animators such as Robert Breer or Jodie Mack that make use of dissimilar images in consecutive frames offer radically different experiences that are not based on the continuity of movement across frames (thus effectively disrupting habitual expectations of animation's presentation of the illusion of life). Karen Beckman, discussing McLaren's and Peter Kubelka's writings on animation, observes that their thoughts reveal that an illusion of movement 'is not a given in animation'; only visual change between frames is necessary (2014: 3).

Animation aesthetics and spectatorship

Considering how difficult it is to establish a single definition of animation or even to identify its unique, yet universal, properties, other approaches to the study of animation instead shift the emphasis from the animation itself to the audience by investigating the diverse ways we *perceive* and *experience* it in its multifarious forms. Indeed, examining animation in spectatorial terms opens up opportunities to explore not only what animation *is* but also what it can *do* – what it can *show* us and enable us to *feel*.

One of the greatest philosophical conundrums of moving images in general, and animation in particular, lies in the complex relation between its ontology (what it is in material terms) and our phenomenological engagement with it (how we perceive and experience it). Building on McLaren's emphasis on the interstices between frames, Keith Broadfoot and Rex Butler note in their contribution to Cholodenko's *The Illusion of Life* that 'what we see, but what cannot be seen, is two images and no image – the space between images – at once' (1991: 271). Animation, as we experience it, is in a constant state of becoming, and when it is arrested for definition or analysis it ceases to be fully what it is while in motion. Our access to animation's illusionistic spectacle is necessarily filtered through our sensorial experience of it. This perceptual paradox is one of the reasons that animation spectatorship is an important aspect of animation studies. As an art form, animation has the potential to produce and manipulate imagery in myriad graphical ways. Thus, studying it often requires taking into consideration the particular ways in which it presents itself, or its formal aesthetics (e.g. the interrelationship between its audiovisual style, technique, medium). Aspects of spectatorial experience, accounted for by means of aesthetic analysis, often inform broader historical, cultural or conceptual analyses and interpretations of the art form.

Animation as a technical process offers artists extraordinary potential for formal experimentation and expressive freedom. It has a remarkable capacity for imaginative visualization, and the diversity of experiences that can arise out of that creative potential is part of what makes animation such a fascinating object of study. Throughout its history, animation's capacity to visualize virtually anything has been put to many different uses. Many scholars have remarked on its limitless artistic potential for the creation of fictional worlds and characters, its ability to recreate events or evoke subjective 'ideas, feelings and sensibilities' in documentary (Honess Roe 2011: 227), and its aptness for the visualization of data, concepts and supra-sensible natural phenomena in science and educational films, and much more besides.

When considering the diverse and distinctive experiences that animations offer us, it becomes quite clear that any one universalizing theory or description of animation spectatorship will not suffice. In her introduction to *Pervasive Animation* Suzanne Buchan writes that 'an effective approach to this complexity is to use pluralist and interdisciplinary methods [...] and, to develop approaches that take into account the differences between celluloid and digital film experience and the platforms these technologies and techniques use' (2013: 2).

Animation appeals to the body and the imagination in many ways that are quite different to live-action cinema – even the most 'invisible' uses of computer animation, in the form of visual effects discussed above, often offer visual experiences that would be impossible to capture with a straightforward cinematographic process. Although animations often make use of live-action filmmaking conventions, they also present their own visual languages that vary enormously across styles, techniques, production contexts, industries, cultures and time periods. Buchan argues that animation often presents its own 'world' that provides spectators with certain phenomenological, psychological and affective experiences that are peculiar to it, demanding of spectators a combination of personal interpretation, real-world understanding and acceptance of the work's own aesthetic logistics (2006: 25). She writes:

> The animation film is utterly unique in its representation of graphic and plastic universes and impossible spaces and in its 'ability' to transcend physical laws which govern our experience. It is therefore crucial to our understanding of animation spectatorship to develop and describe our understanding of this particular set of conditions, which in turn can assist an approach to individual films. (2006: 25)

Because spectatorial experience arises from encounters with the particularities of a specific animation and its own 'set of intricate complexities' (Buchan 2006: 25), investigations of animation spectatorship tend to focus closely on one work or a small number of works at a time. This offers scholars an opportunity to account not only for the historical, cultural or narrative elements of an animation but also for the different ways in which the particular stylistic, technical and technological features of a given animation achieve their effects and 'modes of appearing' (Sobchack 2011: 195). Animations using different styles and techniques will have very different 'modes of appearing', which in turn will affect the kinds of experiences they invite. For instance, a scratch animation such as Norman McLaren's *Blinkity Blank* (1955) that depicts semi-abstract figures that move very rapidly on the shallow surface of a black background in time to a musical soundtrack will elicit different responses than the realist aesthetics of Walt Disney's *Bambi* (1942), with its use of naturalistic two-dimensional-drawn characters moving in relation to detailed painted backgrounds that were shot with a multi-plane camera. These sorts of aesthetic distinctions are equally important in thinking about forms of animation that do not adhere to either short or feature-length narrative paradigms. For instance, a two-dimensional motion graphics-based animation that aims to convey information rather than a narrative will illicit mental and physiological responses that differ to some degree from those evoked by the immersive spectacle of a live-action hybrid like *Avatar* (James Cameron 2009).

Approaching animation spectatorship requires a careful consideration of the way that spectators' experiences of animation can be theorized. These approaches are often founded on the premise that human beings' perceptual faculties respond similarly to particular stimuli, and thus certain experiences can be reasonably assumed to be similar among spectators of an animated work. Phenomenological approaches to animation in particular attempt to address this issue by describing both the objective and subjective aspects of engaging with a moving image work. By rooting investigations of experience in close formal analyses of the works themselves, they aim to ensure that their descriptions of experience are not overly subjective but rather, as Vivian Sobchack notes, 'sufficiently comprehensible and resonant to others who might possibly inhabit [them]' (2009: 438).

Animation scholars use numerous methodologies in their approaches to spectatorship. Scholars including Buchan, Sobchack, Jennifer Barker, Tom Gunning, Aylish Wood and Joanna Bouldin have discussed animation in experiential and/or phenomenological terms. Other scholars such as Torben Grodal (2009) and Dan Torre (2017) have used cognitive theory to interrogate the experiences of animation spectatorship. These and other scholars have addressed the experiential perception of space and 'spatial transformation' (Wood 2006: 133), movement and metamorphosis that are unique to animated moving images. Their works discuss a variety of different material and technological types of animation. Bouldin, for instance, focuses on the relationship between spectators and animated bodies in cartoons, noting that 'animation extends the possibilities of the viewers' embodied responses' (2000: 63). Barker has argued for the tactile appeal of hyperreal computer animations like *Toy Story* (John Lasseter 1995) (2009: 46), and Sobchack describes the unusual sensations evoked by viewing computer-generated morphs (2000: 132). Buchan, in her study of the Quay Brothers' puppet animations, analyses the twofold status of object animation, concentrating on the way that it 'represents a different "world" for the spectator, something between "*a* world," created with the animation technique, and "*the* world" in its use of real objects and not representational drawings' (2006: 21).

Consideration of our embodied responses to movement is integral to this line of enquiry. In his essay 'Moving Away from the Index: Cinema and the Impression of Reality', Gunning works with the film theories of André Bazin and Christian Metz to shift focus away from the photographic index as a marker of realism and onto cinematic motion as a primary impetus for embodied engagement or identification (2007: 38). He thus introduces a theory of cinematic realism that makes room within film studies for a consideration of animation's ability to offer an 'impression of reality' (2007: 45). Gunning stresses the important role that movement plays in rendering animations and films 'believable' (2007: 45). He accounts for the physiological appeal of many forms of animation (2007: 38) by examining how both recorded and animated movement engages spectators' bodies, evokes their 'participation' in the seen movement and offers 'a sense of perceptual richness or immediate involvement in the image' (2007: 42). These ideas help refine our understanding of what is happening, for instance, when we become immersed in an animated spectacle. As he points out, this interest in the physiological appeal of animated motion is not new but was present in the writings of classical film theorists such as Jean Epstein, Germaine Dulac and Sergei Eisenstein (2007: 37). For instance, Eisenstein's writings on Disney in the 1940s demonstrate a fascination with the animated art form's ability to evoke certain synaesthetic, empathetic and ecstatic sensations through watching images move in time. He describes his well-known notion of 'plasmaticness' – the temporal, metamorphosing elasticity of animated bodies, objects and spaces – partly in terms of its profound effects on spectators' bodies (1988: 27).

There has been a somewhat limiting tendency in animation studies to focus on spectatorial experiences of representational forms of animation (e.g. cartoon animation, narrative computer animation, and stop motion puppet animation). This is in part because we are able to relate to figurative types of animation and animated characters because they resemble aspects of the real world enough for us to 'project our somatic knowledge of the world' onto them so that they 'can make "sense" to us' (Bouldin 2000: 60–61). However, this theorization of animation spectatorship does not apply as easily to forms of experimental animation whose primary aims are not to represent or mimic aspects of reality (Buchan 2006: 21). For instance, abstract animation often denies easy sensory assimilation based on recognizable bodies, spaces or states of affairs and calls for a distinct kind of approach to sensory and cognitive intelligibility (Husbands 2018). Other types of experimental animation present different perceptual and conceptual challenges (see Taberham in this volume).

Thinking about what animation can do and the way it can make us feel requires approaches that consider the radically different ways in which animations engage the imagination and the body. They also highlight the fact that the diversity of animation is one of its most prominent features and a variety of interdisciplinary approaches are therefore needed in the field. The differing ways in which animation might engage us raises some compelling questions about our preconceptions of what animation is, and how it has been discussed or defined, requiring us to continue to find new ways of understanding it. As a thoroughly wide-ranging set of techniques, forms, practices and aesthetics, animation deserves the multitudinous approaches on which much of animation studies thrives.

Notes

1 Whereas much of film theory's early enquiry coalesced around issues of
   ontology, and in particular the unique relationship between film and reality
   (see, for example, Bazin 1967), Animation Studies has lacked such a singular
   theoretical enquiry. This is probably due to the fact that animation is not
   'indexical' in the way that film is (i.e. it lacks the direct causal relationship
   between reality and image).

2 To the extent that this term has given title to Johnston and Thomas's (1981)
   behind the scenes book about Disney animation as well as two books on
   animation theory edited by Alan Cholodenko (1991 and 2007).

References

Barker, J. M. (2009), *The Tactile Eye: Touch and the Cinematic Experience*, Los
   Angeles: University of California Press.
Bazin, A. (1967), *What is Cinema? Volume 1*, trans. H. Gray, Berkeley: University
   of California Press.
Beckman, K. (2014), 'Introduction' in K. Beckman (ed.), *Animating Film Theory*,
   1–22, Durham: Duke University Press.
Bouldin, J. (2000), 'Bodacious Bodies and the Voluptuous Gaze: A Phenomenology
   of Animation Spectatorship', *Animation Journal* (Spring): 56–67.
Broadfoot, K. and R. Butler (1991), 'The Illusion of Illusion', in A. Cholodenko
   (ed.), *The Illusion of Life: Essays on Animation*, 263–298, Sydney: Power
   Institute of Fine Arts.
Buchan, S. (2006), 'The Animated Spectator: Watching the Quay Brothers'
   "Worlds"', in S. Buchan (ed.), *Animated 'Worlds'*, 15–38, Eastleigh: John
   Libbey Publishing.
Buchan, S. (2013), 'Introduction', in S. Buchan (ed.), *Pervasive Animation*, 1–22,
   London: Routledge.
Cholodenko, A., ed. (1991), *The Illusion of Life: Essays on Animation*, Sydney:
   Power Institute of Fine Arts.
Cholodenko, A., ed. (2007), *The Illusion of Life II: More Essays on Animation*,
   Sydney: Power Publications.
Darley, A. (2007), 'Bones of Contention: Thoughts on the Study of Animation',
   animation: an interdisciplinary journal, 2(1) March: 63–76.
Denslow, P. K. (1997), 'What Is Animation and Who Needs to Know? An Essay on
   Definitions', in J. Pilling (ed.), *A Reader in Animation Studies*, 1–4, Herts: John
   Libbey Publishing Ltd.
Dobson, N. (2009), *Historical Dictionary of Animation and Cartoons*, Lanham:
   Scarecrow Press.
Eisenstein, S. (1988), *Eisenstein on Disney*, ed. and trans. J. Leyda, London:
   Methuen.
Furniss, M. (1998), *Art in Motion: Animation Aesthetics*, Eastleigh: John Libbey
   Publishing.

Greenberg, R. (2011), 'The Animated Text: Definition', *Journal of Film and Video*, 63 (2) Summer: 3–10.

Grodal, T. (2009), *Embodied Visions: Evolution, Emotion, Culture, and Film*, Oxford: Oxford University Press.

Gunning, T. (2007), Moving Away from the Index: Cinema and the Impression of Reality', *Differences: A Journal of Feminist Cultural Studies*, 18(1): 29–52.

Honess Roe, A. (2011), 'Absence, Excess, and Epistemological Expansion: Towards a Framework for the Study of Animated Documentary', *Animation: An Interdisciplinary Journal*, 6(3): 215–230.

Husbands, L. (2018), 'Fantastical Empathy: Encountering Abstraction in Bret Battey's *Sinus Aestum* (2009)', in C. Holliday and A. Sergeant (eds), *Fantasy/Animation: Connections between Media, Mediums and Genres*, London: Routledge.

Johnston, O. and F. Thomas (1981), *The Illusion of Life: Disney Animation*, New York: Abbeville Press.

Leslie, E. (2014), 'Animation and History', in K. Beckman (ed.), *Animating Film Theory*, Durham: Duke University Press.

Sobchack, V. (2000), '"At the Still Point of the Turning World": Meta-Morphing and Meta Stasis', in V. Sobchack (ed.), *Meta Morphing: Visual Transformation and the Culture of Quick Change*, 131–158, Minneapolis: University of Minnesota Press.

Sobchack, V. (2006), 'Final Fantasy: Computer Graphic Animations of Humanity (or the [Dis]Illusion of Life)', in S. Buchan (ed.), *Animated Worlds*, 173–184, Eastleigh: John Libbey Publishing.

Sobchack, V. (2009), 'Phenomenology', in P. Livingstone and C. Plantinga (eds), *The Routledge Companion to Philosophy and Film*, 435–445, New York: Routledge.

Sobchack, V. (2011), 'Fleshing out the Image: Phenomenology, Pedagogy, and Derek Jarman's *Blue*', in H. Carel and G. Tuck (eds), *New Takes on Film-Philosophy*, 191–206, Hampshire: Palgrave Macmillan.

Torre, D. (2017), *Animation – Process, Cognition and Actuality*, London: Bloomsbury.

Wells, B. (2011), 'Frame of Reference: Toward a Definition of Animation', *Animation Practice, Process and Production*, 1(1): 11–32.

Wells, P. (1998), *Understanding Animation*, London: Routledge.

Wood, A. (2006), 'Re-Animating Space', *Animation: An Interdisciplinary Journal*, 1(2): 133–152.

2

The Cinema of Attractions: Early Film, Its Spectators and the Avant-Garde

Tom Gunning

Here Gunning's discussion relates to early cinema in general which includes both live-action and animation, and indeed they were not distinguished from each other in the early years of cinema. Gunning's notion of a 'cinema of attractions', which he proposed in this article that was first published in 1986 in the journal Wide Angle, *has been widely influential in film and media studies and continues to be relevant to the study of animation in numerous ways: how animation 'presents' itself to us; questions of novelty; the role of comedy, gags and chase sequences; and the function and reception of technology.*

Writing in 1922, flushed with the excitement of seeing Abel Gance's *La Roue* (*The Wheel*), Fernand Léger tried to define something of the radical possibilities of the cinema. The potential of the new art did not lie in 'imitating the movements of nature' or in 'the mistaken path' of its resemblance to theatre. Its unique power was a 'matter of *making images seen*'.[1] It is precisely this harnessing of visibility, this act of showing and exhibition, which I feel cinema before 1906 displays most intensely. Its inspiration for the avant-garde of the early decades of this century needs to be re-explored.

Writings by the early modernists (Futurists, Dadaists and Surrealists) on the cinema follow a pattern similar to Léger: enthusiasm for this new medium and its possibilities; and disappointment at the way it has already developed, its enslavement to traditional art forms, particularly theatre and literature. This fascination with the *potential* of a medium (and the accompanying fantasy of rescuing the cinema from its enslavement to alien and passé forms) can be understood from a number of viewpoints. I want to use it to illuminate a topic I have also approached before, the strangely heterogeneous relation that film before 1906 (or so) bears to the films that follow, and the way a taking account of this heterogeneity signals a new conception of film history and film form. My work in this area has been pursued in collaboration with André Gaudreault.[2]

The history of early cinema, like the history of cinema generally, has been written and theorized under the hegemony of narrative films. Early film-makers like Smith, Méliès and Porter have been studied primarily from the viewpoint of their contribution to film as a storytelling medium, particularly the evolution of narrative editing. Although such approaches are not totally misguided, they are one-sided and potentially distort both the work of these film-makers and the actual forces shaping cinema before 1906. A few observations will indicate the way that early cinema was not dominated by the narrative impulse that later asserted its sway over the medium. First there is the extremely important role that actuality film plays in early film production. Investigation of the films copyrighted in the US shows that actuality films outnumbered fictional films until 1906.[3] The Lumière tradition of 'placing the world within one's reach' through travel films and topicals did not disappear with the exit of the Cinématographe from film production. But even within non-actuality filming – what has sometimes been referred to as the 'Méliès tradition' – the role narrative plays is quite different from in traditional narrative film. Méliès himself declared in discussing his working method: 'As for the scenario, the 'fable,' or 'tale,' I only consider it at the end. I can state that the scenario constructed in this manner has *no importance*, since I use it merely as a pretext for the 'stage effects,' the 'tricks' or for a nicely arranged tableau'.[4]

Whatever differences one might find between Lumière and Méliès, they should not represent the opposition between narrative and non-narrative film-making, at least as it is understood today. Rather, one can unite them in a conception that sees cinema less as a way of telling stories than as a way of presenting a series of views to an audience, fascinating because of their illusory power (whether the realistic illusion of motion offered to the first audiences by Lumière, or the magical illusion concocted by Méliès), and exoticism. In other words, I believe that the relation to the spectator set up by the films of both Lumière and Méliès (and many other film-makers before 1906) had a common basis, and one that differs from the primary spectator relations set up by narrative film after 1906. I will call this earlier conception of cinema, 'the cinema of attractions'. I believe that this conception dominates cinema until about 1906–7. Although different from the fascination in storytelling exploited by the cinema from the time of Griffith, it is not necessarily opposed to it. In fact the cinema of attractions does not disappear with the dominance of narrative, but rather goes underground, both into certain avant-garde practices and as a component of narrative films, more evident in some genres (e.g. the musical) than in others.

What precisely is the cinema of attractions? First, it is a cinema that bases itself on the quality that Léger celebrated: its ability to *show* something. Contrasted to the voyeuristic aspect of narrative cinema analysed by Christian Metz,[5] this is an exhibitionist cinema. An aspect of early cinema which I have written about in other articles is emblematic of this different relationship the cinema of attractions constructs with its spectator: the recurring look at the camera by actors. This action, which is later perceived as spoiling the realistic illusion of the cinema, is here undertaken with brio, establishing contact with the audience. From comedians smirking at the camera, to the constant bowing and gesturing of the conjurors in magic films, this is a cinema that displays its visibility, willing to rupture a self-enclosed fictional world for a chance to solicit the attention of the spectator.

Exhibitionism becomes literal in the series of erotic films which play an important role in early film production (the same Pathé catalogue would advertise the Passion Play along with 'scènes grivoises d'un caractère piquant' [loose scenes of a provocative nature], erotic films often including full nudity), also driven underground in later years. As Noël Burch has shown in his film *Correction Please: How We Got into Pictures* (1979), a film like *The Bride Retires* (France 1902) reveals a fundamental conflict between this exhibitionistic tendency of early film and the creation of a fictional diegesis. A woman undresses for bed while her new husband peers at her from behind a screen. However, it is to the camera and the audience that the bride addresses her erotic striptease, winking at us as she faces us, smiling in erotic display.

As the quote from Méliès points out, the trick film, perhaps the dominant non-actuality film genre before 1906, is itself a series of displays, of magical attractions, rather than a primitive sketch of narrative continuity. Many trick films are, in effect, plotless, a series of transformations strung together with little connection and certainly no characterization. But to approach even the plotted trick films, such as *Voyage dans la lune* (A Trip to the Moon) (1902), simply as precursors of later narrative structures is to miss the point. The story simply provides a frame upon which to string a demonstration of the magical possibilities of the cinema.

Modes of exhibition in early cinema also reflect this lack of concern with creating a self-sufficient narrative world upon the screen. As Charles Musser has sown [*sic*],[6] the early showmen exhibitors exerted a great deal of control over the shows they presented, actually re-editing the films they had purchased and supplying a series of off-screen supplements, such as sound effects and spoken commentary. Perhaps most extreme is the Hale's Tours, the largest chain of theatres exclusively showing films before 1906. Not only did the films consist of non-narrative sequences taken from moving vehicles (usually trains), but the theatre itself was arranged as a train car with a conductor who took tickets, and sound effects simulating the click-clack of wheels and hiss of air brakes.[7] Such viewing experiences relate more to the attractions of the fairground than to the traditions of the legitimate theatre. The relation between films and the emergence of the great amusement parks, such as Coney Island, at the turn of the century provides rich ground for rethinking the roots of early cinema.

Nor should we ever forget that in the earliest years of exhibition the cinema itself was an attraction. Early audiences went to exhibitions to see machines demonstrated (the newest technological wonder, following in the wake of such widely exhibited machines and marvels as X-rays or, earlier, the phonograph), rather than to view films. It was the Cinématographe, the Biograph or the Vitascope that were advertised on the variety bills in which they premièred, not *Le Déjeuner de bébé* or *The Black Diamond Express*. After the initial novelty period, this display of the possibilities of cinema continues, and not only in magic films. Many of the close-ups in early film differ from later uses of the technique precisely because they do not use enlargement for narrative punctuation, but as an attraction in its own right. The close-up cut into Porter's *The Gay Shoe Clerk* (1903) may anticipate later continuity techniques, but its principal motive is again pure exhibitionism, as the lady lifts her skirt hem, exposing her ankle for all to see. Biograph films such as *Photographing a Female Crook* (1904) and *Hooligan in Jail* (1903) consist of a single shot in which the camera is brought close to the main character, until they are in mid-shot. The enlargement is not a device expressive of narrative tension; it is in itself an attraction and the point of the film.[8]

To summarise, the cinema of attractions directly solicits spectator attention, inciting visual curiosity, and supplying pleasure through an exciting spectacle – a unique event, whether fictional or documentary, that is of interest in itself. The attraction to be displayed may also be of a cinematic nature, such as the early close-ups just described, or trick films in which a cinematic manipulation (slow motion, reverse motion, substitution, multiple exposure) provides the film's novelty. Fictional situations tend to be restricted to gags, vaudeville numbers or recreations of shocking or curious incidents (executions, current events). It is the direct address of the audience, in which an attraction is offered to the spectator by a cinema showman, that defines this approach to film making. Theatrical display dominates over narrative absorption, emphasizing the direct stimulation of shock or surprise at the expense of unfolding a story or creating a diegetic universe. The cinema of attractions expends little energy creating characters with psychological motivations or individual personality. Making use of both fictional and non-fictional attractions, its energy moves outward towards an acknowledged spectator rather than inward towards the character-based situations essential to classical narrative.

The term 'attractions' comes, of course, from the young Sergei Mikhailovich Eisenstein and his attempt to find a new model and mode of analysis for the theatre. In his search for the 'unit of impression' of theatrical art, the foundation of an analysis which would undermine realistic representational theatre, Eisenstein hit upon the term 'attraction'.[9] An attraction aggressively subjected the spectator to 'sensual or psychological impact'. According to Eisenstein, theatre should consist of a montage of such attractions, creating a relation to the spectator entirely different from his absorption in 'illusory depictions'.[10] I pick up this term partly to underscore the relation to the spectator that this later avant-garde practice shares with early cinema: that of exhibitionist confrontation rather than diegetic absorption. Of course the 'experimentally regulated and mathematically calculated' montage of attractions demanded by Eisenstein differs enormously from these early films (as any conscious and oppositional mode of practice will from a popular one).[11] However, it is important to realize the context from which Eisenstein selected the term. Then, as now, the 'attraction' was a term of the fairground, and for Eisenstein and his friend Yutkevich it primarily represented their favourite fairground attraction, the roller coaster, or as it was known then in Russia, the American Mountains.[12]

The source is significant. The enthusiasm of the early avant-garde for film was at least partly an enthusiasm for a mass culture that was emerging at the beginning of the century, offering a new sort of stimulus for an audience not acculturated to the traditional arts. It is important to take this enthusiasm for popular art as something more than a simple gesture to *épater les bourgeois* (shock the bourgeois). The enormous development of the entertainment industry since the 1910s and its growing acceptance by middle-class culture (and the accommodation that made this acceptance possible) have made it difficult to understand the liberation popular entertainment offered at the beginning of the century. I believe that it was precisely the exhibitionist quality of turn-of-the-century popular art that made it attractive to the avant-garde – its freedom from the creation of a diegesis, its accent on direct stimulation.

Writing of the variety theatre, Marinetti not only praised its aesthetics of astonishment and stimulation, but particularly its creation of a new spectator who contrasts with the 'static', 'stupid voyeur' of traditional theatre. The spectator at the variety theatre feels directly addressed by the spectacle and joins in, singing along, heckling the comedians.[13] Dealing with early cinema within the context of archive and academy, we risk missing its vital relation to vaudeville, its primary place of exhibition until around 1905. Film appeared as one attraction on the vaudeville programme, surrounded by a mass of unrelated acts in a non-narrative and even nearly illogical succession of performances. Even when presented in the nickelodeons that were emerging at the end of this period, these short films always appeared in a variety format, trick films sandwiched in with farces, actualities, 'illustrated songs' and, quite frequently, cheap vaudeville acts. It was precisely this non-narrative variety that placed this form of entertainment under attack by reform groups in the early 1910s. The Russell Sage Survey of popular entertainments found vaudeville 'depends upon an artificial rather than a natural human and developing interest, these acts having no necessary and as a rule, no actual connection'.[14] In other words, no narrative. A night at the variety theatre was like a ride on a streetcar or an active day in a crowded city, according to this middle-class reform group, stimulating an unhealthy nervousness. It was precisely such artificial stimulus that Marinetti and Eisenstein wished to borrow from the popular arts and inject into the theatre, organizing popular energy for radical purpose.

What happened to the cinema of attractions? The period from 1907 to about 1913 represents the true *narrativization* of the cinema, culminating in the appearance of feature films which radically revised the variety format. Film clearly took the legitimate theatre as its model, producing famous players in famous plays. The transformation of filmic discourse that D. W. Griffith typifies bound cinematic signifiers to the narration of stories and the creation of a self-enclosed diegetic universe. The look at the camera becomes taboo and the devices of cinema are transformed from playful 'tricks' – cinematic attractions (Méliès gesturing at us to watch the lady vanish) – to elements of dramatic expression, entries into the psychology of character and the world of fiction.

However, it would be too easy to see this as a Cain and Abel story, with narrative strangling the nascent possibilities of a young iconoclastic form of entertainment. Just as the variety format in some sense survived in the movie palaces of the 1920s (with newsreel, cartoon, sing-along, orchestra performance and sometimes vaudeville acts subordinated to, but still coexisting with, the narrative *feature* of the evening), the system of attraction remains an essential part of popular film-making.

The chase film shows how, towards the end of this period (basically from 1903 to 1906), a synthesis of attractions and narrative was already underway. The chase had been the original truly narrative genre of the cinema, providing a model for causality and linearity as well as a basic editing continuity. A film like Biograph's *Personal* (1904, the model for the chase film in many ways) shows the creation of a narrative linearity, as the French nobleman runs for his life from the fiancées his personal column ad has unleashed. However, at the same time, as the group of young women pursue their prey towards the camera in each shot, they encounter some slight obstacle (a fence, a steep slope, a stream) that slows them down for the spectator, providing a mini-spectacle pause in the unfolding of narrative. The Edison Company seemed particularly aware of this, since they offered their plagiarized version of this Biograph film (*How a French Nobleman*

Got a Wife through the New York Herald 'Personal' Columns) in two forms, as a complete film or as separate shots, so that any one image of the ladies chasing the man could be bought without the inciting incident or narrative closure.[15]

As Laura Mulvey has shown in a very different context, the dialectic between spectacle and narrative has fuelled much of the classical cinema.[16] Donald Crafton in his study of slapstick comedy, 'The Pie and the Chase', has shown the way slapstick did a balancing act between the pure spectacle of gag and the development of narrative.[17] Likewise, the traditional spectacle film proved true to its name by highlighting moments of pure visual stimulation along with narrative. The 1924 version of *Ben Hur* was in fact shown at a Boston theatre with a timetable announcing the moment of its prime attractions:

8.35   *The Star of Bethlehem*
8.40   *Jerusalem Restored*
8.59   *Fall of the House of Hur*
10.29   *The Last Supper*
10.50   *Reunion*[18]

The Hollywood advertising policy of enumerating the features of a film, each emblazoned with the command, 'See!' shows this primal power of the attraction running beneath the armature of narrative regulation.

We seem far from the avant-garde premises with which this discussion of early cinema began. But it is important for the radical heterogeneity which I find in early cinema not to be conceived as a truly oppositional programme, one irreconcilable with the growth of narrative cinema. This view is too sentimental and too ahistorical. A film like *The Great Train Robbery* (1903) does point in both directions, towards a direct assault on the spectator (the spectacularly enlarged outlaw unloading his pistol in our faces), and towards a linear narrative continuity. This is early film's ambiguous heritage. Clearly in some sense recent spectacle cinema has reaffirmed its roots in stimulus and carnival rides, in what might be called the Spielberg-Lucas-Coppola cinema of effects.

But effects are tamed attractions. Marinetti and Eisenstein understood that they were tapping into a source of energy that would need focusing and intensification to fulfil its revolutionary possibilities. Both Eisenstein and Marinetti planned to exaggerate the impact on the spectators, Marinetti proposing to literally glue them to their seats (ruined garments paid for after the performance) and Eisenstein setting firecrackers off beneath them. Every change in film history implies a change in its address to the spectator, and each period constructs its spectator in a new way. Now in a period of American avant-garde cinema in which the tradition of contemplative subjectivity has perhaps run its (often glorious) course, it is possible that this earlier carnival of the cinema, and the methods of popular entertainment, still provide an unexhausted resource – a Coney Island of the avant-garde, whose never dominant but always sensed current can be traced from Méliès through Keaton, through *Un Chien andalou* (1928), and Jack Smith.

Notes

First published in *Wide Angle*, vol. 8 no. 3/4, Fall 1986.

1   Fernand Léger, 'A critical essay on the plastic qualities of Abel Gance's film *The Wheel*', in Edward Fry (ed.), *Functions of Painting*, trans. Alexandra Anderson (New York: Viking Press, 1973), p. 21.

2   See my articles 'The non-continuous style of early film', in Roger Holman (ed.), *Cinema 1900–1906* (Brussels: FIAF, 1982), and 'An unseen energy swallows space: The space in early film and its relation to American avant garde film' in John L. Fell (ed.), *Film before Griffith* (Berkeley: University of California Press, 1983), pp. 355–66, and our collaborative paper delivered by A. Gaudreault at the conference at Cerisy on Film History (August 1985) 'Le cinéma des premiers temps: un défi à l'histoire du cinéma?'. I would also like to note the importance of my discussions with Adam Simon and our hope to investigate further the history and archaeology of the film spectator.

3   Robert C. Allen, *Vaudeville and Film: 1895–1915, A Study in Media Interaction* (New York: Arno Press, 1980), pp. 159, 212–13.

4   Méliès, 'Importance du scénario', in Georges Sadoul, *Georges Méliès* (Paris: Seghers, 1961), p. 118 (my translation).

5   Metz, *The Imaginary Signifier: Psychoanalysis and the Cinema*, trans. Celia Britton, Annwyl Williams, Ben Brewster and Alfred Guzzetti (Bloomington: Indiana University Press, 1982), particularly pp. 58–80, 91–7.

6   Musser. 'American Vitagraph 1897–1901', *Cinema Journal*, vol. 22 no. 3, Spring 1983, p. 10.

7   Raymond Fielding, 'Hale's tours: Ultrarealism in the pre-1910 motion picture', in Fell, *Film before Griffith*, pp. 116–30.

8   I wish to thank Ben Brewster for his comments after the original delivery of this paper which pointed out the importance of including this aspect of the cinema of attractions here.

9   Eisenstein, 'How I became a film director', in *Notes of a Film Director* (Moscow: Foreign Language Publishing House, n.d.), p. 16.

10 'The montage of attractions', in S. M. Eisenstein, *Writings 1922–1934*, edited by Richard Taylor (London: BFI, 1988), p. 35.

11 Ibid.

12 Yon Barna, *Eisenstein* (Bloomington: Indiana University Press, 1973), p. 59.

13 'The variety theater 1913' in Umbro Apollonio (ed.), *Futurist Manifestos* (New York: Viking Press, 1973), p. 127.

14 Michael Davis, *The Exploitation of Pleasure* (New York: Russell Sage Foundation, Dept. of Child Hygiene, Pamphlet, 1911).

15 David Levy, 'Edison sales policy and the continuous action film 1904–1906', in Fell, *Film before Griffith*, pp. 207–22.

16 'Visual pleasure and narrative cinema', in Laura Mulvey (ed.), *Visual and Other Pleasures* (London: Macmillan, 1989).

17 Paper delivered at the FIAF Conference on Slapstick, May 1985, New York City.

18 Nicholas Vardac, *From Stage to Screen: Theatrical Method from Garrick to Griffith* (New York: Benjamin Blom, 1968), p. 232.

3

Re-Animating Space

Aylish Wood

In an article that first appeared in animation: an interdisciplinary journal *in 2006, Wood argues that animation has the expressive capacity to construct space in ways that is not possible using live-action techniques. Metamorphosis is inherent to this capacity, Wood argues. Although many scholars note the importance of metamorphosis for understanding animation, Wood here provides a sustained analysis of its significance and also helps rethink the concept of cinematic space through animation's capacity for spatial transformation.*

> Space that has been seized upon by the imagination cannot remain indifferent space subject to the measures of the surveyor. (Gaston Bachelard 1994: xxxvi)

Animation has the capacity to re-invigorate how we think about cinematic space. As a technology, cinema seizes space and through the imaginative acts of filmmakers, creates places for a viewer's engagement. Cinematic space is able to represent and be expressive, and its place in generating narrative meaning is taken to be, and indeed is, central to cinema.[1] This view, however, often overlooks another aspect of space, one associated with an expression of intensive spatial experience and other kinds of transformation. We live through and in space, generating intensive experiences through memories and acts of imagination, or transforming through actual activities. This transformative aspect is rarely addressed, perhaps because, even as cinema creates all kinds of engagements with characters, times and spaces, live-action images only infrequently show space itself in the process of change, and so less commonly evoke a more direct experience of that process.[2] By contrast, in many animations space is caught in the act of changing, making it a form of cinema especially relevant to thinking about experiences of spatial transformation.

Such a means of conceptualizing space lies outside more usual conventions of thinking about spatial organizations within cinematic discourse. The latter have tended to consider space in its role of supporting character and narrative, whereas I approach space as an entity in itself. When considering onscreen space, the twin concerns of representing and expressing are central to many discussions. Writing of space as representing and expressing, Richard Maltby (2003) makes clear the ways cinematic space both represent places, the locations of narrative and character action, and express aspects of the narrative, as often described in *mise-en-scène* analyses. Even as this way of thinking seems to privilege space, in effect it instead foregrounds the way in which space serves to support the actions of characters as the main vehicle of the narrative, providing either location or expressive resonance. Film theorists have also articulated the relationship between space and narrative or character. Stephen Heath (1981), for instance, in his influential work on narrative space in Hollywood, used the concept of suture to describe how the flow of images and their central perspective ensured a coherent encounter with the narrative. Gilles Deleuze (1983) has defined two kinds of cinematic images, the movement–image and time–image, each defined by the ability of characters to move or act in given spaces. In the movement–image, space is the background for the movement and action of characters, and gains meaning in its role of supporting characters, a convention typified for Deleuze by Hollywood cinema. As a counterpoint to the movement–image, in the time–image characters are unable to react directly, so a plot-driven imperative of 'what happens next' is less dominant. In the absence of action linking the images, their durational quality gives access to a direct image of time. Though very distinct, both the movement–image and time–image treat space indirectly; the important feature of an image is whether or not a character can act, and in doing so, give meaning to space.

None of these articulations, however, approach space when it exists on the screen as an event in itself, where the actions of characters are set aside, rather than the other way around. Space in this sense escapes the meaning given through character action, allowing for a more direct encounter by a viewer. In emphasizing these encounters, I explore an underdeveloped aspect of cinema studies – the capacity of cinema to evoke intensive experiences of space, revealing more of the ways in which space can be seized upon by filmmakers and viewers. In this article I focus on animation's transformative revitalization of cinematic space. Though there are many ways one might give an account of this revitalized space, the trajectory I take is led by an interaction of form and content. In their different ways *Duck Amuck* (Chuck

Jones 1953), *The Street* (Caroline Leaf 1976), *The Metamorphosis of Mr Samsa* (Caroline Leaf 1977), *Flatworld* (Daniel Greave 1997) and *Nocturna Artificialia: Those Who Desire without End* (Brothers Quay 1979), each involve figures pushing against the boundaries of places or situations in which they find themselves. Especially interesting, in the context of an incipient claustrophobia, is how these animations avoid static constructions of space, re-animating it by drawing attention to spatial transitions and change. To generate this position I formulate a view of space as undergoing processes of reverberation: existing beyond the location of events, fluid and marked by heterogeneity, shifting between familiarity and uncertainty, and finally, as chaotic and potentially unknowable. By paying attention to elements of animated form, I foreground intensive spatial experience and take it to be both a reaction to circumstance and a means of imaginatively taking hold of space. Central to giving space experiential meaning is animation's ability to transfer such character encounters to viewers, allowing them to also find themselves caught between their expectations and the images that resolve on the screen.

Approaching reverberating space

'Animation intrinsically interrogates the phenomena it represents and offers new and alternative perspectives and knowledge to its audiences' (Wells 1998: 11) and among the many alternatives offered are perspectives on space. Animations, especially those striving to break conventions, are suggestive of experiences of space not wholly held captive by narrative. They can achieve an evocation of space that captivates us as it makes meaning, giving locations for movements and gestures, but which also allows the surprise of space emerging in a process of change. In Caroline Leaf's *The Metamorphosis of Mr Samsa* (1977), a version of Franz Kafka's *Metamorphosis*, the story of Gregor Samsa's transformation is created through the technique of sand on glass, a process giving the images an extraordinary fluidity. Waking up, Gregor falls off the bed onto his domed beetle-like back, and rocks from side to side to right himself. Each time he rocks, his multiple insect limbs flap with the motion. As he finally rights himself his limbs follow through in a turbulent circular motion, which resolves into the hand of another inhabitant of the house laying the table for breakfast. This moment of transition, impossible to anticipate from any cues, generates both the disorientating experience of a man who awakens to find himself a bug and also places the viewer in a more uncertain relationship to space. Though the narrative quickly takes hold again, the encounter with uncued space discloses a site of meaningful engagement for a viewer.

In *The Poetics of Space*, Gaston Bachelard draws on Eugène Minkowski's idea of reverberation to reveal the meaningfulness of space. Minkowski writes:

> If, having fixed the original form in our mind's eye, we ask ourselves how that form comes alive and fills with life, we discover a new dynamic and vital category, a new property of the universe: reverberation. (quoted in Bachelard 1994: xvi)

The concept of reverberation enables a shift from the conventional view of space as a place where actions occur, to seeing space as something that visibly re-forms. There are different ways animation can generate unexpected progressions, allowing space to be more directly 'seized upon by the imagination': a wall may appear in mid air, a figure may become rounded, flattened, dimensionally in-between, or interior spaces may exceed the boundaries of their external dimensions. The latter, for instance, occurs in *Pigs in a Polka* (Friz Freleng 1942). As the Wolf chases the three little Pigs through the upper level of the brick house, the hotel-like interior corridors and lift shaft confound a viewer's expectation based on the lower level of the house: the upper levels are far more expansive than the lower ones, extending beyond the dimensional boundaries established in the earlier sequences of the cartoon. Such play yields reverberating spaces through which a viewer can re-encounter the vitality of space. The joke of *Duck Amuck*, for instance, is Daffy Duck's continuous surprise at ruptures in spatial continuity. The cartoon begins with Daffy costumed as a Musketeer in the foreground of a castle. Intent on demonstrating his skill at swordplay, he does not notice his movement from a castle scene into blankness. Daffy's initial absorption in his actions gives way to uncertainty and inaction once he realizes he has stepped outside of a recognizable space for the place of the narrative. This inability to complete the situation defined by the visual cue of the musketeer location reveals both the centrality of space in making sense of actions, while also suggesting that unexpected shifts between familiar and unfamiliar space provoke disorientation. Daffy's experience can be extended further to the viewer, whose relationship with space at the same time becomes less certain. Through this lessening certainty in what comes next, reverberating space is present in two ways: in the images of the animation and in the process of viewing, in adjusting to and making connections between the spatial discontinuities.[3]

Duck Amuck, Pigs in a Polka, and other Warner Bros cartoons such as *Dough for the Do-Do* (Friz Freleng [uncredited] 1949) strikingly show space being made by playing on the relationship between character and space, particularly with how unity and coherence are usually central to the spaces in which a character acts. Their combination of figures encountering confounding spaces with self-reflective cartooning invokes a complex spatiality through an emphasis on form and content. To articulate how the breaking of formal spatial conventions reveals reverberating space I find helpful a quotation by Stephen Heath (1981) in which he discusses how space is conventionally 'used up' in the construction of place or narrative setting in live-action cinema:

> The vision of the image is its narrative clarity and that clarity hangs on the negation of space for place, the constant realization of centre in function of narrative purpose, narrative movement: 'Negatively, the space is presented so as not to distract attention from the dominant actions: positively, the space is "used up" by the presentation of narratively important settings, character traits ... or other causal agents' [Bordwell and Thompson 1976: 42]. Specific spatial cues – importantly, amongst others, those depending on camera movement and editing – will be established and used accordingly, centring the flow of the images, taking place. (p. 39)

The idea of space as 'used-up' is useful here, or rather its opposite is useful; that is, to think about space when it is *not* used-up, when it emerges in an abundance that escapes the setting of place, or the control of character through the manipulation of conventions. This is not to say space is redundant, or in excess, but that it introduces a dimension allowing reverberating space to emerge.

Key to seeing space as 'not used-up', escaping the setting of place is the triadic relationship between character, space and action. As I have already argued earlier, space begins to gain meaning of its own when it no longer solely serves a supporting role by giving meaning to the actions of characters. An essential point of this shift in the balance of the triadic relationship is that conventions of spatial organization are broken. The examples cited earlier, *The Metamorphosis of Mr Samsa*, *Pigs in a Polka* and *Duck Amuck*, though very different kinds of animation, each includes moments where the triadic relationship is shifted to an emphasis on reverberating space rather than supportive space. *Pigs in a Polka* and *Duck Amuck* are the products of the Warner Bros Studio system whose output has included notable pockets of experimentation, and some of this experimentation is evident in the spatial play of these two animations. Given their place within a studio system it is easy to point to the ways the cartoons break with the conventions of that system. However, this is not the only reason for choosing them as examples for study here, as both importantly include a plot in which figures are enclosed within a space, either in the sense of a location or situation, and this double criterion of formal play and enclosure motivated the choices of the other animations considered. The work of Caroline Leaf and the Quay Brothers, for instance, is more usually associated with less commercial animation, so it is perhaps surprising to find them aligned with Warner Bros cartoons in a way that might suggest their formal strategies are equivalent. The discussion of animations in this essay is primarily informed by the specific question of space and, as with any selective criteria, one set of combinations and permutations both includes and excludes, often crossing the boundaries of other criteria, as indeed mine crosses the lines drawn between commercial and art forms of animation. As a consequence, it is not necessarily useful to try to simplistically assert a straightforwardly comparable breakage of convention between all the animations. If one applies the distinction of commercial versus art animation, then the spatio–temporal organizations of *Duck Amuck* and *Flatworld* sit within a different framework of convention than those of *The Street* or *Nocturna Artificialia*. Nevertheless, all these animations include moments in which reverberating space emerges, when space is not used-up in giving meaning to character action.

Whatever the conventional framework within which any animation sits, the idea of space not used up can be allied with approaches that also complicate the content of space. Doreen Massey's work (1993) provides a constructive way of beginning to excavate these possibilities as she sees space as a fluid entity, in which 'spatiality is always in the process of being made'.[4] Massey conceives of this process by taking space not simply to be the place of singular events, but an assembly of different habitations creating multifaceted spaces.[5] Since social and political groupings influence the formation of habitations, when they change so does space, allowing for heterogeneity not only in the sense of a multiplicity of users, but also as a fluid constitution of those users. Through this usage, the concept of space extends beyond the dimensions of a location, to give an account of the interaction of living elements with a dimensional location, one mutually defining both the spaces and the elements within it. Any given space evolves in a complex interplay of location and living elements, a fluid process where space can only be made meaningful by attending to its temporalities.

Reverberating space, then, can be approached through the ideas of fluid and unused space. For example, Caroline Leaf, whose work I discuss more fully later, animates in a variety of ways: sand on glass, oil paint on glass, scratching on film stock. While each of these is a very different technique, they all share the property of fluid spatial construction. Whether created from sand, oil paint or surface scratches, shapes are not only used up in the creation of location, but equally in moving between – images fully metamorphose onscreen as space, objects and figures both emerge and dissolve. Returning to *The Metamorphosis of Mr Samsa* and the sequence discussed earlier of Gregor attempting to right himself, this was created through small changes to an image constructed from sand, in which each change was individually photographed, a process giving the images their marvellous fluidity. The fluidity of form also evokes the complexity of the spatial organization of Gregor's home. When Gregor wakes up, his room is his bedroom but as the animation continues its door becomes a barrier that separates him from the other members of the family. As the technique of the animation metamorphoses so easily between Gregor and his parents on the other side of the door, a paradox emerges. The frequently effortless shifts between the spaces exist in tension with Gregor's entrapment, making his imprisonment appear all the more profound.

While Massey's ideas place an emphasis on the fluidity of space and its complex and multifaceted organization (a view that is undoubtedly pertinent to intensive experiences of space), elements of *The Metamorphosis of Mr Samsa* are also suggestive of a further way of thinking about space: that is, space as both certain and uncertain. Though much of the animation works via cued transitions, there are also moments when the images transform unexpectedly from one space to another, from Gregor's flailing limbs to his mother's hand laying out forks at the breakfast table. Such moments of unexpected transition introduce a quality of uncertainty into the animation. Through its combination of form and content, the animation depicts Gregor's disorientating experience, but these unexpected transitions allow a viewer to also experience moments of uncertainty, of being in-between in an encounter with transforming space. While Massey's view keeps in focus the fluidity of space, individuals can experience space as both static *and* fluid. Space is perceived in terms of stasis when it is certain, when familiarity covers over potential ambiguity. Shifting out of a static engagement with space requires a confrontation with the unfamiliar – returning to a place after the passage of time can destabilize space if actuality and memory no longer coincide. Different experiences of a given spatial organization reconfigure space, forcing the re-discovery that what is mapped out through familiarity is only one dimension of a multiplicity of possibilities. Transformation, then, is not only found in an ongoing intensive experience of space, but in shifting encounters that reveal the multiplicity of meanings from either the perspective of chronology or different points of view.

I now explore these ideas more fully through three distinct animations: *The Street, Flatworld* and *Nocturna Artificialia*. Though each is very different in terms of technique, all share an emphasis on space, where the figures are captivated by space and also encounter unexpected aspects of their storyworld. As these encounters are embedded in both the form and content of the imagery, the unexpectedness or uncertainties of the spaces are transposed into a direct experience for a viewer. As such, they evoke intensive spatial experiences contingent on enclosure, which though offering open and closed experiential possibilities, nevertheless keep space itself as an emergent category. *The Street* is approached through Doreen Massey's ideas about the heterogeneous space of social organizations, a position extended to look at how the fluidity of the animation generates a transforming space for the viewer, occasionally invoking uncertain spaces. This emphasis on certain and uncertain space is continued through a discussion of *Flatworld*. As an animation that plays with dimensionality, it is used to expand on the idea that space is not always encountered in a continual process of change, but also as it shifts between familiar and unfamiliar organizations. To finish, *Nocturna Artificialia* is considered as an account of a figure trapped within a space that proves impossible to abstract from obscurity; in an apparent paradox, although the figure is enclosed, the space remains open to imaginative transformations.

Fluid encounters

Caroline Leaf's animations are known for their fluid transitions, referred to as 'sustained metamorphoses'.[6] The combination of this emphasis on mutability with narratives of confinement in several of her animations (*The Metamorphosis of Mr Samsa, The Street* and *Entre Deux Soeurs*, 1990) makes them very open to thinking about questions of space. *The Street*, perhaps Leaf's most celebrated animation, features images created using under-lit ink on glass, with individual frames generated by small changes to the previous one. This technique, combined with the narrative, produces two senses of space. The first is one of enclosure, while the second is one of transformation. The contrast between these creates the particular spatial dynamics of the animation, where being held in abeyance while waiting for a death in the family has to give way in the end to that inevitable change.

The sense of enclosure of *The Street* is immediately established in the opening sequence. Beginning with the credits, the sounds of a street – the voices of adults and sounds of children playing, the noise of traffic – give way to the sounds of breathing just at the moment that figurative images appear on the screen. The voice-over establishes the context: a hot summer, a dying grandmother, a family unable to go away, held waiting within the space of their home. Being held waiting, trapped within the space of their home, seems to be the essence of the narrative. In this film, the competing sense of transformation emerges through Leaf's use of ink on glass animation, a technique generating spaces and temporalities that combine substantial and insubstantial elements, with change taking precedence. Given often blank or cursory backgrounds, and figures portrayed as sometimes only rudimentary lines rather than being used up in providing locations for action, the changing dimensions take the narrative forward. Despite this quality, the animation is essentially realist rather than abstract (see Figure 3.1). The human figures, while broadly drawn, always evoke the moment of the story – the emotions of weariness, anger, grief and accommodation. It is this aspect that gives substance to the images of time and space in *The Street*. Yet this substance is tempered by the continual transformations of figures and spaces into different figures and spaces, a current of insubstantiality derived from the

FIGURE 3.1 *Still from* The Street *(1976). The mixture of substantial and unsubstantial physicality in the figures of this still captures a quality of the fluidity of the animation.* © *National Film Board of Canada.*

different devices Leaf uses to establish transitions between events, spaces and temporal moments. Up to a point, these transitions recall those of live-action films – straightforward cuts, dissolves and fades – and there even seem to be moving camera-like effects, the most noticeable of which is a 360° panorama of the street. The dissolves, however, are different to those found in live action. Usually a dissolve occurs as one image fades in and another fades out, where both can be discerned briefly competing with each other for a viewer's attention. By contrast in *The Street*, the image literally dissolves and then resolves into another. For instance, the first figurative images of the film emerge as the screen, blank and almost black, resolves into a clasped pair of hands, which in turn dissolve and then resolve into an old woman lying in her bed. In these images the in-between is briefly present onscreen as a hesitation in transformation as one object, seen and comprehended, gives way to another not yet seen and as yet uncomprehended.

The story of a family waiting for a relative to die narrated through a continual mutability of form creates a complex interplay between substantiality and insubstantiality in content and form, one further complicated as *The Street* establishes the different habitations of the space of the home. Following the ideas of Doreen Massey introduced in the previous section, in *The Street* the space of the home is heterogeneous in that each figure interacts with the same space in different ways – the social relations of space are experienced differently – and these different interactions constitute the complexities of the space. For the young boy, the continued life of the grandmother is something of an inconvenience, but one that gives him some status among his friends. Until the grandmother's death he appears eating, sleeping, playing with his friends, or complaining to his parents. For the mother, whose own mother is the ailing woman, it is a time of waiting, marked by filling the day with small activities. This period of waiting filled with action materializes in the sequence that begins with household activities. The visual sequence is structured around a series of transitions across a mixing bowl, combing hair, scrubbing the floors, back to the mixing bowl. Each resolve centres on the repeated motion of an activity, and each gives way to another – the action of the whisk, brush strokes through the hair, the scrubbing of the floor, the wringing of the cloth and the action of the whisk, again. In addition to the passing temporality established in the echoed repetitive action, the return to the mixing bowl is suggestive of a cycle of repetition of quotidian activities only finally interrupted by the cries of the grandmother. Furthermore, since every image of the different activities almost fills the frame, these actions seem to fill not only the time of day but also the space of the home.

The sequence centred on the mother makes an interesting counterpoint to the one which focuses on the father, whose demeanour is one of resignation and relative inaction. Unlike the succession of action-based resolves around the mother, the figure of the father stands almost static to one side of the frame. The other side of the frame is full of nothing, and is mostly in silence until the sound of piano scales intrudes from the street. The figure of the father re-configures into an inactive watcher, hands in pockets at the window, seen first from behind and then through the window. In each of these poses, all he does is take a sweet from his pocket and place it in his mouth. The father is a figure who seems not so much trapped as unable to act, a man who watches as the world goes by him, repeating his ironic and fatalistic mantra: 'what can I say, I was born lucky ... ?' These members of the family (the sister is only rarely glimpsed within the animation) present three distinct yet linked habitations of a home that is marked by the awaited death. Space takes on different meanings according to different lived temporal dimensions; this is a living and heterogeneous space inhabited from the perspectives of individual figures.

The idea of space transformed by different habitations is useful in thinking about the content of Leaf's animation, but it does not fully address another spatial construction within her work: a tendency for the insubstantial quality of the resolves to disassemble the relationship between time, space and action. This allows transformation to enter more forcefully into the organization of the images as the dissolution of an image results not so much in a hesitation but in a complete jump in time and space, where characters resolve from one to another, or objects turn into other objects. In such moments, space can be said to be in use as opposed to used. There are several examples of these in *The Street*: the transitions from the grandmother to the family at table establishing her separation from the family, the boy's hair translating into the children's bedroom, the dissolve from the mother to the nurse and the transformation of the family group into the ambulance. Though these sequences have a dynamic quality, they disrupt the rhythm of fluid transitions by introducing an abrupt change in spatio-temporal continuity. In some of these, the abruptness is bridged by the linked actions of characters. The mother resolves into the nurse, or the family meeting to decide the fate of the grandmother resolves into the ambulance that will take her to a home. The presence of linked action re-establishes a coherence in the images, while also making a point about the transformation of caregiving. In others, however, there is no bridging connection or action, leaving a strong sense of uncertainty in the moments before the image revolves into a distinct time and space. Embedded in the form and content of *The Street*, this sense of uncertainty exists both for the characters and viewers. In the brief moments where the interstitial lingers, before possibilities become definitive actions, there is only transformation, moments that capture the open-ended prospects of beginnings.

Dimensional manipulation

In addition to the continuous transformation of intensive experiences of space, as individuals we also experience space as both fluid and static. To use a different terminology, familiarity erases ambiguity or indeterminacy, and it is only when confronted with something unfamiliar that a shift again occurs. A confrontation with the unfamiliar precipitates the (re)discovery that what is mapped out through familiarity is only one dimension of a multiplicity of possibilities. The idea of dimensional multiplicities extends to animations directed by Daniel Greaves. *Flatworld* and *Manipulation* (1991) constantly pick at assumptions about space by playing with the dimensionality of the image. Noting how filmed objects projected in two dimensions retain a sense of their three-dimensional perspective, Rudolph Arnheim (1958) addressed the precarious dimensionality of projected images, and how a viewer 'sees' the projected image as between two-dimensions and three-dimensions. Although seeing a three-dimensional image projected onto a flat screen, we as viewers also understand images to have depth, even in those works where the illusion of depth is not a particular facet of the work. It is as though we attribute '3-Dness' to the images, even as we know them to be on a two-dimensional screen, and in doing so create a sense of in-between. Arnheim was talking about live-action cinema but his comments are also relevant to animation. Cel-animations generally, or the ink-on-glass technique demonstrated in *The Street*, are two-dimensional images projected on a two-dimensional surface, but depth is introduced through perspective drawing. And because of this, a viewer of animation is able to attribute a sense of depth to two-dimensional animation. While three dimensions have been evident in animation through stop-motion models, puppets, claymation and depth-based sets for many years, the growth of three-dimensional computer animation is currently creating an emergent space in the animation market. In the same way as the later feature-length animations, including the *Shrek* and *Toy Story* films, early shorts showcasing three-dimensional animation such as *Luxor Jnr.* (John Lasseter 1986), *Knick Knack* (John Lasseter 1989) and *The Invisible Man in Blind Love* (Pascal Vuong 1991) sought to achieve the same dimensional qualities evident in live-action cinema. Daniel Greaves's animations are an interesting counterpoint to those aiming for a dimensional equivalence with live-action film, as they constantly call attention to the dimensionality of the image. In calling attention to the dimensionality of space, these animations also evoke another kind of intensive experience of space, where we are confronted with a perspective that makes a familiar space more uncertain.

In both *Manipulation* and *Flatworld*, Greaves creates figures that seem flat, but which subsequently take on additional dimensions. In *Manipulation* a drawn character battles with its animator in ways reminiscent of the Fleischer Brothers' *Out of the Inkwell* series, in which Koko attempts to outwit his animator (a difference here is that the *Inkwell* series made a greater use of animation combined with live-action). The figure in *Manipulation* exists only within the world of paper on drawing board, but draws attention to dimensions as its flat pencil outline is stretched, expanded, squashed and generally manipulated by the fingers of the animator. In retaliation, the figure slides between sheets of paper, steps off the page, moves in three-dimensional space and finally apparently becomes three-dimensional itself. As in live-action or three-dimensional computer animation, this third dimension is only ever an illusion created by perspective since the images themselves are always flat projections on a plane surface. But in watching the shifting dimensions of the animated character a spectator is reminded of the state of being in-between (Figure 3.2). Dimensional space, instead of being in stasis, is in transition; it is as if one were encountering something unexpected in an otherwise familiar territory.

Flatworld extends the play of *Manipulation* into a whole world involving sets and multiple objects. The opening sequence of the animation introduces the key characters: Matt Phlatt, Geoff the Cat and Chips the Fish, who pop up as flat figures. This is followed by an introduction to the planet of Flatworld which looks far from flat, as the dimensions of the space are established through the perspective of the set, and the use of light and shadow and rain effects give perspective even to the surface of the street.

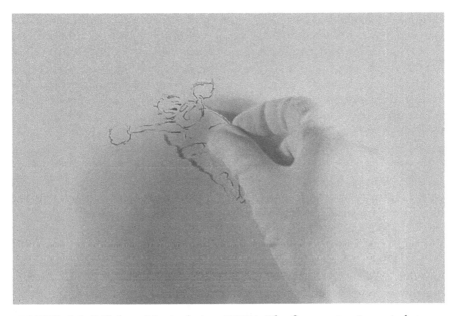

FIGURE 3.2 *Still from* Manipulation *(1991). The figure exists in an in-between state, as both two-dimensional and three-dimensional. Courtesy of Tandem Films Entertainment:* Manipulation *1991.*

Initially, it appears as though the objects of Flatworld are flat, as flat vehicles pass along the streets, and a flat figure sweeps the rubbish. However, as soon as one might have reached this understanding, it is undermined by a flat figure pulling an object with three dimensions. Such shifts continue throughout the animation, and are not cued to help viewers to anticipate the transition: Chips the Fish appears both flat and puffed; Matt can iron part of his leg flat and a chasing dog's face is unexpectedly flattened at a right angle to his body. The play on dimensionality of the objects and characters is a result of the different techniques of drawing, modelling and use of set (with some computer assistance used in the final images). The animation combines conventional cel-animation with flat cut-outs on a three-dimensional set. The cut-outs have shadows, move into depth and behind objects and buildings, and when turning reveal another aspect to their profiles, all of which build the illusion of substance and material dimensions. At other times they are made to slip through impossibly narrow gaps, remain flat when turning, are given heavily drawn outlines which flatten them out, and crumple up like paper. All these reduce the illusion of substance and materiality, especially when the figures and objects are both flat and round, depending on the moment at which they are seen. Through such constant shifts in the dimensions of the characters, *Flatworld* continually explodes assumptions about the spatial dimensions of its characters and objects – as viewers, it turns out that we can never be certain as to what we will see next (Figure 3.3). The manipulations of dimensionality can be thought of as introducing a degree of relativity since the dimension of the objects varies over time. This resonates with the idea of relativity, which has shifted time and space from being seen as absolute dimensions towards the view that they are relative. That is, the measurements given to time and space vary with the positions from which they are observed. Although *Flatworld* is not a commentary on the debates of 20th-century physics, the premise of relativity seems appropriate to the transforming figures of the animation as they are without absolute dimensions, and have aspects changing in time. This relative relationship does not simply introduce uncertainty into the dimensions of space, but also underlines the linkage between space and time. The shifting dimensionality of the characters and objects of *Flatworld* can be seen as a reverberation, of space re-verbed by time.

The uncertain expectation a viewer has for what comes next carries over into the characters of *Flatworld*, as the play on the construction of uncertain dimensions expands into a questioning of the spatial dimensions of the whole planet. This uncertainty of substance also operates on key characters – those

FIGURE 3.3 *Still from* Flatworld *(1991). The image as a whole points to its dual dimensionality, with flat cars driven within a three-dimensional world. Further, the police car in the foreground has a depth absent in any of the others, another moment where the animation denies a viewer certainty. Courtesy of Tandem Films Entertainment:* Flatworld *1991.*

that have been zapped by the multi-coloured aura that escapes the cut cable wires. These characters accidentally fall through puddles from one space into another, and then control access to a myriad of other spaces through the use of a remote control. The introduction of other spaces expands the spatiality of the planet of Flatworld from a singular to a multiple dimension. At first these alternative spaces seem like a means to escape from the chase – the colours of the characters become brighter and vivid, except for the thief who remains in his original grayscale. But it also becomes clear that each world has its own set of rules: heterogeneity does not simply reside in the existence of parallel spaces but also in their distinct organizations. As Matt, the thief, the policeman, Geoff, Chips and the police dog channel hop, the different spaces present new domains, though ones ultimately limited by generic TV conventions. For instance, the events in the Western channel culminate in a Spaghetti-Western style shoot out; Geoff gets bounced on the basketball channel; trapped in a microwave on the cookery show; threatened by a rattlesnake in a romantic desert saga and so forth. The chaotic yet always structured chase breaks down completely when Chips eats the remote, and the channels and spaces begin to leak into each other, or rather they begin to leak into Flatworld itself. The rules of each world cease to operate as everything begins to emerge within a single space, with elements of warfare, nature programmes, a sports channel all running around in the same space. The laws of Flatworld in the end transcend these intrusions, suggesting perhaps that while there may be a multiplicity of possibilities, there are also rules to be followed.

Lost in space

The idea that space emerges from simultaneous interactions, ones that may be unexpected and chaotic, can flip in turn to a view of space as not easily defined, and which may even remain obscure, without any rules to follow. The work of the Brothers Quay is open to this view as films by these puppet animators frequently feature complex spaces established by strange and opaque relations and interactions. These are often frustrating constructions of space which defy any simple definition as it is impossible to grasp what is occurring at any given moment. The places of these animations have locations and realities that remain ambiguous; series of actions rarely result in any clear outcome as cause and effect is convoluted and frequently deferred. The spaces are also uncertain because of their fluctuating dimensions. This fluctuating dimensionality is especially clear in *The Cabinet of Jan Svankmajer* (1984) during the sequences entitled 'The Child's Divining of the Object' and 'The Migration of Forms', when the child discovers drawers that hold expanding spaces (Figure 3.4). Pulling open a drawer in this imaginary world reveals drawers inside drawers inside drawers that look

FIGURE 3.4 *Still from* The Cabinet of Jan Svankmajer *(1984). The boy-like figure opens drawers whose spatial organization expands beyond expected dimensions. Stills courtesy of Koninck.*

into sets of cabinets that open of their accord, and exchange their contents. In *The Cabinet of Jan Svankmajer* there seems to be the suggestion that we should look beyond the obviousness of spaces, and not simply understand them through the measurable set of three dimensions.

The animations of the Brothers Quay, though in detail very distinctive, share a feature with the animations of Caroline Leaf and Daniel Greaves – a sense of space that is both substantial and insubstantial. The minutiae of details – tiny objects, dummies, dust, railings, mechanisms – fill the image, yet the connections between the different elements of the whole do not seem to ever coincide within any given location; instead, each element spirals outwards, seeming to reach beyond the visible boundaries. This combination of substantial and insubstantial space is evident in *Nocturna Artificialia: Those Who Desire without End*, one of the first of the Brothers Quay stop-motion animations. The animation has eight sections, each of which is introduced by a cryptic phrase given in four languages: English, French, German and Polish. The action centres on a single room that seems to have no means of escape, though it does have a number of small windows. The room is inhabited by a single trapped puppet figure, but is vibrantly filled with sounds and shadows that keep this closed space from implosion. Throughout, a series of actions defines at least two spaces, the actual space inhabited by the figure and a second space whose status is uncertain – it is either a fantasy or memory, or a combination of the two – but which is constructed around a tram journey. The first space is indicated partly through the décor of fading patterned wallpaper, bits of furniture and also by the ways in which the figure looks and reaches out of the various apertures of the room. The second space, although apparently separate, in the sense that it can be looked out on, or reached into, is connected to the first by permeable and uncertain boundaries. Given substance in the point of view shots of the figure, the second space is more strongly inferred from shadows and sounds that enter into the enclosed space of the room via the windows and ventilation grilles, and also through objects heard and seen inside the room. The sounds are of a tram passing, creaking wood, metallic clangs, a bell, the twang of cable losing tension and the operation of an electrical engine; the shadows, which at first seem like those of tree branches, are of the cables and passing pantograph, variously still or in motion. The figure, whose movements are captured by stop-motion animation, imagines it is travelling with the tram, at times inside as a passenger and at times as the driver, and finally as the pantograph. The continual shifting between the different spaces, rather than ensuring that they emerge as distinct places, establishes an insubstantial quality that exists in tension with the more substantial enclosing walls of the room, so much so that the boundaries between appear to dissolve. This dissolution of boundaries is further seen in the transitions effected within a shot. At one moment a movement past foregrounded objects may go screen left within the room (clearly delineated by the wallpaper), in the next the same objects (posts) are still being passed, but the background has changed, to perhaps a tunnel, or maybe the darkness of night.

The extensive shifting and permeability of boundaries in *Nocturna Artificialia* creates a figure that inhabits an indeterminate yet curiously lively space. Even when the illusion of the imagined journey literally crashes down, and the figure falls in its attempt to travel the length of imaginary wires transfigured into a pantograph, the ground of the illusion is retained as it feels the cold metal tracks on the cobbles of its floor. As the animation closes on the figure lying prone, still touching this ground, the actuality of the story-world never becomes apparent (Figure 3.5). Just as the status of the spaces remains uncertain, so does the uncertainty of what anything might mean. In *Nocturna Artificialia* it seems impossible to be sure of the reality of this peculiar space – does it suggest a captive figure, held by impossible yet irresistible fantasies of movements outside; or does it suggest a prisoner who retains a connection beyond the prison by refusing to stop immersing itself inside its fantasies, even when confronted with its absurdities; or does it suggest something altogether different? Making a choice would seem to be beside the point, as that seems to be about retaining uncertainty. As Michael

FIGURE 3.5 *Still from* Nocturna Artificialia: Those Who Desire without End *(1979). The figure falls to the ground, yet the space still carries the uncertain status of the figure's actuality in its shadows, and the visual echoing of earlier imagery. Stills courtesy of Koninck.*

Atkinson (1994) has commented: 'Flamboyantly ambiguous, retroactively archaic, obeying only the natural forces of a purely occult consciousness, Quay films are secret, individuated knowledge for each and every viewer' (p. 36). For viewers, the experience is one of disorientation as they are confronted with a space that refuses to become familiar, refuses to allow an abstraction from uncertainty to certainty. Unlike the figure held in the thrall of this space, space itself remains beyond capture.

Re-animating space

Animation's mutable form endows it with an ability to generate the 'illusion of life'; in giving movements to inanimate objects and figures, it challenges assumptions about constructions of time and space, as well as movement, in the cinema. My aim in this article has been to extend this challenge to spatiality. Though all kinds of cinema dynamize form, animation has a particular capacity to reconfigure space. Through the technologies of cinema, space is almost always captured and organized in some way, and its ability to establish the setting for action is without doubt in both animated and live-action filmmaking. Animation has a further facility to create a reverberating space that is in itself a meaningful site for a viewer's engagement, where the process of transformation is able to emerge. Being in space, living through experience, carrying out actions, drawing on memories, imagining possibilities, all generate complex reverberations in our relationships with space. In carrying out these activities, space is inhabited in all sorts of ways, not only in terms of a multiplicity of social relations, but also through continually shifting understandings and experiences from which identities, memories and imaginative possibilities emerge. The diversity of techniques collected together under the term 'animation' yields a rich resource for thinking about how cinema can show being in space. Though there are many ways that space can be explored in animation, the examples considered here bring their formal strategies to bear on enclosure, enlivening their narrative's focus on experiencing transformations in the spaces they inhabit, whether these spaces open out or remain closed and captivating. The sustained metamorphoses of resolving transitions, the dimensional play and space which defies abstraction variously reveal the versatility of animation to depict spaces where possibilities have not yet fully subsided.

Space, then, is a complex phenomenon and animations allow its multiple aspects to emerge in a myriad of ways. Doreen Massey (1993) states:

> It seems to me important to establish the inherent dynamism of the spatial, at least in the sense that the spatial is not simply opposed to the temporal as its absence, as a lack. The argument thus releases the spatial from the realm of the dead. (p. 4)

While Massey's work addresses spatiality in the actual world, my intention here has been to invoke animation as a cinema allowing a re-encounter with the dynamism of space. Animation shows space in the process of being made and re-vivifies cinematic experiences of space, dis-locating it from setting and place. As debates in film studies have shown, we are very aware of the temporalities brought into play by moving images, but spatiality remains an underexplored terrain. To rephrase Gaston Bachelard, space seized upon by the imaginative possibilities of animation, and other kinds of filmmaking, ought not to remain an indifferent space.

Acknowledgement

I would like to thank the Leverhulme Trust for their award of a Research Fellowship.

Notes

1 See, for instance, Gibbs (2002).

2 Almost all films use space as locations for imaginative acts, and sets are often beautifully designed and crafted, but the places created do not themselves change. This is less true of digital effects films where it is possible to find crafted sets that transform. For instance, *Dark City* features a set that morphs under the control of an alien species.

3 In all the animations discussed in this article, the spatial discontinuities are visual as the soundscapes maintain continuity, primarily through music but also through action-based sounds.

4 Massey makes this comment in conversation with Karen Lury (Massey and Lury 1999: 234).

5 Doreen Massey's work belongs in the context of other spatial geographers such as Edward Soja and Henri Lefebvre. See, for instance, Edward Soja (1989) and Henri Lefebvre (1991).

6 Paul Wells explores this idea in an interview with Caroline Leaf, published in Wells (2002: 101–11).

References

Arnheim, R. (1958), *Film as Art*, London: Faber.

Atkinson, M. (1994), 'The Night Countries of the Brothers Quay', *Film Comment*, 30(5): 36–44.

Bachelard, G. (1994), *The Poetics of Space: The Classic Look at How We Experience Intimate Spaces*, Boston: Beacon Press.

Bordwell, D. and Thompson, K. (1976), 'Space and Narrative in the Films of Ozu', *Screen* 17(2): 41–73.

Deleuze, G. (1983), *Cinema 1: The Movement Image*, London: The Athlone Press.

Gibbs, J. (2002), *Mise-en-scène: Film Style and Interpretation*, London: Wallflower Press.

Heath, S. (1981), *Questions of Cinema*, Bloomington: Indiana University Press.

Lefebvre, H. (1991), *The Production of Space*, Oxford: Basil Blackwell.

Maltby, R. (2003), *Hollywood Cinema*, Oxford: Blackwell Publishers.

Massey, D. (1993), *Space, Place and Gender*, Oxford: Polity.

Massey, D. and Lury, K. (1999), 'Making Connections', *Screen*, 40(3): 229–238.

Soja, E. (1989), *Postmodern Geographies: The Reassertion of Space in Critical Social Theory*, London: Verso.

Thomas, D. (2001), *Reading Hollywood: Spaces and Meanings in American Film*, London: Wallflower Press.

Wells, P. (1998), *Understanding Animation*, London: Routledge.

Wells, P. (2002), *Animation: Genre and Authorship*, London: Wallflower Press.

4

Realism and Animation

Mihaela Mihailova

The title of this chapter is not meant to be provocative. And yet, placing animation and realism in the same sentence still tends to raise eyebrows. Perhaps this is due to animation's production process itself and its status as '"other" to the more dominant live-action cinema' (Bukatman 2014: 309). After all, as Stephen Rowley points out, 'the inherent artificiality of animation means that the slippery concept of realism becomes even more suspect than in the live-action context' (2005: 67). And yet, questions of realism have been at the centre of animation aesthetics and discourse since the earliest days of cinema. This chapter outlines key concepts, historical developments and debates on the subject of realism, from classical Hollywood cel animation to contemporary augmented and virtual reality works.[1]

Realism and classical animation techniques

Casey Riffel (2012: 4) has argued in favour of seeing animated realism 'as a technological achievement [and] a historically situated process, rather than merely as a monolithic style or aesthetic'. Indeed, the early history of animated realism in America is intrinsically bound to two technological inventions that fundamentally altered animation production: the rotoscope and the multiplane camera. The rotoscope, patented by Max Fleischer in 1917, allows the animator to trace over live-action footage of an actor, capturing human movement with more fluidity and higher accuracy than previously possible in cartoons (Furniss 2007: 76). The Fleischer Studios would go on to become synonymous with rotoscope animation, thanks in part to its *Out of the Inkwell* series (1919–27), which pioneered the use of this technique through the character Koko the Clown, who was often shown interacting with Max Fleischer, setting an early standard for combining live-action and cartoon imagery in the same frame. The Disney studio quickly adopted and often relied on rotoscoping as well, particularly for the titular female characters in its mid-twentieth-century princess features, whose graceful movements were achieved by animating over footage of female performers.

While Disney's multiplane camera was not the first, it was the studio's particular technical design, used for its first feature-length film *Snow White and the Seven Dwarfs* (1937), that contributed to a fundamental shift in animation aesthetics that would have a lasting and international impact on commercial animation. The multiplane camera introduced to drawn animation a realistic sense of perspective and depth and a more convincing illusion of three-dimensional space. This is achieved by painting different layers of the image on separate movable planes of glass that are placed directly below each other. As the camera moves vertically through this setup, all the separate elements of the frame remain in perspective (Wells 1998: 23).

Since Disney's adoption of the multiplane camera, the studio's house style would be defined by a balancing act between faithfully recreating the physical world and embellishing it for stylistic and narrative purposes. Paul Wells (1998: 25) has dubbed this approach 'hyper-realism' and defined its key conventions: 'it approximates live-action film's representation of reality', obeys the laws of the physical world and features sound that 'corresponds directly to the context from which it emerges'. Similarly, Chris Pallant (2011: 35) argues that 'Disney-Formalism' – his term for the aesthetic style forged in the earliest Disney features – 'prioritized artistic sophistication, "realism" in characters and contexts, and, above all, believability'. However, as Casey Riffel (2012: 4) has aptly observed, Disney's approach to cel animation also revealed a gap between realism and the fantastic, exemplified by the tension between 'emotive anthropomorphism and accurate animal anatomy' and between 'romantic depictions of nature and the role of these romanticized backgrounds in "naturalizing" the seemingly coherent space of the animated image'.

It is such negotiations that hold the key to Disney's animated realism. As evident in the following quote by the veteran Disney animator Joseph Gilland (2009: 156), this aesthetic developed out of the belief that 'what sets animation apart from other mediums [is] our ability to exaggerate reality, to push it farther, into a more fantastic, and ultimately entertaining version of reality'. Or, as Ollie Johnston put it, 'Good [Disney] animation is not about "copying" real life. Good animation is about caricaturing real life. It is Life-Plus' (Sito 2013: 202).

Even though Disney's 'life-plus' approach quickly emerged as a globally dominant one, the Golden Age of American animation (roughly defined as the period between the late 1920s and late 1960s) also gave rise to a parallel movement towards stylization, anti-naturalism and expressionistic use of colour as exemplified by United Productions of America's cartoon shorts. UPA, as the studio came to be known, was active for three decades (early 1940s to 1970). Its notable works include *Gerald McBoing Boing* (Robert Cannon 1950), *Rooty Toot Toot* (John Hubley 1951) and several *Mr. Magoo* cartoons. Formed shortly after the Disney animator's strike of 1941, UPA responded to Disney's animated realism by developing a limited animation aesthetic (limited animation involves fewer drawings between keyframes) influenced by modern and abstract art. In contrast to Disney's obsession with depth and simulating three-dimensional space, UPA's flat, two-dimensional cartoons are 'unequivocally *drawings*, not meant to be mistaken for anything else' (Abraham 2012: 87, emphasis in original).

UPA was not alone in embracing animation's potential to break away from the constraints of the physical world. Studios such as Warner Bros and Hanna-Barbera, which shaped television animation in America during the Golden Age of cartoons, solidified the principles and visual style of 'cartoon physics', a set of 'physical laws [and] restrictions that operate in the service of humor [and] propose an alternative set of means by which bodies navigate space: momentum trumps inertia, gravity is a sometime thing, solid matter often isn't' (Bukatman 2014: 303). As anyone who has seen Wile E. Coyote's indestructible body or the Flintstones' logic-defying household appliances can attest, animated Hollywood has toyed with the impossible as much as it has flirted with the real.

While cel animation has been instrumental in bringing questions of realism to the fore of animation process and production, the theories outlined in relation to drawn imagery are not necessarily applicable to animated media as a whole. Indeed, any attempt at a comprehensive overview of animation and realism is further complicated by the wealth of existing animation techniques and their distinct aesthetic concerns and characteristics. In particular, stop-motion's relationship to reality is much more immediate and direct because this type of filmmaking relies on objects that exist in the world. For example, the films of the Quay Brothers feature both puppets and organic materials which 'as in live action, as materials, are what they represent photo-indexically' (Buchan 2011: xxiii). At the same time, the movement created via stop-motion is often noticeably uneven since, as Maureen Furniss (2007: 161) has noted, 'footage created with frame-by-frame photography lacks the "motion blur" that occurs naturally when a figure moving in real time performs before a live-action camera'. Nevertheless, there are stop-motion productions, notably the feature films of studio Laika, which strike a balance between caricaturing and emulating reality that is not unlike the classic Disney approach. Still, there are other types of animation, such as the direct or drawn-on-film experimental films of Len Lye and Stan Brakhage, which typically eschew or reject figural representation altogether. In such abstract works, rhythm of movement and colour composition are often prioritized over approximating the look of the physical world.

In fact, despite Disney's impact on global animation, the studio's vision of animated realism as 'life-plus' is by no means a universally accepted approach. Non-Western national animation traditions interpret animated media's relationship to reality in a variety of distinct ways, some of which reject imitation, or emulation-based, definitions of realism. For example, some of Russia's most celebrated animators remain sceptical about animation approaches that prioritize the approximation of photographic accuracy in the drawn image. According to Yuri Norstein (2014: 9), 'realistic art should not be confused with simple photographic imaging'. In his opinion, contemporary commercial animation – computer animation in particular – depicts only exteriors without delving into the inner experiences of characters and the depth of a situation, whereas it is this ability to go beyond the surface that constitutes animation's relationship to reality (Norstein 2014: 9–15). Andrei Khrzhanovsky's (2014) interpretation of animated realism focuses on animation's capacity to create a specific atmosphere or convey a believable relationship through carefully chosen details. Thus, he argues that a film about two paper napkins in love can still be realistic because it is based on a recognizable human relationship – a position which favours a narrative-driven approach to realism. Examples of films that would be considered realistic according to this definition include Jan Švankmajer's 1989 stop-motion short *Meat Love,* featuring flirtatious chunks of meat, and Garri Bardin's 1988 *Vykrutasy,* a stylized short featuring characters and environments constructed out of wire.

In Japan, achieving visual similarity to physical reality is not a necessary prerequisite for animated realism, either. According to certain Japanese animation critics, realism is not a question of resemblance to the real, but 'first and foremost a set of conventions proper to historically produced configuration of a given medium'. In this context, animation is considered a medium that, instead of replicating realism, 'provides the basis for "animation-like" work within a different media form' (Steinberg 2014: 289). While anime's relationship to reality is too broad and distinctive to adequately cover here, such definitions of realism and its connection to animated media hint at the need to go beyond hegemonic Hollywood approaches and explore these questions in a transnational context.

Animated realism in the digital age

While some of the key approaches towards defining animated realism have been formulated in relation to two-dimensional drawn animation, in the last two decades animation's relationship to reality has been most rigorously theorized in the context of digital imagery and visual effects. The ubiquity of sophisticated computer-generated imagery in global media – both live-action and animated – has given new urgency to questions about animation's relationship with reality.

One of the most persistent interpretations of computer-generated realism defines it as fundamentally based on imitating the representational strategies of live-action cinema and photographic imagery. This reading is perhaps best exemplified by Lev Manovich and Andrew Darley's work. Despite disagreeing on the characteristics of the resulting realism and its meaning vis-à-vis the evolution of digital-era filmmaking, both scholars propose that, instead of engaging reality directly, computer animation emulates existing cinematic representations of the world. Specifically, Manovich (2001: 200) argues that 'what computer graphics have (almost) achieved is not realism, but rather only *photorealism* – the ability to fake not our perceptual and bodily experience of reality but only its photographic images'. For his part, Darley (2000: 75) writes that computer imaging achieves a 'second-order' realism wherein classical cinematic conventions of realistic representation – such as three-point lighting, depth of field, lens flare and motion blur – are emulated by software. For example, *WALL-E* (Andrew Stanton 2008) takes advantage of virtual camera software designed to simulate both the perspective and the visual imperfections typical of the 1970s classic science-fiction films that the Pixar feature nostalgically evokes (Herhuth 2014: 68).

A prominent alternative to theories describing animated realism as quintessentially derivative of live action is the idea that animation's relationship with reality hinges on going beyond the photographic image and into an aesthetic territory accessible only to animation itself. Scholars who have approached the issue from this angle include Vivian Sobchack and Michele Pierson. In their writing on computer-generated imagery, both theorists explicitly question the framing of photographic representation as an ideal that digital imagery aspires to; instead, they suggest that computer-generated animation, unfettered as it is by any direct links to the physical world, may in fact be working towards transcending the goal of capturing reality and focusing on (re)creating it. To quote Pierson (2002: 87), much of early-1990s computer-generated imagery represented 'a hyperreal electronic aesthetic that took the cinematographic image as a possible point of departure'. Meanwhile, Sobchack (2006: 173) argues that 'perhaps insistent on its own discrete metaphysics, animation might desire not "integral realism," but "integral *irrealism*" – and thus be guided by an alternative ideal founded on the "total" creation (not re-creation) of the world in its own image'. Moreover, as Sobchack's analysis of *Final Fantasy: The Spirits Within* (2001) illustrates, digital animation's obsession with photorealism, with its over-investment in replicating minute visual detail, can lead to a distracting and ultimately unsatisfactory spectatorial experience, as viewers who have been primed to expect an imitation of reality end up fixating on CGI's limitations instead.

As these various interpretations suggest, defining and theorizing digital animation's relationship with reality remains an epistemologically slippery endeavour. While some scholars tend to undermine and underestimate animation's uniqueness as a visual medium, others run the risk of overdetermining its exceptionality. To avoid generalization, and account for the ongoing evolution of digital animation techniques and their representational modes, it is productive to study contemporary digital animated realism not as a monumental entity, but as a phenomenon shaped by specific national, historical, industrial and political contexts.

Contemporary Hollywood animation: A case study

While the tools available to today's animators are much more sophisticated and versatile than the multiplane camera, what they offer is an enhanced version of the same illusion of movement within a cohesive deep space that classical animators established as essential to cartoon realism. Relatedly, the tendency to bend – but rarely break – the rules of physics that can be traced back to Disney's pre-digital output (as discussed earlier in this chapter) remains a key feature of Hollywood animation features. Indeed, American digital animation often blends highly precise technologically-enabled fidelity to physical phenomena with elements of stylized cartoon imagery. In other words, contemporary US animated media's relationship to reality is the product of a balance between the accurate reproduction of light, shading, texture, perspective and movement, and the distortion of these same parameters for aesthetic or narrative reasons. For example, Sully's fur in *Monsters, Inc.* (Pete Docter 2001) is designed to look naturalistic in texture, density and movement without detracting from the blue creature's cartoonish and otherworldly appearance. Similarly, in the Dreamworks feature *How to Train Your Dragon* (Chris Sanders and Dean DeBlois 2010), the titular creature Toothless is designed as an adorable catlike hybrid (but with amusingly doglike behaviour), but his flight movements are meticulously modelled on actual birds and calibrated to convey the appropriate sense of speed and weight.

Furthermore, contemporary Hollywood animation remains indebted to the rules of classical Hollywood storytelling. Since its earliest features, the Disney studio has always been careful to incorporate reasons for any anti-realist appearance or behaviour of its characters into the films' storylines, legitimizing aesthetic experimentation via conventional narrative. For instance, Dumbo's simultaneous defiance of the laws of gravity and the animal kingdom is motivated by his enormous ears (Ajanović 2004: 46).

This brand of animated realism, which developed under the influence of live-action cinema, sets the tone for contemporary animated features, which favour convincing appearance, movement and behaviour in combination with continuity editing. In recent Disney/Pixar features (*Brave, Frozen, The Incredibles*), any escape from the basic laws of nature is attributed to magic or superpowers. Even an event as unbelievable as an entire house taking flight in *Up* (Pete Docter and Bob Peterson 2009) is given an explanation: a mountain of balloons which could conceivably overcome the house's weight.

Historical continuity and the lasting influence of Disney have had a major impact on contemporary digital realist aesthetics, but they are not the only factors worth considering. For example, it is important to note Pixar's early work in commercials and the essential role that animated realism played in their success. As D. A. Price (2008: 110) explains, 'Pixar's ability to create photorealistic versions of inanimate objects and turn them into expressive characters was novel to television audiences'. Indeed, the widespread adoption of computer-generated imagery capable of both emulating and creatively distorting reality can be attributed to a combination of factors, including the needs of other industries – such as advertising, the military and video games – all of which have historically benefitted from advances in sophisticated visual simulation.

From an ideological standpoint, digital animation's relationship to reality is often presented as synonymous with technological superiority. Computer-generated imagery's capacity to both create a highly precise impression of reality and use it as a baseline for formal experimentation – resulting in what Ed Catmull, the current president of Pixar, has fittingly dubbed 'stylized realism' – is often cited by members of the industry as one of the medium's defining artistic features (Pallant 2011: 133). What is more, it is seen as a criterion of quality and sophistication, both technologically and aesthetically. For instance, Jodi Whitsel (2002), Blue Sky's Lighting Lead on *Ice Age* (Chris Wedge and Carlos Saldanha 2002), boasts that the company's renderer is 'so physically accurate that [the team] can place lights and do things just like you would in the real world and it pretty much comes out right'. At the same time, the freedom to diverge from the laws of nature for aesthetic reasons is often celebrated as a sign of both technological progress and artistic superiority. Such technophilic accounts of the digital animation process as a journey beyond the limitations of reality demonstrate that – to quote filmmaker Jane Shadbolt (2012) – 'the rhetoric of digital filmmaking is the promise of the infinite'.

Digital visual effects

Digital visual effects produced for live-action cinema share many of the aesthetic features and approaches described above, including the tendency to gently embellish reality through 'careful cheats in the interest of style and tone' (Prince 2012: 70). However, they also pose additional challenges to defining animated realism because they are meant to convincingly coexist on screen with non-animated characters and landscapes. According to Stephen Prince's (2012: 32) theory of perceptual realism, this means that filmmakers need to convince viewers that the creatures or worlds created via digital effects exist in the same perceptual reality and follow the same laws of physics as the real world. Prince (2012: 32) posits that digital effects achieve this by recreating 'contextual cues designating a three-dimensional world', including 'principles of motion and anatomy and the physics involved in dynamic systems such as water, clouds, and fire'. This is especially relevant to live-action films centred on interactions between actors and computer-generated creatures – such as *Fantastic Beasts and Where to Find Them* (David Yates 2016) and *War of the Planet of the Apes* (Matt Reeves 2017) – because the success of these productions is largely predicated on the digital beasts functioning as believable characters occupying the same diegetic space as the humans.

In order to achieve this, many contemporary features rely on a technique called motion capture which is used to achieve physically accurate and convincing motion in computer-animated film and video game characters by using reference data collected from the digitized footage of human actors wearing specialized suits with sensors. Visual effects artists rely on this data as a starting point when animating the digital body, working with what Lisa Purse (2013: 56) has described as 'an abstraction of the actor's movements' in order to alter and edit it in the service of realistic movement and gestures. Notable recent examples of live-action features using motion and performance capture (a more sophisticated technique which includes facial capture) include *Star Wars: The Force Awakens* (J.J. Abrams 2015), *Avatar* (James Cameron 2009), and *Beowulf* (Robert Zemeckis 2009). Certain video game franchises have also featured motion-captured lookalikes of Hollywood actors, such as Kevin Spacey (*Call of Duty: Advanced Warfare* 2014) and Sigourney Weaver (*Alien: Isolation* 2014), largely in order to draw on the star power of these performers to enhance the game's marketability.

In addition to realism of movement, contemporary cinema is likewise concerned with simulating realism of behaviour, particularly as it applies to animated crowds. Animated multitudes appear more convincing if the individual behaviour of their members and their behaviour as a group are integrated successfully and feature a certain number of variations. For example, the MASSIVE software used in *Lord of the Rings* enabled animators to introduce an element of spontaneity in large battle scenes, giving the actions of separate Orcs and Uruk-hai a certain measure of randomized uniqueness (Whissel 2014: 79).

Contemporary superhero franchises are also preoccupied with showcasing computer animation's capacity to manipulate elements of the physical world. Both *X-Men: Days of Future Past* (Bryan Singer 2014) and

X-Men: Apocalypse (Bryan Singer 2016) feature representative visual effects scenes involving the mutant Quicksilver, whose incredible speed appears to make time literally stop flowing, allowing him to re-order the space around him according to his needs. In both films, the mutant's effortless mastery over his environment is underscored through a series of random cheeky acts he performs in the middle of high-stakes crisis situations. In the 2014 film, he pauses to steal a hat from someone's head, while in the 2016 sequel he takes time to sip from a soda can, moonwalk and fix a boy's hair. While ostensibly designed for comic relief, such gestures also serve to emphasize contemporary visual effects' capacity to transcend the natural flow of movement in time, thereby also altering physical space in objectively impossible ways. If, at the turn of the twentieth century, film promised to capture and decode reality, now it dreams of re-ordering and (computer-) programming it.

Emerging media and realism

The past decade has seen the rapid proliferation of emerging digital art forms whose functions and visual design rely on redefining the relationship between computer-generated imagery and physical space. Considering animated imagery's relationship with reality will be among the key factors in conceptualizing the development of such media. Virtual and augmented reality, in particular, are already being shaped by realism debates. According to some, the key to creating a convincing sense of reality in VR experiences is not visual verisimilitude, but engaging the user's proprioception (their sense of the position and movement of their own limbs in space that is independent of vision) (Vanderbilt 2016). This is particularly relevant to current research into virtual reality projects that aim to create the illusion of exploring immersive virtual spaces. Such projects benefit from a technique called 'redirected walking', which uses 'subtle visual clues' and misdirection to trick head-mounted display users walking in a confined space into believing that they are moving through a large area (Zhang 2015).

Augmented reality applications rely on a more immediate relationship with the surrounding world designed around the interplay between animated and physical realities. Take, for example, Niantic's 2016 cell phone game *Pokémon Go*. Unlike virtual reality applications, which create the illusion of placing the user into digitally generated environments, *Pokémon Go* involves navigating actual cities in order to discover – by making use of the phone's built-in camera – digital creatures which are virtually overlaid onto existing locations. Here, animation's relationship with reality is no longer representational; the cartoon dimension merges with real space – and in real time – and adds a new layer of meaning to existing landmarks.

Animation's central role and expanding presence in emerging media raise questions about the evolving definitions and attitudes towards animated realism in the digital age. How might virtual and augmented reality's emphasis on movement in space – both simulated and physical – expand and reshape the aesthetic and industrial imperatives of digital realism? What new forms of realism may arise out of the digital hybridization of physical environments? Virtual and augmented reality technologies are still relatively new, and their place within the larger twenty-first-century media landscape remains to be defined. However, it is clear that examining animation's role in (re)ordering the world will be central to understanding emerging global modes of negotiating physical reality and social landscapes.

Note

1 Questions of animated realism are especially relevant to – and productively illuminated by – animated documentary filmmaking, which is examined in detail in a separate chapter of this volume.

References

Abraham, A. (2012), *When Magoo Flew: The Rise and Fall of Animation Studio UPA*, Middletown, CT: Wesleyan University Press.

Ajanović, M. (2004), *Animation and Realism*, Zagreb: Hrvatski filmski savez/ Croatioan Film Clubs' Association.

Buchan, S. (2011), *The Quay Brothers: Into a Metaphysical Playroom*, Minneapolis, MN: University of Minnesota Press.

Bukatman, S. (2014), 'Some Observations Pertaining to Cartoon Physics; or, The Cartoon Cat in the Machine', in K. Beckman (ed.), *Animating Film Theory*, 301–316, Durham, NC: Duke University Press.

Darley, A. (2000), *Visual Digital Culture: Surface Play and Spectacle in New Media Genres*, New York: Routledge.

Furniss, M. (2007), *Art in Motion: Animation Aesthetics*, rev. edn, Eastleigh: John Libbey Publishing.

Gilland, J. (2009), *Elemental Magic: The Art of Special Effects Animation*, Burlington, MA: Focal Press.

Herhuth, E. (2014), 'Life, Love, and Programming: The Culture and Politics of *Wall-E* and Pixar Computer Animation', *Cinema Journal*, 53(4): 53–75.

Khrzhanovsky, A. (2014), Interview by author, October 20, recording.

Manovich, L. (2001), *The Language of New Media*, Cambridge, MA: The MIT Press.

Norstein, Y. (2014), 'Yuri Norstein: To Be Responsive to Life', interview by Kamila Boháčková, *Homo Felix: The International Journal of Animated Film*, 5(1): 9–15.

Pallant, C. (2011), *Demystifying Disney: A History of Disney Feature Animation*, New York: Continuum.

Pierson, M. (2002), *Special Effects: Still in Search of Wonder*, New York: Columbia University Press.

Price, D. A. (2008), *The Pixar Touch: The Making of a Company*, New York: Vintage.

Prince, S. (2012), *Digital Visual Effects in Cinema: The Seduction of Reality*, New Brunswick, NJ: The Rutgers University Press.

Purse L. (2013), *Digital Imaging in Popular Cinema*, Edinburgh: Edinburgh University Press.

Riffel, C. (2012), 'Dissecting *Bambi*: Multiplanar Photography, the Cel Technique, and the Flowering of Full Animation', *The Velvet Light Trap*, 69: 3–12.

Rowley, S. (2005), 'Life Reproduced in Drawings: Preliminary Comments upon Realism in Animation', *Animation Journal*, 13: 65–86.

Shadbolt, J. (2012), 'Matter Meets Anti-Matter: An Excursion into Annihiliation through Hybrid Stop-Motion Animation', The Anime Machine: 24th Annual Society for Animation Studies Conference Proceedings, Melbourne, 25–27 June 2012.

Sito, T. (2013), *Moving Innovation: A History of Computer Animation*, Cambridge MA: MIT Press.

Sobchack, V. (2006), 'Final Fantasies: Computer Graphic Animation and the [Dis] Illusion of Life', in S. Buchan (ed.), *Animated 'Worlds'*, 171–183, Eastleigh: John Libbey Publishing.

Steinberg, M. (2014), 'Realism in the Animation Media Environment: Animation Theory from Japan', in K. Beckman (ed.), *Animating Film Theory*, 287–301, Durham, NC: Duke University Press.

Vanderbilt, T. (2016), 'These Tricks Make Virtual Reality Feel Real', *Nautilus*, 7 January. Available online: http://nautil.us/issue/32/space/these-tricks-make-virtual-reality-feel-real (accessed 1 August 2017).

Wells, P. (1998), *Understanding Animation*, London: Routledge.

Whissel, K. (2014), *Spectacular Digital Effects: CGI and Contemporary Cinema*, Durham, NC: Duke University Press.

Whitsel, J. (2002), 'The Making of Ice Age', disc 2, *Ice Age*, Blu Ray, directed by Chris Wedge, Greenwich, CT: Blue Sky.

Zhang, S. (2015), 'You Can't Walk in a Straight Line – and That's Great for VR', *Wired*, 21 August. Available online: https://www.wired.com/2015/08/cant-walk-straight-lineand-thats-great-vr/ (accessed 1 August 2017).

5

The Uncanny Valley

Lisa Bode

For many viewers of *Rogue One: A Star Wars Story* (2016), the digital face of Grand Moff Tarkin seems sepulchral, and not quite human, his gaze even icier than the original played by the late Peter Cushing in 1977 (McMillan 2016). A side-by-side comparison of Cushing and his replica, however, reveals the two to be very nearly indistinguishable. It is difficult to pin down why the digital face does not quite work: Is there something a little blank and unseeing about the eyes, or something diminished in the face's micro-expressions? Or is the discomfort entangled with the knowledge that it is a technological resurrection of a deceased actor? Whatever the reason, viewer responses to the digital Tarkin are in line with those elicited by earlier 3D digitally animated human faces – that are at one and the same time very realistic but not quite realistic enough, or 'uncanny'.

Myriad reviewers of *Final Fantasy: The Spirits within* (Hironobu Sakaguchi 2001) have similarly described the characters as cold, soulless and mechanical mannequins. Writing on Robert Zemeckis's screen adaptation of *The Polar Express* (2004), reviewer Manohla Dargis claimed that the characters were 'creepily unlifelike' with an 'eerie listlessness' (2004). Watching Zemeckis's later film, *Beowulf* (2007), Peter Bradshaw felt that the characters were 'disconcertingly only almost human [...] There is something about the way the eyes are drawn which makes them look distant or even blind' (2007), while Kevin Maher complained that the 'synthespians look like rubber-faced automatons' (2007). Various explanations have been put forth for why animated figures that aim for lifelike photorealism tend to strike us as vaguely unpleasant or not fully 'alive', and largely these are tied to 'the uncanny valley' hypothesis. Here I examine some of these explanations in relation to photorealistic animation of human and human-like figures, as well as uncanniness in animation more generally, in order to deepen our understanding of spectatorial unease with particular kinds of moving images.

The term 'uncanny valley' was coined by Japanese roboticist Masahiro Mori in 1970. He wrote, 'I have noticed that, in climbing toward the goal of making robots appear like a human, our affinity for them increases until we come to a valley, which I call the uncanny valley' (2012: 98). Mori plotted a graph visualizing what he saw as the correlation between levels of viewer affinity and various kinds of human-like objects (puppets, robots, dolls), and marked a tipping point where simulations of life, whether prosthetic limbs, androids or moving waxworks, become 'too real' or 'too human-like', and our affinity and warmth towards them slides steeply down into aversion. The greater the proximity to human likeness in appearance, he argued, the deeper the repulsion. Mori proposed that this aversion might be due to evolutionary biology, connected to the explanations we have for other emotions such as disgust: if the skin on a prosthetic limb looks unalive or unhealthy, or if a face looks only semi-conscious, it may trigger something hardwired in our brains that leads us to avoid sickness, death or other things that may bring us physical harm. Whatever the underlying causes, he concluded that robot designers should pull back from the pursuit of simulating human likeness, and instead experiment with abstraction and stylization in their designs if they wished to avoid the possibility of uncanniness being triggered in the viewer (2012: 99).

Despite Mori's recommendations, in the 2000s further strides have been made in the verisimilitude of android design and the 3D animation of photorealistic human figures for movies and games. As a result, the uncanny valley has re-emerged as an important topic for researchers in fields such as animation studies, film studies, robot–human interaction and cognitive science. Since 2005, various empirical studies have tested viewer responses to replica human images of different kinds. Such studies have sought to ascertain what might guarantee, amplify or decrease the uncanny effect, to determine whether or not it is a universal experience, and to understand its underlying cognitive roots or evolutionary purpose (MacDorman and Chattopadhyay 2016: 190–191). Research using adults, children, infants and other primates seems to support the reality of the phenomenon (MacDorman and Chattopadhyay 2016: 190); however, some studies support less a 'valley' than a 'cliff', suggesting a much steeper aversion correlation with synthetic human likeness – one that may not tilt upwards again towards affinity. The idea of an 'uncanny cliff' implies that the pursuit of absolute human verisimilitude is a failed project: that it will never be possible to circumvent the complexity of the ways our brains process faces and facial expressions. No matter how lifelike and human synthespians become, we are hardwired to spot the fake.

Film theorist Stephen Prince (2012) disagrees, suggesting that under the right economic and technological conditions, it is possible for animated digital humans to 'cross' the uncanny valley. He points out that while marker-based motion capture systems are great for capturing body motion, they are inadequate for facial expressions, as these are produced through surface deformation. Our faces contain fifty-three muscles in thin sheets, which are not attached to bone but 'from skin to skin' (2012: 123). Marker-based systems produce incomplete and crude character expressions that have required substantial, painstaking supplemental animation based on video reference of the actors. Much rendering and animation is needed not just for skin and facial muscles but everything to do with the eyes, such as gaze direction, blinks, saccades and minute expansions and contractions of the pupils in response to light or emotional arousal. For these reasons, Prince concludes that 'the amount of labor from digital animators necessary to provide all the subtle expressions of character that a live actor might contribute would be far too expensive to create. Thus calculations of cost-efficiency contribute to the phenomenon of the uncanny valley' (2012: 123).

Films such as *Beowulf* and *Final Fantasy: The Spirits Within* attempt to compensate for diminished facial verisimilitude by instead attending to the tiny surface details of fabric textures, skin and hair, such as age spots, veins, peach fuzz on a cheek catching the light or nostril hair. Prince reports that with *Beowulf*, 'the visual effects supervisor felt that by adding more detail, the actor's performances would become more engaging' (2012: 125). While gorgeous to look at, the 'hyperbole' of this detail appears to have been counterproductive. This is something Vivian Sobchack notes of *Final Fantasy* and the way the film lingers on such visual details cuing a 'heightened and hyperbolic form of judgemental attention' (2006: 179). Because our attention is drawn away from the inner life of the characters 'to the character's skin, their liver spots, their freckles and wrinkles [...] the physics of clothing, movement, and [...] the way hair falls', the experience, she argues, is 'not so much uncanny as it is unmoving' (2006: 180). While our evaluative centres are in such a state of alert, we are distanced from the characters, and any chance of an empathetic engagement with them is dissolved. I would argue too that our heightened attention continues to be primed by promotional paratexts discussing synthespians, photorealistic animated human figures and the uncanny valley phenomenon itself. In other words, there may be a neurological basis to the uncanny valley effect, but it is likely amplified and sustained by the entertainment media buzz around digital 3D humans, which invites us to test our perception by framing each new synthespian as an illusion to be critiqued rather than a compelling screen character.[1]

For some, the uncanny valley is seen as a problem to be solved, or investigated, in order to better understand the complexities of spectatorship. Other animation scholars take the uncanny valley as something to be avoided by animators, and engage with Mori's recommendation to pull back from absolute verisimilitude. They make a case for abstraction, caricature or the plasmatic qualities traditionally valued in animation and are wary of the pursuit of digital photorealism, because, they argue, pushing animation to mimic live-action conventions obscures the visual markers of animation labour and creativity. Matthew Butler and Lucie Joshko have drawn on Mori's work in order to compare viewer engagement with the 'burlesque' caricatured animation style of Brad Birds' *The Incredibles* (2004) against what they see as viewer disconnection from *Final Fantasy*'s 'frighteningly realistic' 3D characters. Through this comparison they argue that caricature, abstraction and distance from verisimilitude in animation character design allows viewers to deploy their imaginations in recognizing and projecting familiar characteristics from their own experience onto the characters, and this projection leads to a deeper engagement and the kind of 'affinity' noted by Mori. By contrast, 'ultra-realistic (or photorealistic) animation offers no visual space for viewers to engage their imagination in order to form a unique experience' (2009).

While we might be able to pinpoint the specific qualities of animation that may cue an uncanny experience, this is a different matter from understanding the underlying principles of that experience. It is these principles that allow us to see the connections between the uncanniness of photorealistic animation and other kinds of animation. German psychologist Ernst Jentsch in his 1906 essay 'The Psychology of the Uncanny', determined that uncanniness was first and foremost a kind of 'psychical uncertainty': a sensation in which what we perceive might be fleetingly at odds with our rational understanding about the way things are (p. 9). He provides a list of scenarios or phenomena that may arouse this feeling: masked balls (what if the being behind the mask is not human? What if there is nothing behind the mask?); illusions, conjuring tricks (is magic real?); a moving tree branch (the wind, or?); before arguing that the uncanny was most regularly aroused by 'doubt as to whether an apparently living being is animate and conversely, doubt as to whether a lifeless object may be in fact inanimate' (p. 11). Listing corpses, waxworks and porcelain dolls among objects likely to arouse the uncanny, he noted that 'the life-size automata that perform complicated tasks, blow trumpets, dance, and so forth, very easily give one a feeling of unease' (p. 12). In an argument that pre-figures Mori, he said 'the finer the mechanism, and the truer to nature the formal reproduction, the more strongly will the special effect also make its appearance' (p. 12). Sigmund Freud later took Jentsch's argument further into discussions of castration anxiety, but for our purposes here, he also usefully emphasized that the uncanny is 'a class of the frightening which leads back to what is known of old and long familiar' (1955 [1919]: 220). For Freud, the uncanny arises when the old buried fantastical fancies of our childhood seem momentarily confirmed in the rational universes of our adult selves.

Jentsch's ideas imply that what is troubling about photorealistic animation is that it tends to make us uncertain about the ontological status of what it is we are seeing. This notion of uncertainty is borne out by Mark Langer who suggested that the problem with *Final Fantasy* was the 'liminality' of its aesthetics which cued an uncertain wavering as to whether he was watching living actors or the work of animation (2002: 5). In order to dispel that uncertainty, we scour the image for clues, and if we can find ways to categorize it as a facsimile, this allows us certainty.

Jentsch's focus on uncertainty and doubt, specifically in relation to categories like real/unreal, human/inhuman, living/dead, animate/ inanimate has tremendous resonance for thinking about the uncanniness of other kinds of animation, beyond just the kinds of photorealistic characters examined so far. Maureen Furniss, Suzanne Buchan and Paul Wells have all observed that stop motion, object or puppet animation, as it involves endowing 'objects that we know to be inanimate' with life, gives us a different order of viewing experience from that provided by drawn animation, which as Furniss observes is 'more clearly marked as being fabricated, rather than something of the "real world"' (Furniss 2007: 169). Buchan's phenomenological work on the Quay Brothers' 1986 film *The Street of Crocodiles* expands on the particular qualities of puppet animation in this film, saying that it creates something between 'a world' (the fictional world of animated dolls and other objects such as screws) and 'the world', the material one in which we coexist with inanimate dolls and other objects (Buchan 2006: 15–38). The haunted strangeness of the Quay Brothers' work can be in part attributed to this 'between' quality of inanimate material objects from our world endowed with impossible movement.[2]

Paul Wells argues that, because the objects in object animation are part of our world, their use in animation is 'the re-animation of materiality' (1998: 90). According to this view, objects are never unalive just because they are inanimate, but instead have 'secret inner lives'. These 'secret inner lives' are essentially the invisible traces left from all the ways in which objects have been made, held, used and invested by us with life and 'kinetic energy', or how, as silent and still presences in our lives, objects have absorbed our memories and emotions (1998: 90). Through this perspective, object animation is uncanny in the Freudian sense of resonating with our old childhood beliefs that our toys have feelings.

Human actors too can be rendered uncanny through animation techniques, as Laura Ivins-Hulley has explored in relation to 'human pixilation' animation, such as we see in Norman McLaren's *Neighbours* (1952) and Jan Švankmajer's *Food* (1992), in which stop-motion techniques are used to animate living actors. As Jentsch argues, uncanniness can be aroused when doubts emerge as to whether an 'apparently living being' is animate, and Ivins-Hulley puts it well when she says Švankmajer '"objectifies" the actors, paradoxically taking away much of their human agency even as he so often grants agency to non-living objects through stop motion' (2013: 268). Here we see people become like mechanized puppets, their still poses captured in increments and joined in the editing suite, moving at the will of the animator. The result is both amusing and disquieting.

To further think through the implications for the way the concepts of animate and inanimate relate to those of 'living' and 'dead', it is useful to turn to animation theorist Alan Cholodenko. Cholodenko considers animation within a long-standing series of debates

> 'from classical times onward between the animists, who believed that the world was alive with organic or spiritual substance, that all that moved was alive (even things that did not move could be considered as alive), and the mechanists, who believed that the motion of matter was obedient to physical laws and necessitated no presumption of organic or spiritual vivifying agency' (2007: 487).

The term 'to animate' has a doubled definition: to endow with life, and to endow with motion. But these two meanings are not always synonymous, for instance, machines and zombies move, but we do not say they are 'alive', while the magic of animation can bestow inanimate objects such as the Pixar lamp or Jan Švankmajer's beefsteaks with an illusion of living consciousness. A strong impression of living consciousness and agency may be key to the dissolving of unintended uncanny effects in animation, as it dispels uncertainty about what is driving the movement of a character. We can think, for example of *Toy Story* (John Lasseter 1995), a film that playfully dramatizes our lingering childhood fantasies and uncertainties about the secret 'life' of material objects in its depiction of vivified toys, their friendships and adventures, when humans are not around to observe. In our games and ludic animation of our toys, we endow them with our own living agency. But the uncanny is not present in the midst of such play. Rather, as Robyn Ferrell suggests, it is to be found in 'the sly turn of a doll's head, the imperceptible flicker of a statue's stone eyelids, the animal whose expression is for a moment almost human' (1991: 132). Indeed, consider those moments in *Toy Story* where a human enters the playroom, and the toys, a moment ago so full of life and conversation, instantly fall silent, flinging themselves in haphazard configurations on the floor, their eyes glassy and seemingly unseeing.

Toy Story provides more useful examples through which to understand the uncanny. There is a moment where Buzz and Woody get into Sid's bedroom. Sid, the bully who lives next door, likes taking toys apart and putting them back together in mutant form. To Buzz and Woody's horror, these mutant toys come to very sinister life: a shaved baby doll's head with one blinking blue eye atop a Meccano spider body; or human doll body parts hybridized with machine toys such as skate boards and hooks, like little toy cyborg mutants. The way in which they move – sliding and creeping in jerky fits and starts – is very different from the comical and consistent motions of the 'normal' toys next door. But perhaps the biggest key to their uncanniness is not just movement, it is that they do not speak, and so unlike Woody and Buzz, they do not have legible interiority and intentions. Sid's toys elicit, then, that troubling uncertainty about whether they are 'alive' or 'dead', and about whether they move through animistic or unthinking mechanical means. This moment in *Toy Story* is arguably inspired by the Quay Bros, but, while using digital 3D instead of object animation, the sequence works on a 'meta' level. Woody and Buzz's untroubling liveliness is contrasted against the uncanny undead qualities of Sid's toys, setting in play the twin definitions of animation as 'endowing with life' and animation as 'endowing with motion'.

Let us take these twin definitions, and the uncertainty they engender, and return back to where we began: to a consideration of the uncanny valley and the pursuit of verisimilitude in animated humans and androids. At the Society for Animation Studies conference at the University of Southern California in 2013, an android 'portrait' of the late science fiction writer Philip K. Dick held court in the lobby, responding to questions from fascinated and curious fans. Dick, whose stories have been the source of films such as *Blade Runner* (Ridley Scott 1982), *Total Recall* (Paul Verhoeven 1990/ Len Wiseman 2012), and *A Scanner Darkly* (Richard Linklater 2006) seemed an appropriate subject for such a portrait, as his work has explored simulation, artificial intelligence, and the nature of human life and consciousness. 'He' sat with his legs crossed, face set in a faintly benevolent dreamy expression, lips slightly parted, and his eyes blinking intermittently. Wires ran from the back of his head to a laptop. An indistinct tinny voice issued barely audible phrases taken from novels and interviews with the author, from somewhere inside. From a distance, if you didn't see the wires, you saw a slightly rumpled bearded man in a bad polyester shirt and trousers, surrounded by people with their phones out, taking pictures or poking him and jumping back with a nervous titter. Proximity, however, triggered unease, if you were close enough to see or feel the pink rubbery skin on his hands and face and the limited range of expressions, or to hear the muffled electronically mediated voice. But still, if you squinted, you could instead re-imagine the figure as an ageing man whose faculties had deteriorated as the result of too many brain scrambling drugs, but who, at times, could give the impression that his consciousness was on a higher plane. The unseeing gaze seemed, in that benevolent slowly blinking face, to be seeing beyond. My point is: the uncanny effect was strongest if I focused on the fact that the android's motions had a purely technological cause. There was no interiority: just a dead doll made to slightly move. However, the uncanny effect dissipated if I projected recognizably human qualities and interiority onto the figure. Then, its slight movements evoked signs of low-key life, rather than signs of mechanism.

The figure itself, like a 3D photorealistic digital actor, was liminal, and it was up to me to create certainty out of uncertainty: to look for the clues for human-ness and aliveness or technological artifice and un-aliveness, in the process thinking through the ways in which living humans can seem machine-like at times, or lacking agency, on automatic pilot, absent-minded. Similarly, watching the digital Moff Tarkin of *Rogue One*, and noting the signs of slight inhumanity, these can be reframed in the viewer's mind to enhance an impression of the character's calculating coldness. Tarkin, after all, does not require our empathetic engagement. He is meant to give us the creeps. Perhaps, then, depending on the type of character, the uncanny valley does not have to be a 'problem'.

We can see Jentsch's 'psychical uncertainty' as the key to understanding uncanniness in animation of many kinds and how central stillness as well as movement is to the generation of this uncertainty. The ways in which we experience the uncanniness of photorealistic animation of human figures have points of connection with the uncanniness of other forms of animation, such as object animation, human pixilation and stop-motion puppet animation incorporated in live-action contexts, as well as animation that might be more clearly fabricated but takes up themes of objecthood and agency. Each is tied in its way to some kind of in-betweenness that may momentarily make us question our knowledge or beliefs about the foundations or definition of reality, organic life, humanness and agency. Such ongoing questions are central, as Cholodenko recognizes, to the very meaning of animation.

Notes

1 It is also apparent that when the proportions of character faces are not aiming for human likeness, highly detailed surface rendering in digital animation can be a sensual, haptic invitation into the story world, rather than a distraction. Pat Power discusses 'low and high modality cues' for human-ness in 3D animation, noting that when it comes to animation of the human form, 'due to our cognitive sensitivity [...] lower modality stylized cues can be more effective or expressive, and are less likely to cue dissonance, as in, for example, the uncanny valley effect' (2009: 113). In other words, despite the attention lavished on the surface details of skin, hair and eyes of characters like Gollum in Peter Jackson's *Lord of the Rings* (2001, 2002, 2003) or Neytiri in *Avatar* (James Cameron 2009), neither character evokes the uncanny valley because their facial design proportions follow low human modality principles.

2 This also explains why the benign plasticine universes produced by Aardman avoid uncanniness. Because they are fashioned from plasticine and follow principles of caricature and stylization, Aardman's characters clearly occupy their own fictional world, separate from the one in which we live.

References

Bradshaw, P. (2007), 'Beowulf', *Guardian*, 16 November. Available online: http://www.guardian.co.uk/film/2007/nov/16/actionandadventure.animation (accessed 2 May 2017).

Buchan, S. (2006), 'The Animated Spectator: Watching the Quay Brothers' "Worlds"', in S. Buchan (ed.), *Animated 'Worlds'*, 15–38, Eastleigh: John Libbey.

Butler, M. and L. Joshko (2009), 'Final Fantasy or The Incredibles: Ultra-Realistic Animation, Aesthetic Engagement and the Uncanny Valley', *Animation Studies*, 4: 55–63.

Cholodenko, A. (2007), 'Speculations on the Animatic Automaton', in A. Cholodenko (ed.), *The Illusion of Life II: More Essays on Animation*, 486–529, Sydney: Power Publications.

Dargis, M. (2004), 'Do You Hear Sleigh Bells? Nah, Just Tom Hanks and Some Train', *New York Times*, 10 November. Available online: http://www.nytimes.com/2004/11/10/movies/do-you-hear-sleigh-bells-nah-just-tom-hanks-and-some-train.html (accessed 2 May 2017).

Ferrell, R. (1991), 'Life Threatening Life: Angela Carter and the Uncanny', in A. Cholodenko (ed.), *The Illusion of Life: Essays on Animation*, 131–144, Sydney: Power Publications.

Freud, S. (1955), 'The "Uncanny"', in J. Strachey and A. Freud (eds), *The Standard Edition of the Complete Psychological Works of Sigmund Freud Vol. XVII (1917–19)*, 219–252, London: Hogarth Press and Institute of Psychoanalysis.

Furniss, M. (2007), *Art in Motion: Animation Aesthetics*, rev. edn, Hertfordshire: John Libbey.

Ivins-Hulley, L. (2013), 'A Universe of Boundaries: Pixilated Performances in Jan Švankmajer's Food', *animation: an interdisciplinary journal*, 8(3): 267–282.

Jentsch, E. (1995 [1906]), 'On the Psychology of the Uncanny', *Angelaki*, 2(1): 7–16.

Langer, M. (2002), 'The End of Animation History', *Society for Animation Studies*. Available online: http://asifa.net/SAS/articles/langer1.htm (accessed 2 July 2003).

MacDorman, K. F. and D. Chattopadhyay (2016), 'Reducing Consistency in Human Realism Increases the Uncanny Valley Effect, Increasing Category Uncertainty Does Not', *Cognition*, 146: 190–205.

Maher, K. (2007), 'Beowulf', *The Times*, 17 November. Available online: http://entertainment.timesonline.co.uk/tol/arts_and_entertainment/film/film_reviews/article2870848.ece (accessed 2 May 2017).

McMillan, G. (2016), '"Rogue One": That Familiar Face Isn't Familiar Enough', *Hollywood Reporter*, 18 December. Available online: http://www.hollywoodreporter.com/heat-vision/rogue-one-grand-moff-tarkins-familiar-face-isnt-familiar-957178 (accessed 30 October 2017).

Mori, M. (2012 [1970]), 'The Uncanny Valley', trans. K. F. MacDorman and N. Kageki, *IEEE Robotics & Automation Magazine*, June, 98–100.

Power, P. (2009), 'Animated Expressions: Expressive Style in 3D Computer Graphic Narrative Animation', *animation: an interdisciplinary journal*, 4(2): 107–129.

Prince, S. (2012), *Digital Visual Effects in Cinema: The Seduction of Reality*, New Brunswick, NJ: Rutgers University Press.

Sobchack, V. (2006), 'Final Fantasies: Computer Graphic Animation and the [Dis] Illusion of Life', in S. Buchan (ed.), Animated 'Worlds', 171–182, Eastleigh: John Libbey.

Wells, P. (1998), *Understanding Animation*, London and New York: Routledge.

6

Animation and Performance

Annabelle Honess Roe

The concept of performance, imbued as it is with ideas of embodiment and the corporeal, would initially seem to have little relevance to animation. After all, many animated characters are virtual and intangible, unlike the physical, 'real' bodies that typically come to mind when we think of something or someone 'performing'. Animated figures, as Norman McLaren's definition of animation reminds us, only come to life by virtue of what happens in-between the frames that we see on screen (see Furniss 1988: 5). This is true even of physical objects, such as puppets, that are animated via stop-motion. Animated characters, unlike a human actor, have no physical autonomy. They rely on the animator to move and, therefore, to come alive.

Because animation is often defined in opposition to live-action cinema – in terms of what animation can do that live-action cannot, and vice versa – and because the physical body is inherent to live-action cinema in a way that it is not to animation, the importance of performance for animation has often been overshadowed by animation studies' tendency to focus on areas such as animation's material and aesthetic properties. This chapter will demonstrate, through an exploration of the history of performance *in* animation as well as the idea of animating as *a type of* performance, that performance is in fact central to animation.

Early animation and the presence
of the performing animator

Much early animation is characterized by the appearance of the animator in the frame. From Emile Cohl's very early animation *Fantasmagorie* (1908) to the *Out of the Inkwell* series made by the Fleischer Brothers between 1918 and 1929, it was very common to see the animator's hand draw the characters and bring them to life on screen. Scott Bukatman (2012: 109) suggests that this tendency was because 'animation was too new, and perhaps too mysterious, to simply emerge fully formed onscreen'. Similarly, David Clark thinks of the presence of the hand of the animator as a way for animators of the period to 'come to terms with the strangeness of this new medium' (Clark 2005: 144). Thus, inserting the means of creation – the hand and the pen of the animator – into this 'strange and foreign parallel world' (p. 144) overcame the ontological challenges presented by early animation to audiences unfamiliar with this new form. Also typical of this period is the presence of the animator as a performer within the cartoon. In *Betty Boop's Rise to Fame* (1934) the animated, coquettish, Betty flirts with 'Uncle Max' Fleischer who appears with her on screen. Although Fleischer is playing himself, this is nonetheless clearly a performance, one that also features his brother Dave posing as a reporter doing a story on Betty, who herself is constructed as a 'vaudevillian' performer in the film (Crafton 2013: 27).

The appearance of the animator's hand, or even their entire body, is a reminder of animation's close relationship to an earlier type of performance-based mass entertainment – vaudeville. Several early animators had previously worked in this context as lightning sketch artists – onstage performers who created virtuosic drawings live in front of an audience – and many early animated films are, essentially, lightning sketch films, in which 'the spectator is never allowed to forget that he [*sic*] was observing a theatrical performance' (Crafton 1993: 57). James Stuart Blackton's performance in his 1907 *Lightning Sketches*, in a way that is typical of animation of this period, has much in common with that of a magician, from the presentation of the blank canvas at the outset of the film – similar to a magician 'proving that his hat and sleeves are empty' – to the sartorial signifier of the conjuror's formal evening wear (Crafton 1993). Even in later animations that don't include the act of lightning sketching, the relationship between animation and vaudeville performance is still apparent, as exemplified by Winsor McCay's *Gertie the Dinosaur* (1914). Prior to making animated films, McCay was an accomplished and successful comic strip artist and lightning sketcher (see Bukatman 2012: 110–130). The original animated film of *Gertie* was used as part of McCay's live act, in which he 'interacted' with the animated dinosaur, the brontosaurus seeming to respond to the commands McCay issued from the stage (see Crafton 1993: 110–113). In the subsequent version of the film for release in cinemas, McCay's from-stage commands are replaced by intertitle cards, and McCay performs himself in the film's live-action bookend sequences in which he enters into a wager with a group of fellow animators to bring a dinosaur to life. In these examples, and countless others from the first decades of animation, we can see that the animator often took on the role of onscreen performer.

Live action performance as a basis for animation

Later, after the onscreen presence of the animator fell out of cultural fashion, live-action performance once again became significant to animation, but in a different way – as part of the production process. Disney animators Frank Thomas and Ollie Johnston (1981) recall the important role filmed live-action came to play in the animation process during the studio's first heyday in the 1930s and 1940s. This first came about when 'burlesque comedian' Eddie Collins was recruited to help with the animation of Dopey during the production of *Snow White and the Seven Dwarfs* (1937). Dopey was suffering from a lack of personality, the '"leftover" dwarf' as he was called by the animators working on the film (Thomas and Johnston 1981: 320), so Collins was brought into the studio to perform 'innovative interpretations of Dopey's reactions' to help 'breathe life into the little cartoon character' (Thomas and Johnston 1981). This strategy proved so successful that it became a standard tool used at Disney to help animate other characters.

The Disney animators used this material in two key ways: as 'resource material' to give 'an overall idea of a character, with gestures, attitudes, an idea that could be caricatured' (Thomas and Johnston 1981: 320–321) or as 'a model for the figure in movement' where it 'could be studied frame by frame to reveal the intricacies of a living form's actions' (p. 321). Initially live-action filmed material was used for general reference in these two ways, but later the studio began 'shooting film for specific scenes or special actions' (p. 323) for a particular sequence they were trying to animate. For example, to help the animators create the titular character in *Snow White* dancer Marjorie Belcher 'was filmed as she acted out [her] parts' (Furniss 2017: 104).

When the animators at Disney used an actor as a frame-by-frame reference for how an animated character moved, this involved a modified version of the process called rotoscoping, where live-action performance is filmed and then traced frame by frame.[1] At Disney in the 1930s, the studio's processing lab devised a system by which frames of film were individually printed out onto 'photostats' – sheets of paper that could fit onto the pegs of an animation desk so the animator could 'study the action by flipping "frames of film" backward and forward just as he did his drawings' (Thomas and Johnston 1981: 321). This revealed the complexities of the human form in action as it performed. Rotoscoping has been used more widely in animation, often to help create realistic movement in human characters and it can be thought of as the ancestor of the contemporary process of motion or performance capture, in which live-action performance is used as the basis for creating digital, computer-generated animation.[2] This will be discussed later in the chapter.

At Disney, the animators first traced over the live action images, which they then set aside. They then worked from the traced drawings to create the cartoon character, 'choosing only those actions that relate to the point of [a] particular scene' (Thomas and Johnston 1981: 323). This was because, as Thomas and Johnston note, problems came about with the use of live-action performance as the basis for their animation if they tried to stay too close to the filmed reference of movement: 'The moves appeared real enough, but the figure lost the illusion of life [...] it was impossible to become emotionally involved with this eerie, shadowy creature who was never a real inhabitant of our fantasy world' (Thomas and Johnston 1981: 323). This is a common criticism of rotoscoped animation – that it somehow deadens the animated character. This might be because too slavishly following a reference in some way inhibits the animator's own input into the creation of a character, and it implies that the authenticity of an animated character's 'performance', and how engaging or empathy-inducing it is, is more than simply recreating realistic movement. Indeed, Brad Bird (director of films including *The Iron Giant* [1999] and *The Incredibles* [2004]) asserts that 'when you watch an animated film, the performance you're seeing is the one the animator is giving to you' (quoted in Crafton 2013: 15). Before moving on to explore this idea of the animator as a type of invisible performer, we first need to establish what 'performance' means.

Performance

'Performance' is a contested concept – not only do scholars working in the interdisciplinary field of performance studies tend to not agree precisely on what the term 'performance' means, but, more importantly, its contested status is inherent in its meaning and 'disagreement about [its] essence' is 'built into the concept' of performance itself (Carlson 2004: 68). However, one undisputed idea is that performance entails bringing something into being in the moment that the performance takes place. Most obviously, this might be an actor performing a role in a play or a film. Less obvious is the notion that performance is a part of everyday life, something we all do when we interact with other people. In fact, as Richard Schechner (2002: 2) notes, performance is 'any action that is framed, presented, highlighted, or displayed' and this will range from simple everyday interactions with our fellow human (and non-human) beings, such as greetings, through to more complex communications, social actions and rituals, as well as cultural performances such as plays and performance art.[3] The nature of performance means that to study it involves thinking more about behaviours and actions than analysing texts or things in themselves. Furthermore, treating 'any object, work, or product "as" performance [...] means to investigate what the object does, how it interacts with other objects or beings, and how it relates to other objects or beings. Performances exist only as actions, interactions, and relationships' (Schechner 2002: 24).

Two concepts that are frequently cited as inherent to performance will be particularly significant as we go on to consider animation as a type of performance. One is the idea that performance implies a process of 'doubling' and the second is the significance of 'embodied knowledge' to understanding and interrogating performance. Marvin Carlson notes that 'all performance involves a consciousness of doubleness, through which the actual execution of an action is placed in mental comparison with a potential, an ideal, or a remembered original model of that action' (2004: 71). This idea of doubling goes hand-in-hand with the notion mentioned above of performance bringing something into being. The 'something' that is 'being brought in to being' is the thing that is being doubled. This could be a character that an actor is performing, in that the character pre-exists the performance either in prior performances or simply as an idea written on the page or in its creator's imagination. Doubling is also part of the performance of everyday actions such greetings, in that we base this 'performance' on our already existing knowledge of how such actions should be carried out in the social situation we are in – knowledge that we begin to develop in childhood.

In all cases, the 'performance' involves some sort of comparison (either by ourselves and/or an audience) to some other 'elusive "other" that performance is not but which it constantly struggles in vain to embody' (Carlson 2004: 71). Thus, we might think about how the notion of authenticity is valued in performance, and how this entails a performer effectively or convincingly embodying the thing they are doubling. We can see this idea at play in the example of the Disney studio using live action performance as a reference for creating animated characters discussed above; in particular, the way that 'it became increasingly important to choose just the right actor for this type of action, since it would have such an influence on the development of a character's personality' (Thomas and Johnston 1981: 327). Here Thomas and Johnston are pointing to the idea that certain actors will be better able to enact, or bring into being, a character by embodying that role.

Embodiment is inherent to the process of performance. In performance studies, scholars are interested in how actions are carried out by bodies and how particular knowledge carried by those bodies, or embodied knowledge, might impact on, or influence, the performance. At the most basic level, we might think that we are able to most authentically or convincingly perform an action that we already have some physical experience of. This helps explain why an actor who was already adept at burlesque, physical comedy worked so well to help the animators bring life to the character of Dopey in *Snow White*.

Animation as a type of performance

As suggested at the outset of this chapter, embodiment might seem initially to have little relevance to animation that does not use live action in some way as a basis for creating animated characters, or 'regular animation' as Thomas and Johnston (1981: 319) call it, 'which develops entirely from an artist's imagination'. After all, how could an animated, completely imagined and virtual character that does not exist beyond the animation in which it appears, have any embodied knowledge? However, reflecting on the importance of acting to animation production can help reveal the significance of embodied knowledge for animation. This is because even though the animator is usually no longer physically present in the frame and their body remains invisible to audiences, it is the animator's actions, be that drawing with a pencil or moving a stop-motion puppet, that bring characters to life. Such actions require a certain element of performance from the animator. This makes sense if we think of performance as bringing something into being, as discussed above. The process of animation also involves bringing something into being.

Richard Williams (2001) suggests that the pathos of animation comes from the animator's ability to instil a character with soul and emotion. We might think of this ability as embodied knowledge. Williams gives an example from the feature film *Who Framed Roger Rabbit* (1988), on which he worked as animation director. Williams had wanted a certain animator, who was feeling particularly lonely at the time, to animate a 'shot of Roger sitting on a garbage can in a back alley crying about what he thought was his wife's infidelity' (Williams 2001: 318). Another animator, one who was experiencing a much happier personal life, ended up animating the shot. As a result, Williams felt 'we missed having another dimension to the character which would have given a much stronger emotional pull with the audience' (p. 318). This anecdote points to the idea that an animator will bring to bear on a character their embodied knowledge of their personal and life experiences.

The suggestion made by Williams that the animator's job is to 'get inside the character or characters' and also 'show clearly what they're thinking' (Williams 2001: 326) is echoed by Wells and Moore (2016: 94) who suggest that 'whether working through the pencil, a puppet or pixels, the need to express thought, emotion and action is fundamental to effective animated sequences'. However, this ability comes not just from an animator tapping into her or his own experiences, as Williams's example above might imply, but also through developing the skills of a performer. The importance of learning these skills was acknowledged at the Disney studio in the 1930s in their adoption of Stanislavsky-type theories of method acting as part of the animation process (see Crafton 2013: 36–48).

Thus, the similarities between acting and animation have often been observed (see Wells 1998: 104–107) and are frequently emphasized in books oriented at people wanting to learn how to animate (see, for example, Hooks 2017). The affinity between acting and animation is similarly observed by animators reflecting on their own practice. For example, stop-motion animator Richard Haynes likens his animation of the Aardman character Shaun the Sheep to the performance of a silent comedy actor and suggests that the anthropomorphism of characters such as Shaun 'depends on animators successfully translating something in their own physicality via the process of animation' (Haynes forthcoming). Haynes's description of his animation work implicitly argues that doing animation is in itself a type of physical performance where 'the animator must essentially use the techniques employed by the actor to project the specificities of character' (Wells 1998: 104). Thus, we can think of the process of animation *as a type of* performance, the ultimate aim of which is to turn 'cartoon characters into embodied actors' (Crafton 2013: 37).[4]

Motion capture: The animation of performance

Motion and performance capture, as did their predecessor, the Rotoscope, use filmed live-action performance as the basis for animation. The green (or blue) screen performance of an actor is recorded digitally using sensors that are attached to a suit the actor wears. In performance capture, the addition of sensors to the actor's face means that facial gesture and expression can be captured as well as body movement. The data collected from the sensors provides a basis for the creation of a digitally animated character. Perhaps the best-known example of such a character is Gollum in the *Lord of the Rings* trilogy played by Andy Serkis (Peter Jackson 2001–2003).

There has been a long-running intellectual and industrial debate over whether or not motion capture is animation (see Freedman 2012). This wrangling has led to a parallel debate about who can claim 'ownership' of a motion or performance capture character. Much of the press and publicity surrounding motion and performance capture promotes the idea that the actor is exclusively responsible for the character. New Line's push for Andy Serkis to receive an Oscar nomination for the role of Gollum in *The Lord of the Rings: The Two Towers* (Peter Jackson 2002) implied that 'Serkis's performance was the whole performance' and elided the role of the animation team who realized Gollum in the final film (Freedman 2012: 44). 'Gollum, according to the studio, was not animation […] He was pure performance, and motion capture was simply the means of recording this performance' (p. 44) However, as Mihaela Mihailova (2016) argues, this cultural discourse ignores the significant technical and creative labour required by animators and visual effects artists to translate the digital data, which usually does not 'readily correspond to the desired end product', into an empathetic and believable onscreen animated performance by presenting 'motion capture as a technological miracle capable of directly translating an actor's performance into a digital creature, as if by magic' (p. 43). In other words, the popular understanding of motion and performance capture typically downplays the process of animation *as a type of* performance in favour of solely recognizing and celebrating the actor's original profilmic performance. As such, motion and performance capture can be thought of as a site in which the two types of performance and animation explored in this chapter come into conflict: performance *in* animation and animation *as a type of* performance.

Conclusion

The discussion of performance could be taken even further if we consider the suggestions by Scott Bukatman and Donald Crafton that we should be wary of deterministic approaches to the animation process and that in addition to considering the performance that brings animation into being we should also think about the animated character itself as a performer.[5] Bukatman (2012: 133–134) argues that animated characters have a degree of autonomy and that, especially in studio production with its factory-like division of labour, it is hard to ascribe the enlivening of an animated character to 'the' animator because so many people would have been involved in bringing one character 'to life'. In addition, Crafton points to the 'responsive performances by the viewers' (2013: 17) of animation and contends that 'performance isn't a sender-receiver communication model, but rather a galaxy of relationships, many of which remain unknowable' (p. 18). Here Crafton emphasizes the significance of the viewer in 'creating' animated performances that are autonomous from their original animation, an autonomy that is enabled by animators' creation (or performance) of believable characters that entails less control 'over how the characters would be understood and used by the films' audiences' (Crafton 2013: 48). Crafton's observations also remind us of the importance of remembering that the reception of animated characters is historical and culturally specific.[6]

In many ways, Crafton's and Bukatman's thoughts on the autonomy of the animated character refigure, from a different (historical) perspective, the debate around motion capture, and who can claim credit for an animated performance. Such debates caution against any teleological presumption of a linear evolution of the intersection of animation and performance, in which we are moving, historically, from the appearance of the performing animator on screen towards some final point at which the performance of the animator becomes entirely invisible or erased. Such a teleological perspective would potentially accept 'performance as the exclusive domain of the actor (and, by extension, of live-action cinema)' (Mihailova 2016: 43). Instead, as this chapter has demonstrated, animation has always utilized and implied 'performance' in a variety of rich and complex ways.[7] Both animation and performance entail a process of 'coming into being', something that Sergei Eisenstein, that unlikely but ardent fan of Mickey Mouse, claimed as inherent to animation and fundamental to our human desire for omnipotence (see O'Pray 1997). With this in mind, and as demonstrated by this chapter, animation and performance have a close affinity, the recognition of which can lead to a fuller understanding of what animation is.

Notes

1 The Rotoscope was invented by the Fleischer Brothers and patented by Max Fleischer in 1915. Dave later took on the role of Koko the Clown, his rotoscoped performance forming the basis for the popular animated character.

2 Bob Sabiston's Rotoshop process, used in *Waking Life* (Richard Linklater 2001) and *A Scanner Darkly* (Richard Linklater 2006) and many short films directed by Sabiston, is another digital descendent of the Rotoscope.

3 And, indeed, gender identity (see Butler 2003).

4 The same can be argued of abstract and non-character animation. See Dobson (2015) for a discussion of performance in Norman McLaren's work.

5 When thinking about the performance *of* the animated character, Crafton distinguishes between 'embodied' and 'figurative' acting. For Crafton, this distinction is also partly a historical one, with embodied characters coming about with the alignment of acting and animation at the Disney studio in the 1930s, at which point the animated character begins to become an avatar for the animator, replacing the hand of the animator seen on screen in early animation. Although, as Crafton notes, much animation combines both figurative and embodied approaches. See Crafton (2013: 15–57)

6 Laura Ivins-Hulley (2008), in a discussion of puppet animation, similarly points out the importance of taking 'the audience into consideration to determine how performance is constituted'.

7 For example, real-time animation and the use of animation in live performance. See Tomlinson (2013).

References

Bukatman, S. (2012), *The Poetics of Slumberland: Animated Spirits and the Animating Spirit*, Berkeley, CA: University of California Press.

Butler, J. (2003), 'Performative Acts and Gender Constitution', in H. Bial (ed.), *The Performance Studies Reader*, 154–166, London: Routledge.

Carlson, M. (2004), 'What Is Performance?', in H. Bial (ed.), *The Performance Studies Reader*, 68–73, London: Routledge.

Clark, D. (2005), 'The Discrete Charm of the Digital Image: Animation and New Media', in C. Gehman and S. Reinke (eds), *The Sharpest Point: Animation at the End of Cinema*, 138–151, Toronto: YYZ Books.

Crafton, D. (1993), *Before Mickey: The Animated Film 1898–1928*, Chicago, IL: University of Chicago Press.

Crafton, D. (2013), *Shadow of a Mouse: Performance, Belief, and World-Making in Animation*, Berkeley, CA: University of California Press.

Dobson, N. (2015), 'Dancing to the Rhythm of the Music: Norman McLaren, the Body and Performance', *Animation Studies Online Journal*, 10. Available online: https://journal.animationstudies.org/nichola-dobson-dancing-to-rhythm-of-the-music-norman-mclaren-the-body-and-performance/ (accessed 21 February 2018).

Freedman, Y. (2012), 'Is It Real … or Is It Motion Capture? The Battle Redefine Animation in the Age of Digital Performance', *The Velvet Light Trap*, 69 (Spring): 38–49.

Furniss, M. (1988), *Art in Motion: Animation Aesthetics*, Bloomington, IN: Indiana University Press.

Furniss, M. (2017), *Animation: The Global History*, London: Thames and Hudson.

Haynes, R. (forthcoming), 'Shaun the Sheep: Buster Keaton Reborn?', in A. Honess Roe (ed.) *Beyond Stop-Motion Film: Production, Style and Representation in Aardman Animations*, London: I.B. Tauris.

Hooks, E. (2017), *Acting for Animation*, 4th edn, London: Routledge.

Ivins-Hulley, L. (2008), 'The Ontology of Performance in Stop Animation', *Animation Studies Online Journal* 3. Available online: https://journal.animationstudies.org/category/volume-3/laura-ivins-hulley-the-ontology-of-performance-in-stop-animation/ (accessed 21 February 2018).

Mihailova, M. (2016), 'Collaboration without Representation: Labor and Issues in Motion and Performance Capture', *animation: an interdisciplinary journal*, 11 (1): 40–58.

O'Pray, M. (1997), 'Eisenstein and Stokes on Disney: Film Animation and Omnipotence', in J. Pilling (ed.), *A Reader in Animation Studies*, 195–202, London: John Libbey.

Schechner, R. (2002), *Performance Studies: An Introduction*, London: Routledge.

Thomas, F. and O. Johnston (1981), *Disney Animation: The Illusion of Life*. New York: Abbeville Press.

Tomlinson, L. (2013), 'Animation and Performance', *Animation Studies2.0*, 30 September. Available online: https://blog.animationstudies.org/?p=555 (accessed 13 February 2018).

Wells, P. (1998), *Understanding Animation*, London: Routledge.

Wells, P. and S. Moore (2016), *The Fundamentals of Animation*, 2nd edn, London: Fairchild.

Williams, R. (2001), *The Animator's Survival Kit*, London: Faber and Faber.

7

Animation and Memory

Victoria Grace Walden

In Pixar's *Inside Out* (Docter and Del Carmen 2015), Joy and Sadness navigate around their host Riley's long-term memory where coloured orbs representing different events in her past are stored on shelves. The film imagines memory as fixed content that can be recalled as needed. However, developments in the interdisciplinary field of memory studies now consider memory to be much more complex than this. Like the term 'realism' (see Mihailova in this volume), memory is a slippery thing – it is better understood as always in a state of becoming, as related to the present as much as the past, and as a creative, networked process rather than as a simple transmission of historical data. After introducing some of the broad ideas related to contemporary studies of media and memory, this chapter focuses on the ways in which we can remember the past through and with animation, and how the form can represent memory, concentrating particularly on issues of trauma and witnessing, collective memory and identity, and nostalgia.

Understanding memory

Memory is a familiar term, yet it can be difficult to define without confusing it with the past – events that have happened – and History – the telling of such events. If History (and I use the capital H here purposely to refer to the practice of historians) is the construction of narratives of the past following a cause and effect logic, often detailed with empirical data, then memory refers to our experience of the past in the present. Memory highlights the fragmentary nature of temporality and refers to our bodily and sensual relations to events that have previously happened. Memory is incomplete, inaccurate, messy and subjective. It is not fixed, but rather it is fluid. Memory is a creation that is never complete and involves an assemblage or network of actors – human and non-human – contributing to its continuous development (Garde-Hansen, Hoskins and Reading 2012: 7). Memory is something felt and is often shared and developed with others. Although when we colloquially use the word 'memory' we tend to mean the things we personally remember, the concept 'memory' encapsulates personal, collective and collaborative experiences with the past and how these relate to each other. It is important to remember that 'the past is not preserved but is reconstructed on the basis of the present' (Halbwachs 1992: 40). Thus, in studying memory, we come to understand as much about the current situation as we do about the events being remembered.

Media, such as animation, play an important role in the creation of memories today as our engagement with the past is extensively mediated (Garde-Hansen 2011; van Dijck 2007). Marshall McLuhan's seminal book *Understanding Media* (1964) introduced the idea that media might be able to extend human experience. Following such thinking in relation to memory, Alison Landsberg (2004) argues that films can serve as prosthetics, encouraging us to feel emotionally and bodily engaged with a past we neither witnessed nor know much about. Landsberg here emphasizes the assemblage nature of memory – that it involves the interaction of organic and inorganic agents in its creation (Garde-Hansen, Hoskins and Reading 2012: 11) as media can inspire the spectator to remember. Memory is not solely situated within our minds; rather it emerges through social collaborations. Given that animation often foregrounds the subjective – with its often handmade quality and ability to resist photographic traditions of representation – the form can help encourage the types of affective responses to historical events that we tend to define as memory.

Memory and animation

Animation can highlight issues related to memory in many ways. First, the creativity and imagination that inform memory are often highlighted in animated works, particularly when their frame-by-frame production is emphasized, such as with stop-motion and pixilation films, or when the physical imprint of the animators is materialized onscreen, such as in the finger marks on the surfaces of clay figures. Film phenomenologist Jennifer M. Barker, in her analysis of the Quay Brothers' *Street of Crocodiles* (1986), argues that the foregrounding of the creative process in stop-motion films is indicative of play (2009: 130–132). Pixar's first feature film *Toy Story* (Lasseter 1996) also highlights animation's relationship to play, despite its use of digital animation rather than stop-motion, as we watch the adventures of Andy's toys when they come alive, and follow the narrative of Woody, an old toy, with whom Andy no longer wants to play when he receives his new Buzz Lightyear figure. The emphasis on play in *Toy Story*, as in many animations, is shrouded in nostalgia for childhood. Nostalgia is a particular feeling about the past discussed in more detail later in this chapter.

Secondly, animation particularly foregrounds embodiment. Even if we do not see the animator's hands moving objects onscreen, we are aware of the human agency acting between frames, which enables the creation of movement. Material, non-human forms in animations can also provoke the spectator to feel bodily sensations in reaction to historical events. For example, in the Estonian short *Body Memory (Keha mälu,* Pikkov 2011) about the deportation of Estonians by Soviet officials – objects encourage deep visceral affect for the audience. The film includes anthropomorphic figures, which are made of twine, placed inside a model of a cattle car. The figures are seen being violently jerked around until they are untangled and destroyed. Barker claims that when film draws attention to a sense of corporal discontinuity, such as with stop-motion, this can evoke feelings of bodily vulnerability within the spectator because it encourages them to recognize that the unity of the film – its body – is actually constructed of fragile, individual elements and the failure of any of these could threaten the existence of the whole (Barker 2009: 21). In *Body Memory,* such affect is not only suggested through the staccato temporality of the film, but also through the unravelling and metamorphosis of the twine figures, which encourage us to consider how our own body could be torn to pieces or changed by external forces. Such a sensation can enable the tragic past of Soviet deportations to resonate deep within the spectator's body and thus it is through an embodied relationship with the animation that they can become invested in remembering this past.

Thirdly, animation's ability to emphasize subjective reality (Wells 1998: 27) enables it to explore the sensual responses of people to historical events rather than to show them photographically. Animation has long been interested in depicting things which are impossible to represent in live action, and the embodied, fluid experience of memory is certainly something that a photograph or live-action film cannot satisfactorily depict. This is particularly significant when animations deal with events that are questionably real. For example, Paul Vester's *Abductees* (1994) uses animated drawings to accompany the vocal testimony of individuals who describe their experiences of being abducted by aliens. The artwork attempts to both illustrate the interviewees' memories and question the reliability of subjective narratives of the past with interjections of iconic fantasy images, such as Bambi. This approach is also particularly useful for confronting trauma.

Traumatic memory

'A traumatic event is often understood as an aporia in subjective experience and also for the possibilities of representation' (Honess Roe 2013: 156), thus while photographic-based live-action images might struggle to engage with trauma through traditional narratives, animation can offer an aesthetic response (p. 153). Following the psychoanalytical work of Sigmund Freud, trauma theorist Cathy Caruth defines trauma as a 'double wound' (1996: 3). By this she means that it is a 'breach in the mind's experience of time, self and the world' and that as it reappears in flashbacks to the survivor, trauma is always 'experienced too soon' and 'too unexpectedly to be fully known' (1996: 4). Therefore, trauma causes the survivor of a horrific experience to be confronted with the past in fragments. Furthermore, as Shoshana Felman and Dori Laub (1992), and Janet Walker (2005) argue, because trauma can never be fully known, it is also shaped by fantasy and 'disremembering'. Walker uses the term 'disremembering' to refer to the process through which fragments of the past allow us to begin to work through trauma even when we cannot remember the original event.

Laub argues that survivors of horrific experiences cannot recognize their trauma until they testify to the events (1992: 57). While video (analogue and digital) is often used to record such testimonies, it only presents the survivor telling their story – it cannot show events as they happened or illustrate memories of them. Often, particularly in the case of wars or genocides, there are few images evidencing horrendous crimes. If they do exist, they are often shot by the perpetrators, thus do not present the victims' point-of-view. This is perhaps why there has been an increasing number of animated documentaries as well as fictional interpretations of traumatic events such as the Holocaust told from a personal perspective. Animation helps draw attention to an individual's subjective response to events, rather than claiming to represent official or purportedly objective accounts of an event. In the case of horrific events it might also be a 'means for overcoming the effacement of the past blocked by traumatic experience' (Honess Roe 2013: 155). This is illustrated in the feature-length animated documentary *Waltz with Bashir* (Folman 2008) in which the filmmaker uses animation to try to discover his missing memories of his time as a soldier in the Lebanon War.

Another example, the short Canadian animation *I Was a Child of Holocaust Survivors* (Fleming 2010), foregrounds the complexity of memory and the significance to it of imagination. Fleming's animated film is a post-memory work (Hirsch 2012), which means it explores the relationship that a member of the second generation (Bernice Eisenstein) has with her parent's traumatic past (the Holocaust) which she did not experience first-hand. At one point in the film, Bernice tries to reconcile the image of her father as she knows him with imagery of the concentration camps and imagines him as a sheriff (as if from a Western film) fighting the Nazis. She cannot recall a past she did not experience, but she can feel affected by it and still invest imaginatively in it – remembering it from a deferred position.

However, to think about animated films like *I Was a Child of Holocaust Survivors* that confront real experiences of trauma simply as an exchange between the testifier and the viewer is to ignore the significance of both the animators and their imagery. What we see on screen is not simply the testimony – unless the animation is also created by the person telling their story – so whose memory is it? The animators are interpreting the interviewees' narratives, thus bringing their own imagining of the past to the representations and drawing attention to their presence as well as that of the person giving testimony (Honess Roe 2013: 87). Furthermore, with the ubiquity of computers in our everyday lives, our media engagements are now mostly composed of a 'convergence of matter (human memory [and image]) with information (silicon memory)' (Garde-Hansen, Hoskins, Reading 2012: 13). We must not assume that digital media, including animation, offer a more complete record of the past, such as the myth of the 'total archive' (Hoskins 2009),[1] however, the blurring of the human and machine, as well as the combination of first-hand witnesses and the post-memory generations – those born after the event – in the production of animated documentaries about traumatic pasts draw attention to the ways in which memory works as an assemblage of the organic and non-organic, and of the past and the present for the future. We can see this in the short animated documentary *My Good Fortune in Auschwitz* (*Mijn Geluk in Auschwitz,* Dosky 2012) which uses rotoscoped images of actors performing a survivor's memories with live-action footage of the survivor telling his story, all of which were compiled by animators who did not experience this past.

Although trauma has often been defined as something that needs to be worked through (Friedländer 1996; LaCapra 1998), the recent phenomenon of stop-motion Lego 'brickfilms' about the Holocaust on YouTube suggests that perhaps post-memory generations need to *play through* traumatic pasts in order to feel bodily invested in them (Walden forthcoming). While 'working through' necessitates a critical distance and is most appropriate for first-hand witnesses, playing through enables those who did not experience the past in question to get close to it through bodily engagement with objects. Post-war generations' playful engagement with the Holocaust can help them to materialize their imagined memory of it (Young 2000: 42), as they take on the responsibility for remembering a past they did not experience first-hand in bodily ways. This is not to suggest that their experience of playing through affords them factual knowledge about real events from the past, but that playing through helps them to connect to it. It is in such ways that events like the Holocaust can become part of collective, rather than just individual, memory.

Collective memory and national identity

The term 'collective memory', popularized by sociologist Maurice Halbwachs, suggests we do not remember the past as isolated individuals, but aggregate and recollect memories as part of a society (1992: 38). Collective memory helps to formulate our 'imagined communities' (Anderson 2016) – those groups to which we see ourselves belonging and from which others are excluded. Each community might thus share a particular memory about a historic event, which might conflict with the way another group remembers it. Thus, each community remembers its own 'version of the past' (Neiger, Meyers and Zandberg 2011: 5). Collective memory, then, is key to identity formation. Yet it does not suppress the importance of the individual, rather the notion of collective memory recognizes that people share memories and help each other to remember events from the past. How then might animations speak to this discourse about collective memory?

It is possible to see how certain animations might appear to contribute to the imagining of specific communities. For example, the cuddly bear-like figure *Cheburashka* became an icon of Soviet animation and has since been the official mascot for the Russian Olympic team in the respective summer and winter games of 2004, 2006, 2008 and 2010. Japanese science-fiction anime's Mecha characters often embody a renewed Japanese identity after the nation's American occupation. As Joon Yang Kim argues, *AstroBoy* (Osamu Tezuka et al. 1963–1966) became a 'national icon for a dream of the reconstruction of Japan' (2013: 179). He represented not only the other becoming accepted as equal to the human rulers, but that the answer to Japan's identity of the future would be technology (2013.).

Yet, if we consider collective memory to be less fixed to a specific notion of identity and more fluid, melding together the recollections and experiences of different individuals and things, then we can understand animations as representing a plurality of relations to the past. Although an icon of Soviet culture, *Cheburashka* was created by a number of Jewish Holocaust survivors working for the state animation studio in the USSR. Acknowledging the creators' background enables one to identify small features of *Cheburashka*'s story that challenge the idea that he represents a specific collective Soviet identity. His arrival in a crate of Jaffa oranges and the suitcase that he carries point to the plight of Jewish refugees suggesting that there are a number of levels on which this figure can be read (Katz 2016).

While the anime *Akira* (Katsuhiro Ôtomo 1988) is, as is typical of anime science fiction, concerned with ideas of the post-human in the future, it is also a film that points to group identity as something that is always in flux. *Akira* is set in a dystopic metropolis – a symbol of capitalism as corruption brought to Japan by its American occupiers – yet it amalgamates this imagery and the greed of its protagonist with ideals about masculinity which are deeply rooted in Shinto culture. Although set in the future, *Akira* explores the entanglement of different layers of the past in forming contemporary notions of Japanese identity. Indeed, the film's finale sees technology and human body amalgamate into a monstrous figure as Tetsuo is transformed, which questions the proposals made by other works such as *Astroboy* about technology as Japan's future. Technology is as much a negative import of the occupying forces (consider, for example, the devastating impact of Hiroshima and Nagasaka) as it is a part of Japan's future in *Akira,* as the film ends with Kaneda riding off in search of a new beginning on his high-spec motorbike. Both *Cheburashka* and *Akira* present the boundaries of collective identity as neither clearly defined nor stable, but feature an assemblage of references to different experiences of the past which speak to various notions of identity in their own times. They present identity as something constructed through the collaboration of various discourses about the past, rather than precedented on a specific collective memory. In some respects, *Akira* draws attention to the tension between a nostalgic longing for Japan's Shinto traditions and the rapid changes of modernization.

Nostalgia

Nostalgia has been characterized as a rose-tinted, and thus unproductive, view of the past (Bal 1999: xi). The word 'nostalgia' takes its meaning from the Greek *Nostos* – return to the native land and *Algos* – suffering of grief. Thus nostalgia combines both a longing for the past and a mourning for a lost time that cannot return. Although the term was originally used in the 1600s to diagnose the illness of mercenaries far from home, the cultural definition, which we are more familiar with today, gained traction in the late nineteenth century. The idea of nostalgia as a certain feeling towards the past emerged during the Enlightenment – a period of rapid modernization, and thus many scholars have considered it in the context of a crisis of temporality in which contemporary society is so future focused that we don't have the chance to register the present or reflect on the past. Media engagements with nostalgia 'could indicate a twofold phenomenon: a reaction to fast technologies, despite using them in desiring to slow down, and/or an escape from this crisis into a state of wanderlust and a homesickness that could be cured through media consumption' (Niemeyer 2014: 2). As such, nostalgia should not simply be dismissed as sentimentality towards the past.

Nostalgia suggests two sensations: first, that things are changing too rapidly, therefore we long to return to a time that seemed slower or at least more constant than the late-capitalist era with its obsessive drive towards the future. Secondly, that the present feels much disconnected from the past that we remember, and a past that we see as fundamental to shaping our personal and collective identity. Robin L. Murray and Joseph K. Heumann (2009) argue that nostalgia might not only help us to 'learn from the past but also to recuperate real community'. Niemeyer (2014) suggests that media can play a role in offering a nostalgic, albeit temporary, cure for a desire to return to a more familiar time. There is of course a paradox here. It is often digital media, such as Pixar animations, that offer nostalgic value – allowing us to feel comfortable in a past we seem to recognize. However, they are also products of modern advancement and often depict post-human worlds, and their means of production (computer-generated animation) technologically threaten the existence of the old media forms that characterized the eras to which we often longingly look back.

The narratives of Pixar's films are usually informed by nostalgia, for example the conflict between Woody and Buzz Lightyear in *Toy Story* alludes to the cultural shift from the traditional American cowboy to the Space Age. In the recent *Cars 3* (Brian Fee 2017), Lightning McQueen longs to return to the glory age of traditional racing. *WALL-E* (Andrew Stanton 2008) shows a future world in which our sympathies are drawn to the 'old technology' embodied by the titular mechanical robot, abandoned in the wastelands of Earth while humans live on a space cruiser, reduced to obese passivity by the digital technology that does everything for them.

Pixar's nostalgic turn is rooted in not only its narratives, but also its films' aesthetics. As Murray and Heumann (2009) note, *WALL-E* takes influence from Charlie Chaplin films and includes clips and music from *Hello Dolly* (Gene Kelly 1963). In *Cars 3* (Brian Fee 2017), Lightning McQueen looks back at his former successes in newspaper clippings – a pre-digital media form drawn in the film as digital images. Pixar films, then, often depict the paradoxical nature of mediated nostalgia as they express longing for a past in which they could not exist. Yet they create this past via digital technology, which threatens to replace the formats, such as analogue films and newspapers, represented onscreen.

We have seen in this chapter how animation can help us to remember the past, how they represent dimensions of memory such as trauma, post-memory and nostalgia, and how we can look at the history of animation production to explore how the form contributes to the construction of identities that inform national, collective memory. Animation is particularly salient for exploring issues related to memory because it often foregrounds creativity, embodiment and the subjective, which are fundamental to memory. As animations often involve assemblages of objects and people in their creation and within their representations, they also draw attention to the complex, collaborative dimensions of memory. We do not simply remember on our own; rather our relationships with the past are shaped by our encounters with people, things, places and ideas. We must remember, though, not to solely look at the representational values of animation when thinking about memory, but interrogate their technological, material and aesthetic dimensions as well, in order to examine what the form can specifically contribute to our understanding about memory and the past.

Note

1 The 'total archive' refers to the idea that digital technologies could one day completely replace human memory because of our use of them to record everything in our lives.

References

Anderson, B. (2016), *Imagined Communities: Reflections on the Origin and Spread of Nationalism*, London and New York: Verso.

Bal, M. (1999), 'Introduction', in M. Bal, J. Crewe and L. Spitzer (eds), *Acts of Memory: Cultural Recall in the Present*, vii–xvii, Hanover: University Press of New England.

Barker, J. M. (2009), *The Tactile Eye: Touch and the Cinematic Experience*, Berkeley, CA: University of California.

Caruth, C. (1996), *Unclaimed Experience: Trauma, Narrative, and History*, Baltimore, MD and London: The Johns Hopkins University Press.

Felman, S. and D. Laub (1992), *Testimony: Crises of Witnessing in Literature, Psychoanalysis, and History*, Abingdon: Routledge.

Friedländer, S. (1996), 'Trauma, Transference and "Working Through" in Writing the History of the *Shoah*', *History and Memory*, 4(1): 39–59.

Garde-Hansen, J. (2011), *Media and Memory*, Edinburgh: Edinburgh University Press.

Garde-Hansen, J., A. Hoskins and A. Reading (2012), 'Introduction', in *Save As … Digital Memories*, 1–26, Basingstoke: Palgrave Macmillan.

Halbwachs, M. (1992), *On Collective Memory*, trans. L. A. Coser, Chicago, IL and London: The University of Chicago Press.

Hirsch, M. (2012), *The Generation of Postmemory: Writing and Visual Culture after the Holocaust*, New York: Columbia University Press.

Honess Roe, A. (2013), *Animated Documentary*, Basingstoke: Palgrave Macmillan.

Hoskins, A. (2009), 'Digital Network Memory', in A. Erll and A. Rigney (eds), *Mediation, Remediation, and the Dynamics of Cultural Memory*, 91–108, Berlin: de Gruyter.

Katz, M. B. (2016), *Drawing the Iron Curtain: Jews and the Golden Age of Soviet Animation*, New Brunswick, NJ: Rutgers University Press.

Kim, J. Y. (2013), 'The East Asian Post-Human Prometheus: Animated Mechanical "Others"', in S. Buchan (ed.) *Pervasive Animation*, 172–194, New York: Routledge.

LaCapra, D. (1998), *History and Memory after Auschwitz*, New York: Cornell University.

Laub, D. (1992), 'Bearing Witness, or the Vicissitudes of Listening', in S. Felman and D. Laub, *Testimony: Crises of Witnessing in Literature, Psychoanalysis, and History*, 57–74, Abingdon: Routledge.

Landsberg, A. (2004), *Prosthetic Memory: The Transformation of American Remembrance in the Age of Mass Culture*, New York: Columbia University Press.

McLuhan, M. (1964), *Understanding Media: Extensions of Man*, New York: McGraw-Hill.

Murray, R. L. and J. K. Heumann (2009), '*WALL-E:* From Environmental Adaptation to Sentimental Nostalgia', *Jump Cut: A Review of Contemporary Media*, 51. Available online: http://www.ejumpcut.org/archive/jc51.2009/WallE/text.html (accessed 22 February 2018).

Neiger, N., O. Meyers and E. Zandberg (2011), 'Introduction', in *On Media Memory: Collective Memory in a New Media Age*, 1–26, Basingstoke: Palgrave Macmillan.

Niemeyer, K. (2014), 'Introduction: Media and Nostalgia', in *Media and Nostalgia: Yearning for the Past, Present and Future*, 1–26, Basingstoke: Palgrave Macmillan.

Van Dijck, J. (2007), *Mediated Memories in the Digital Age*, Redwood City, CA: Stanford University Press.

Walden, V. G. (forthcoming), *Cinematic Intermedialities and Contemporary Holocaust Memory*, Basingstoke: Palgrave Macmillan.

Walker, J. (2005), *Trauma Cinema: Documenting Incest and the Holocaust*, Berkeley, CA: University of California Press.

Wells, P. (1998), *Understanding Animation*, London and New York: Routledge.

Young, J. E. (2000), 'David Levinthal's *Mein Kampf:* History, Toys, and the Play of Memory', in *At Memory's Edge: After-Images of the Holocaust in Contemporary Art and Architecture*, 42–61, New Haven, CT: Yale University Press.

8

Some Thoughts on Theory–Practice Relationships in Animation Studies

Paul Ward

Perhaps even more so than film and media studies more broadly, animation studies has always enjoyed a productive fluidity between theory and practice and much animation scholarship is written by people who are also animators. Ward, in this article that was originally published in animation: an interdisciplinary journal *in 2006, provides an important analysis of this relationship between theory and practice in animation studies that focuses on 'communities of practice' and argues that animation studies is an interdisciplinary field and must be understood as such.*

Introduction

The relationship between practice and theory is especially acute in the field of Animation Studies. This is due to the notions of craft and artistry that are attached to animation as an activity, and also the fact that animation is so diverse. Animation is at one and the same time a rich, multifaceted activity, seemingly existing in many different places at once, and it is an intuitive, magical process. Both of these factors make attempting to pin down animation in a theoretical way – to understand what is going on and why – an extremely difficult enterprise.

In this article I am going to make some tentative moves towards a more critical understanding of how theory and practice relate to one another in this rich and vibrant area. I shall do this by examining animation in relation to some concepts derived from education and pedagogy. Certainly with animation studies, the assumption often seems to be that learning *the craft* is the most vital thing, and the way that animation is talked about and theorized is therefore shaped by a specifically craft (some would say vocational) mentality. This is all very well – after all, what is animation without people to actually *do* the animating? – but tends to close off some of the more interesting critical avenues. Animation as a craft becomes too easily 'attached to' or placed in the service of particular paymasters. If animation really is as diverse and exciting a field as the rhetoric tells us, then we need to ensure that it is allowed to flourish as well as it can. This means being alive to every possible theoretical (as well as practical) possibility, and attuned to how theory and practice are inter-related.

With this in mind, I am going to discuss animation as an intersecting, discursive field, and draw upon three main concepts. First of all, I shall concentrate on Jean Lave and Etienne Wenger's (1991) notion of 'legitimate peripheral participation', which is derived from their work on 'socially situated learning'. Secondly, I shall talk about the notion of 'critical practice', drawing in particular on the recent work of Mike Wayne (2001) in this area. Finally, the concept of 'recontextualization', as proposed by sociologist of education Basil Bernstein (2000), will link discourses about animation – and especially how it is seen as a craft, and taught and learned as such – to broader and very important debates about pedagogy. These debates are central to understanding how animation practice actually functions.

Animation as 'legitimate peripheral participation'

One of the key theoretical and practical considerations for anyone trying to offer an outline of animation – as a mode of practice, a pedagogy, a knowledge area – is its multi-sitedness. That is, how can we discuss a wide range of people, doing what can appear to be very diverse things, as if they constitute a coherent group? Animation as a category includes the cartoons produced during the classical Hollywood era by studios such as Warner Brothers, MGM, Disney and the Fleischers, the formal experiments of Norman McLaren, the surreal worlds of Jan Švankmajer and the Quay Brothers. It also encompasses those who engage with animation techniques in order to capture, analyse or otherwise render particular types of motion or specific spaces – e.g., physical fitness instructors might use motion capture software as a tool to analyse a runner's movements or architects might construct a virtual version of a planned building. Therefore it is important to recognize that there *is* diversity within the category of animation, while at the same time concentrating on how particular participants interact with and coincide with one another in very specific material contexts. There will be occasions when people actively involved in different aspects of animation will come into each other's orbit. This may lead to one-off discussions, disputes and collaborations, or may lead to an ongoing/ permanent engagement. The point is that the interaction and engagement is not a static thing or a simple exchange but is something that is in flux and any learning and communication that occurs is 'socially situated'. I am using this term in Lave and Wenger's (1991) sense, and they explain the related term 'legitimate peripheral participation' as follows:

> Legitimate peripheral participation provides a way to speak about the relations between newcomers and old-timers, and about activities, identities, artifacts and communities of knowledge and practice. It concerns the process by which newcomers become part of the community of practice. A person's intentions to learn are engaged and the meaning of learning is configured through the process of becoming a full participant in a sociocultural practice. (p. 29)

Therefore, people will position themselves in relation to knowledge communities by thinking through what *they* do and think to what *others* – perceived to be already part of the knowledge community in question – do and think. Lave and Wenger's underlying point is that *all* learning (not simply school-based teaching) is a social activity and we therefore need to grapple with social context in order to understand this. For Lave and Wenger, all activity (potentially, at least) involves learning; I would suggest that they are correct in this assumption, but that for actual learning to take place there has to be some *critical reflection* on the activity and the fact that something is being learned. In terms of animation it is easy to discern how Lave and Wenger's concepts are useful. Certain activity might be central to one specific inquiry, yet peripheral to another. How it is viewed depends on the relative position of the person viewing it, and the activities in which they are engaged (Ward 2003). To rephrase this in a way that makes it more germane to the current discussion, someone's engagement with animation might be deemed peripheral by certain others, until there comes a time when (due to specific socio-historical circumstances) that engagement moves to become more central. As Lave and Wenger (1991) make clear, 'peripheral' and 'central' are of course relative terms, not concrete ones, and it is the dialectical relationship between participants and contexts that produces meaning. As they say: 'Agent, activity, and the world mutually constitute each other' (p. 33).

For example, classically trained cel animators will have close connections to those who work in the same area, but a particular project might bring them into collaboration with animators working in other forms of animation, such as computer rendering, direct animation or clay animation. As they move away from their specific community and interact more with the other community, working practices will be questioned, challenged, may become entrenched and so on.[1] An interesting example of this kind of movement is outlined by Brad Bird, director of *The Iron Giant* (1999) and *The Incredibles* (2004). He was asked during an interview about his time working as a consultant on the television series *The Simpsons*, and he points to the ways in which different working practices can be channelled and changed. Bird states:

> When I first got into it, the visual language of television animation was very, very rudimentary. There was a standard way of handling things ... When I got in there with the storyboard artists, they were approaching things that way because that's the way they were trained. I said, 'No, come on, man! We're doing a take on *The Shining* here. Let's look at how Kubrick uses his camera. His camera always has wide-angle lenses. Oftentimes, the compositions are symmetrical. Let's do a drawing that simulates a wide-angle lens' At first they were completely bewildered, and very soon they were into it. I said, 'Look, we can't spend a lot of money on elaborate animation, but we can have sophisticated filmmaking'. (quoted in Robinson 2004)

Here, the entrenched working practices of television animation come into contact with someone who is thinking in terms of a rather different approach, and how animation might usefully be related to other forms of expression. The specificities of different communities of animation practice are usefully compared in Bird's statement; he is asking the animators to think carefully about the broader interrelationships at play, and something that was previously not done then becomes a distinct possibility, something that was peripheral becomes more central.

In terms of animation studies and its relationship to other knowledge areas, we can see a similar process at work. For instance, as one researches particular areas, one will encounter and engage with different communities of practice or nodes of animation inquiry. For example, the teaching and researching of animation of the classical Hollywood era ostensibly requires a radically different approach and set of collaborators than does animation's application to the development of new techniques in Sports Science or Veterinary Medicine. However, while these clearly represent very different communities of practice in Lave and Wenger's (1991) meaning of the term, they are all engaging with animation in some shape or form. Furthermore, animation's multifaceted character is what needs to be explored by drawing out the way it links such apparently unrelated communities of practice. A traditional Film Studies-inflected approach to animation, and sports science- and veterinary medicine-inflected approaches to animation appear, on the surface, to have very little common ground (apart, that is, from their use of/interest in animation). Yet I would argue that the commonalities not only go much deeper than they appear, but that this common ground is precisely the terrain on which we need to build. Thus, debates about realism and representation in Hollywood cartoon animation might take us into an analysis of naturalistic drawing styles, studios' use of live-action film to help artists capture 'natural' movement and use of devices such as the rotoscope. It was common practice, for example, for classical-era Disney animators to use a range of techniques and technologies to ensure that character movements were as realistic as possible – see 'The Uses of Live Action in Drawing Humans and Animals' in Frank Thomas and Ollie Johnston's book *Disney Animation: The Illusion of Life* (1981: 319–366). Likewise, although its acceptance as an animation technique is somewhat more contested, the rotoscope was invariably used to help capture the specificity of human movement in an animated context. The fact that the resulting animation often looked strange, eerie, or out of place emphasizes both the difficulty of rendering naturalistic movement in animation and the importance of rotoscoping and other motion capture technologies from the perspective of animation studies research (see Bouldin 2004; Ward 2004). It is precisely the interstitial qualities of animation that relies on pre-capturing or previsualizing movement that makes it of such interest – whether we are talking about the very first uses of the original rotoscope by Max Fleischer in his *Out of the Inkwell* cartoons, or more recent use of motion-capture technology in animating Tom Hanks's multiple performances in *The Polar Express* (2004).

At the same time, the sports scientist or veterinary researchers might be examining how motion capture devices and digital imaging can help them in their research. The various techniques for gathering data on how athletes move in specific contexts is of obvious relevance to sports science, but the application of these data in broader contexts, using animation technology, is of potential use to anyone with an interest in kinesiology (the study of human movement). Animation used in one context could therefore be of use to physiotherapists, medical staff, people working within robotics – the list could be extended. Veterinary studies of animal locomotion, often using the same technology as that used in some sports science contexts, and that used for motion capture in Computer Animation and Games Design – for example, the Qualisys ProReflex 3D Motion Analysis System – have clear value to animal husbandry and training, but the information gathered in such a context can again be more broadly applied. The underlying questions being asked in this instance by apparently unrelated communities of practice (film studies, sports science, and veterinary medicine) are actually very similar. They have to do with the clear and accurate capturing of motion via specific animation techniques – and, despite their differences (indeed, I would maintain, *because* of them) there is a lot to be learned from a critical dialogue between them. In this respect, animation has the potential to usefully collapse some of the boundaries that still exist between broadly Arts and Science orientations. We need to keep in mind that apparently stable knowledge areas or disciplines should be more accurately thought of as *interacting communities of practice*: they may overlap a great deal or not at all; they may have practitioners who collaborate a lot or rarely. What is certain is that it is in the process of actively engaging with different contexts that one learns anything. It therefore follows that knowledge about something is produced by constantly critically (re-)evaluating what that something is, and how it relates to its (many) contexts.

Animation and critical practice

In his recent work examining media production practices Mike Wayne has developed a useful typology of cultural practitioners. Although he does not refer to animation specifically, his typology can clearly be applied to animation. As Wayne (2001) says, his aim is to explore 'different modes and ambitions of being self-conscious about what it means to understand cultural production' (p. 30). By this he means there are different extents to which one can be self-conscious about one's work, existing on an overlapping continuum, but characterized by attention to specific domains, namely the 'process of production, the text itself and the context of production and consumption' (p. 30). In a moment, I shall suggest how people working in animation might be located on this continuum. First of all, we need to summarize the main points on the continuum. At one end is the *reflexive* practitioner, who is able to reflect on the production process, but with a tendency to focus on the minutiae of this, often leading to a debilitating concentration on technology to the detriment of other factors. The *theoretical* practitioner, on the other hand, tends to dwell on the importance of *the text* as the site of meaning. As Wayne points out, though, 'being able to discuss how an editing sequence constructs meaning is not the same as being able to situate the text within a broader context of power' (p. 30). This brings us to the most desirable form of practitioner – and the most difficult to produce and sustain – the *critical* practitioner. They are 'able to interrogate the politics of representation. This requires a movement from the text ... to context' (p. 31). A truly critical practitioner is therefore someone who is willing and able to think through the implications of what they do, and place it in its social, historical and political contexts.

It seems clear from the wealth of points raised in email exchanges I have had with colleagues engaged in animation studies and animation production that Wayne's typology is especially useful.[2] I think this has to do with the way that animation is often subsumed within other theoretical or disciplinary structures, and also with how much of the discussion of animation centres on the role of technology. Animation's overlapping relationship with film and other media has meant that the theoretical paradigms applied to these other areas are often applied to animation, without first fully thinking through how animation's theory and practice might inform *them*.

Similarly, the rationalizing and instrumental trajectory of discourses of technology tends to mean that animation as a practice is often placed in a problematic relationship with those very technologies. The value of critical practice is that it *interrogates* those potentially problematic relationships rather than taking them at face value. The concept of critical practice is also invaluable because it dovetails with the notion of legitimate peripheral participation. As people's activities will depend on the specific material context in which they are operating at any particular moment, it is important to discuss this within a framework that places emphasis on their ability to *critique* their shifting practices. The critical practitioner in the field of computer animation, for example, would ideally be attuned to the possible applications of what they do, across the broad spectrum of arts and sciences alluded to earlier. It is certainly the case that the categories Wayne suggests can overlap, or rather, that a person can occupy *different* positions according to their conditions of practice at any one moment. To go back to a point raised earlier, I think we can take Wayne's typology one step further by stating that there can be a high degree of *mobility* in how people engaged with animation might be defined and define themselves. For instance, there are a considerable number of people whose teaching of animation practice, for one reason or another, seems to fall into the reflexive practitioner category. In other words, they concentrate on the production process and particularly 'the *technology* of cultural production' (Wayne 2001: 30, emphasis added). My point here would be to stress that the discourse of many courses tends to be instrumentalist in nature. Another way to put this would be to say that these courses are more or less vocational in the way they concentrate on the mastering of techniques and technology. Indeed, the technology is often seen as the *main* selling point of the courses.

Despite the fact that an animation teacher might well fall into the reflexive practitioner category in terms of their day-to-day teaching, it is evident (from email discussion group exchanges) that many of them are also acutely aware of debates and issues that would seem to be the preserve of theoretical and critical practitioners. One email respondent states 'conceptually, I feel that Animation Studies means the study of animation, inclusive of both theory and practice. What I do professionally is teach animation practice'. This is an example of the tension noted earlier – i.e. that someone might have a set of ideas ('conceptually') about something, yet be required to do only one *part of* that something in the course of their (educational) job. Also evident from this comment is the discourse of a 'profession'; that there are certain duties and responsibilities that someone in this position must fulfil. Namely, that someone could have a personal view about what constitutes animation, yet that view might not (be allowed to) feature in their actual teaching. Someone might personally be a highly sophisticated critical practitioner in Wayne's sense of the term, yet they recognize the pragmatic dimension of their teaching, and this will mean that their teaching is more or less reflexive (again, in Wayne's sense of this term, reflecting predominantly on the production process, and the related technological issues and debates).

It certainly seems to be the case that the concerns of a reflexive practitioner feature in a lot of animation courses. But they are often in tension with the impulse towards being a more critical practitioner. Evidence of this can be seen in a recent extended debate in the *Animation Journal* discussion group about the role of computer technologies in animation courses. There will always be a tendency towards the fetishization of technology in those courses that are predominantly merely reflexive, simply because what is being reflected upon is the production process (rather than, as Wayne (2001) argues, the broader theoretical and contextual dimensions). A question posted by a member of the group (actually a dissertation working title) prompted a discussion of the role of computer technology. The question was 'are computers in danger of putting "the cart before the horse" in relation to human resource training in the animation industry?' A lively discussion ensued, with a consensus seeming to form around the idea that knowing the 'basics' is more important, and should be seen as a prerequisite for using any form of computer technology. One contributor states:

> I find the cart and horse analogy is accurate since there is a worship of technology and a suspicion of anything 'artistic' in a great many computer animation courses ... Fortunately there are students who are aware of the disproportionate emphasis on technology and who have honed their 'traditional' skills.

The general thrust seems to be that 'the horse' (creativity) must go before, or lead, 'the cart' (the computer technology). The important thing is then seen to be a careful and considered reflection on how the new technology impacts upon the traditional way of doing things.

What is missing to a great degree here though is anything that moves the debate beyond the merely reflexive level. The fact is, a majority of the contributors simply discuss the new technology in a fairly simplistic 'is it better than what we had previously?'-type way (with most reaching a conclusion of 'no, not really', or rather, 'no, not without *building upon* what we had previously, rather than *replacing* it'). There is little theorizing of the broader contextual issues at stake. One contributor edges towards this important ground though:

There is a very strong pressure (from students and institutions) for animation curricula which focus mostly on technology. I think this is in part a consequence of how difficult 3D technology still is for most students. It is also because it is more difficult to assess and quantify the artistic side of animation than the technical aspects. I don't like the cart and horse analogy, because it implies that one thing necessarily comes before the other or dominates. I think that you will find that the best schools always include both, and they walk side by side. You don't find architects debating if their students should learn either to make buildings stand or be expressive – both are fundamental.

This contribution certainly makes some interesting points, not least stating that the analogy used suggests that one part of the equation is actually driving the other. Extending the analogy, we could think of the horse as creativity and the cart as the technology (whether this is computer technology, as it is being debated here, or pen and paper which, lest we forget, are a form of technology too), but add that the practitioner will usually be seated in the cart and drive/control it. Not only that, but they will drive/control the technology by actively using their creativity. This reformulation places *human agency* back in the frame: this is something which is in danger of being effaced entirely (by people who see the technology as the main driving force), or talked about in insufficient terms, that is, couching it only in terms of creativity or artistry, which can tend to imply a transcendental realm, where only people with the requisite artistic temperament can comment on things. The cart, in this analogy, is a *vehicle*, so of course it has to be guided somewhere. But a lot of people in this debate were talking as if merely placing the horse and cart in the correct positions was all that was needed and forgot that both horse and cart are nothing without a real, human agent, actively bringing both creativity and technology under control of their *practice* (under specific conditions).

In other words, the creativity and the technologies that allow the expression of that creativity must be seen as existing in a dialectical relationship. This sees neither one as dominant or prior to the other (falling into either a technologically determinist trap, or one that sees artistry as transcending material conditions), but recognizes that they feed off one another. Developments in computer technology, for example, have arguably produced a good deal of poor animation,[3] where the tendency has been to hope that the 'flashiness' of the new technology will distract. However, it is vital to note that this is a factor whenever any new technology arrives on the scene; it takes time for the technology's limits and possibilities to be fully mapped and realized. This is not helped by inevitable hyperbole that accompanies new technologies. For instance, recent developments in digital video – an extremely cheap way to generate broadcast-quality images that are eminently manipulable – have led some commentators to talk of the 'end of Hollywood'. Such statements are absurd and it only takes a cursory look at the evidence to see that any new developments in an area *will* make some sort of impact, but that they will usually be adapted to or subsumed by the existing power structures (see Bolter and Grusin 1999).

Returning to the cart-and-horse analogy, one respondent offers this observation about special effects wizards, Industrial Light and Magic (ILM):

> ILM used to have an example of bad animation from a fictional 'Cee Student' which displayed everything bad, dumb, and ugly sent to ILM from students who think learning software (and not even all that thoroughly) is all that is required to be hired by a big 3D company. It was apparent from the fictional 'reel' that the good people at ILM have had to look at a lot of crap, and as a result are resentful.
>
> In an information packet that can be downloaded from ILM's web-site is the following regarding the position of character animation: 'Character Animators are generally from a traditional hand-drawing "cel" animation background who now take a computer modelled character or object and bring it to life via the computer.'
>
> Translation: horse first, cart second.

Here we have the view of one of the cutting-edge special effects and animation studios and it is clear that they see the technology as a means to an end and not the end in itself. Their belief is that there is a foundation of good practice (as seen in the reference to 'a traditional hand-drawing "cel" animation background') and that this is mobilized in the context of cutting-edge computer technology. This mobilization of a specific discourse in a new context is an example of what educational theorist Basil Bernstein referred to as 'recontextualization'. A good example of such recontextualization in relation to animation is the recent work of Bob Sabiston and his updating of the principles of rotoscoping via his computerized 'Rotoshop' software (e.g. *Waking Life* 2001). The traditions and foundations of rotoscoped animation, where live-action footage was traced over and animated one frame at a time, meant particular working practices and training: the personnel needed to be trained 'cel' animators to work in this context. The Rotoshop system has been designed so that not just computer experts can use it, and people from other animation and broader art traditions have worked on Sabiston's films. In some cases, even people who have no animation background to speak of have successfully used Rotoshop. This not only demonstrates how the principles of one animation tradition can be mobilized in another, using new technology; it has also caused debate (and some controversy) over how animation is actually defined and who can legitimately be called 'an animator' (Ward 2004: 41–44).

Technology's impact on animation, and the way that animation has had to change due to commercial pressures, is therefore one of the key areas in need of analysis. This is something that Keith Bradbury, Lecturer in Animation at Queensland College of Art (affiliated to Griffith University in Australia), has commented on regarding the role of animation practitioners and scholars.[4] Bradbury asks the question 'is animation a new skill or an old skill?' He continues:

> Essentially I think ... that animation's identity has been fractured by its need to attach itself [and] locate its practice within other commercial industries. The educational neglect of animation ... has further compounded animation's identity as either Disney or special effects or advertising. Advertising has special needs of animation and thus contain[s] its use. Discrete courses on traditional animation practice are rare and thus for a generation of people animation is a skill that needs to be re-discovered not simply revived.

This comment is useful as it points to how a knowledge area and its related practices can be impacted upon by social/material forces. Bradbury is implicitly arguing that the emergence of specific courses, where training will be at the forefront, is the result of shifts in the perceived function and uses of animation (as a set of textual artefacts). This could be characterized as a 'we need more people who can' approach – which is to say, a form of instrumentalism. This ultimately has the effect of undermining the pedagogic and epistemological underpinnings of the knowledge area, as it is seen increasingly as mere 'training' for an already delimited set of options – in Bradbury's example, 'Disney or special effects or advertising'. Also interesting is the contention that an arena such as advertising, having a role for animation to play, tends to try and *keep* animation playing that role, and therefore itself has a role in defining what animation actually *is*. This is a similar argument to that of Thompson (1980) or Ward (2000) on the place of animation within an institutional structure such as Hollywood – that is, it does X well, so it should *only* do X.

Bradbury's key point (see note 4) is 'that animation's identity has been fractured by its need to attach itself [and] locate its practice within other commercial industries'. This is something that really warrants extra thought – the idea that a cultural practice can be fractured in this manner. It is a point that goes some of the way to explaining why some educators or artists working in animation might have a personal view that would make them fit into the critical practitioner category, but that they recognize the reality of their material conditions of practice, and this results in them playing out the role of reflexive practitioner. As I have tended to argue throughout this article, the reflexive practitioner, in the sense I am using it, is likely to be someone who thinks long and hard about the technology and tools at their disposal, but does not take that thinking the one (or more) step(s) further to actually *critique* their conditions of practice and the wider power structures in which they operate. This is why the notion of critical practice is crucial for animation: it needs to offer a critique in order to define itself, but also in order to negotiate its place in relation to the reconfiguring of digital technologies and aesthetics. As Bradbury makes clear, it is easy for animation as a field and set of practices to become fractured, and this possibility has been increased by the rapid diffusion of new media technologies, where animation is a considerable presence. Animation studies' relative youth as a putative (inter-)discipline makes it all the more important that those involved retain a critically informed overview of all the areas where animation has a stake.

The new facility at Brunel University called BitLab[5] was developed initially as an Electronic and Computer Engineering facility to help with teaching and research into multimedia. Recent and ongoing developments have explored the ways in which the facility could be used to increase the connections between arts- and technology-based teaching and research. At present BitLab deals with a great deal of animation-related work, but the vast majority falls under the umbrella of science in the sense that it is scientific applications that use animation (engineering applications, systems analysis, computer modelling and so on). However, there are clear applications for other knowledge areas to exploit, whether they are Performance Studies, Film and Media Studies, Robotics, or even Biology, Sports Science, and the like. My point here would be that what connects these diverse knowledge areas is animation. These communities of practice are engaging with animation on some level, and this is what can give us some critical purchase on both the communities and animation as social phenomena. I have outlined elsewhere the ways in which animation should be considered a discursive field, operating in a number of places (Ward 2003). What we see happening in a facility such as BitLab is animation becoming a potential *catalyst* for the critical practice I have referred to earlier. We have a situation where a variety of disciplinary knowledges are coming together, in a context where they have traditionally been separate: the arts–science–technology interface at Brunel is something that is still in the process of becoming established. The common ground that teachers, researchers and practitioners are finding is animation: whether issues of digital performance, 3D rendering, how new technology impacts upon narrative and more traditional time-based media, the predictive power of modelling programmes, the use of motion capture devices for a plethora of reasons – all of these applications are concerned with animation. As well as underlining the reasons why a sense of critical practice is important, this also means we have to attend to the notions of recognition and community and how they are inflected in debates about disciplines.[6] As established disciplinary boundaries are transgressed, we need a way of critically evaluating what is happening and the social uses to which such practice is being put (hence the need for *critical* practice). We also need to be able to map and predict specific points of contact (hence the need for a theory of academic community in the face of such apparent diversity). Again, Lave and Wenger's (1991) conceptual framework is useful, as it outlines questions of community, but more specifically addresses these notions of centrality, peripherality and what happens when the new meets the old.

Animation as a recontextualized discourse

As noted earlier, different tendencies and skills within animation can come into conflict with each other (e.g. the notion of so-called traditional drawing skills and cutting-edge technology supposedly replacing them). It is also the case, as Bradbury suggests, that animation as a (set of) practice(s) has had to attach and locate itself within a range of other contexts. This brings us to Basil Bernstein's (2000) concept of 'recontextualization': this refers to when and how specific pedagogic discourses are relocated and transformed by their use in other contexts (pp. 41–63). The teaching of particular filmmaking or animating skills will be inflected differently in different courses: the 'same' skill will be recontextualized according to whether it is being taught in a vocational training course, a theoretically inclined course, a film-related course or a multimedia-related course. Clearly, recontextualization can have a commonsense meaning and seem deceptively straightforward. But it is important to understand that such apparently obvious terms are often misunderstood, or their complexities are glossed over, and it is especially important we analyse such terms carefully in as rich and diverse an area as animation.

One of Bernstein's key theoretical innovations was to suggest that the way social practices (such as teaching, forms of cultural production) are *classified* and *framed* has ideological implications (Bernstein 1973, 1977). To take the example of strong classification and strong framing, the argument would go something like this. Strong classification works on the basis of a rigid separation of different types of particular social practices, clearly demarcated from one another. In the case of animation, the suggestion would be that it has its own logic and methods and it should be learned and dealt with as an autonomous discipline. Animation would encounter clearly recognizable animation problems and would use animation methods and procedures to solve them. The implication is that there should be a perfect fit between the kinds of knowledge problems encountered and the methods and practices used to engage with them, and that such a fit, by definition, means that the same knowledge problems cannot be engaged with (or solved) using different methods and practices. The converse is equally true: particular methods and practices can only be applied to the specific knowledge problem in question, not applied to a range of other problems.

Weak classification, on the other hand, approaches the situation differently, by working on the basis that there are inevitable overlaps, and that the fit just alluded to is a fantasy. This approach will engage with particular research problems and issues, but take into account anyone who has something interesting to say on the matter, rather than exclude someone because they are not part of a recognized disciplinary community. Exploring issues in animation might therefore involve listening to a range of researchers and students from a number of different disciplinary backgrounds. The focus becomes the actual epistemological problems (i.e. what counts as valid and interesting knowledge in this context?) rather than some notion of disciplinary purity. Clearly these are difficult issues when viewed in the full context of higher education, that messy place where competition for research funds, recognition from one's peers and so on can mean nailing one's colours to a particular mast as a matter of convenience. Yet, for animation studies (and a good many other knowledge areas, not least film and media studies), the weakly classified route seems to be the most fruitful one to explore. The central dilemma to be addressed is how the strong classification mindset tends to reproduce particular hegemonic discourses and practices. If the general tendency is to see knowledge areas as existing in a strongly classified relationship – where disciplines are separated from each other – then very often only certain (kinds of) answers will be sought and legitimated. This is because only certain people are seen as *able* to answer those questions.

Mark Langer has addressed some of these issues in relation to animation in his polemical essay 'The End of Animation History' (2001). The essay focuses on how the distinction between animation and live-action has dissolved to such an extent that we need to rethink the ways we approach both of them as objects of study (indeed, approaching them 'both', i.e. as distinct 'objects', is part of the problem). Langer's argument is not so much that animation has ceased to be useful as a critical category, but that those thinking about animation need to be attuned to a broader set of debates than is usually the case. He states:

> The entire nature of the relationship between the animated image and the live, real-world spectator is something that is being renegotiated by technology, but that renegotiation is being ignored by scholars in animation studies in specific and film studies in general. [However,] this is not to say that it is being ignored by scholars elsewhere.

Although not said in so many words, Langer is pointing out how the *strong classification* of animation knowledge problems perhaps means that some very apposite answers are not being heard. We can no longer afford to look at animation history (and included here is animation theory and all other variants) as a highly specific (which is to say, *strongly classified*) knowledge area. People who are researching animation can and should learn things from philosophers, engineers, those in performance arts, computing and so on. In short they should follow a pathway of weak classification. This will always be the ultimate test: Is what someone is arguing coherent and of interest, rather than 'does this belong in animation studies?' I would suggest this approach needs to be developed in a way that foregrounds the *critical* potential of animation: we can recognize the diverse material contexts in which animation operates, but in tandem with this we need to also develop a critical perspective that can respond to this diversity.

The concept of recontextualization as outlined by Bernstein can be usefully compared with that of 'remediation' (Bolter and Grusin 1999). This latter term is proposed as a way to understand what happens when new media emerge, with Bolter and Grusin arguing that, far from new media simply replacing existing media forms, what happens is that the new refashions the old. The different media enter into a relationship of co-existence characterized by the interrelated logics of immediacy and hypermediacy:

> Although each medium promises to reform its predecessors by offering a more immediate or authentic experience, the promise of reform inevitably leads us to become aware of the new medium as a medium. Thus immediacy leads to hypermediacy. (p. 19)

This is certainly the impulse we see at work in relation to some recent computer graphics (CG) animation, where the attempt to render in CG imagery a photorealistic human leads to the viewer becoming *more* aware of the mediation at work. In *Final Fantasy: The Spirits Within* (Hironobu Sakaguchi, Moto Sakakibara 2001), for example, there is a paradox evident in the rendering of the human characters – they are at one and the same time too real and not real enough; the viewer knows he or she is watching an animated film, but there is an indeterminacy about the human figures that leads to a heightening of the mediation. What appears to be an attempt at *immediacy* (i.e. increased transparency and realism) results in *hypermediacy* (i.e. increased opacity and noticeability of the medium itself). While Bolter and Grusin are talking about media (and, inevitably, technology), I believe it is useful to think about discourses and ideas in a similar way. If we are to move towards a truly interdisciplinary way of conceptualizing animation, it is important to ensure that we are being as critical as possible, yet open to the very wide range of disciplinary voices that come together in animation's name. The logic of weak classification demands this, and the recontextualization of animation-related discourses in a variety of contexts implies that we need a hypermediated awareness of the potential of animation studies as a discipline, rather than a belief in its immediate or transparent nature.

Conclusion

As animators and animation scholars work within their specific material contexts, producing certain artefacts, using certain technology and so on, they form strategic alliances. Animation is far too diverse to be simply categorized as one single entity, and it is in the attention to the specific working practices, alliances and recognitions between diversely situated people that the particular character of animation will emerge. It is for this reason that I have pointed in this article to the three conceptual frameworks of legitimate peripheral participation, critical practice and recontextualization. Each of these concepts addresses the complex ways in which discourses and sets of knowledges overlap and interact. They openly acknowledge how different people might use the same discourses, but do so in what appear to be entirely different contexts.

As Wayne's (2001) typology of practitioners makes clear, the critical practitioner is someone who is able to identify and reflect upon the occasions when such recontextualization of discourses is occurring. I would add that such a critical thinker will also be attuned to the ways in which he or she is participating in communities of practice (to use these terms in Lave and Wenger's [1991] sense). The fact that animation exists at the conjunction of a very wide range of discourses – about film, fine art, philosophy, technology, aesthetics, individual expression, among others – means that it *takes and recontextualizes* those discourses, but also that it, in turn, is *taken and recontextualized*. A critical reflection on what animation is and what it might be – its conditions of practice and the many different contexts in which it operates – therefore requires that we understand how specific knowledges are positioned by and in relation to other discourses, and how these discourses are in turn positioned by animation. It is this dialectic that is at the heart of animation and all of the knowledges that it has a hand in producing.

Notes

1 Communities of practice can of course be a negative force in the sense that people can retreat into them if they feel threatened.

2   The emails are mainly drawn from the *Animation Journal* e-discussion forum at http://groups.yahoo.com/group/animationjournal/; (you have to join the moderated group in order to view the message archive), plus some personal email exchanges.

3   The idea of 'poor' animation is of course a value judgement that requires explanation and contextualization. Discussions of 'poor' animation in relation to debates about technology usually invoke a lack of 'traditional' animation ability (i.e. the ability to draw, or the ability to move an audience with storytelling and character construction), and suggest that a fetishization of technology occurs in place of this lack of ability.

4   These comments were made in a personal email to the author.

5   BitLab is the name for the Brunel University Information Technology Laboratory, a state of the art facility which includes a range of animation related technology and software, including a motion capture suite, render farm and 3D scanner.

6   On 'recognition' in the sense I am using it here, see Taylor (1995); on 'community' and how it impacts on academic and disciplinary behaviours, see Becher and Trowler (2003) and Lave and Wenger (1991).

References

Becher, T. and P. Trowler (2003), *Academic Tribes and Territories: Intellectual Enquiry and the Cultures of Disciplines*, Milton Keynes: Society for Research into Higher Education and Open University Press.

Bernstein, B. (1973), 'On the Classification and Framing of Educational Knowledge', in R. Brown (ed.), *Knowledge, Education and Cultural Change*, 363–392, London: Tavistock Publications.

Bernstein, B. (1977), *Class, Codes and Control*, Vol. 3: *Towards a Theory of Educational Transmissions*, 2nd edn, London: RKP.

Bernstein, B. (2000), *Pedagogy, Symbolic Control and Identity: Theory, Research, Critique*, rev. edn, London: Taylor and Francis.

Bolter, J. D. and Grusin, R. (1999), *Remediation: Understanding New Media*, Cambridge, MA: MIT Press.

Bouldin, J. (2004), 'Cadaver of the Real: Animation, Rotoscoping and the Politics of the Body', *Animation Journal*, 12: 7–31.

Langer, M. (2001), 'The End of Animation History', paper delivered at the 13th Society for Animation Studies annual conference, Concordia University, Montreal, Canada. Available online: http://asifa.net/SAS/articles/langer1.htm.

Lave, J. and Wenger, E. (1991), *Situated Learning: Legitimate Peripheral Participation*, Cambridge: Cambridge University Press.

Robinson, T. (2004), 'Interview with Brad Bird', *The A.V. Club*, 3 November. Available online: http://avclub.com/content/node/23273.

Taylor, C. (1995), 'The Politics of Recognition', in *Philosophical Arguments*, 225–256, Cambridge, MA: Harvard University Press.

Thomas, F. and Johnston, O. (1981), *Disney Animation: The Illusion of Life*, New York: Abbeville.

Thompson, K. (1980), 'Implications of the Cel Animation Technique', in S. Heath and T. De Lauretis (eds), *The Cinematic Apparatus*, 106–120, London: Macmillan.

Ward, P. (2000), 'Defining "Animation": The Animated Film and the Emergence of the Film Bill', *Scope: An Online Journal of Film Studies*. Available online: http://www.nottingham.ac.uk/film/journal/articles/defining-animation.htm.

Ward, P. (2003), 'Animation Studies, Disciplinarity and Discursivity', *Reconstruction* 3(2). Available online: http://www.reconstruction.ws/032/ward.htm.

Ward, P. (2004), 'Rotoshop in Context: Computer Rotoscoping and Animation Aesthetics', *Animation Journal*, 12: 32–52.

Wayne, M. (2001), 'Problems and Possibilities in Developing Critical Practice', *Journal of Media Practice*, 2(1): 30–36.

PART TWO

Forms and Genres

Introduction

Not only can animation take a variety of material forms, it also exists across a wide range of formats and is distributed in various media. This part explores the significance of these different forms and genres of animation. From TV (Dobson) to video games (Pallant), for purposes including advertising (Cook) and propaganda (Herhuth) and for audiences of different ages (Ratelle). As animation is also commercially prevalent in short form and feature length (Holliday), exists in a variety of modes including experimental (Taberham), and non-fiction (Honess Roe), the chapters in this part aptly demonstrate the diversity and ubiquity of animation.

9

Absence, Excess and Epistemological Expansion: Towards a Framework for the Study of Animated Documentary

Annabelle Honess Roe

This article was first published in animation: an interdisciplinary journal *in 2011 and outlined ideas that Honess Roe would go on to explore in more detail in her book* Animated Documentary *(Palgrave Macmillan 2013). Here she points out that animation and documentary, while perhaps superficially antithetical, have a long history of hybridization. She argues that animation has a particular capacity to expand the range and depth of what documentary can tell us about the real world through functioning in ways that make up for the shortcomings of live-action.*

The marriage of animation and documentary may seem like an odd union, a matching of opposites, complicated by their different approaches to representing our experiences of the world. The former conjures up thoughts of comedy, children's entertainment and fantasy; the latter carries with it (often misplaced) assumptions of seriousness, rhetoric and evidence. The long history, however, of the hybridization of animation and documentary, one that stretches back to the earliest days of the moving image, would suggest that, as in many things in life, opposites can attract in a meaningful way. Animation, for example, has long been used in non-fictional contexts to illustrate, clarify and emphasize. The past twenty to thirty years, however, have seen an increase in the production of what has become known as the 'animated documentary'. In addition to frequently appearing in the line-up of animation and documentary festivals worldwide, feature-length animated documentaries have received mainstream theatrical releases – for example, *Chicago 10* (Brett Morgen 2007) and *Waltz with Bashir* (Ari Folman 2008) – and digital animation has been a staple of primetime television documentary series since prehistory was brought back to life by the BBC in *Walking with Dinosaurs* (Tim Haines and Jasper James 1999).

Despite this long shared history, which is explored in more detail later, the cross-pollination of animation and documentary has been relatively neglected by documentary studies. This neglect is rooted in several possible causes. Animated documentaries are most often made by those who are animators first and documentary-makers second; that is, by filmmakers trained in the craft and art of animation, who have chosen to turn their attention to non-fiction subject matter. As such, animated documentaries might be argued to fit more easily into the animation canon (of both films and scholarly literature). Furthermore, there is little question that animated documentaries are animated films. There is, however, potential debate as to whether animation is an acceptable mode of representation for documentary.

Bill Nichols comments in *Blurred Boundaries* (1994: 29) that the documentary is 'dependent on the specificity of its images for authenticity'. The authenticity of a documentary and the power of its claim to be such a type of film are deeply linked to notions of realism and the idea that documentary images bear evidence of events that actually happened, by virtue of the indexical relationship between image and reality. Animation presents problems for this documentary ontology and, as such, animated documentaries do not fit easily into the received wisdom of what a documentary is. Anecdotally, I can attest to this. A frequent response to mention of animated documentaries – 'Does such a thing exist?' – is founded on the widely held assumptions regarding what a documentary should look like and what sorts of images it should contain. The presumption goes that documentaries should be observational, unobtrusive, bear witness to actual events, contain interviews and, even, be objective.[1]

In fact, it could be argued that documentary does not, and never has fully upheld these characteristics. John Grierson's (1933: 8) definition of documentary as 'the creative treatment of actuality' has demonstrated longevity through seventy years of flux and change in the boundaries of documentary. The attraction lies, in part, in the broadness of this definition. It is easy to mould it to the user's requirements and it is applicable to such a large range of approaches and styles that it has proved resilient to aesthetic, ideological and technological developments in documentary making. It is, for example, equally as applicable to the non-interventional films of the 1960s Direct Cinema filmmakers, as to Errol Morris's interviews and stylized re-enactments and, indeed, to animated documentary.

There is a promise in this Griersonian definition, however, as well as in the colloquial understanding of documentary, that these sorts of films should be about the events, experiences and people that exist in the actual world. As Nichols (2001: xi) suggests, documentaries 'address *the* world in which we live rather than *a* world imagined by the filmmaker' (emphases in original). Nichols and Grierson help us think of animation as a viable means of documentary expression. After all, if Grierson's definition allows re-enactment, why not also animation as a way of creatively treating actuality? And thinking of a distinction between *the* world and *a* world helps us differentiate between animation that is non-fictional and that which is based on make-believe.

Animation is no less complex a term to define than documentary. Norman McLaren's definition of animation as 'not the art of drawings that move but the art of movements that are drawn' is as attractive in its broadness as his one-time mentor Grierson's definition of documentary (quoted in Furniss 1998: 5). For this project, however, we might take our lead from Charles Solomon, who identifies two key factors inherent to animation. That is, that 'the imagery is recorded frame-by-frame' and 'the illusion of motion is created, rather than recorded' (quoted in Furniss 1998: 5). These ideas, of frame-by-frame manipulation and the construction of an illusion of motion, are ones that apply to both handmade and digitally produced animation. Furthermore, they encompass the broad range of techniques and styles that can be considered animation including cel animation, puppet animation, claymation, three-dimensional computer-generated animation and so on.

Mindful of all this, I would suggest that an audiovisual work (produced digitally, filmed or scratched on celluloid)[2] could be considered an animated documentary if it: (i) has been recorded or created frame-by-frame; (ii) is about *the* world rather than *a* world wholly imagined by its creator and (iii) has been presented as a documentary by its producers and/or received as a documentary by audiences, festivals or critics. This last criterion is significant as it helps us differentiate two aesthetically similar films that may be motivated by different intentions by their respective producers or received in different ways by audiences. It also helps to narrow the field; advertising, scientific, educational and public service films, arenas in which animation is frequently utilized, fall beyond what I would consider an animated documentary because they are neither intended, nor received as documentaries.

This article is intended to contribute to a deeper and more nuanced examination of animated documentary by exploring the theoretical foundations and framework for such work. I contend that, while animation may at first seem to threaten the documentary project by destabilizing its claim on the real, the opposite is the case. Rather than questioning the epistemological viability of documentary, as has been done by some authors, I propose that animation broadens and deepens the range of what we can learn from documentaries. One way it does this is by showing us aspects of life that are impossible to film in live-action. Ancient history, distant planets and forgotten memories are just some of the unseeable aspects of reality that animation manifests for the documentary viewer. However, animation goes beyond just visualizing unfilmable events. It invites us to imagine, to put something of ourselves into what we see on screen, to make connections between non-realist images and reality. Animation enriches documentary and our experience of viewing it. Animation is, quite simply, doing something that the conventional live-action material of documentary cannot. I suggest that this is a fruitful way to think about the animated documentary – to consider how the animation functions in the documentary context. This is not a case of attempting to crowbar animated documentary into existing ways of thinking about the documentary, again something that has been suggested by some critics, but a way of thinking about the unique epistemological potential of the animated documentary in itself. This exploration of the functionality of animation in animated documentary will be contextualized by a brief look at the history of animated documentary as well as by the way it has been conceptualized in the scholarly literature.

Animation and documentary's shared history

Rather than re-hashing a history of animated documentary, much of which has been covered in the existing literature (Del Gaudio 1997; Wells 1997; Strøm 2003; Patrick 2004), this section aims to point out some significant tendencies in the early intersections between animation and documentary, as well as suggest a turning point towards the development of the animated documentary as a form in its own right. It would be tempting to trace a neat linear history that takes us teleologically from these early intersections of animation and documentary to the more recent examples. However, the genesis of the animated documentary reveals a more convoluted trajectory. In *Remediation*, Jay Bolter and Richard Grusin (1999: 21, note 1) cite the Foucauldian concept of genealogy in making a connection between new and old media technologies and practices. They seek out 'historical affiliations or resonances and not origins', adapting genealogy to relationships of power to 'formal relations within and among media'. Thomas Elsaessar (2006: 18), on the other hand, rejects the concept of genealogy altogether in favour of the notion of archaeology in his examination of the relationship between new media and the early cinema. He tells us:

> An archaeology is the opposite of genealogy: the latter tries to trace back a continuous line of descent from the present to the past, the former

knows that only the presumption of discontinuity and the synecdoche of the fragment can hope to give a present access to its past.

Elsaessar maps film history as a network, rather than 'discrete units' and, as such, he draws attention to Foucault's (2008 [1969]: 6) claim that history is not continuous, but is rather a process of breaks, mutations and transformations.

Just as Bolter and Grusin (1999) and Elsaessar (2006) point to the folly of examining new media technologies as discrete from the history of cinema and visual arts, so too would one fall foul of an attempt to mark out contemporary animated documentary as separate, yet linearly descended, from the history of these two forms. Instead, the precedent for contemporary animated documentaries must be mapped as a network of both interweaving and independent threads. If we think of animated documentaries as 'new media', relative to the 'old media' of hand-drawn animation and documentary, then we reveal a history of mutual enrichment. What is also revealed is the wide variety the historical hybridization of these two forms takes. The intertwined history of animation and documentary is not, however, a teleological progression towards the current trend of animated documentaries. Just as Foucault's archaeology of the history of ideas 'does not seek to rediscover the continuous, insensible transition that relates discourses, on a gentle slope, to what precedes them, surrounds them, or follows them'(Foucault 2008 [1969]: 115), the history of the overlaps between animation and documentary is not one of easy continuities. There is no single beginning, but rather many concurrent, international examples can be found that demonstrate the instinct that documentary can be strengthened by animation, and vice versa. Similarly, there is no terminal point towards which this history progresses. What is important to take from this history, however, is that, early on, animation was seen to have a unique representational function for the non-fictional moving image, one that could not be fulfilled by the conventional live-action, photographic-based alternative.

In 1918, pioneer American animator Winsor McCay made what is widely dubbed as the 'first animated documentary', *The Sinking of the Lusitania* (Wells 1997: 42, 1998: 16; Patrick 2004: 36). McCay, who was better known for his flamboyant vaudeville lightning sketch performances and animated high jinx with *Gertie the Dinosaur* (1914), turned to non-fiction upon the sinking of the British passenger liner *Lusitania* by a German submarine in 1915. Shocked at the death of innocent civilians, many of them American, but stymied by the absence of original footage or photographs, McCay recreated the events, as retold by the survivors, using animation.[3] His aesthetic approach to the material was modified from his usual animation style to suit the subject matter and the look of the 12-minute long film resembles newspaper editorial illustrations and newsreels of the time.[4]

Significantly, *The Sinking of the Lusitania* contains several textual implications of the suitability of animation to the representation of real life, a sentiment that is echoed in extra-textual material surrounding the film. An early intertitle tells the audience: 'You are looking at the first record of the sinking of the Lusitania' and, in general, the images' perspective resembles those of an imaginary eyewitness, viewing the events from a distance (see Figure 9.1). The *Lusitania* is mostly seen in 'long shots' that allow us, for example, to watch its slow but inevitable disappearance after the torpedo strike. Even the live-action prologue, in which we see McCay and his colleagues setting to work on drawing the film's images, suggests an unproblematic application of animation as a medium for an actuality subject. McCay makes no distinction between live-action and animation in terms of their ability to show us reality and contemporary reviewers seemed equally content to accept that the film offered audiences a chance to '*witness* the whole tragedy, from the moment of the first attack to the heartrending ending' (Bioscope 1919: 74, emphasis added). *The Sinking of the Lusitania* demonstrates the early use of animation as a substitute for missing live-action material.

While McCay's film was the first commercially released 'animated documentary',[5] there are earlier examples of animation being used in a non-fiction context. In particular, animation has historically been used as a tool of illustration and clarification in factual films. British filmmaker

FIGURE 9.1 *The perspective of an imagined witness in Winsor McCay's* The Sinking of the Lusitania *(1918).*

Percy Smith made a series of films, including *Fight for the Dardanelles* (1915), that used animated maps to depict battles of the First World War. In the United States, Max Fleischer made animated films for the military as early as 1917 that were used to train soldiers heading to the battle zones in Europe. The realization that animation could clarify and explain more effectively and efficiently than live-action led to an even greater uptake of the medium by the US government and military in the Second World War. The Walt Disney Studios were commissioned to make numerous educational and training films and also provided the animated sections for Frank Capra's *Why We Fight* series of seven propaganda films (1942–5). In these types of films we see animated maps, moving illustrations of military equipment and diagrams that explain military strategy. This use of animation demonstrates that envisioned information is easier to understand and retain, and that much factual information is communicated more efficiently via animation than the spoken word. These films, however, often conveyed more than facts through their animation by using it for emphasis and visual association. Simple symbolism prevails throughout the *Why We Fight* series, such as pitting dark hues for enemy nations against paler colours for the Allies. This type of symbolism is established in the series' first animated sequence, in *Prelude to War* (1942), when a dark, black inky stain spreads across Japan, Italy and Germany as the narrator notes the cultural differences between these countries and the United States (see Figure 9.2).

FIGURE 9.2 *The inky stain of fascism spreads across an animated map in* Why We Fight: Prelude to War *(Frank Capra 1942).*

Apart from wartime, there is a long history of putting animation to educational use. While still working in the mid-West before moving to California, Walt Disney was commissioned to make two films on dental hygiene.[6] With these early pedagogic endeavours, he was following many of the pioneers of animation and cinema. As early as 1910, Thomas Edison made instructional films that included animated sequences and, according to Richard Fleischer (2005: 27), Randolph Bray made partially animated educational films for the US Government prior to 1916. Subsequently, animators from the Soviet Union to the United States would use animation to explore the physical world. From the Fleischer Brothers' *Einstein's Theory of Relativity* (1923) to Vsevolod Pudovkin's *The Mechanics of the Human Brain* (1926), animation was used as a prescient tool to explain, clarify and visualize.

There are plenty of contemporary examples of animation being used in documentary for a specific purpose. Animated segments are still used in a non-fictional context to clarify, explain, illustrate and emphasize. The use of animated maps, charts, graphs and diagrams in mainstream formats ranging from television news to theatrical documentary are too numerous to mention. This illustrative function of animation has become so commonplace to the point of being inconspicuous. Similarly, natural history, science and history programming now use digital animation as a matter of course to bring to life objects and events that are impossible to capture with the live-action camera. For example, the BBC's recent *Wonders of the Solar System* (2010) displays CGI close-up images of far-off planets that would be impossible to film or photograph.

A frequent, and perhaps relatively recent, use of animation is in live-action documentaries that use animation to create moments of, often ironic, interjection. In films such as *Bowling for Columbine* (Michael Moore 2002), *Blue Vinyl* (Judith Hefland and Daniel B. Gold 2002) and *She's a Boy I Knew* (Gwen Haworth 2007), animation is rendered in a humorous and cartoonlike style as a way of contrasting with the seriousness of the documentaries' subject matter. Emily Hubley's simple line-drawing style animation in *Blue Vinyl* punctuates Hefland's argument regarding our self-destructive reliance on PVC. The animated segments in *Bowling for Columbine* evoke the anarchic humour of television show *South Park* and highlight the absurdity, as perceived by Moore, of America's relationship with firearms. In *She's a Boy I Knew*, Gwen Haworth interjects animated sections into the autobiographical account of her gender transition. Retro adverts and magazine extracts are brought into motion in a segment entitled 'how to be a girl … by Mom' that accents, in a light-hearted way, the issues Gwen's mother has with her take on being female. Hawthorn has commented that she included animation to 'lighten the mood' and add humour to her film as she was concerned it might otherwise become too intense and serious.

However, with the exception of *The Sinking of the Lusitania*, none of these films or television programmes would be described as animated documentaries, either by their makers or their audiences. They lack the sense of animation and documentary cohering into a single form in which the animation works to enhance our knowledge of an aspect of *the* world and to the extent that the separation of the animation from the documentary is either impossible, or would render the inherent meaning of the film incomprehensible. Examples as varied as *Waltz with Bashir, Walking with Dinosaurs* and the *Animated Minds* series (Andy Glynne 2003, 2009) communicate meaning because of their complex and inseparable interplay of animation and documentary. The first person accounts of mental health issues in *Animated Minds* are more than just radio documentaries. The animation adds something very specific to the way we interpret and understand the experiences being recounted. *Walking with Dinosaurs* depends on its realistic animated reconstructions of prehistoric life, in a style that copies the familiar aesthetic of natural history programming, to deliver its scientific hypotheses about the way dinosaurs lived. Ari Folman's personal journey to unearth suppressed memories of his role in the Sabra and Shatila massacre during the 1982 Lebanon War in *Waltz with Bashir*, resonates thematically via the style of animation and the film's refusal to make an aesthetic distinction between past and present.

The animated documentary is archaeologically linked, as suggested previously, to the earlier examples of the use of animation in non-fiction scenarios, just as it is connected to contemporary examples of documentary utilizing animation for specific purposes. The possibilities for the convergence of animation and documentary into a coherent form, however, were anticipated in the United States by the work of John and Faith Hubley and, in the United Kingdom, by Aardman Animation. John Hubley, a key figure in the left-leaning and aesthetically innovative United Productions of America (UPA) animation company, worked with his wife Faith to set up their independent company in 1953. In 1959, they made *Moonbird*, a fantastical flight of fancy that matches animated visuals to a soundtrack of their young sons playing. They followed this up with two further films, *Windy Day* (1967) and *Cockaboody* (1973), which similarly pair documentary tape recordings of their children at play with animated imaginings of their make-believe world. What we see in these films is often directly connected to what we hear the children talk about as they play; thus, when they talk about finding a rabbit, one pops into the scene. The Hubleys' visualization of their children's imaginations is enhanced by the films' expressive aesthetic, with their hand-drawn quality that resembles children's drawings.[7]

Aardman began combining stop-motion animation of plasticine puppets with documentary soundtracks in the 1970s. David Sproxton and Peter Lord produced two short films for the BBC in 1978 under the collective title of *Animated Conversations*. Both films, *Confessions of a Foyer Girl* and *Down and Out*, use documentary sound as their basis and malleable puppets are stop-motion animated against an audio track of eavesdropped conversations. This led to a commission from Channel 4 to make five more shorts, under the banner *Conversation Pieces*, that 'demonstrated how real people's voices could be characterized with insight, humour and sensitivity'.[8] The soundtracks of the five *Conversation Pieces* were again recorded by openly 'eavesdropping' in locations such as workplaces and community centres.

Ultimately, this trend in Aardman's work led to 1989's *Lip Synch* series, one of which was the *Creature Comforts* short film of plasticine zoo animals animated to the musings of interviewees on their living conditions and domestic amenities, which won the studio its first of many Academy Awards.[9] By this stage, Sproxton and Lord began more formally interviewing and recording their subjects, often using a trained radio journalist to do the interviews, which they later cut out of the final soundtrack.[10] While *Creature Comforts*, and its subsequent 'sequels' and spin-offs, may be read as making astute observations on the human condition, with its matching and mismatching of animal form and human voice, it is rarely presented or understood as a documentary. The film does, however, effectively integrate documentary and animation into a coherent whole – in this case a comedy short. The critical and commercial success of this piece of genre integration elevated the profile of the now very successful animation studio and signalled the creative possibilities for the convergence of animation and documentary.

This brief survey illustrates a long-standing relationship between animation and documentary. Historically, documentary makers have utilized animation to illustrate, clarify, visualize and emphasize, using animation to make up for the shortcomings of live-action material. Concurrently, animators have turned their attentions to events occurring in *the* world. This shared history suggests animation and documentary are more compatible than they at first seem. This was confirmed by the Hubleys and Aardman Animation, who clearly demonstrated the potential for the seamless integration of animation and documentary material to create short films that were far more than the sum of their parts.

Interpreting animated documentaries

In the two decades since Aardman's *Creature Comforts*, the production of animated documentary has proliferated. Despite this, and their increased exposure through festival, conferences and public viewing outlets, there is still a relative paucity of scholarly work on the form. In 1997, two essays appeared on the subject: Sybil DelGaudio's 'If Truth be Told, Can 'toons Tell It? Documentary and Animation' in the journal *Film/History* (1997) and Paul Wells's 'The Beautiful Village and the True Village: A Consideration of Animation and the Documentary Aesthetic' in a special (1997) edition of *Art & Design Magazine* guest edited by Wells. These first forays into examining the existence and nature of animated documentaries were followed several years later by two further essays (Renov 2002; Strøm 2003), and Eric Patrick's 'Representing Reality: Structural/Conceptual Design in Non-Fiction Animation' (*Animac Magazine* 2004). Then, in 2005, the March issue of the online animation magazine *FPS* (*Frames per Second*) made animated documentaries its cover story and included three articles on the topic by both animators and scholars. The same year saw the publication of Paul Ward's short book *Documentary: The Margins of Reality*, which includes a chapter on animated documentary.

Much of this early scholarship on animated documentary takes as its foundation key ideas from documentary studies. In particular, the desire to fit animated documentary into the organizational structure of documentary 'modes' first suggested by Bill Nichols in *Representing Reality* (1991).[11] Ward argues for certain types of animated documentaries, namely ones that include documentary voiceover and interviews with participants, as fitting into the 'interactive' mode. He casts these animated documentaries as interactive not just because of the nature and origin of their audio tracks, but also because their production involves the collaboration of the documentary subject(s). DelGaudio (1997: 192) prefers to class animated documentaries within the 'reflexive' mode because, she claims, 'animation itself acts as a form of "metacommentary" within a documentary'. She is suggesting here that by adopting animation as a medium of representation, animated documentaries are necessarily passing comment on live-action's ability, or lack thereof, to represent reality. This is especially the case, she argues, in animated documentaries that document events and topics that were not, or could not have been, captured on camera.

Both Strøm and Patrick see animated documentaries as examples of Nichols's 'performative' mode. According to Nichols (2001: 131), the 'performative documentary underscores the complexity of our knowledge of the world by emphasizing its subjective and affective dimensions'. His conceptualization appears to welcome animation as a mode of representation, not least because of the necessarily subjective nature of much of animation production. Patrick (2004: 38) identifies this appeal with his claim that 'the very nature of animation is to foreground its process and artifice'. Furthermore, when Nichols (2001: 131) tells us that 'the world as represented by performative documentaries becomes, however, suffused by evocative tones and expressive shadings that constantly remind us that the world is more than the sum of the visible evidence we derive from it', it is as if he could be speaking directly to animation.

I would suggest, however, that to shoehorn the animated documentary into one of Nichols's modes threatens to limit our understanding of the form. Ward's ascription of animated documentaries to the interactive mode is, as he admits, only applicable to certain types of animated documentary. Not all animated documentaries have a documentary voiceover and even fewer are produced through an interactive relationship between producer and subject. Similarly, DelGaudio's definition of animated documentaries as reflexive excludes those films that are not necessarily critiquing live-action's capabilities to represent reality. Furthermore, even if animation is doing something live action cannot, it does not necessarily follow that the resulting film is passing comment on the representational abilities of either approach. I contend that the assignment of animated documentaries to the performative mode is equally limiting. Nichols's (2001: 131) explanation of the performative mode is, at times, nebulous. While these types of documentary foreground subjectivity, they also 'demonstrate how embodied knowledge provides entry into an understanding of the more general processes at work in society'. This is a definition of the performative documentary that is far harder to reconcile with animation.

We might question, then, how useful it is to try to fit animated documentaries into Nichols's modes of documentary production. Both Wells and Patrick come up, instead, with different typologies that may be more fruitful for a discussion of this form. Wells re-figures the modes of documentary production outlined by Richard Barsam and examines how animated documentaries fit into, and expand, these modes. In so doing, he reconstitutes Barsam's categories into four 'dominant areas within the field of animation' (Wells 1997: 41). By tracing similarities in overall tone, subject matter, structure and style, Wells determines these four dominant areas as the imitative mode, the subjective mode, the fantastic mode and the post-modern mode.

Films in the imitative mode 'directly echo the dominant generic conventions of live-action documentary' (p. 41). As such, Wells claims, these films are often intended to educate, inform and persuade. The subjective mode often challenges the notion of objectivity through creating tension between the visual and the aural by combining humorous animated representations with 'serious' documentary voiceovers or by connecting to broader social issues through the individual expression of the animator (p. 43). Ultimately, the subjective mode uses animation to 're-constitute "reality" on local and relative terms' (p. 44). The fantastic mode extends the subjective mode's commentary on realism and objectivity to the extent of rejecting realism entirely as 'an ideologically charged (often politically corrupt) coercion of commonality' (p. 44). The fantastic mode further challenges accepted modes of documentary representation by presenting reality through the lens of surrealist animation that bears little or no resemblance to either the physical world or previous media styles. The postmodern mode adopts the general characteristics of postmodernism in 'prioritising pastiche, rejecting notions of objective authority, and asserting that "the social", and therefore "the real", is now fragmentary and incoherent' (p. 44). Wells claims that one of the fundamental pursuits of the documentary project is the attempt 'to engage in the annunciation of commonality and the social dimension of the real' (p. 45). This pursuit is undermined, Wells contends, by the postmodern mode's questioning of the possibility of knowledge in itself.

Patrick (2004: 39) adopts the notion of 'structures' to categorize animated documentaries, suggesting 'in making any kind of film, structure tends to be the skeleton that the content lives on'. He proposes three primary structures – the illustrative, narrated and sound based – and a fourth, the 'extended structure', which is an extension of Wells's fantastic mode (p. 39). 'The four structures encompass the range of possible approaches to animated documentaries without initial regard to concept, techniques or aesthetics' (p. 39). Patrick takes a different conceptual approach from that of Wells, looking through the lens of storytelling rather than the films' relationship to reality. 'Illustrative', Patrick (2004: 40) contends, is a more apt term to describe the films discussed by Wells under the imitative mode. These films illustrate 'events based on historical or personal evidence' and use this to structure the storytelling. The narrated structure uses a script to tell the story and these animated documentaries often use 'voiceover that recounts and connects the elements of the story' (p. 40). The sound-based structure, by contrast, 'uses sound that has either been found or recorded in an unmanipulated, uncontrived way as the primary structuring device' (p. 41). Patrick notes that this aural link between film and reality gives these films all at once a 'naturalistic or improvised' and 'dramatic and cinema verité' feel (p. 41). Patrick dubs Wells's fantastic mode as 'expanded structure' because it 'expands the possibilities of the documentary form by transmuting the traditional storytelling method' (p. 42). Like Wells, Patrick notes the highly subjective nature of this approach and how films in this category eschew a direct relationship or commentary on reality, preferring instead a more surreal, symbolic or metaphoric approach. Patrick then goes on to observe conceptual trends within each mode, by which he means 'the very essence of the film ... the content of what the filmmaker is talking about' (p. 43). So, for example, the sound-based and narrated structures tend to be memorials or portraits of individuals or groups, and films with an illustrative structure often have a historical basis.

This discussion of two different approaches to categorizing animated documentaries, however, raises the question of the purpose of such an exercise. Patrick suggests that his structures are 'a springboard for studying the nature of the form' (p. 45). While, in the early days of scholarship on animated documentaries, the work of Patrick and Wells helped to make the case for its identification as a discrete form, it is questionable whether their modes and structures help us understand this type of film or fulfil much of a purpose beyond a self-serving one of being able to divide films up into their suggested categories. This question of usefulness and purpose is exacerbated if one queries the founding assumptions of their approaches. For example, it is unclear whether 'illustrative', 'narrated' and 'sound-based' are actually structures of storytelling rather than modes of delivery. Patrick's omission of a detailed explication of what he understands by the terms 'structure' and 'storytelling' further muddies these waters.

Wells's approach, which devises categories that speak to the relationship between representation and reality, can be seen as responding to the so-called crisis of postmodernism in documentary. The year before Wells published his essay, an article by Noël Carroll appeared in the collection co-edited with David Bordwell, *Post-Theory: Reconstructing Film Studies* (1996) entitled 'Nonfiction Film and Postmodernist Skepticism'. In this chapter, Carroll takes issue with several theorists' (including Michael Renov, Bill Nichols and Brian Winston) discussion of the fictional elements or stylistic tendencies in some non-fiction. Carroll extrapolates (and, one could argue, misinterprets) these discussions to be a wholesale rejection of a connection between documentary and reality. He characterizes this as a new trend in scepticism regarding the documentary project, one that is inflected by postmodernism more generally. Even earlier than this, in 1993, Linda Williams's (1993) essay 'Mirrors without Memories: Truth, History and *The Thin Blue Line*' uses the lens of postmodernism to examine that film and suggests truth is relative and contingent. While Wells does not cite either of these essays directly, his modes highlight the supposed ineffectuality of conventional documentary representation (as in, live-action) to access or show reality. Furthermore, he suggests a teleology developing towards the postmodern mode that ultimately questions the coherence of reality itself.

However, the existence of a postmodern crisis in documentary has since been debunked. Michael Renov (2004: 137) points out that the targets of Carroll's censure 'rarely addressed postmodernism in any direct way in [their] writings on documentary film'. Renov counters that Carroll's critique is a 'documentary disavowal' that fails to recognize that the form has long since abandoned such rationalist goals as objective, disinterested knowledge. Instead, he suggests documentary is more often concerned with 'contingency, hybridity, knowledge as situated and particular, identity as ascribed and performed'. Renov's words remind us that contemporary documentary studies rarely question the notion that the form coveys knowledge. Rather, the pertinent questions are *how* this knowledge is conveyed and what *type* of knowledge it is.

In response to these debates, I would suggest that Wells's modes of animated documentary are entrenched in a now rejected postmodernist doubt regarding the viability of the documentary project and the very possibility of representing reality. It remains true, however, that there are different types of animated documentaries that present their subject matter through a variety of styles and techniques. Furthermore, animation is not used in the same way in all animated documentaries. It may still be useful, therefore, to demarcate different types of animated documentaries. One means of doing this is to consider how the animation functions. In other words, what is the animation doing that the conventional alternative could not?[12] I suggest that animation functions in three key ways: mimetic substitution, non-mimetic substitution and evocation. I believe this is not just categorization for the sake of it, but rather a way to help understand how animated documentaries work. In particular, sorting these films into categories of functionality helps us understand *what* we learn from animated documentaries and *how* we learn it. This, in turn, will aid consideration of whether, and if so how, the epistemological status of the animated documentary differs from the non-animated documentary and what the implications of such a difference are. By considering the functionality of the animation along epistemological lines this is not an exercise in postmodern doubt regarding the *possibility* that documentary can teach us something about *the* world. Nor is it a by-product of questioning the existence of the real altogether. Furthermore, I am not suggesting that animated documentaries are a subset of Nichols's reflexive mode. Rather, this process embraces the epistemological potentiality of the documentary form by suggesting that animation has the capacity to enhance and extend this potential.

One way that animation functions in animated documentaries is in a substitutive way. In these instances, the animation illustrates something that would be very hard, or impossible, to show with the conventional live-action alternative and often it is directly standing in for live-action footage. The animation here is substituting for something else. This is, in fact, one of the first ways animation was used in non-fiction scenarios in, as discussed earlier, Winsor McCay's *The Sinking of the Lusitania*. More recent examples of substitutive animation can be seen in the BBC's 1999 natural history series *Walking with Dinosaurs* and Brett Morgen's *Chicago 10* (2007). In *Chicago 10*, motion-capture and traditional animation are used to recreate the trial of Abbie Hoffman and the other members of the anti-war movement accused of inciting riot in the run-up to the 1968 Democratic National Convention in Chicago. No filmed record of the courtroom exists and these sequences are based on the transcripts of the legal proceedings, which often descended into a circus-like state of chaos as the defendants refused to adhere to the proceeding's rules and regulations. In *Walking with Dinosaurs*, prehistoric creatures are created using 3-D computer animation that is superimposed on backdrops that had previously been filmed at suitable-looking locations.

In both these examples, the animation is used to stand in for live-action. This is necessitated for similar reasons in both cases, as well as in older examples such as *The Sinking of the Lusitania*, that there exists no live-action footage of the events being portrayed. In these examples, therefore, animation functions as a kind of re-enactment of historical events and this kind of animated documentary works in much the same way as a reconstruction documentary. In that sense, it calls on the viewer to make certain assumptions and allowances and, similar to a reconstruction, says: 'This is a reasonable likeness of what these events looked like the first time they happened and we have chosen to reconstruct them, or in this case animate them, because we don't have a filmed record of that first time they happened.' Substitutive animation is, in these cases, made to closely resemble reality, or rather, the look of a live-action recording of reality. In most of the examples in this category, the animation is created using digital computer techniques, which are achieving ever-increasing levels of verisimilitude. *Walking with Dinosaurs* was celebrated at the time of its release for the realistic CGI images of the dinosaurs. However, the series also inserts extra details, which are extraneous to the narrative, to further imply that the imagery we are seeing is what would have been captured by a camera, had one been around in prehistoric times to track these ancient beasts. In one instance, for example, a T-Rex turns and roars right into the 'lens' of the camera, splattering it with spittle. There are many other examples of other animated documentaries that use these kinds of techniques to make it seem as if the material has been shot on film, even though we know it has not. The History Channel's *Battle 360* (2008), for example, uses digital animation to reconstruct the exploits of a Second World War aircraft carrier and the digital footage is often manipulated to look like aged film.

There are other animated documentaries that also substitute animation for live-action. However, whereas the animation in *Chicago 10* and *Walking with Dinosaurs* attempts to mimic the look of reality, these other films are not so constrained. Animated interview documentaries often use this approach, where a documentary soundtrack is loosely interpreted through animated visuals. The 2002 Swedish film *Hidden* (Heilborn, Aronowitsch and Johansson) animates a radio interview with a young illegal immigrant. Unlike *Chicago 10*, this film has less concern for making the characters resemble their real-life counterparts. Similarly *It's Like That* (Southern Ladies Animation Group, 2004) animates young asylum seekers as knitted puppets of small birds (see Figure 9.3). In these animated documentaries, the animation works as non-mimetic substitution. There is no sense of trying to create an illusion of a filmed image in these examples. Instead, they work towards embracing and acknowledging animation as a medium in its own right, a medium that has the potential to express meaning through its aesthetic realization.

In both mimetic and non-mimetic substitution, the animation could be considered a creative solution to a problem: the absence of filmed material. Animation functions in both cases to overcome limitations of a practical nature. In the case of several animated documentaries, the existence of original filmed material is impossible. The dinosaurs preceded the motion picture camera by several millennia; no cameras were allowed to film the

FIGURE 9.3 *Child asylum seekers are animated as knitted puppets: still from* It's Like That *(2003).* © *Southern Ladies Animation Group.*

trial of Abbie Hoffman and his co-defendants; there is no visual record of the interviews with the Swedish and Australian child immigrants. In these examples, animation is one of many choices available to the filmmaker who could, conceivably, have used another documentary device such as reconstruction or archival material. Often, too, there are ethical considerations at play. The filmmakers of *Hidden* had a responsibility to protect the anonymity of their child subject. In Liz Blazer's *Backseat Bingo* (2003), a short animated documentary about the sex lives of senior citizens, she gained consent to interview her subjects by promising that they would not appear on camera.[13] In both cases, animation becomes an alternative to the silhouetted figure familiar from television interview documentaries and current affairs programming.

Evocation is a third function of animation in animated documentaries that responds to a different kind of representational limitation. Certain concepts, emotions, feelings and states of mind are particularly difficult to represent through live-action imagery. Historically, filmmakers have used various optical devices, such as wavy lines, blurring the edges of the image and alterations of colour palette and film stock, to indicate the representation of subjective states of mind. Similarly, certain camera angles inform the audience that they are seeing the world from a particular character's point of view. Animation, however, is increasingly being used as a tool to evoke the experiential in the form of ideas, feelings and sensibilities. By visualizing these invisible aspects of life, often in an abstract or symbolic style, animation that functions in this evocative way allows us to imagine the world from someone else's perspective. In *Feeling My Way* (1997), Jonathan Hodgson uses animation to communicate his train of thought on his daily walk to work. *Animated Minds* (Andy Glynne 2003) combines animated visuals with a soundtrack on which an interviewee speaks of their experience of living with mental illness. The style of animation reflects the experiences being described on the soundtrack and gives us a visualization that aids our understanding of these internal worlds.

This evocative functionality of animation has particularly been used to evoke the reality experienced by the films' subjects, realities that are often quite different from those experienced by the majority of society. In these instances, animation is used as an aide-imagination that can facilitate awareness, understanding and compassion from the audience for a subject-position potentially far removed from their own. Samantha Moore's 2009 film *An Eyeful of Sound* is about synaesthesia, the neurological condition of experiencing normally separated sensations at the same time (such as seeing a sound or tasting a noise). In the film, Moore focuses on people who have audiovisual synaesthesia, or who see sounds. Like much animated documentary, she combines animated visuals with an audio track of interviews with participants with first-hand experience of synaesthesia. The film works to evoke, rather than represent, the experiences we hear being described and Moore's images respond to the film's musical score in a way that a synaesthete's brain will trigger images in response to sounds (see Figure 9.4). Moore is attempting to evoke the synaesthetic experience for her viewers through the interplay of animation, documentary soundtrack and musical score.

These three functions – mimetic substitution, non-mimetic substitution and evocation – are the three key ways that animation works in animated documentary. In the case of mimetic substitution, in examples such as *Chicago 10* and *Walking with Dinosaurs*, the animation tends to be offering us knowledge of something that we could have all seen if we had been alive in prehistoric times or a spectator in Judge Julius Hoffman's courtroom. This is, perhaps, the kind of knowledge that the documentary is, traditionally, evidential of: knowledge that is out there, in the shared historical world, which we all could have accessed equally if we were eyewitness to it. In non-mimetic substitution, such as *It's Like That*, the animation begins to add something, to suggest things through its style and tone; the film makes a point about the incarceration of innocents with the representation of the young asylum seekers as soft, knitted birds. This shift from the observable is furthered through the evocative use of animation. Instead of pointing outwards, pieces such as *Feeling My Way, Animated Minds* and *An Eyeful of Sound* are pointing inwards towards the internal. These films, through the use of animation, are proposing documentary's ability and suitability to represent the world *in here* of personal experience as well as the world *out there* of observable events. Extending on from this, films that engage with the personal memories of the filmmakers, such as *Waltz with Bashir* (Folman

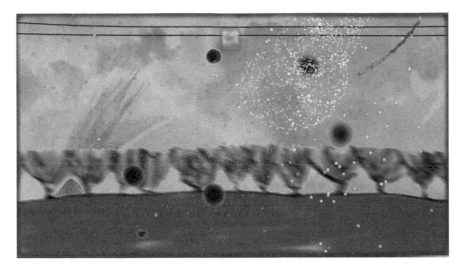

FIGURE 9.4 *Animation evokes the synaesthetic experience: still from Samantha Moore's* An Eyeful of Sound *(2010). © Samantha Moore.*

2008) and *Silence* (Yadin and Bringas 1998), use animation as a tool to explore and reveal hidden or forgotten pasts, demonstrating the medium's capacity for documenting the world from a subjective point of view.

Conclusion

Looking at how the animation functions in animated documentary allows us to draw some conclusions regarding the epistemological status of these types of films. While all documentaries purport to teach us something about *the* world, animating documentary broadens the epistemological potential of documentary by expanding the range of what and how we can learn. Through mimetic substitution, non-mimetic substitution and evocation, animation compensates for the limitations of live-action material. Rather than questioning the viability of knowledge-through-documentary, animated documentaries offer us an enhanced perspective on reality by presenting the world in a breadth and depth that live-action alone cannot. Life is rich and complicated in ways that are not always available to observation, something that is reflected in the diversity of style and subject matter of contemporary animated documentaries.

This is a decisive moment for the study of animated documentary. We no longer need to marvel at its mere existence; that was the job of the forward guard scholarship, discussed earlier. Now, the heterogeneity of animated documentary demands we go beyond general observation, towards specification and theorization. The question of the epistemology of animated documentary is just one place to start, one that addresses some fundamental assumptions of documentary. Animation and documentary have co-enriched each other since the earliest days of cinema, and we can hope they will continue to do so for a long time yet. As the form evolves, so too must the questions we ask of it.

Notes

1   These are some of the most frequent assumptions I have heard expressed by students in undergraduate documentary courses.

2   For brevity, I will refer to the audiovisual texts under discussion as 'films', even though many of them are produced on digital video and are not intended for projection on the big screen.

3   A process that took two years and required 25,000 individual drawings.

4   This emulation was clearly effective as the film was included in the Universal Weekly newsreel shown in movie theatres (see Crafton 1982: 116).

5   While it was not labelled as such at the time of its production or initial reception, an argument can be made for it being understood as such, according to the criteria set out earlier.

6   *Tommy Tucker's Tooth* (1922) and *Clara Cleans Her Teeth* (1926), both for Dr Thomas B McCrum of the Deener Dental Institute in Kansas City, Missouri (see Shale 1976: 112).

7   One of the Hubleys' daughters, Emily, became an animator and some of her work appears in Abraham Ravett's autobiographical documentary, *Everything's for You* (1989) and Judith Helfand and Daniel B. Gold's *Blue Vinyl* (2002).

8   http://www.aardman.com/html/history.asp (accessed 15 February 2009). The five films are *On Probation, Sales Pitch, Palmy Days, Early Bird* and *Late Edition* (all 1983).

9   This also led to many commissions for television commercials; see http://www.aardman.com/html/history.asp (accessed 15 February 2009). The other films in this series are *Going Equipped, War Story, Next!* and *Ident.*

10   David Sproxton, email message to author, 1 October 2008.

11   Nichols initially suggested four modes: the expository, the observational, the interactive and the reflexive. He later added the poetic and the performative and re-named the interactive as the participatory mode (see Nichols 1991, 1994, 2001).

12   By 'conventional alternative', I mean the types of photo-based media familiar to documentary, such as observational filming, archival footage, reconstruction, interviews, photographs and so on.

13   However, once they had seen the finished film, the senior citizens agreed to their photographs appearing in its credits (Liz Blazer, email message to author, 17 February 2009).

References

Bioscope (1919), 'Unsigned Review of *The Sinking of the Lusitania*', *Bioscope*, 41(650) 27 March: 74.

Bolter, J. D. and Grusin, R. (1999), *Remediation*, Cambridge, MA: MIT Press.

Carroll, N. (1996), Nonfiction Film and Postmodern Skepticism', in N. Carroll and D. Bordwell (eds), *Post-Theory: Reconstructing Film Studies*, 283–306, Madison, WI: University of Wisconsin Press.

Crafton, D. (1982), *Before Mickey: The Animated Film 1898–1928*, Cambridge, MA: MIT Press.

DelGaudio, S. (1997), 'If Truth Be Told, Can 'toons Tell It? Documentary and Animation', *Film History*, 9(2): 189–199.

Elsaesser, T. (2006), Early Film History and Multi-Media, in W. Hui Kyong Chun and T. Keenan (eds), *New Media Old Media: A History and Theory Reader*, 13–25, New York: Routledge.

Fleischer, R. (2005), *Out of the Inkwell: Max Fleischer and the Animation Revolution*, Lexington, KY: University Press of Kentucky.

Foucault, M. (2008 [1969]), *The Archaeology of Knowledge*, trans. A. M. Sheridan Smith, London: Routledge.

Furniss, M. (1998), *Art in Motion: Animation Aesthetics*, Sydney: John Libbey.

Grierson, J. (1933), 'The Documentary Producer', *Cinema Quarterly*, 2(1): 7–9.

Nichols, B. (1991), *Representing Reality*, Bloomington, IN: Indiana University Press.

Nichols, B. (1994), *Blurred Boundaries*, Bloomington, IN: Indiana University Press.

Nichols, B. (2001), *Introduction to Documentary*, Bloomington, IN: Indiana University Press.

Patrick, E. (2004), 'Representing Reality: Structural/Conceptual Design in Non-Fiction Animation', *Animac Magazine no. 3*, 36–47.

Renov, M. (2002), Animation: Documentary's Imaginary Signifier, Paper presented at Visible Evidence conference X, Marseilles, France.

Renov, M. (2004), *The Subject of Documentary*, Minneapolis, MN: University of Minnesota Press.

Shale, R. (1976), *Donald Duck Joins Up: The Walt Disney Studio during World War II*, Ann Arbor, MI: UMI Research Press.

Strøm, G. (2003), 'The Animated Documentary', *Animation Journal*, 11: 46–63.

Ward, P. (2005), *Documentary: The Margins of Reality*, London: Wallflower Press.

Wells, P. (1997), 'The Beautiful Village and the True Village: A Consideration of Animation and the Documentary Aesthetic', in P. Wells (ed.), *Art and Animation*, 40–45, London: Academy Editions.

Wells, P. (1998), *Understanding Animation*, London: Routledge.

Williams, L. (1993), Mirrors without Memories: Truth, History and *The Thin Blue Line*, Film Quarterly, 46(3): 9–21.

10

Experimental Animation

Paul Taberhman

Experimental animation offers a distinct set of formal challenges to the spectator. Watching a commercial animation, the viewer is typically compelled to speculate on how the narrative conflicts might be resolved, and they are also invited to reflect on the characters featured and the themes raised by the story. The viewing strategies required when engaging with experimental animation are different, and so the aim of this chapter is to elucidate what it is the viewer should keep in mind when they encounter this type of film.

One of the principal distinctions one may make between commercial and experimental animation is the way in which imagery is used. In commercial animations, the visual details are always subordinated to the story they serve, and they will not play as big a part of the experience once they have been integrated into the larger, more 'meaningful' form of an overarching story. By contrast, the visceral dimension of experimental animations, the colours, movements and visual textures more fully comprise the film's aesthetic appeal. The earliest explorations of this sensuous experience of animation took the form of visual music, which may be understood as non-figurative animation that visually aspires to the dynamic and non-objective qualities of music. While not all experimental animations try to do this, abstraction still warrants particular attention in this discussion, since it played a key part in the development of experimental animation. In the early twentieth century, artists of the time were concerned about what was considered a 'misuse' of cinema. Robert Russett explains that they 'envisioned motion pictures not as a form of popular entertainment, but rather as a new and dynamic expression, one closely allied with the major art movements of the day' (Russett 2009: 10).

Painter Wassily Kandinsky claimed in 1911 that visual art should aspire to the achievements of music and he sought a visual equivalent to music in contemporary painting. This led to abstract (non-figurative) art. In *Concerning the Spiritual in Art*, he argues:

> A painter […] in his longing to express his inner life cannot but envy the ease with which music, the most non-material of the arts today, achieves this end. He naturally seeks to apply the methods of music to his own art. And from this results that modern desire for rhythm in painting, mathematical, abstract construction, for repeated notes of colour, for setting colour in motion. (Kandinsky 2010: 32)

Contemporaries of Kandinsky such as František Kupka and Paul Klee possessed similar creative aspirations, and by the 1920s, European abstract painters Walter Ruttmann, Viking Eggeling and Hans Richter extended their craft to animation, with the musical organization of film time as their central concern. Concepts from musical composition such as orchestration, symphony, instrument, fugue, counterpoint and score were applied. For example, Richter's *Rhythmus 21* (1921) strips visual information back to its core element – motion in time. An assortment of squares and rectangles (sometimes white on black, other times black on white) expand and contract on the screen at different speeds. Each visual articulation, like a series of musical motifs, repeats and makes variations. Like music, the movements are variously fast, slow, aggressive, smooth, graceful and abrasive. Just as two or more musical melodies can move in counterpoint, so too can shapes in motion move contrapuntally around one another.

Following these early pioneers who sought to visually express music, experimental animation later assumed a variety of different forms. While no two experimental animations are the same, we can begin to think about some common tendencies that feature in these types of films. The following list of features does not include essential characteristics but rather *tendencies*.[1]

First, the context of distribution and production may be outlined in the following way:

- It may be created by a single person or a small collective.
- The film will be self-financed or funded by a small grant from an arts institution, without expectation to make a profit.
- Instead of undergoing commercial distribution, experimental films are normally distributed independently online, or through film cooperatives to be exhibited by film societies, universities and galleries.

Second, the aesthetics of experimental animation may be characterized thus:

- They *evoke* more than they *tell*. They don't offer a clear, unambiguous 'message'.
- The materials of animation may be consciously employed in a way that calls attention to the medium.
- The personal style and preoccupations of the artist will be easily discernible.
- Psychologically defined characters with identifiable motivations and goals do not feature.

Maureen Furniss has discussed the difference between commercial and experimental animation, and prudently makes the point that these two categories exist on a continuum. She rightly comments that both represent extremes 'to which few cultural products could adhere completely; but, evaluating a particular text in terms of the various paradigms, it is possible to see a given work as generally being related to one mode of production or the other' (Furniss 2008: 30). This is a productive way to think about categories such as commercial or experimental animation, since it is seldom a tidy distinction.

   With an outline of the tendencies of experimental animation in place, we can now consider some of these characteristics in closer detail.

The artist and the spectator

An experimental animation creates meaning in a different way to a narrative-based animation that tells a traditional story. In commercial, mainstream animation events are generally depicted to be interpreted unambiguously. Stories follow a causal chain, with protagonists typically overcoming an internal obstacle to achieve a goal with wide-reaching consequences and ultimate resolution. For example, Simba in *The Lion King* (Allers and Minkoff 1994) overcomes internal doubt to challenge the tyranny of his wicked uncle Scar, and regain his place as the rightful king. In *How to Train Your Dragon* (Sanders and DeBlois 2010), Hiccup, a timid and physically weak teenager, learns to use his intelligence and compassion to reconcile his Viking community with a horde of dragons. In both instances, the theme of the importance of self-belief is easily discernible. Experimental animation, by contrast, is more likely to defy straightforward description; ideas are expressed in an indirect way, they *provoke* rather than *tell*. In turn, the viewer is left to interpret the work according to their own dispositions. There isn't a hidden meaning set up by the artist which the viewer needs to identify; rather, the viewer should respond to the experience imaginatively, as if the work was a mirror reflecting back what the spectator sees and what they bring to the experience. If a spectator is concerned that they don't 'understand' a film, they may instead ask themselves how it made them *feel*. A film might create a feeling of ambient entrancement, agitation, relaxation or disorientation, for instance. If the viewer chooses to focus on the feelings generated by the film, this is an adequate response to the work. It may, thus, be experienced as an *enchantment*, rather than a story.

In addition to the experience of the spectator, one may also consider the creative process of the artist. The creation of experimental animation may be more heavily conceived as a process of discovery, rather than a film that is pre-planned and then subsequently executed. The artist might reflect on a given subject and a series of images will come to mind. Using a form of non-rational intuition, the meaning might be highly internalized and various references won't necessarily be apparent to the viewer. Even if the spectator does not know what originally motivated the images, he/she may nonetheless understand that there was a creative rationale behind them. In turn, understanding this and ceding to the artist's guiding light of intent informs their viewing experience. For example, consider Robert Breer's *Bang!* (1986): on the surface, this film, which combines animation with brief sequences of live-action, appears to feature a string of dissociated images, but there is a discernible theme to those who look for it. Broadly speaking, the film deals with Breer's own childhood and adolescence (Camper 1997). Instead of telling a linear story, the film is more like a daydream in which images 'skip around the way thoughts do' (Breer, quoted in Coté 1962/63: 16).

Bang! presents Breer's own boyhood fascinations – outdoor activities (the forest, rafting, a waterfall), sport (football and baseball) and Tarzan. Fighter pilots and the face of Adolf Hitler also briefly appear, a figure who will have been widely recognizable to all Americans in the 1930s and 1940s. Images evoking pubescent, burgeoning sexuality are also featured, such as drawings of a nude woman, a drooling man and sperm swimming. The spectator is free to ruminate on themes raised in the film such as nostalgia, regret and conflict (both in war and sport). Breer used his own childhood memories to generate images for his film, but didn't count on spectators to 'decode' each image shot-by-shot. Artists accept that they create works, send them into the world where viewers will make their own interpretations. As with all experimental animation, there is no single 'correct' reaction to *Bang!*. Even if the theme of childhood and autobiography passes unnoticed, the viewer may still be engaged by Breer's distinctive range of materials used to make the film such as felt-tip pen, pencil, filmed television, photographs and childhood drawings. In addition, his use of a loose sketch style and flickering imagery is also enough to hold the viewer's interest.

Some artists, such as those during the Gothic period did not consider their work to be a form of personal expression; rather, they were channelling God's will. Today, the creative act is less commonly understood in these terms, but the notion of drawing from an exterior force (divine or otherwise) still persists. One artist who did consider his work to draw creatively from a sacred force is Jordan Belson, who produced experimental animation between 1947 and 2005. He drew inspiration by practising meditation and then recreating his inner visions through film. In *Allures* (1961), the viewer's attention is continually drawn back to the centre of the frame. We see intersecting dots, flicker effects, distant spirals and revolving mandalas. A similarly mysterious soundtrack, featuring bells, a deep hum, distorted gongs and electronic sounds, works with the imagery to create a unified experience of entrancement. An abstract work such as this seems to defy interpretation altogether, so how does one talk about it? In a sense, the images may be understood and appreciated in a pre-conscious way; indeed, Belson encouraged this interpretation. He has commented that his films 'are not meant to be explained, analyzed, or understood. They are more experiential, more like listening to music' (Belson, quoted in MacDonald 2009: 77).

Nonetheless, images can be imaginatively interpreted in a way that could enrich one's experience of *Allures*. For instance, one may say that the opening images, with swirling dots that lead to the centre of the frame, create the impression that the spectator is being pulled through a cosmic tunnel into the imaginative space of the film. Likewise, when the screen is awash with light, it may be interpreted as representing enlightenment. Aimee Mollaghan has suggested that the high-pitched electronic sounds accompanied by a lower beating rhythm resemble the inner-bodily nervous and circulatory systems. In addition, the film's 'fields of dots and dashes super-imposed over each other reflect the speed and activity of the neural pathways as they enter even deeper into the state of meditation' (Mollaghan 2015: 89). As such, by looking at the specifics of this wholly abstract film, it is possible to discern the theme of inner-consciousness. Conversely, Gene Youngblood (1970: 160) has suggested that the film depicts the birth of the cosmos. Suffice to say, both interpretations of this film – that it expresses the small and large, the micro and macro – are accommodated in the work. The spectator is free to see it both ways.

We may say, then, that experimental animation is poetic and suggestive instead of concrete and specific in meaning.[2] Artists use non-rational intuition to create images which viewers can respond to imaginatively. There is no single correct reading of an experimental animation, and the film may be designed to create a feeling which cannot be articulated through spoken word or a conventional story.

Creative individuality

Ordinarily, mainstream animated films and TV shows are not marketed as the work of an expressive individual. In part, this is because commercial animations are collaborative and need a large working crew. Auteurs such as Hayao Miyazaki, Pendleton Ward and Genndy Tartakovsky are an exception to this – directors who are associated with a particular visual style and approach to storytelling. More broadly this is not the case, general audiences do not tend to remember who directed the Disney feature animations *Lady and the Tramp* (1955), *Aladdin* (1992) or *Frozen* (2013), to name a few examples.

When viewing an experimental animation, the artist's creative presence can be more vividly felt. Since they generally work alone and do not produce animations commissioned by a studio with an expectation to make a profit, experimental animators will have the freedom to express more personal visions than commercial directors. In experimental animation, the artist is the creative force who 'communicates' (what is the film *saying?*) and who 'expresses' themselves (what is the artist's *personal style?*) rather than striving to 'entertain'. Familiar viewers will watch films by an artist expecting certain themes and techniques the director has used previously. The film, in turn, becomes understood as part of a larger oeuvre.

While this chapter deals principally with broad, governing principles for engaging with experimental animation, there are also more localized principles which apply to specific artists. Robert Breer, for instance, uses a range of materials to create his films and images loosely relate to each other in a manner similar to a daydream; Jordan Belson works with abstract images that evoke impressions of inner-consciousness and also the larger universe.

Established artists tend not to aim for profundity when creating work, but rather simply remain true to their creative instincts. They are sometimes drawn to depicting extreme psychic states or madness. Jan Švankmajer has associated his own animations with the surrealist art movement (Jackson 1997), in which the artist draws creatively from the part of the mind that remains untouched by rationality, social convention and the laws of nature, that is most readily accessed through dream. Even if experimental animators tend to look inwards and create something that feels internalized, they still try to create a work of art that will offer a meaningful experience to viewers. Otherwise, there would be no reason to share it with others.

Experimental animators may also express their creative individuality by questioning premises that can otherwise go unquestioned in commercial animation. For instance, do stories need to make sense? Should animated movement be smooth? Is technical competence necessary? Do images need to be visually appealing by conventional standards, or can grotesque imagery also be compelling? Jan Švankmajer's *Dimensions of Dialogue* (1982), for example, includes crudely rendered heads made from metal, paper, wood, meat, vegetables and plastic. They eat, and vomit one another out in turn until both become bland copies of each other. The effect is both compelling and disconcerting.

David Theobold's authorial presence can be vividly felt in his films since they frame a philosophical question in a distinctive way. He is known for producing high-quality computer-generated animation, but featuring minimal onscreen movement. His films implicitly ask, does a significant event need to happen in a film? Lilly Husbands explains:

> Although his works might resemble the visual aesthetic of [...] commercial studios, Theobald's animations spend their entirety focusing on places and objects that would appear in a Pixar animation only very briefly and most likely somewhere in the background. The intensive labour that goes into Theobald's animations is perversely used to produce images of everyday objects and scenarios that would normally be deemed unworthy of prolonged attention. (Husbands 2015)

For example, Theobald's three-minute *Kebab World* (2014) features a single, static shot that looks into a kebab takeaway window. Most of the frame remains motionless, though the kebab slowly rotates and the neon lights of the shop sign blink. The soundtrack features an ongoing radio, with intermittent police sirens. Red and blue flashing lights illuminate the contents of the frame, although we never see any cars. The seemingly mundane subject matter and absence of a story can be interpreted as humorous to those who are attuned to Theobold's creative concerns. The film asks: Why would anyone create, or watch, a film as uneventful as this? Why test your own patience when watching an animation? His other works such as *Jingle Bells* (2013) and *Night Light* (2016) are similarly uneventful. Theobald's creative presence is readily discernible in these films because they make a philosophical statement in an aesthetically provocative way. As Husbands explains, 'Theobald's refusal to cater to conventional narrative expectations, denying spectators their attendant gratifications, serves to remind them of the fact that everything is not always selfishly, anthropocentrically, *for us*' (Husbands 2015).

The examples of films by Breer, Belson and Theobald illustrate that the creative force behind experimental animation is more vividly present than it typically is in commercial animation.

Exposing the medium

Commercial animation does not typically invite viewers to actively contemplate the materials used to produce the film, such as cels, clay (for stop-motion) or CG models. Experimental animation, by contrast, sometimes invites viewers to consider the way in which the medium is being put to use. This tendency harks back to the early twentieth century. Clement Greenberg discusses the transition from realistic paintings to modernist art:

Realistic, naturalistic art had dissembled the medium, using art to conceal art; Modernism used art to call attention to art. The limitations that constitute the medium of painting – the flat surface, the shape of the support, the properties of the pigment – were treated by the old masters as negative factors that could be acknowledged only implicitly or indirectly. Under Modernism these same limitations came to be regarded as positive factors, and were acknowledged openly. (Greenberg 1991: 112)

Modernist painters such as Pablo Picasso, Henri Matisse and Piet Mondrian stressed the flatness of their painting canvases rather than concealing it with illusions of visual depth, for instance. Flatness was unique to pictorial art, and was in turn embraced.

Exposing the materials used to create an animated film can be done in a variety of ways. When artists like Len Lye or Steven Woloshen scratch directly onto the film stock, for example, their physical presence can be felt in the markings. Stop-motion animators like Švankmajer can leave their fingerprints in the clay. Caleb Wood's *Plumb* (2014) begins with a hand drawing pictures on a wall with a marker pen. This is followed by a wide shot of the various markings, and then each individual mark is shown in rapid succession, creating an animated sequence. The CG-animated *Black Lake* (2010) by David O'Reilly pulls the viewer through an uncanny, hallucinatory underwater landscape with rocks, fish, a house and other objects. After a minute and a half, the same items are seen again, but in wire-frame form, exposing the way in which they were digitally generated.

The materiality of an animation may also be exposed by allowing the audience to visually register the frame rate of the film. If consecutive frames are sufficiently different, a flicker effect occurs which prevents the viewer from relaxing their eyes into the impression of smooth motion. Instead, every frame (i.e. 24 per second) visually registers, creating a flicker effect. Robert Breer's *Recreation* (1956) applied this technique, as did Paul Sharits's *T:O:U:C:H:I:N:G* (1968). The technique is still applied today with more recent films like Thorsten Fleisch's *Energie!* (2007) and Jonathan Gillie's *Separate States* (2016).

The techniques used to create an animation are therefore something that may be exposed and celebrated in a variety of ways, in opposition to commercial animation's tendency to make the techniques of production invisible.

Additional topics

There are a range of other issues and questions, in addition to those focused on above, that can be considered when exploring experimental animation. First of all, alternative methods of exhibition may also have been explored such as multiple projection work, gallery-specific animation or projecting onto the sides of buildings. Also, the recent adoption of .gif files (brief, looped digital films) as found in the work of artists like Lilli Carré and Colin MacFadyen could be considered, as well as David O'Reilly's recent forays into videogame production.

Secondly, the connections between experimental and commercial animation may also be briefly considered. Just as the term *avant-garde* means 'advance guard', implying pioneers who lead the way in their artistic field, experimental animators influence mainstream aesthetics. This can occur in the realm of special effects, where artists like Michel Gagné can produce abstract animations like *Sensology* (2010) and also use the same style for special effects in *Ratatouille* (2007). Title sequences can also be influenced by experimental animation such as the opening to *Scott Pilgrim Vs. the World* (2010) which is a homage to the scratch films of Len Lye and Norman McLaren. Animator Gianluigi Toccafondo began his career producing experimental animations like *La Coda* (1989) and *La Pista* (1991) and later produced title sequences for films such as *Robin Hood* (2010) with an aesthetic adapted from his earlier style. Finally, music videos have also been influenced by experimental animation. Singer Robyn's 2007 music video *With Every Heartbeat* features a homage to Oskar Fischinger's *Composition in Blue* (1935), and the music video to *Where Are Ü Now* (2015) by Skrillex, Diplo and Justin Bieber draws directly from the sketchy, flicker aesthetic pioneered by Robert Breer.

Conclusion: Approaching experimental animation

The central aim of this chapter has been to elucidate the underlying viewing strategies needed when engaging with experimental animation. Some of the central principles have been detailed: the notion that these films evoke, rather than tell, the discernible presence of the creative force behind the films, and exposing the materials used to make the films. One may ask then, when writing about experimental animation, what does one discuss? How does one talk about a kind of film that tries to express the inexpressible? This four-step plan may offer a helpful starting point:

- Vividly describe the artwork. This will show that you were sensitive to the details of the film rather than just experienced them as a flurry of vague, generalized images.

- Summarize existing material on your chosen artist case study. Outline what their 'larger project' or general approach is. This has happened briefly in this chapter in relation to Jordan Belson and David Theobald.

- Articulate the creative aspirations of the artist by matching it with specific moments of their film.
- If you can discern one, offer your own interpretation of a film that has not been expressed elsewhere.

In experimental animation, images come from the quick-of-the-soul. An artist follows his/her individual inspiration, and shares his/her vision with the outside world. As the viewer, your principal duty is to keep an open mind, and let the film do its work. Sometimes a work of art creates a vivid experience, while at other times it creates a persistent memory. Some offer both, while others provide neither. A film might hold you captive for two hours, and then promptly be forgotten. While experimental animation and commercial animation are no different in this respect, experimental animation can put a premium on the long-term resonance over the immediate impact. You may be left with an itch, or a feeling that there was something about a film that you haven't yet fully grasped which needs to be revisited. Even if a concrete meaning remains out of reach, one's experience of a work of art can change at different periods of your life.

Notes

1   This list was first published in: Taberham, P. (2018). It is adapted from Paul Wells (1998: 36) and Maureen Furniss's (2008: 30) discussions of experimental animation.
2   This is not to imply that narrative filmmaking cannot also be ambiguous, or open to thematic interpretation. Nonetheless, in the absence of narrative-dramatic scenarios, experimental animation can be notably elusive.

References

Camper, F. (1997), *On Visible Strings*. [online] Chicagoreader.com. Available online: https://www.chicagoreader.com/chicago/on-visible-strings/ Content?oid=893567 (accessed 27 October 2017).
Coté, G. (1962/63), 'Interview with Robert Breer', *Film Culture*, Winter: 17–18.
Furniss, M. (2008), *Art in Motion: Animation Aesthetics*, London: John Libbey.
Greenberg, C. (1991), 'Modernist Painting', in S. Everett (ed.), *Art Theory and Criticism: An Anthology of Formalist Avant-Garde, Contextualist and Post-Modernist Thought*, 1st edn, 112, London: McFarland.

Husbands, L. (2015), 'Animated Alien Phenomenology in David Theobald's Experimental Animations', *Frames Cinema Journal*. Available online: http://framescinemajournal.com/article/animated-alien-phenomenology-in-david-theobalds-experimental-animations/ (accessed 22 February 2018).

Jackson, W. (1997), 'The Surrealist Conspirator: An Interview with Jan Švankmajer', *Animation World Magazine*, 2(3). Available online: https://www.awn.com/mag/issue2.3/issue2.3pages/2.3jacksonsvankmajer.html (accessed 22 February 2018).

Kandinsky, W. (2010), *Concerning the Spiritual in Art*, Whitefish, MT: Kessinger Publishing.

MacDonald, S. (2009), *A Critical Cinema 3: Interviews with Independent Filmmakers*, Berkeley: University of California Press.

Mollaghan, A. (2015), *The Visual Music Film*, Hampshire: Palgrave Macmillan.

Russett, R. (2009), *Hyperanimation*, London: John Libbey.

Taberham, P. (2018), 'Defining and Understanding Experimental Animation', in M. Harris, L. Husbands and P. Taberham (eds), *The New Experimental Animation: From Analogue to Digital*, London: Routledge.

Wells, P. (1998), *Understanding Animation*, London: Routledge.

Youngblood, G. (1970), *Expanded Cinema*, London: Studio Vista.

Further reading

Buchan, S. (2011), *The Quay Brothers: Into a Metaphysical Playroom*, Minneapolis: University of Minnesota Press.

Dobson, T. (2007), *The Film Work of Norman McLaren*, London: John Libbey.

Hames, P. (2008), *The Cinema of Jan Švankmajer*, London: Wallflower Press.

Horrocks, S. and R. Horrocks (2010), *Art That Moves: The Work of Len Lye*. Auckland: Auckland University Press.

Keefer, C. and J. Guldemond (2013), *Oskar Fischinger, 1900–1967: Experiments in Cinematic Abstraction*, London: Thames & Hudson.

11

Features and Shorts

Christopher Holliday

Just as 'animation' is a term that covers a diverse range of forms, modes, practices, image-making materials and technologies, a glance at the many origins and pre-histories of the medium reveals that it equally operates in a variety of lengths and screen durations. From independently funded shorts, fleeting web animations and commercial logos lasting only a few seconds, to episodic television animation and theatrically exhibited blockbuster features normally the reserve of larger film studios, the continued proliferation of animation within a number of multimedia contexts has created an art form that comes in all shapes and sizes. Animation is itself a time-based media, and, as multiple scholars have explained (Cholodenko 1991; Pilling 1997; Wells 1998), it evokes the illusion of life and creates unbroken movement incrementally frame-by-frame, rather than through traditional photographic-based processes of live-action film. Animation is therefore both a series of techniques, and their comprehension or spectatorship, which may encompass proto-animated forms (magic lanterns, flip books) and toys of the Victorian era (Thaumotrope [1826], Phénakisticope [1833], Zoetrope [1834], Praxinoscope [1877]) as much as the contemporary digital landscape of spectacular computer graphics.

Numerous animation scholars and historians have confronted the medium 'at length', as it were, identifying its aesthetic and cultural importance through its versatility of duration and multiplicity of forms. However, the relationship between short and longer animated forms does not reflect a break within animation history between 'then' and 'now'. Nor does the shift from early animated shorts or visual effects to feature-length films imply a teleology of inevitable maturation. Rather, the entwined connection between the two formats exemplifies how animation as a creative medium has undergone a series of significant and fundamental changes that have struck at various moments throughout its history.

The long and the short of animation

Although both longer and shorter live-action films coexisted with similar commercial success throughout the formative days of silent film production, early animation was universally of a shorter kind. Many of the medium's early pioneers working in the first decade of the nineteenth century tested the capabilities of moving images and techniques of photography in a range of exploratory animated shorts. Particularly significant within critical studies of animation's expansive history and multiple genealogies (Bendazzi 1994; Furniss 2016) are the eminent names of Winsor McCay and J. Stuart Blackton (United States), Raoul Barré (Canada), Arthur Melbourne Cooper and Walter R. Booth (United Kingdom), and Émile Cohl, Émile Reynaud and Georges Méliès (France), who all contributed to the development of early animated media in a variety of national contexts.

The brevity of these early animated shorts can be traced back to the spectacle of stage entertainment and nineteenth-century amusements. Paul Wells (1998) has argued that initial experiments in proto-animation, such as those undertaken by Reynaud during the 1890s, were almost immediately 'incorporated into theatrical shows, often with simulated sounds to accompany the illusion of narrative action' (1998: 2). Predating the Lumière brothers' public screening of the cinématographe on 26 December 1895, Reynaud's Théâtre Optique moving picture performances in October 1892 in Paris offered spectacular shows of around ten minutes. Other early filmmakers, such as Booth (an amateur magician) and Méliès (an illusionist) are cited by those historians of animation who consistently situate 'trick' photography as central to the medium's origin story (Wells 1998; Furniss 2016). Quickly subsumed by the live-action realist tradition of the Lumières and, later, the rhythms of Classical Hollywood narration (Bordwell, Staiger and Thompson 1985), 'trick' films with animated effects and fleeting durations illustrate the importance of the medium to the temporality of Tom Gunning's 'cinema of attractions' (1986, reprinted in this volume) conceptualization of early film.

Lasting anywhere between ninety seconds (as with Blackton's *The Enchanted Drawing* [1900] and Cohl's *Fantasmagorie* [1908]) and the twelve-minute short *Gertie the Dinosaur* (McCay 1914), the length of early animation was informed by the expenditure involved in the production of animation that had not yet been shaped into an industrial art form. Leonard Maltin (1987) documents the prohibitive cost of early animation techniques (including the price of materials), and the subsequent impact of economics on animation's mode of exhibition. Maltin notes the pressures felt by early practitioners (particularly McCay) who were overstretched 'to make the cartoon the screen equivalent of the comic strip – and produce it nearly as often' (1987: 1). Charlie Keil and Daniel Goldmark's more recent account of early Hollywood animation recognizes that 'the labor-intensive nature of animation dictated that it be restricted to the short format' (2011: 6).[1] But even when animation reached full institutional maturity within the system of Hollywood mass production in the 1930s, a little over two decades after McCay's *Gertie*, cartoons remained shaped by 'economically enforced limitation (that is, profoundly restricted budgets compared to live-action features or shorts)' (Keil and Goldmark 2011: 4). Relegated to 'nonfeature production', American cartoons were quickly awarded a particular kind of narrative, assigned a comedic function by necessity given that 'the feature format was generally reserved for more "weighty" material' (2011: 4–6).

Many early animators not only raided the vocabulary of a comic strip form already established in the American print media industries since the late-1890s, but also drew from the lightning sketch cultural tradition (Cook 2013). Animation historian Donald Crafton (1979, 1993) has been fundamental to the critical understanding of early animation and the cartoon's 'lightning sketch' origins. Adopted by Crafton from the title of Booth's 1906 short of the same name, the 'hand of the artist' trope of audacious self-figuration showcased the artist as the 'mediator between the spectator and the drawings' (Crafton 1979: 414). In making a performance out of the act of drawing, the earliest animated shorts emphasized the rapidity of the 'lightning' sketches within the spectacle of quick change. Blackton's *Humorous Phases of Funny Faces* (1906) and *Lightning Sketches* (1907) both explored the power of animation within a shortened and condensed duration, quick on the draw and replete with fleeting 'animated' effects that fuelled the dreamlike excess and oneiric mystifications of early screen media.

America's golden age

American animator John Randolph Bray was the first to frame the short within industrial parameters, and founded in 1914 his Bray Productions studio, which became the dominant facility in America during the First World War (Wells 2002). In terms of storytelling, shorts permitted a degree of seriality across narratives and offered the pleasure of repeating characters, many of whom became animated 'stars', a few minutes at a time. Pat Sullivan and Otto Messmer's *Felix the Cat* (1919–36) series contained approximately 200 animated shorts, while *Out of the Inkwell* was a series of silent-era animated cartoons that premiered around the same period.

Produced by Max Fleischer between 1918 and 1929, and largely starring Koko the Clown, these popular *Out of the Inkwell* cartoons were released through Paramount (1919–20), and later Goldwyn (1921), totalling over 100 individual shorts.

Michael Barrier (1999) offers an exhaustive account of the thousands of Hollywood studio cartoons produced between 1928 and 1966, a period bookended by the release of Walt Disney's first short *Steamboat Willie* (1928) and the progressive downturn in theatrical animated shorts due to the arrival of 'prime-time' television animation in the late 1950s (Stabile and Harrison 2003). Barrier's important work surveys the main studios and key figures that supported the Golden Age of American animation, including the Leon Schlesinger Studios; the team of Hugh Harman and Rudy Ising (creators of Bosko in 1928 and founders of Warner Brothers' animation division); Metro-Goldwyn-Mayer; United Productions of America (UPA); the short-lived Ub Iwerks Studio that briefly ran in the 1930s and created Flip the Frog and Willie Whopper; the creator of *Woody the Woodpecker* shorts during the 1940s Walter Lantz; New York–based Terrytoons company; and the Hanna-Barbera studio in Los Angeles, California, founded in 1957 by former MGM animation directors William Hanna and Joseph Barbera.

As animation coalesced into an industry and a popular form of big-screen mass entertainment, the animated cartoons by these major film production companies in Hollywood during the early-sound era remained principally short, rather than feature-length, subjects that made up part of a varied film bill that included animated shorts, newsreels and feature films (Ward 2000). In fact, shorter cartoons came to dominate studio-era animation in America as an industrial product, packaged alongside feature-length (typically live-action) films, and screened as part of theatrical exhibition programmes well into the 1940s and 1950s (Keil and Goldmark 2011). The waxing and waning of animated shorts attached to theatrical exhibition has therefore been used to chart the broader rise and fall of the American animation industry. Christopher Lehman notes that the major US animation studios (Disney, MGM and UPA) all ceased production of theatrical shorts by the late 1950s, only to return to shorter cartoon production in 1961 as a topical response to the Vietnam War, with cartoons that provided veiled 'commentaries on the federal government, the armed forces, the draft, peace negotiations, the counterculture and pacifism' (2007: 4). The Golden Age era of the American cartoon remains a major area of scholarly investigation (Peary and Peary 1980; Maltin 1987; Klein 1993; Smoodin 1993; Sandler 1998; Goldmark 2005; Keil and Goldmark 2011), and a focal point for understanding the 'evolutionary change from lightning cartoonist films to the true animated cartoon' (Crafton 1990: 138).

The shift in animation's priorities away from vaudeville elements of performance and 'lightning sketch' traditions to more character-based action has enabled the American cartoon short to be understood through long-standing characters with distinctive personalities. The Golden Age, in telling rudimentary tales in episodic form with familiar characters, developed animation's most enduring stars. The era of Bugs Bunny, Tweety Pie and Daffy Duck also provided a counterpoint to the abstract graphic animation produced across Europe. Often understood through the rubric of modernism and the avant-garde (Holloway 1983; Hames 1995), the work of Viking Eggeling, Oskar Fischinger, Hans Richter and Walter Ruttman in the 1920s, and later the Eastern European (Czechoslovakia, Poland) puppet and stop motion traditions of Jan Švankmajer and Jiří Trnka, divided the animated short between the narratives of mainstream US cartoon production and more experimental, unorthodox styles.

Perhaps the most sustained consideration of the American cartoon's repeated motifs, character archetypes and structuring principles, has been provided by Norman Klein (1993). Klein argued that the seven-minute US cartoon could be specifically understood as organized around the 'blistering chase' (1993: 99), a plot device that impressed ordered economy onto the anarchy of the short. Many Tom and Jerry and Wile E. Coyote/Road Runner shorts cut to the chase, establishing a narrative template that was repeated across Warner Brothers' output (including in the 48 Wile E. Coyote/Road Runner shorts produced between 1949 and 2003). For Klein, the treatment of the chase narrative structure implemented by Tex Avery at the Warner Brothers' studio resulted in the collision between the chaos of the early sound cartoon, and the illusionist style of animation that would emerge at the Walt Disney Studios across a multitude of shorter cartoons and, a few years later, in full length colour features.

The Disney effect

Disney was foundational in developing an extensive programme of shorts that became crucial sites of formal experimentation, affording the studio opportunity to test out visual styles, narrative structures (Merritt 2005) and 'ecstatic' manipulations of form (Eisenstein 1986).[2] The assessment of the Disney shorts by J.P. Telotte (2008) notes the studio's desire to harness the possibilities of cinema technology in formalizing certain stylistic principles. *Steamboat Willie* was the second animated short to be produced using synchronized sound (the first was *Dinner Time* [1928] made at the Van Beuren studios), while *Flowers and Trees* (Burton Gillett 1932) pioneered the virtuosity of three-strip Technicolor for which Disney had negotiated an exclusive three-year contract in the early 1930s.[3] Chris Pallant notes that 'Disney's increasing drive for ever more realistic animation led to a number of in-house developments' (2011: 27), and it was within the shorter film format that the studio honed its influential full animation style.

Disney's nine-minute *The Old Mill* (Wilfred Jackson 1937) marked an early experiment in depth and dimension using the multi-plane camera, just as subsequent shorts have been utilized by the studio as a testing ground for new techniques and technologies. For example, hand-drawn techniques were combined with emergent computer graphics in the Disney shorts *Off His Rockers* (Barry Cook 1992) – attached to the theatrical exhibition of *Honey, I Blew up the Kid* (Randal Kleiser 1992) – and more recently *Paperman* (John Kahrs 2012), which accompanied *Wreck-It Ralph* (Rich Moore 2012).

The solidification of animation as a viable economic industry in North America during the late 1920s and early 1930s was, however, founded upon the increased popularization of the theatrical cartoon short (up until the 1960s), *and* the simultaneous emergence of the feature-length animated film. US-centric accounts, such as those by Maltin (1987) and Barrier (1999), examine the drive to produce cartoons both longer in duration and more impressive in scope. Maltin in particular notes that in the case of Walt Disney, 'expansion was the lifeblood of his business, and feature-film production was not only logical but inevitable' (1987: 43). At the same time, the 'unknown' of extended duration prompted widespread industry scepticism over whether audiences 'would *want* to see a feature-length cartoon' (1987: 53). Yet although many American audiences were unaware of them, feature-length animated films *had* been produced outside the United States by the time the Disney studio finished work on their landmark colour feature *Snow White and the Seven Dwarfs* (1937).

Coming almost a decade prior to Lotte Reiniger's sixty-five-minute silhouette animation *The Adventures of Prince Achmed* (1926) that was released on 2 July 1926 (and nearly twenty years before Disney's *Snow White*), *The Apostle* (1917) was a stop-motion cut-out feature film produced by Italian-born Argentine Quirino Cristiani, a filmmaker since neglected by film history. An animation pioneer and cartoonist who forged the early cut-out style of animation, Cristiani went on to make *Without a Trace* (1918), and a few years later, *Peludópolis* (1931). In his history of animation film, Giannalberto Bendazzi (1994) described *Peludópolis* as a biting political satire about the then-Argentine president, Hipolito Yrigoyen, whose progressive social reforms were not enough to oust him from government a year into *Peludópolis*'s production. Bendazzi's exhaustive account of global animation history places Cristiani as a key figure within the emergence of feature-length animation. Bendazzi (1994: 49) argues that while there remains some contestation over whether *The Apostle* (1917) 'was actually a feature film' (given that the film is now considered lost), it was thanks to Cristiani and his collaborators Alfonso de Laferrère (a politician) and musician José Vázquez Vigo that Argentina was able to lay claim to ushering animation from 'one-minute sketch' films to more elaborate feature-length productions.

In the wake of Cristiani's early features (which ran to around sixty minutes), many countries in Europe and beyond developed indigenous animation industries whose own origin stories have been the subject of much critical investigation. The history of early animation pre–Mickey Mouse offered by Crafton (1993), for example, discusses the desire by many European filmmakers to make 'a monumental feature length animated film' (1993: 258) as a way of fully realizing the potential of the art form. Richard Neupert's (2011: 63) own interest in the birth of French animation positions *Le Roman de Renard* (*The Tale of the Fox*) (1930) as 'the longest and perhaps most successful film' made by Ladislas Starevitch, and the first feature-length animation to be produced in France. Other important milestones in feature animation include *The New Gulliver* (Aleksandr Ptushko 1935), a seventy-five-minute Soviet stop motion retelling of Jonathan Swift's *Gulliver's Travels*, and the fairytale feature *The Seven Ravens* (Ferdinand Diehl and Hermann Diehl 1937) produced in Germany. Another version of Swift's eighteenth-century novel, *Gulliver's Travels* (1939), was made at the Fleischer Studios as their first feature-length animated film, and was the second made by an American studio after Disney's *Snow White*. While it is clear that stop-motion predominated over early experiments in feature-animation, the viability of cel-animation as a replacement for drawing was quickly realized despite its expense (see Barrier 1999, who discusses how cels could be washed and reused, unlike paper). Directed by Raoul Verdini and Umberto Spano, *The Adventures of Pinocchio* (1936) was intended as the first Italian animated film and would have been the first produced entirely through cel-animated techniques (predating *Snow White*); however, it was never finished.

The digital renaissance

Nowhere has the reciprocal relationship between animated features and cartoon shorts been more evident than in contemporary Hollywood. The economic renaissance of Disney feature animation (Pallant 2011) that unfolded during the 1990s, and the subsequent arrival of the computer-animated feature film with *Toy Story* (John Lasseter 1995), reignited the commercial and critical popularity of feature-length theatrical animation. But while the success of Disney's animated musicals – including *The Little Mermaid* (Ron Clements and John Musker 1989) and *Beauty and the Beast* (Gary Trousdale and Kirk Wise 1991) – alongside the animation/live-action hybrid *Who Framed Roger Rabbit* (Robert Zemeckis 1988) and television series *The Simpsons* (Matt Groening 1989–) combined to remind audiences of animation's drawing powers, the medium's resurgence likewise cued a return to short film production in a manner not seen since the seven-minute cartoon of the Golden Age.

Beginning with the short *The Adventures of André and Wally B* (Alvy Ray Smith 1984), which was produced under The Graphics Group banner (a division of the Lucasfilm company), Pixar Animation Studios reinvigorated the possibilities of the short film format in the digital era. Daniel Goldmark argues that 'Pixar had been producing shorts for years before it attempted to tackle a feature-length film, thus following the precedent set by Fleischer and Disney' (2013: 219). The success of Pixar's films *Luxo Jr.* (John Lasseter 1986), *Red's Dream* (John Lasseter 1987), *Tin Toy* (John Lasseter 1988) and *Knick Knack* (John Lasseter 1989) helped solidify Pixar 'as a force in animation, following a similar path to Disney's some sixty years earlier' (2013). Pixar's approach to the animated short has much in common with that of the Disney studio; with the shorter film format running to only a few minutes, it offers up an important creative space in which Pixar's animators can rigorously test the application of innovative digital techniques. Alongside their commercial projects in the early 1990s, Pixar's short film programme represented a particularly significant place of research and development into early photorealist design, including the behaviour of light and shadow (*Luxo Jr.* and *Red's Dream*) and the simulation of surfaces and textures such as metal (*Tin Toy*) and glass (*Knick Knack*), thereby presenting audiences with many experiments in the early visual possibilities of digital animation. It comes as little surprise that, at the turn of the new millennium, scholars of computer-generated imagery and new media technologies (e.g. Wells 1998; Darley 2000) used the Pixar shorts to examine the visual possibilities of emerging computer graphics to represent a certain 'realism'.

While the Pixar shorts have attracted ongoing scholarly attention in relation to film sound (Wells 2009; Goldmark 2013; Whittington 2012) and characterization (Neupert 2014), one significant avenue through which the features and shorts relationship has been understood is that of the domestic consumption of animated cinema. Critical accounts of DVD and Blu-ray home video technology formats (Bennett and Brown 2008; Brereton 2012; Tryon 2013) have discussed the role played by animation, from intricate animated menus to the inclusion of bonus cartoon shorts as a supplement to the main feature. In addition to their theatrical shorts programme that accompanies their feature films, Pixar have established the 'Home Entertainment Shorts' series, which are short 'spin-off' cartoons packaged exclusively on DVD releases. Current Hollywood rivals to Pixar, including DreamWorks Animation, Blue Sky Studios and Illumination Entertainment, have all followed a similar template, producing DVD-specific shorts as part of a wider shift towards franchises, series and cycles. The upsurge in shorts has even prompted Disney to combine feature film production with a return to the theatrical short with *Get a Horse!* (Lauren MacMullan 2013), the first Mickey Mouse theatrical animated short since *Runaway Brain* (Chris Bailey 1995).

Conclusion

The global history of animation across a variety of contexts and institutions has been well covered in stories of the medium's most significant films and filmmakers, and its increasingly pervasive place within wider moving image and visual cultures. However, the heterogeneous category of 'animation' and its historical evolution has been supported by the perseverance and coexistence of short and feature film production. It is possible to read much of popular animation's screen history through the stakes of the feature/shorts relation, around which is wrapped a series of questions concerning film history, industry, audiences, exhibition and distribution practices, as well as formal elements of design, structure and coherency of characterization. The concise means of expression afforded by shorter animation makes them the ideal place to explore narrative economy and technical experimentation, just as the extended duration of feature-length animation requires a more detailed underlying conceptualization of plot, character and setting that enables stories to be told across a longer running time. It is therefore in the continual interplay and repeated exchange between animated feature films and shorter forms that traditions of innovation and shifts in the medium's creative possibilities are to be found.

Notes

1 The labour of animation has often been co-opted into the subject matter of a number of animated films, forming the bedrock of what Wells (2002) has labelled 'deconstructive' cartoons that reflexively fall back on the contexts of their very creation to stress the visible process of moving image production. From early British series *Jerry the Tyke* (Sid Griffiths 1925–7) through to the irreverent Chuck Jones cartoon *Duck Amuck* (1953), numerous shorts have disclosed the mechanics and unravelled the constituent parts of animated production (page, paint, ink, brush and even film strip) all laid bare in a comic feat of anti-illusionism.

2 These included the *Alice Comedies* (1923–7), which mixed live-action with cel-animation; the *Oswald the Lucky Rabbit* (1927–8) series (before the character migrated to Winkler Productions and Universal, only returning to Disney in 2010); and the *Silly Symphonies*, a series of seventy-five theatrical shorts produced between 1929 and 1939, which were parodied by Warner Brothers for their subsequent Looney Tunes and Merrie Melodies series.

3 This perhaps explains why Disney's shorts 'were about twice as expensive as those of most other studios, typically costing in excess of fifty thousand dollars each' (Barrier 1999: 393).

References

Barrier, M. (1999), *Hollywood Cartoons: American Animation in Its Golden Age*, Oxford: Oxford University Press.

Bendazzi, G. (1994), *Cartoons: One Hundred Years of Cinema Animation*, London: John Libbey.

Bennett, J. and T. Brown, eds (2008), *Film and Television after DVD*, New York: Routledge.

Bordwell, D., J. Staiger, and K. Thompson (1985), *The Classical Hollywood Cinema: Film Style and Mode of Production to 1960*, London: Routledge.

Brereton, P. (2012), *Smart Cinema, DVD Add-Ons and New Audience Pleasures*, New York: Palgrave Macmillan.

Cholodenko, A., ed. (1991), *The Illusion of Life: Essays on Animation*, Power Publications in association with the Australian Film Commission, Sydney.

Cook, M. (2013), 'The Lightning Cartoon: Animation from Music Hall to Cinema', *Early Popular Visual Culture*, 11(3): 237–254.

Crafton, D. (1979), 'Animation Iconography: The "Hand of the Artist"', *Quarterly Review of Film Studies*, 4 (Fall): 409–428.

Crafton, D. (1990), *Émile Cohl, Caricature, and Film*, Princeton, NJ: Princeton University Press.

Crafton, D. (1993), *Before Mickey: The Animated Film 1898–1928*, Chicago, IL: The University of Chicago Press.

Darley, A. (2000), *Visual Digital Culture: Surface Play and Spectacle in New Media Genres*, London: Routledge.

Eisenstein, S. (1986), *Eisenstein on Disney*, trans. Jay Leyda, London: Methuen.

Furniss, M. (2016), *Animation: The Global History*, London: Thames and Hudson Ltd.

Goldmark, D. (2005), *Tunes for 'Toons: Music and the Hollywood Cartoon*, Berkeley, CA: University of California Press.

Goldmark, D. (2013), 'Pixar and the Animated Soundtrack', in J. Richardson, C. Gorbman and C. Vernallis (eds), *The Oxford Handbook of New Audiovisual Aesthetics*, 213–226, New York: Oxford University Press.

Gunning, T. (1986), 'The Cinema of Attractions: Early Film, Its Spectator and the Avant-Garde', *Wide Angle*, 8(3): 63–70.

Hames, P., ed. (1995), *Dark Alchemy: The Films of Jan Švankmajer*, Westport, CT: Greenwood Press.

Holloway, R. (1983), 'The Short Film in Eastern Europe: Art, Politics of Cartoons and Puppets,' in D. W. Paul (ed.), *Politics, Art and Commitment in the East European Cinema*, 225–251, London: Palgrave Macmillan.

Keil, C. and D. Goldmark, eds (2011), *Funny Pictures: Animation and Comedy in Studio-Era Hollywood*, Berkeley, CA: University of California Press.

Klein, N. (1993), *Seven Minutes: The Life and Death of the American Cartoon*, London and New York: Verso.

Lehman, C. (2007), *American Animated Cartoons of the Vietnam Era*, Jefferson, NC: McFarland & Company.

Maltin, L. (1987), *Of Mice and Magic: History of American Animated Cartoons*, New York: Penguin Books.

Merritt, R. (2005), 'Lost on Pleasure Islands: Storytelling in Disney's Silly Symphonies', *Film Quarterly*, 59(1): 4–17.

Neupert, R. (2011), *French Animation History*, Malden, MA: Wiley & Sons Ltd.

Neupert, R. (2014), 'Melancholy, Empathy and Animated Bodies: Pixar vs. Mary and Max', in D. Roche and I. Schmitt-Pitiot (eds), *Intimacy in Cinema: Critical Essays on English Language Films*, 215–224, Jefferson, NC: McFarland & Company.

Pallant, C. (2011), *Demystifying Disney: A History of Disney Feature Animation*, London: Bloomsbury.

Peary, D. and G. Peary, eds (1980), *The American Animated Cartoon: A Critical Anthology*, New York: E.P. Dutton.

Pilling, J., ed. (1997), *A Reader in Animation Studies*, London: John Libbey.

Sandler, K. S., ed. (1998), *Reading the Rabbit: Explorations in Warner Bros. Animation*, New Brunswick, NJ: Rutgers University Press.

Smoodin, E. (1993), *Animating Culture: Hollywood Cartoons from the Sound Era*, Oxford: Oxford University Press.

Stabile, C. and M. Harrison, eds (2003), *Prime Time Animation: Television Animation and American Culture*, New York: Routledge.

Telotte, J. P. (2008), *The Mouse Machine: Disney and Technology*, Chicago, IL: University of Illinois Press.

Tryon, C. (2013), *On-Demand Culture: Digital Delivery and the Future of Movies*, New Brunswick, NJ: Rutgers University Press.

Ward, P. (2000), 'Defining "Animation": The Animated Film and the Emergence of the Film Bill', *Scope: An Online Journal of Film Studies*, December. Available online: https://www.nottingham.ac.uk/scope/documents/2000/december-2000/ward.pdf (accessed 22 February 2018).

Wells, P. (1998), *Understanding Animation*, London: Routledge.

Wells, P. (2002), *Animation: Genre and Authorship*, London: Wallflower Press.

Wells, P. (2009), 'To Sonicity and Beyond! Gary Rydstrom and Quilting the Pixar Sound', *Animation Journal*, 17: 23–35.

Whittington, W. (2012), 'The Sonic Playpen: Sound Design and Technology in Pixar's Animated Shorts', in T. Pinch and K. Bijsterveld (eds), *The Oxford Handbook of Sound Studies*, 367–386, New York: Oxford University Press.

12

Advertising and Public Service Films

Malcolm Cook

Animation and advertising have been entwined from the earliest days of moving images, and every major animator and animation studio has contributed to films promoting goods, services and ideas. In the past animation studies has ignored or marginalized this central activity, seeing it as detracting from animation as an art form. The importance of animation to digital techniques and technologies, which are now pervasive in advertising and all moving pictures, demands a reassessment of this position, and is supported by a new attention within film studies to 'useful cinema', including 'films that sell' (Acland and Wasson 2011a; Florin, de Klerk and Vonderau 2016). By looking again at key examples of animated advertising, and consulting recent pioneering research in this area, we can recognize the way each field shaped the expansion of the other. Vital qualities of animation were recognized and developed for their suitability within advertising, including the animator's control and manipulation of the image, the subsequent transformation and 'plasmatic' nature of those images, and the ability to bring to life and anthropomorphize inanimate objects. Animation would not exist in the form we understand today without advertising. Much of this history remains to be uncovered and many questions are still unanswered, indicating this as one of the most exciting avenues for future animation research.

Advertising and animation history

While animation is today characterized by a diversity of techniques, three methods have dominated animation history and define it for most audiences: drawn or cel animation, stop-motion animation and computer animation. In each case, the earliest developments of these techniques were bound up with advertising in a way that suggests animation was not simply a pre-existing tool adopted by advertisers, but rather its very definition and elaboration were predicated on its promotional potential. There are countless examples of this, but three formative moments, one for each technique, indicate this foundational relationship.

Advertising and selling underpin some of the very earliest steps towards drawn animation. James Stuart Blackton is often cited as 'the father of animation' (Beck 2004: 12–13) and in his first film in collaboration with the inventor and film pioneer Thomas Edison the promotional impulse is prominent. *Blackton Sketches, No. 1* (1896), also known as *Inventor Edison Sketched by World Artist*, shows Blackton performing a lightning sketch on a large sheet of paper (Musser 1994: 120–121). As Charles Musser (2016: 86) observes, all the early Edison films should be considered a form of advertising because they promoted Edison's moving picture technologies and the Edison name, qualities that are evident in this example. Furthermore, Blackton conspicuously displays his own name and that of his employer, the *New York World* newspaper, ensuring both were publicized by the film. This film is not animated in the sense we understand that term today, as it does not utilize intermittent frame-by-frame construction, but given the significance of the lightning sketch to animation history (See Crafton 1982; Cook 2013) this constitutes a nascent co-development of drawn animation and filmed advertising in the earliest days of moving images.

While Blackton was innovating early drawn animation techniques in conjunction with the promotion of his own and his employers' names, British animator Arthur Melbourne-Cooper's *Matches Appeal* (dated as early as 1899 by some sources) provides an embryonic demonstration of the use of stop-motion animated films to deliver a persuasive message (Vries and Mul 2009). The film depicts a puppet made of matchsticks that, through stop-motion animation, writes a message on the wall, encouraging viewers to donate one guinea to buy matches for soldiers serving overseas. This very short film serves a public service function of supporting troops and encouraging charitable donation. It also serves as a commercial stimulus: increasing the sponsor's (Bryant & May Matches) sales and raising brand awareness and loyalty by connecting the company to social altruism. At that time, the stop-motion technique was a novelty that would have especially attracted the attention of the spectator and made them receptive to the message of the film, but it also allowed the product being promoted to come alive, a process that would be vital to later animated advertising.

While drawn and stop-motion animation emerged alongside the earliest moving pictures, the third dominant animation technique appeared much later. As Tom Sito (2013) has shown, computer graphics technology was developed within a number of contexts after the Second World War and the promotion of products, services and brands became an important component of that early computer animation, such as the relationship between John Whitney and IBM in the 1960s (Stamp 2013).

The early history of Pixar provides a vivid case study of this mutual relationship between computer animation and advertising, both because of the central role that company has played in defining and popularizing computer animation and because it demonstrates the value of thinking beyond the animated film itself and considering the production and exhibition contexts in which they appeared. It is well documented that Pixar produced a large number of television commercials after their spin-off from Lucasfilm in 1986, promoting household brands such as Tropicana, Listerine and Lifesavers. Most popular histories of the studio recognize the economic importance of this work in financially maintaining the studio and advancing skills and infrastructure prior to the production of *Toy Story* (1995) (Paik and Iwerks 2007: 64–68; Price 2008: 109–111). However, the studio has not given their commercials the same status as other short films, which have been included as DVD extras and released in standalone collections.[1] This is typical of a prevailing deprecation of the role advertising has played in other famous studios, such as Aardman and Halas & Batchelor, where a simple art/commerce binary division has often been applied (Cook Forthcoming; Stewart 2016). The role of advertising in Pixar's history is far more pervasive than such a division allows.

Most early Pixar films had very little prospect of directly generating revenue, but instead served to advertise and sell their other products and services. The 'one-frame movie' *The Road to Point Reyes* (1983), produced while the group was part of Lucasfilm, served to demonstrate to George Lucas that computer-generated images could be incorporated into feature films at high resolution and, as such, promoted the company's internal Computer Division (Cook 2015). Early films *The Adventures of André and Wally B.* (1984) and *Luxo Jr.* (1986) were designed to showcase the group's expertise to SIGGRAPH, the major computer graphics conference (Lasseter 2001). Equally, *Luxo Jr.* opens and closes with the original Pixar logo that closely resembled the fascia of the Pixar computer hardware, which was the company's only commercial proposition at the time. This logo had a computer-generated grey square with bevelled edges and a central concave circle creating complex variations in computed shadows and highlights (see Figure 12.1). The logo not only acted as product placement, but was also an active demonstration of the lighting and shading techniques that the computer could achieve, as was the film as a whole. Later shorts, including *Tin Toy* (1988) and *Knick Knack* (1989), would similarly function as indirect advertisements for Pixar's Renderman software. These films would

FIGURE 12.1 *The original Pixar logo, which resembles the company's hardware. Screengrab from* Luxo Jr. *(dir. John Lasseter, 1986). Produced by Pixar.*

also court Hollywood studios and advertisers, promoting the availability of Pixar's talent for new projects. A purely film-based approach might simply interpret such films as commercial entertainment; however, the value of the questions raised by the study of 'useful cinema' is evident here. It is necessary to take into consideration how these films were commissioned, circulated and exhibited to understand their very different function, use and economic value, where the film is not an end product or principal profit generator (Elsaesser 2009: 23; Acland and Wasson 2011b: 1–7; Vonderau 2016: 4).

The centrality of advertising to Pixar is evident in their successful and celebrated feature films, in many of which television commercials become a prominent and recurrent narrative feature. Beyond this explicit citation of advertising vernacular, a number of scholars have noted the more persistent use of advertising strategies within Pixar's aesthetic, suggesting a substantial reassessment of the studio and its output is necessary in this light (Gurevitch 2012; Herhuth 2017; Holliday 2017).

Advertising and the emergence of animation studies

Given this close relationship between animation and advertising, landmark works of animation studies necessarily acknowledged advertising to some degree. In his 1982 book *Before Mickey* Donald Crafton (228–237) devoted several pages to silent-era European advertising and instructional films, including relatively unknown figures who devoted their career to these fields, such as Julius Pinschewer in Germany and Robert Collard in France, also known as Lortac. However, this discussion was framed in terms of an art/commerce binary wherein advertising subsidized aesthetic experiments by the likes of Walter Ruttmann and Oskar Fischinger (Crafton 1982: 235). Writing in 1998 Paul Wells noted that 'animation is particularly appropriate to the needs of advertising' (249n2) and described its capacity to bring products to life and create product identity. Yet it is revealing that this insight was relegated to an endnote, symptomatic of Wells's primary goal of elevating animation to an independent art form worthy of study in its own right. This was equally apparent in his discussion of Len Lye's *A Colour Box* (1935), a landmark animated advertisement for the British General Post Office. Wells dismissed the advertising message of this film as a 'glib coda', distancing the aesthetic value of the film from its funding and distribution contexts.

Maureen Furniss, also in 1998, explored the influence of advertising on animation history. Drawing on the work of Karl Cohen, she situated advertising's influence as primarily an economic and technological one, with 1940s television commercials innovating the low-cost limited animation techniques that became typical for post-war television animation (Furniss 2007: 142–144; Cohen 1992). In 1993 Norman M. Klein likewise offered an ambivalent account of post-war animated 'consumer graphics', and he expressed amazement at Tex Avery's comfort in the 'ulcerous' advertising world (206, 216). Klein adopted an elegiac tone as he saw the rise of this consumerist mode of animation contributing to the death of the seven-minute theatrical cartoon. In each case, these pioneering animation scholars recognized the significance of advertising within animation history, but saw this as negative or tangential to animation as an art form. Recent research has started to recognize that rather than being antagonistic, the mutual relationship between advertising and animation has deeply shaped and defined each field. Fundamental qualities ascribed to animation, including control, abstraction and figuration, transformation and anthropomorphism were not simply utilized by advertisers, rather their identification and growth was a direct product of their suitability for selling and promotion. Instead of being essential and universal, our very definition of animation and its qualities emerged historically because of their use in advertising.

Advertising and recent animation theory

Crafton (1979: 409–428; 1982: 11) has established the importance within animation history of the controlling influence of the animator, encapsulated in the pervasive recurring iconography of the 'hand of the artist'. The intricate frame-by-frame construction typical of animation techniques offers unprecedented control over the moving image, and this was undoubtedly one of the reasons advertisers adopted animation. Michael Cowan has recently addressed this central idea in relation to animated advertising in Germany in the 1920s. The control afforded by animation was understood in practical terms of the novelty and plasticity of the image, which could attract viewers and maintain design principles from marketing material in other media or the product itself. However, Cowan (2016: 108) shows that control could also operate at a psychological level, with practitioners intending that '"applied animation" would serve to control spectatorship at every level by capturing and directing attention, provoking psychological reactions and stimulating acts of consumption through film'.

As Cowan demonstrates, the growth in advertising psychology expertise in Germany in this period was intimately connected with the parallel growth in abstract animation from Walter Ruttmann, Hans Richter, Lotte Reiniger and Oskar Fischinger, among other celebrated animators. Rather than being 'compromises or opportunistic means of financing the artists' more "serious" experimental projects', there was an affinity and mutually beneficial influence between experimental animation and advertising psychology (Cowan 2013: 50–51). Both fields were looking to establish an essential or elemental form of visual control that could appeal and communicate with spectators in immediate and affecting ways. A central characteristic of animation, control through the hand of the artist, is here inextricably bound up with advertising, as are a number of celebrated animation artists.

Cowan's work on Walter Ruttmann's advertising films also associates them with another central area of animation theory, the balance between figuration and abstraction (Cowan 2013). This division is evident in many accounts of animation and its specificity, for example Furniss foregrounds a continuum between mimesis and abstraction, while Wells makes these central to his theory of animation (Wells 1998: 33–34, 36; Furniss 2007: 6). Through the close analysis of Ruttmann's animated advertising films Cowan indicates how 'the particular quality of these films lies in the way they seem to hover between absolute formalism and denotative referentiality' (2013: 53). This tension is again not simply a product of aesthetic experimentation or choice, but is linked with the advertising psychology of the time and the wider political, social and cultural context of Germany in the 1920s and 1930s (Cowan 2013: 65).

The conflict between figuration and abstraction is also central to Vivian Sobchack's (2008) discussion of the animated line. For Sobchack the line is sufficient to define a work as animation and distinguish it from photoreal cinema, because the line does not exist in the latter (2008: 252). The line is two things at once, a liminal entity that is always in a state of becoming, it is '*both* geometric base *and* figural superstructure' (Sobchack 2008: 257). Sobchack chooses to illustrate this general principle with a series of television advertisements made by German animator Raimund Krumme for Hilton Hotels, transmitted originally in 2005–6. In these advertisements, a horizontal line on the screen dynamically assumes human shapes engaged with a range of imagery associated with travel: a hammock, a sand castle, a sunset. Initially Sobchack discounts these films' status as advertising: the qualities of their lines are apparent 'even if in the service of an advertising campaign' (2008: 251). Yet her discussion of the promotional message contained in the films indicates that it is no mere coincidence that advertisements offer such an exemplary instance of a vital quality of animation. The commercials are not intended simply to offer a rational promotion of Hilton's services, but to foster an emotional bond with the brand and ideals it hopes to encompass: 'the Hilton ads momentarily relieve real-world existential conditions by offering up fantasies of painless travel … and by presenting the visibly unbroken (if irregular) flow of the line itself' (Sobchack 2008: 260). The duality of the line communicates the duality of the promotional message. Like Cowan's discussion of Ruttmann's work, it would seem these animated qualities exist because of their advertising intentions, not despite them. Crucially it is not simply the line that is important to Sobchack, as this exists in many forms of print advertising, but the *animated* line and the quality of transformation or metamorphosis this entails, which are also commonly seen as defining animation.

Similar uses of transformation and metamorphosis can be seen in many other advertisements, and not necessarily those dependent upon the animated line. Numerous stop-motion advertisements by British studio Aardman Animations use clay or plasticine to enact metamorphoses from abstract, amorphous materials to figurative representations. In *Fairground* (1991), *Balloon* (1991) and *Rollercoaster* (1994) the chocolate of a Cadbury's Crunchie bar transforms into a series of vibrant scenes, such as a dog chasing its tail or Tiller girls dancing, that communicate the unrestrained joy and freedom of the 'Friday Feeling' the confectionary hopes to sell. Transformation allows a shift from the rational benefits of a product to its emotional engagement. As with other examples discussed here qualities often seen as essential and defining of animation, in this case transformation or metamorphosis, become central to films' advertising function.

These examples from Aardman of transformation and metamorphosis also encompass the final recurring quality of animation addressed in this chapter, anthropomorphism. The attribution of human characteristics to animals or objects is common in animation, along with the inverse zoomorphism in which animal characteristics are attributed to humans. As Paul Wells suggests, it might be argued that anthropomorphism is an 'essential component of the language of animation' (2009: 2). Anthropomorphism has commonly been utilized by advertisers, and its association with animation is inextricably bound up with that relationship. The basic appeal of anthropomorphism for advertisers is readily apparent as it provides a way to give motion and life to an inanimate product (thereby giving it a personality) and associate it with less tangible values that will appeal to consumers at an emotional level. As such anthropomorphism provides an extension of the practice of creating brand mascots or spokespersons for products, in which the product itself is given a personality rather than simply represented by one (Dotz and Husain 2015).

Several scholars have commented on this basic practical function of anthropomorphism and noted its more complex political implications. Both Esther Leslie and Michael Cowan raise Karl Marx's description of commodity fetishism and link it to animation and the anthropomorphism of inanimate objects (Leslie 2002: 6–9; Cowan 2016: 99). Marx's theory suggests that within capitalism commodities seemingly take on an independent life of their own, while workers are alienated from their labour and dehumanized: 'Humans become things; things become human' (Leslie 2002: 7). Leslie and Cowan discuss advertisements from Germany in the 1920s and 1930s to illustrate this, but this tendency is evident in a wide range of examples, including the Melbourne-Cooper, Pixar and Aardman films already discussed. Another Aardman advertisement, *Conveyor Belt* (1995) for the Polo brand of confectionary, is especially apt in highlighting this quality. The advertisement is set in a factory and shows a long line of anthropomorphized Polo sweets hopping along a conveyor belt in a childlike manner. Importantly, in contrast to these 'living' Polos, there are no human workers seen in this factory, only automated machines that operate in a regimented and systematic fashion. In short, this advertisement shows the commodity has gained independent agency and human personality, while the work of production has been dehumanized. This exemplifies the widespread use of anthropomorphism within advertising to give a sense of life and personality to products and its encapsulation of the commodity fetish, but it might also be taken as a reflection on animation. Animation is itself a product in which inanimate objects take on movement, life and an apparent independent agency, while the labour involved in their production, often in factory-like settings, is increasingly hidden or automated.

Conclusion

Animation and advertising are inextricably linked historically and conceptually. The earliest developments of all the major techniques and technologies were bound up with the use of animation for advertising. This suggests that these techniques, and the very definitions of animation they produced, were shaped by being put to use for promotional ends. It is fitting, therefore, that the emerging scholarship on animated advertising to date should centre on qualities that have been considered central to animation: control, abstraction and figuration, transformation and anthropomorphism.

Yet there remain many unresearched paths and many unanswered questions to this reciprocal relationship.

In his celebrated and often-cited account of animation's specific qualities, Russian filmmaker and theorist Sergei Eisenstein puts forward the neologism 'plasmatic' to describe the appeal of animation as 'a rejection of once-and-forever allotted form, freedom from ossification, the ability to dynamically assume any form' (1986: 21). While commonly treated as simply a synonym for transformation, Eisenstein's term encompasses more than the shape shifting of one form into another. Rather, it is a rejection of categorization and boundaries between things, and it describes anything that has a simultaneous duality or plurality. Transformation, anthropomorphism and the dualities of the drawn line are not synonyms of the plasmatic but are individual examples of this more encompassing quality of the plasmatic. Sobchack acknowledges this by citing Eisenstein when discussing the duality of the line as both graphic abstraction and figurative representation (2008: 253). Equally, Eisenstein discusses the role of anthropomorphism in his description of Mickey Mouse, who rarely transforms but is nevertheless plasmatic because 'he is both human, and a mouse ... this unity is not dynamic' (1986: 96n59).

This serves as further evidence that the qualities of animation that advertisers have embraced are precisely those that have been seen as characteristic or essential to defining animation by many commentators. Beyond this, however, Eisenstein's comments are especially important at this point because of the relationship he sees the plasmatic having with capitalism. He writes that Disney's animation, as the exemplar of the plasmatic, 'bestows precisely this upon his viewer, precisely obliviousness, an instant of complete and total release from everything connected with the suffering caused by the social conditions of the social order of the largest capitalist government' (Eisenstein et al. 1986: 8). For Eisenstein the plasmatic qualities of animation offer a respite from the rationalizing and categorizing imperatives of capitalism. Yet in this brief overview we have seen those same qualities put to work for advertising, one of the engines of capitalism. Those plasmatic qualities were defined as central to animation because it expanded in conjunction with advertising. There remains a great deal more work to be done to unpick this contradiction, to reassess the role of advertising in the histories of well-known animators and studios, and to discover the parallel industry of animation advertising production that is currently afforded no place in canonical histories.

Note

1 Pixar's advertisements are, however, easily accessible online.

References

Acland, C. R. and H. Wasson, eds (2011a), *Useful Cinema*, Durham, NC: Duke University Press.

Acland, C. R. and H. Wasson (2011b), 'Introduction: Utility and Cinema', in C. R. Acland and H. Wasson (eds), *Useful Cinema*, 1–14, Durham, NC: Duke University Press.

Beck, J., ed. (2004), *Animation Art: From Pencil to Pixel, the History of Cartoon, Anime & CGI*, London: Flame Tree.

Cohen, K. (1992), 'The Development of Animated TV Commercials in the 1940s', *Animation Journal*, 1(1): 34–61.

Cook, M. (2013), 'The Lightning Cartoon: Animation from Music Hall to Cinema', *Early Popular Visual Culture*, 11(3): 237–254.

Cook, M. (2015), 'Pixar, "The Road to Point Reyes", and the Long History of Landscapes in New Visual Technologies', in C. Pallant (ed.), *Animated Landscapes: History, Form and Function*, 51–72, London: Bloomsbury Academic.

Cook, M. (forthcoming), '"All You Do Is Call Me, I'll Be Anything You Need": Aardman Animations, Commercials, and Music Videos', in A. Honess Roe (ed.), *Beyond Stop-Motion Film: Production, Style and Representation in Aardman Animations*, London: I.B. Tauris.

Cowan, M. (2013), 'Absolute Advertising: Walter Ruttmann and the Weimar Advertising Film', *Cinema Journal*, 52(4): 49–73.

Cowan, M. (2016), 'Advertising and Animation: From the Invisible Hand to Attention Management', in B. Florin, N. De Klerk and P. Vonderau (eds), *Films That Sell: Moving Pictures and Advertising*, 93–113, London: BFI/Palgrave.

Crafton, D. (1979), 'Animation Iconography: The "Hand of the Artist"', *Quarterly Review of Film Studies*, 4(4): 409–428.

Crafton, D. (1982), *Before Mickey: The Animated Film, 1898–1928*, Cambridge, MA: MIT Press.

Dotz, W. and M. Husain (2015), *Meet Mr Product: The Graphic Art of the Advertising Character*, Vol. 1, San Rafael, CA: Insight Editions.

Eisenstein, S., J. Leyda, A. Upchurch, and N. I. Kleiman (1986), *Eisenstein on Disney*, Calcutta: Seagull.

Elsaesser, T. (2009), 'Archives and Archaeologies: The Place of Non-Fiction Film in Contemporary Media', in V. Hediger and P. Vonderau (eds), *Films That Work: Industrial Film and the Productivity of Media*, 19–34, Amsterdam: Amsterdam University Press.

Florin, B., N. De Klerk, and P. Vonderau, eds (2016), *Films That Sell: Moving Pictures and Advertising*, London: BFI/Palgrave.

Furniss, M. (2007), *Art in Motion: Animation Aesthetics*, rev. edn, New Barnet: John Libbey. Original edition, 1998.

Gurevitch, L. (2012), 'Computer Generated Animation as Product Design Engineered Culture, or Buzz Lightyear to the Sales Floor, to the Checkout and Beyond!', *animation: an interdisciplinary journal*, 7(2): 131–149.

Herhuth, E. (2017), *Pixar and the Aesthetic Imagination*, Oakland, CA: University of California Press.

Holliday, C. (2017), 'Driving off the Production Line: Pixar Animation Studios' *Cars* (2006–2017)', *Animation Studies 2.0.*, https://blog.animationstudies. org/?p=2137.

Klein, N. M. (1993), *Seven Minutes: The Life and Death of the American Animated Cartoon*, London: Verso.

Lasseter, J. (2001), 'Tricks to Animating Characters with a Computer [Original presentation given in 1994]', *Computer Graphics*, 35(2): 45–47.

Leslie, E. (2002), *Hollywood Flatlands: Animation, Critical Theory, and the Avant-Garde*, London: Verso.

Musser, C. (1994), *The Emergence of Cinema: The American Screen to 1907*, *History of the American Cinema: 1*, Berkeley, CA: University of California Press.

Musser, C. (2016), 'Early Advertising and Promotional Films, 1893–1900: Edison Motion Pictures as a Case Study', in B. Florin, N. De Klerk and P. Vonderau (eds), *Films That Sell: Moving Pictures and Advertising*, 83–90, London: BFI/ Palgrave.

Paik, K. and L. Iwerks (2007), *To Infinity and Beyond!: The Story of Pixar Animation Studios*, London: Virgin.

Price, D. A. (2008), *The Pixar Touch: The Making of a Company*. New York: Alfred A. Knopf.

Sito, T. (2013), *Moving Innovation: A History of Computer Animation*, Cambridge, MA: MIT Press.

Sobchack, V. (2008), 'The Line and the Animorph or "Travel Is More than Just A to B"', *animation: an interdisciplinary journal*, 3(3): 251–265.

Stamp, R. (2013), 'Experiments in Motion Graphics – or, when John Whitney met Jack Citron and the IBM 2250', *Animation Studies 2.0.*, https://blog. animationstudies.org/?p=426.

Stewart, J. (2016), 'Robin Hood and the Furry Bowlers: Animators vs Advertisers in Early British Television Commercials', in B. Florin, N. De Klerk, and P. Vonderau, *Films That Sell: Moving Pictures and Advertising*, 239–250, London: BFI/Palgrave.

Vonderau, P. (2016), 'Introduction: On Advertising's Relation to Moving Pictures', in B. Florin, N. De Klerk and P. Vonderau (eds), *Films That Sell: Moving Pictures and Advertising*, 1 18, London: BFI/Palgrave.

Vries, T. de and A. Mul (2009), *'They Thought It Was a Marvel': Arthur Melbourne-Cooper (1874–1961) Pioneer of Puppet Animation*, Amsterdam: Amsterdam University Press.

Wells, P. (1998), *Understanding Animation*, Abingdon: Routledge.

Wells, P. (2009), *The Animated Bestiary: Animals, Cartoons, and Culture*, New Brunswick, NJ: Rutgers University Press.

13

Political Animation and Propaganda

Eric Herhuth

Political activity arises from living with others. It has an aesthetic dimension that includes appeals to the senses, to pleasure and to the non-instrumental qualities found in art and recreation. How this dimension is understood varies across historical and cultural contexts. Classical Greek philosophy distinguished rhetoric, the art of persuasion, from philosophy, the love of wisdom and pursuit of truth. This divide presented a fundamental dilemma for political actors: should service to their community be realized through rhetoric or philosophy, should it be grounded in persuasion or truth? In *The Republic*, Plato argues for philosophy but this does not preclude his usage of poetic devices such as the allegory of the cave, which famously aligns animation (shadow puppets at least) with illusion, ignorance and captivity. Likewise, Plato's argument for basing politics on philosophy includes concern for the capacity of poetry and music to disrupt social order and generate enthusiasm that can be manipulated for political purposes.

Contemporary animation is no less political. Even though today's arguments about aesthetics and politics take place on a different terrain, there remain concerns that aesthetic experience, that taste and sensorial pleasure, is thoroughly organized by structures of power. This implies that the experience of liking/disliking an animated film is social. It presupposes the presence of others who may judge the film differently or similarly. Spectator experience emerges through a complex intersection of identities (race, class, occupation, gender, sexuality, etc.), each of which has specific meaning and value in a given social order. And animation itself, whether created by independent artists, a state government or transnational media company or some combination of these, likewise emerges through a matrix of intentions, practices, beliefs and materials. Social order and political power organize these complex fields.

To explore this complexity, this chapter follows two intersecting lines of inquiry: (1) the animation of politics and (2) the politics of animation. The former refers to animated films, media and performances that do politics, that support a position or make an argument that intervenes in a political debate or social crisis. The latter refers to the debates, issues, ideological differences and conflicts that exist within animation production, consumption and spectatorship. For brevity, I will restrict my comments to animation that directly engages politics and that remains prevalent today – namely caricature, cartoons, satire and propaganda. This focus is distinctly modern in that it primarily considers nation-state politics, industrial media and cel animation, which means the long history of puppets and politics has been omitted.[1]

The historical frame of this chapter is a reminder of the situatedness of the animation scholar. A key question for those studying animation is to ask how their political commitments inform their analyses. Analysis takes place within historical contexts shaped by political events and by the ideas and concepts in circulation. When organized into a structure such concepts constitute a theory or critical framework that can guide research questions and analysis. My approach draws upon the history of dialectical theory in that it considers the animation of politics and the politics of animation. By dialectical I do not mean that these two considerations lead to a synthesis, but that they facilitate shifting one's view of a problem or concept to expose different sets of inconsistencies and contradictions that are not necessarily resolvable. These include animation's contradictory aesthetic expressions, its relation to discursive power (systems of symbols, a social imaginary) and its relation to institutional power (the State/media companies) in production and reception.

Caricature and political cartoons

Political animation has historical roots in many art forms, including theatre and literature, but the graphic arts of caricature and cartooning provide an especially rich heritage. Caricature can arguably be found in ancient cave drawings, but historians often trace the first political cartoon back to 1360 BC in Egypt, and there is a long history across many cultures of using zoomorphic images to marshal insults and discredit opponents in political disputes (Keane 2008). While 'caricature' is not medium specific, 'cartoon' refers to drawing on paper and is the more recent term. In the modern era of political cartoons, early significant artists include William Hogarth (1697–1764) in England, Francisco Goya (1746–1828) in Spain, Honoré Daumier (1808–79) in France and Thomas Nast (1840–1902) in the United States. There is also a strong correlation between the rise of democracy, with its commitment to free expression, and the expansion of political cartoons (Keane 2008: 853–854). Such political and artistic developments function in concert with the invention and development of printing technology and contribute to the growth of political media, which begins to include animated films around the turn of the twentieth century.

In nineteenth-century France, caricature was commonly used to critique bourgeois society and political elites and featured prominently in illustrated magazines. By the beginning of the twentieth century this custom had evolved in response to political and technological changes. During this period the graphic artist Emile Cohl transitioned from political caricaturist to comic strip artist and then to animated filmmaker (Crafton 1990). Cohl's case, recounted by Donald Crafton, demonstrates how political, technological and artistic developments intersect within a person and a historical period. Cohl's evolution helps explain how the oppositional politics of caricature remain part of the legacy of animated cartoons that ridicule and parody everyday life.

In the United States, the longest-running scripted primetime TV series, *The Simpsons*, is an animated satire famous for irreverence and caricature aesthetics, including the occasional celebrity guest. Prior to *The Simpsons* and the glut of adult, satirical animation programming it inspired, the oppositional politics of caricature were evident in the work of the Warner Bros. animators of the 1930s and 1940s. Many of these animators used caricature to criticize Hollywood and its iconic star system and to expose the second-class status of animators working within the entertainment industry. Caricature remained a tool for aggression and criticism; it enabled animators to gain fictional control over their enemies by rendering them as two-dimensional caricatures, at once highly recognizable and grossly disfigured (Crafton 1993: 227).

This association between caricature and anti-elitism can also be traced back to nineteenth-century illustrated magazines in the United States which employed 'artist-reporters' or 'pictorial journalists' who commonly combined art and politics in an effort to serve and protect average citizens. This approach is famously represented by Thomas Nast's editorial caricatures. But caricature aesthetics are not restricted to anti-elitist, oppositional politics. Even in Nast's work caricatures of racial and ethnic minorities were commonplace and the lasting impacts of these prove that caricature aesthetics can be incredibly harmful. This is evident in the vestigial presence of blackface minstrelsy in contemporary American commercial animation (see Sammond 2015, reprinted in this volume).

The caricature's political capacity exists alongside its amusing incongruity in that it simultaneously presents a person's iconic traits and exaggerates them to such an extent that it dissolves the sanctification of the representational image. The image remains representational – it effectively refers to a person – but it breaks with the norms of representation. This makes the image and its referent more available to critique, play, but also disrespect. As Freud posited, the caricatured image of a person of high status degrades that status and renders that person more vulnerable to critique and ridicule (Freud 1905: 144). Caricatures of persons of low status affirm or exacerbate their vulnerability. This degradation effect can be approached through different questions. Are caricatures and cartoon aesthetics being used to render elites vulnerable to critique, or are they used to marshal stereotypes and prejudices against oppressed/marginalized groups? And how exactly do these biases, prejudices and stereotypes inform animation production and reception? Is there evidence of discrimination or political activity within the studio? Is reception influenced by a longer history of artistic/entertainment conventions?

Propaganda: The intersection of discursive and institutional power

Animated propaganda is a common source for caricatures, stereotypes and political satire. The twentieth century, the age of cinema, was rife with global conflicts between nation-states and propaganda was crucial to mobilizing populations and promoting competing ideals and values during times of war. Many well-known animators active during the first half of the twentieth century produced propaganda using a variety of animation techniques. Albert E. Smith and James Stuart Blackton, for instance, made some of the earliest propaganda films in the United States during the Spanish-American War. Reportedly, *The Battle of Manila Bay* (1898) was filmed in a bathtub and *The Battle of Santiago Bay* (1898) was filmed using photographic cut-outs of battleships and cigarette smoke to simulate smoke from canon fire (Dewey 2016: 60–61). Winsor McCay's *The Sinking of the Lusitania* (1918) is an early animated documentary and propaganda piece, intended to promote the US entry into the First World War, that demonstrates the dramatic capacity of cel animation. Propaganda utilizes all media forms of course, but as many governments and artists learned, cel animation and cartoon aesthetics were particularly effective at communicating factual, instructional content, comedic and dramatic scenarios, and satirical, disparaging attacks. During the Second World War, many governments had established departments of propaganda that utilized animation or maintained working relations with animation studios. The Soviet Union, for example, established its Department of Agitation and Propaganda (agitprop) in the early 1920s. Imperial Japan relied on its Propaganda Department for animated propaganda shortly before and during the Second World War. And Nazi Germany developed its own German Animation Company, although it produced fewer animated propaganda films than the USSR or the United States (Bendazzi 2016: 148). Animated propaganda in the United States was produced commercially, but government contracts with animation studios were common and these effectively kept the Disney animation studio running during the war years. Likewise, British animation companies were contracted by the British Ministry of Information (MOI) to make propaganda.

As a media category, 'propaganda' is a challenging term because its meaning has changed over time and vernacular usage is inconsistent. The term originates from the Latin word *propagare* which means to propagate, and its institutional history began when the Catholic Church created a Congregation for Propagating the Faith in 1622. The subsequent modernization and secularization of the term has resulted in a series of pejorative connotations around media designed to spread ideals and values by non-rational or emotional means. Recent history has demonstrated that messages communicated through animated, audiovisual media and that employ culturally specific symbols, narratives and artistic conventions (discursive power) are likely to be compelling and fascinating despite a lack of rationality. From the beginning of the twentieth century onwards, propaganda has become more pervasive and intensive through the industrialization of media production under the auspices of private capital/ state funding (institutional power). It is clear from the growth of advertising and public relations that creating media that embody and promote ideals and values can be used to mobilize all kinds of groups, whether voters, consumers, employees or students. The pejorative connotations of the term derive from this condition and they gesture towards broad social problems. Large-scale propaganda campaigns diminish the amount of media space for truth-oriented content and they place a burden on individuals to exercise critical analysis. Propaganda's primary function is to advance a political cause. Its commitment to truth is negligible, which is why it often does not contribute to politics as directly as it purports. Propaganda injects a dose of distortion into a media environment which, even if helpful in the short term, can perpetuate confusion and harmful myths in the long term.

In practice, there are at least two basic kinds of propaganda: supporting propaganda, which embodies specific ideals and contributes to realizing them; and undermining propaganda, which embodies specific ideals but does not contribute to realizing them (Stanley 2015: 53). Distinguishing between supporting and undermining propaganda is often a matter of analysis and argument. Analysing animated propaganda might begin by following a series of inquiries. First, there is the sometimes difficult process of distinguishing propaganda from media that happen to have propagandistic elements. Most studies of propaganda begin by outlining parameters (based on region, historical period, medium, political system, etc.) and by distinguishing between propaganda and media that have latent ideological content. Advertising and news media, for instance, do promote values, but in many cases this promotion is understood as secondary to the primary function of selling a product or reporting facts. Second, there is the process of identifying the communities, ideals and values involved, and then determining if the propaganda really contributes to realizing those values and ideals. This procedure may not be as straightforward as it sounds.

Consider, for example, the Oscar-winning Disney production *Der Fuehrer's Face* (1943). This cartoon is a famous example of American anti-Nazi propaganda created using cel animation and composed in the Disney style. As was common to war propaganda, the short's comedy and plasmatic possibility provided comedic relief to audiences suffering from conditions of war (Sharm 2009: 76–77). But *Der Fuehrer's Face* also presents a degradation effect. The short consists of an extended dream sequence in which Donald Duck is subjected to the horrors of a hyperbolic totalitarian society. By depicting the restrictions of living under totalitarianism, the film supports American ideals of freedom. By caricaturing Nazis and Hitler, it degrades the American enemy, giving confidence to American soldiers and civilians. Granted, it is equally true that the cartoon trivializes the horrors of the Nazi regime and creates a safe distance from that reality, and it does not provide many historical facts for political deliberation. One might argue that it supports the defence of American democracy, and therefore is an instance of supporting propaganda, but it is not in itself the most democratic form of expression since it dismisses and disrespects the Nazi perspective. And that seems entirely acceptable given the Nazi threat at the time and their crimes against humanity.

The complication for democratic society is that freedom of expression protects propaganda, but propaganda is rarely conducive to reasonable, respectful political debate (Stanley 2015: 94). In this sense, propaganda tactics are not politically beneficial in democratic processes in which one hopes to be treated reasonably by a political opponent and may need to work with that opponent in the future. *Der Fuehrer's Face*'s promotion of American values to American audiences is not part of a democratic process but demonstrates the one-sidedness and disinterest in other perspectives that is common to wartime propaganda. It also highlights the intersection of commercial and political interests facilitated by nationalism. Commercially produced animated propaganda can be both profitable and political through its use of culturally specific techniques and aesthetics. This intersection was common in American animation during the Second World War (Shull and Wilt 1987), and earlier examples can be found in British animated films from the First World War (Ward 2003 and 2005).

The historical and cultural specificity of animated propaganda provides opportunities to investigate the symbols and associations that constitute the social imaginary that propagandists and audiences draw upon.[2] For example, the Second World War propaganda films feature distinct aesthetic strategies that relied on cultural traditions and government-coordinated media campaigns. Nazi propaganda tended to utilize live-action newsreel footage more than staged or animated film, and this correlated with their totalitarian ideology which sought to control reality (Kracauer 1942). Cel animation was common in American and Japanese propaganda from the Second World War and both included instances of speciesism: when racial/ ethnic identities are translated into human and non-human animal relations. Speciesist depictions are regularly used to dehumanize an opponent in order to justify military action. Thomas LaMarre observes, however, that although Japanese and American Second World War animations give representation to the racialized imaginaries of both countries, these imaginaries varied and led to different deployments. American wartime animation commonly depicted Japanese characters as savage animals. Japanese wartime animation did not depict Americans as animals, but as 'failed human beings, as demons, ogres, or fiends' (LaMarre 2008: 76). When Japanese animation did deploy speciesism, it translated the identities of other Asian cultures into 'cute, friendly, and accommodating' animal characters (LaMarre 2008: 78 and 2010). These depictions were hardly innocent as they correlated with Imperial Japan's hierarchical vision of its colonies, but they suggest a significant difference between Asian colony and American enemy in the Japanese imagination at the time. These different usages of speciesist imagery indicate how racial/ethnic associations and zoomorphic depictions have distinct patterns of circulation and meaning. It is precisely these patterns and traditional associations that propaganda seeks to invoke and possibly redeploy.

LaMarre, like many media scholars, bolsters his analysis of aesthetic and symbolic elements with an analysis of political economy, which considers the economic and political institutions and relations involved in the production of media. This creates a fuller picture of an animation's ideals, values and political dynamics. Consider, for instance, the first British animated feature film *Animal Farm* (Halas and Batchelor 1954), an adaptation of George Orwell's novella published in 1945 which critiques the rise of Stalinism in the Soviet Union through an allegory in which animals on a farm overthrow their human master only to be later subjugated by the farm's pigs. The film was covertly funded by the American Central Intelligence Agency (CIA) through American producer Louis de Rochemont. Although removed by several layers, the CIA monitored the production and insisted on changes when they thought it necessary (Leab 2005: 238–241). The film's production speaks to the ideological alliance between the United States and Britain and it demonstrates how state power can operate through commercial channels.

In general, state-produced propaganda, such as Soviet agitprop, differs from commercially produced propaganda, such as that in the United States, at the level of animator autonomy. The simple formulation is that in a liberal democratic society non-governmental entities are free to produce whatever they want. Despite the chaos of this freedom, ideology, or a shared system of ideas, is reproduced and gains an organic appearance because there are, in theory, no top-down, restrictions over media production (hence, the significance of *Animal Farm* as a counter example). In modern democracy, media power is often described as a means for engineering or manufacturing consent because it is through media that ideas are voluntarily shared and affirmed. In an authoritarian state in which the government controls media production, there is a straightforward acknowledgement of top-down ideological programmes. In these cases, it is usually more interesting to analyse the continued creation of subversive media and subversive interpretations of media. The general point here is that closer examinations often reveal case-specific negotiations between state power and commercial power and between individual actors and the systems within which they operate.

Conclusion: Modernism and critical theory

The early twentieth century was a formative period for animated propaganda, but at the same time, animation more broadly defined attracted many modernist artists, especially for its capacity to resist and trouble representation. Like the degrading effect of caricature, the animated line can disrupt and resist representational and realistic aesthetics. In the early twentieth century, these aesthetics were maligned for concealing class conflicts, inequality, and the reality of political, social and technological changes – not unlike commodities that do not disclose how they are made or which groups benefit the most from their production. Individual artists and movements (e.g. Dadaism, Futurism, Soviet constructivism and Surrealism, among others) turned to animation techniques for different reasons. But for many of these artists, animation techniques had a politics to them, whether it was challenging conventions of representational, perspectival painting or experimenting with the possible combinations of photography and motion or using cartoons to parody or critique ideological positions (Leslie 2004). These techniques facilitated aesthetic responses to modernity, specifically the shocks, fragmentation and alienation associated with the industrialization of labour, the rationalization of time, increasing urbanization, the growth of capitalism, and technological changes in media and transportation. This legacy persists in animation forms that align the subversion of representational/perceptual norms with the subversion of social and political norms. This legacy counters the valuation of accurate iconic representation – that the image resembles the person or thing to which it refers. As many animation theorists point out, the further removed from recognizable reality a cartoon becomes, the less likely it is to be judged seriously (Wells 2002: 108). This can be useful for artists seeking to evade censorship and/or deliver biting criticism.

In dialogue with the critical work of artists, theorists studying the political consequences of cinema and mass media developed new methodologies during the twentieth century. Scholarship produced during the 1930s by theorists associated with the Institute for Social Research at the Goethe University Frankfurt (also known as the Frankfurt School) analysed popular culture for the purposes of understanding deep political problems within societies. In a well-known argument, Walter Benjamin, writing in the 1930s, suggested that cartoons such as Mickey Mouse facilitated collective laughter and fantasy as a kind of therapy or expression of playful possibility that answered the conditions of modernity. Theodor Adorno countered that Disney cartoons merely present the violence and mutilation of modern life in a humorous, seemingly benign form (Hansen 1993, 2012). The shadow of these oppositional claims persists today in that cartoons still tend to express possibility and metaphysical relief, but also violence, futility and industrial rationalization. Such dialectical readings of cartoons and animation find their fullest articulation in Sergei Eisenstein's (2011) writings from the 1940s, but they remain common and typically highlight competing expressions of life and death, movement and stasis, and freedom and constraint. Such expressions have purchase on a host of political issues ranging from hierarchical valuations of life (Chen 2012) to the alienation of labour (Leslie 2013).

Animation labour has been a consistent topic for critical study given political concerns over exploitation and discrimination and the capacity for cartoon aesthetics to conceal the conditions of their production. Concerns range historically from the industrial era to today's global, digital production environment, and they range from studies of gender-based discrimination to studies of the precarious conditions of international workers. Although labour issues are beyond the scope of this chapter, they are central to understanding the history of media conglomerates, globalization and digital infrastructure. Within the last twenty-five years, digital media practices have blurred the lines between consumer, viewer, user and producer, and raised new questions about animation labour and politics. This includes the categorization of fan activity and how it serves/complicates the interests of powerful media companies. The pervasiveness of animation in today's media environment has shaped politics quite broadly through the continued use of caricature, cartoons, satire and propaganda, and in quotidian ways through the expansion of digital tools and the use of animated computer graphics to enhance just about everything – from local news to the websites of political organizations. Understanding these developments and intervening in them requires critical enquiry into discursive and institutional forms of power, which means asking questions about animation forms and aesthetics and their intersections with people, practices and ideas.

Notes

1 For my view of how puppets and animated cartoons engage modern philosophy and political theory, see Herhuth (2015).
2 Scott Lash and Celia Lury use the term 'social imaginary' to refer to the collective memory and imagination of media users and audiences (2007: 182).

References

Bendazzi, G. (2016), *Animation: A World History*, Vol. 1, Boca Raton, FL: Taylor & Francis.

Chen, M. Y. (2012), *Animacies: Biopolitics, Racial Mattering, and Queer Affect*, Durham NC: Duke University Press.

Crafton, D. (1990), *Emile Cohl, Caricature, and Film*, Princeton, NJ: Princeton University Press.

Crafton, D. (1993), 'The View from Termite Terrace: Caricature and Parody in Warner Bros Animation', *Film History*, 5(2): 204–230.

Dewey, D. (2016), *Buccaneer: James Stuart Blackton and the Birth of American Movies*, Lanham, MD: Rowman & Littlefield.

Eisenstein, S. (2011), *Sergei Eisenstein: Disney*, ed. O. Bulgakowa and D. Hochmuth, trans. D. Condren, Berlin: Potemkin Press.

Freud, S. (1905), *Jokes and Their Relation to the Unconscious, SigmundFreud.net.* https://docs.google.com/viewerng/viewer?url=http://www.sigmundfreud.net/jokes-and-their-relation-to-the-unconscious.pdf (accessed 21 February 2018).

Hansen, M. B. (1993), 'Of Mice and Ducks: Benjamin and Adorno on Disney', *The South Atlantic Quarterly*, 92(1): 27–61.

Hansen, M. B. (2012), *Cinema and Experience: Siegfried Kracauer, Walter Benjamin, and Theodor W. Adorno*, Berkley, CA: University of California Press.

Herhuth, E. (2015), 'The Politics of Animation and the Animation of Politics', *animation: an interdisciplinary journal*, 11(1): 4–22.

Keane, D. (2008), 'Cartoon Violence and Freedom of Expression', *Human Rights Quarterly*, 30(4): 845–875.

Kracauer, S. (1942), *Propaganda and the Nazi War Film*, Ann Arbor, MI: Edwards Brothers, Inc.

Lash, S. and C. Lury (2007), *Global Culture Industry: The Mediation of Things*, Cambridge: Polity Press.

LaMarre, T. (2008), 'Speciesism, Part I: Translating Races into Animals in Wartime Animation', *Mechademia*, (3): 75–95.

LaMarre, T. (2010), 'Speciesism, Part II: Tezuka Osamu and the Multispecies Ideal', *Mechademia*, (5): 51–85.

Leab, D. J. (2005), 'Animators and Animals: John Halas, Joy Batchelor, and George Orwell's *Animal Farm*', *Historical Journal of Film, Radio and Television*, 25(2): 231–149.

Leslie, E. (2004), *Hollywood Flatlands: Animation, Critical Theory and the Avant-Garde*, New York: Verso.

Leslie, E. (2013), 'Animation's Petrified Unrest', in S. Buchan (ed.), *Pervasive Animation*, New York: Routledge.

Sammond, N. (2015), *Birth of an Industry: Blackface Minstrelsy and the Rise of American Animation*, Durham, NC: Duke University Press.

Sharm, R. (2009), 'Drawn-Out Battles: Exploring War-Related Messages in Animated Cartoons', in P. M. Haridakis, B. S. Hugenberg, and S. T. Wearden (eds), *War and the Media: Essays on News Reporting, Propaganda and Popular Culture*, 75–89, Jefferson, NC: McFarland & Company, Inc.

Shull, M. S. and D. E. Wilt (1987), *Doing Their Bit: Wartime American Animated Short Films, 1939–1945*, Jefferson, NC: McFarland & Company, Inc.

Stanley, J. (2015), *How Propaganda Works*, Princeton, NJ: Princeton University Press.

Ward, P. (2003), 'British Animated Propaganda Cartoons of the First World War: Issues of Topicality', *Animation Journal*, (11): 65–83.

Ward, P. (2005), 'Distribution and Trade Press Strategies for British Animated Propaganda Cartoons of the First World War Era', *Historical Journal of Film, Radio and Television*, 25(2): 289–201.

Wells, P. (2002), *Animation and America*, New Brunswick, NJ: Rutgers University Press.

14

TV Animation and Genre

Nichola Dobson

General audiences have only been exposed to one type of animation, that
of popular, funny and usually American, cartoons, as if there were only
"pop" music and no other kind (Halas in Langer 1997: 149)

As the part of this book in which this chapter appears indicates, animation
can refer to a variety of forms, practices and formats. This multifariousness
of animation extends also to content and subject matter. The quote from
animator John Halas above implies, however, that the US cartoon format
has come to dominate the perception of animation. This is problematic not
only for those who want to produce and market animation that falls outside
of this category, but also presents challenges for theorizing animation genre.
By exploring the extent to which the cartoon continues to dominate the
Western TV landscape, this chapter suggests that there is, in fact, a much
wider variety of animation television genres than Halas's quote, and,
arguably, popular perception, would first suggest.

Animated TV

Steve Neale (2001: 3) argues that genre has a 'multi-dimensional' function,
in that it can categorize and group similar work for creation and marketing
and also for analysis. This categorization can come from the institutions
which created the work, the theorists who analyse the work, and from the

systems of understanding which audiences use to differentiate the work from other genres and from texts within the same genre. Each genre has a set of recognizable characteristics that enable categorization; these are repeated and reinforced through what Altman (1999) refers to as 'cycles' and can be seen in patterns in TV history. Cycles are not static or temporally discrete and new elements can change the genre to create new ones, or old ones can come back into favour (Altman uses the example of adding music to comedy to create the musical comedy).

As Halas suggests in the above quote, the Hollywood cartoon dominated the creation, and thus the industrial development, of the animation TV series and thus came to shape the audience's 'system of expectations' that they bring to each animated 'text' (Neale 1990: 46). The history of animation, and in particular animation on American television, reinforces rather than challenges any expectations and the mainstream continues to present animation which is broadly categorized and thus understood as 'cartoon'. The aesthetic of the cartoon, derived from the comic strip, remains commonplace and adds to assumptions of generic uniformity. Though the range of genres available within the animated form is as vast as that in live-action (TV and cinema), television is dominated by animated comedy, though within comedy this can take the structural form of the short gag sketch and serialized, sitcom formats. While each of these forms has different characteristics within them, they all fall under the generic dominant of comedy; they are funny and are intended to make audiences laugh (Neale 1990). This dominance is why it is easy to think of all of animated TV as comedy without perhaps considering that there might be variation within the genre, even while animation is used, for example, to satirize or comment on other aspects of genre. Paul Wells argues that 'the animated form inherently embraced the self-figurative, self-reflexive, self-enunciating characteristics' (2002: 110) seen in so-called postmodern texts. This self-reflexivity is evident in many animated TV series particularly from the early 2000s, such as *Family Guy* (1999–).[1]

Comedy's dominance of TV animation can be traced through the birth of TV in the United States which saw a need to fill the schedule with material for younger viewers, as well as a family audience, gathered around one focal point.[2] This was initially the re-packaged work from the major studios of animation's Golden Age such as MGM and Warner Bros., as well as Walt Disney. Many of these short films had their origins in the comic strip, and the comedic visual gags became a mainstay for the fledgling medium, and with it, the generic dominance of animated comedy on television.

As the technology of television broadcasting improved and the market expanded, more content was required and networks turned to production companies which were already well versed in comedy, such as the newly formed Hanna-Barbera. The studio grew out of William Hanna and Joseph Barbera's work together at MGM, notably the *Tom and Jerry* (1940–58) series. They began creating more narrative comedy in a serialized form, which was structured around the requirements of advertising sponsors on television. This along with the new form of the sitcom in live-action saw the creation of the animated sitcom, or anicom (Dobson 2003, 2009), in 1960. This genre of animation would dictate the course of TV animation for decades to come.

The anicom adopts the narrative strategies of the live-action television sitcom (originally based on radio comedies) conforming to narrative space, structure and character groupings, but capitalizes on the particularities of the language of animation to produce something distinct. If the animated form highlights what Wells (1998, 2002) refers to as its 'animatedness' by defying physical laws and using narrative strategies such as metamorphosis,[3] we note their difference from live-action, even in something as simple as series featuring characters who never age, such as Bart, Lisa and Maggie in *The Simpsons*.

The first anicom, Hanna-Barbera's *The Flintstones* (1960–6) was consciously modelled on live-action counterparts, such as *The Honeymooners* (1955–6), in order to appeal to the same audience. The series was a comedic portrayal of 1950s married life, but in a Stone Age setting complete with jokes on gender roles and relationships. The show thus fulfilled what Neale (1990) and Todorov (1981) describe as genre's 'verisimilitude'; that is, the way it conforms to audience expectations of a particular genre, which in this case is a sitcom about working class family life. This successful series set a precedent for the development of the anicom genre which flourished in the 1960s, declined in the 1970s and 1980s, but by the 1990s cycled back to immense success with *The Simpsons*, which is currently airing its 29th season.

The Hanna-Barbera anicoms were made with an adult audience in mind, in terms of themes, and this was signalled to the audience by its prime time (early evening) scheduling. Their later shows such as *The Jetsons* (1962–3), would also follow this pattern, but as the television landscape altered and children were being increasingly catered to as a separate audience group, their subsequent shows moved away from adult comedy – comedy that dealt with socio-cultural or political themes – and were no longer scheduled in prime time. The only exception to this was in their last anicom, *Wait 'til Your Father Gets Home* (1972–74), which featured storylines about communism and increasing paranoia in the United States as well as one on pregnancy in later life (which hinted at abortion), whereas their series aimed for children such as *The Magilla Gorilla Show* (1964–6) and *The Atom Ant/Secret Squirrel Show* (1965–6) included more slapstick humour, anthropomorphism and less socio-political commentary.

Animation on television was increasingly seen throughout the 1960s and 1970s as something for children and scheduled accordingly with the ratings for the primetime anicom reducing and the market for children's television increasing. In fact there were no primetime anicoms on US TV between

1974 and 1989. While the animation that was broadcast was industrially categorized for children and broadly fell within the catch-all TV cartoon genre, there was much diversity. In Hanna-Barbera's output alone, there was still an echo of the live-action sitcom genre, albeit in a comedic, and curiously satirical fashion with the development of the detective action series seen in *Josie and The Pussycats* (1970), *Scooby Doo Where Are You?* (1969–70), *Captain Caveman* (1977–80) (often with musical interludes), the boys' adventure series in *Jonny Quest* (1964–5) and sci-fi adventures with *Birdman and the Galaxy Trio* (1967–9) and *Space Ghost* (1966–8). This diversity was replicated by other studios, notably Filmation, with sci-fi and adventure shows such as *Rod Rocket* (1963), *The New Adventures of Superman* (1966–70), *Journey to the Centre of the Earth* (1967–9) and musical comedy in *The Archies* (1968–9). These shows reflected the popular genres in live-action of comedy, sci-fi and musical comedy, such as *The Partridge Family* (1970–74), in TV and cinema as well as broader popular culture such as comic books and pop music. The variation within TV animation has not readily been acknowledged by animation scholarship, arguably because it was aimed at children and therefore deemed less worthy of attention.

Television animation remained primarily considered 'just for kids' until the late 1980s when both television and cinematic feature animation began to target more adult audiences with *Who Framed Roger Rabbit* (1987) in the cinema and *The Simpsons* (1989–) on television. This also coincided with the launch of MTV in 1981 (and Channel 4 in the UK, see Kitson 2008) which provided a platform for short experimental animation in different forms beyond the traditional 2D cel animated work commonly seen on TV. Many of these animators, like Bill Plympton and Mike Judge, had been brought up with Saturday morning TV animation and were now starting to work in a newly revitalized industry with new opportunities for interesting and subversive work on cable and the new FOX network, all open to new content. This also led to a new genre cycle of anicom oriented at both the primetime family and adult audience and scheduled in early and late evening time slots, including *King of the Hill* (1997–2010), *Family Guy* (1999–), *South Park* (1997–) and *Futurama* (1999–2013).

Despite this development in the animation offering on television, the industrial categorization of animation for children persisted and occasionally became problematic. A notable, and well-documented example from 1992 is the Nickelodeon series *Ren and Stimpy* created by John Kricfalusi, an animator highly influenced by Bob Clampet and others of the 1940s and 1950s (Langer 1997). Kricfalusi's approach to comedy presented a retro style with an element of satire and subversion, which Langer refers to as 'animatophilia' (1997: 143) and was very popular critically. However, the network presented this as a children's show – it was rated as TV-Y7, suitable for children age seven or older, and promoted via a Mattell toy company merchandising deal – and thus the industrial genre signalled it as comedy suitable for children in what Nickelodeon considered the classic Warner Bros. *Looney Tunes* model. As Langer points out, the initial pitch of a multi layer/multi audience show (a strategy seen in earlier family animated TV series such as *The Flintstones*) suited Nickelodeon's corporate strategy (though puzzlingly they also aired a late-night screening on MTV which demonstrated its success with an adult audience). However, it was when Kricfalusi began to deliver shows which needed editing by the network in order to be suitable for the show's designated family audience or, as they claimed, failed to deliver on budgets and deadlines, that they fired him. Kricfalusi refused to compromise his ideas and alter the tone of the show to be more family-friendly and Nickelodeon went on to produce a more sanitized version of the series. Kricfalusi later presented a new version, *Ren & Stimpy 'Adult Party Cartoon'* on the TNT network in 2003. It was full of the scatological humour which had been an early hallmark of the show but fans were not as receptive this time round and the series was cancelled before a second season aired.

This example could be described as a case of creative differences (and is written as such, see Langer 1997), but I would argue that the more fundamental issue is that the industrial genre was wrongly assigned due to a lack of understanding of what the series actually was, beyond the appeal of its visual style. 'Nickelodeon sought to find styles and characters that would create a distinctive product identity ... *Ren & Stimpy* was to become a mass-marketable form of cultural capital for Nickelodeon' (Langer 1997: 150). They liked the style of the 1940s animation which Kricfalusi produced, but his interest went beyond this to subvert the content and 'deliberately violated the norms of good taste' (p. 151). Langer outlines the use of the MTV network by Nickelodeon's parent company Viacom to increase the popularity and reach of the show to an adolescent audience, but 'this was done in order to get the MTV audience and bring it to Nickelodeon for Sunday morning *Ren & Stimpy* cablecasts' (p. 155). By airing the series in a child-friendly time slot, the system of expectation set up for the audience by the network was for a show suitable for young children. However, this expectation was erroneous and the 'cartoon' aesthetic was arguably the only element taken into account when promoting, scheduling and commissioning the series. The bottom line for the company was connected to their deal with Mattel 'to licence *Ren & Stimpy* products to children ... Positioning *Ren & Stimpy* outside of a juvenile taste group might have jeopardised the popularity of the series among potential Mattel toy purchasers' (p. 157). Kricfalusi had little intention of changing his own personal animatophile tastes to cater to the younger Nickelodeon audience and as a result they saw increasing interference from the network in script editing, and eventually parted ways.

The *Ren and Stimpy* example shows how merchandising can lead to confusion regarding the generic classification of popular mainstream animated shows. Due to the 'cartoon' style of many of these shows, the merchandise often has a 'cute' or child-friendly style, despite the show itself often being inappropriate for a children's audience. Another example of this is in the soft toy products sold to promote the animated sitcom *South Park* during the 1990s. The series is scheduled in a late-night slot, and the opening title card explains that the show is offensive, deliberately so, however the merchandise has an appeal to children who may not be aware of the true content of the show. This becomes a problem when adults, unfamiliar with the content, make assumptions based solely on the animated form and ignore the aspects of the industrial genre, the scheduling, in favour of the other industrial codes, the marketing. In the UK in 1999, a parent launched an awareness campaign about *South Park*, at her local school to tell parents how 'the merchandise seems to be specifically aimed at youngsters' and 'A lot of parents don't realise what their kids are watching' ('South Park Is not Suitable for Youngsters Says Mum' 1999).[4] Many of these misconceptions can be traced back to the assumptions made by the mainstream audience as outlined at the start of the chapter, ones that are also largely reinforced by the industrial categorization of TV animation as one entity.

While the generic dominance of comedy has persisted throughout the history of TV animation, in mainstream US television the most prevalent generic alternative to comedy has been in sci-fi and fantasy, largely developed from imported Japanese anime. More recently these have tended to be scheduled in late-night slots and therefore not aimed at a mainstream audience.[5] However, in the mid 1960s and 1970s, US television schedules were filled with sci-fi adventure series, including *Birdman and the Galaxy Trio* and *Space Ghost*. The first Japanese television series *Astro Boy* (1963–6) was highly successful and established the market for television animation in Japan and abroad and led to the creation of *Battle for the Planets* (1978–80), a Westernized version of the Japanese series *Science Ninja Team Gatchaman* (1972–4). In the UK, television producer Gerry Anderson released the highly successful *Stingray* (1964), *Thunderbirds* (1965) and *Captain Scarlet and the Mysterons* (1967) using his unique puppet animation. As previously noted, in the United States, Hanna-Barbera ventured into sci-fi by combining it with the domestic sitcom in *The Jetsons*. Matt Groening later emulated this approach with the production of his second anicom, *Futurama* (1999–2013), which combines the narrative of the workplace sitcom with the tropes of the sci-fi genre, creating a hybrid.

The transnational exchange of series between East and West, which started with *Astro Boy*, has seen an increased audience for alternatives to the anicom, such as sci-fi and fantasy with different forms and styles of animation and for different age groups. The growth in animated television generally, and the increase in platforms for viewing on cable and streaming

TV as well as internet channels, has seen a rise in innovative TV animation, for both children and adults. Shows which challenge ideas of genre (mixing sci-fi with fantasy and absurdist comedy) as well as shows which challenge dominant norms of gender and sexuality, such as *Adventure Time* (2007–10) and *Steven Universe* (2013–), or that deal with issues of mental health such as *Rick and Morty* (2013–), are very far removed from the slapstick of the *Looney Tunes* or the aforementioned musical detective shows of the 1960s. It is interesting that these shows are all shown on the cable channel Cartoon Network, which since the early 1990s has pioneered and celebrated diverse animation in terms of content and style. We might argue that by classifying and containing all of these shows in one place as 'cartoon' they limit the perception of animation genre, but instead they have in fact provided audiences with a site for the development of new genres and sub genres, as well as for exposure to content outside of the mainstream.

Other recent examples of this type of subversion that challenge dominant generic expectations can be seen in late-night television sketch shows in the UK, such as *Modern Toss*, *2DTV* (2001–04) and *Monkey Dust* (2003–05) (see Norris 2014). In the United States the late-night offering ranges from *South Park* (1997–), the output from the Adult Swim project (2001–) including *Venture Bros.*, *Robot Chicken* and *Rick and Morty*, to the even more adult and absurd *Bojack Horseman* (2014) on the streaming service Netflix. Though these again all fall under the generic dominant of comedy, they use their animatedness to extend sub genres of comedy and, in the case of *Bojack*, the nature of television itself. A notable example of this in *Bojack* can be seen in season 4, episode 6 entitled 'Stupid Piece of Shit' which uses different styles of animation to reveal Bojack's thought processes and his confused mental state. Bojack's role as a 'washed-up' TV sitcom star in itself refers to the formulaic nature of TV genre and in numerous episodes critiques the problem of child stars, Hollywood and celebrity. Dramatic genres which deal with serious aspects of real life rarely occur in TV animation, and I would suggest are harder to produce (to fund or commission) due to the success and dominance of comedy in contemporary TV animation. That said, *Bojack Horseman* could arguably be categorized as a bleak black comedy, which deals with very dramatic, and very adult themes such as drug and alcohol addiction, casual sex and depression. However, it is not broadcast on a mainstream network, but instead on a streaming service which has greater liberty to offer edgier content.

The post-network era, described in detail by Amanda Lotz (2014), demonstrates that a diverse audience exists which is not always catered for by standard industrial genres and that therefore do not need to be directed towards certain genres in the same way. For these audiences, scheduling is less important and marketing is often done by word of mouth on social media. The discourse surrounding series such as *Bojack* enables prospective audiences to discover television animation which suits a variety of tastes at a time convenient to them. The audience is no longer content to be confined to network schedules and traditional 'flow' of the TV medium (see Williams 1975). That many of these shows have found an increased 'grown up' audience speaks of several factors. Like the generation before them, the audience has been raised on multiple forms of animation thanks to the success and visibility of shows like *The Simpsons* and the pervasiveness of animation more generally; the diversity of platforms allows for and presents a variety of content, and as such traditional systems of generic expectations are arguably less important to a show's continued success.

Although the generic categories of TV animation are not always as clearly defined by industrial practices in marketing and scheduling as their live-action counterparts, this chapter has shown that there is generic diversity within the catch-all term 'TV animation'. That this is relatively recent, and most likely enabled by the diversification of viewing platforms, perhaps suggests that the dominance of comedy persists. However as new transnational, increasingly experimental TV animation emerges and finds an audience, this generic catch-all categorization of 'TV animation' will most likely change further. Williams argues, 'As genres change over time, [...] their audiences become more and more self-conscious' (Williams in Neale 1990: 59). This self-conscious audience may become more open to difference and development within the genre and new genres of TV animation may well emerge.

Notes

1   Each of these series, over their run, have included episodes which are about television, with *Family Guy* including several, with one episode centred around 'that episode of Who's the Boss... ' the 1980s US live-action sitcom ('Love Thy Trophy', season 2 episode 5, 2000).

2   See Sandler (2002), Burke and Burke (1998), Mittell (2004) and Ratelle (in this volume) for further discussion of the history of animation for children on TV.

3   See Paul Wells on the narrative devices and strategies used which are particular to animation, including metamorphosis, in *Understanding Animation* (1998) chapter 3.

4   The parent admitted that the show was scheduled post watershed but claimed that young children would still be watching then. See 'South Park Is not Suitable for Youngsters Says Mum' (1999)

5   Cartoon Network's 'Adult Swim' late-night animation block which was set up in the late 1990s to broadcast adult only animation began a dedicated anime slot 'Toonami' in 1999. This was generally scheduled at midnight though later often included popular anime within the Cartoon Network's daytime schedule.

References

Altman, R. (1999), *Film/Genre*, London: BFI Publishing.

Burke, K. and T. Burke (1998), *Saturday Morning Fever: Growing up with Cartoon Culture*, New York: St Martin's Press.

Dobson, N. (2003), 'Nitpicking the Simpsons: Critique and Continuity in Constructed Realities', *Animation Journal* (2003): 84–93.

Dobson, N. (2009), *Historical Dictionary of Animation and Cartoons*, Lanham, MD: Scarecrow Press.

Kitson, C. (2008), *British Animation: The Channel 4 Factor*, London: Parliament Hill Publishing.

Lotz, A. (2014), *The Television Will Be Revolutionized*, New York: New York University Press.

Langer, M. (1997) 'Animatophilia, Cultural Production and Corporate Interests', in J. Pilling (ed.), 143–162, *A Reader in Animation Studies*, Sydney: John Libbey.

Mittell, J. (2004), *Genre and Television: From Cop Shows to Cartoons in American Culture*, New York: Routledge.

Neale, S. (1990), 'Questions of Genre', *Screen*, 31(1): 2–17.

Neale, S. (2001), 'Studying Genre', in G. Creeber (ed.), *The Television Genre Book*, London: BFI publishing.

Norris, V. (2014), *British Television Animation (1997–2010): Drawing Comic Tradition*, London: Palgrave Macmillan.

Sandler, K. (2002), 'Movie Ratings as Genre: The Incontestable R', in S. Neale (ed.) *Genre and Contemporary Hollywood*, 201–217, London: BFI.

'South Park Is not Suitable for Youngsters Says Mum' (1999), *Warrington Guardian*, June. Available online: http://www.warringtonguardian.co.uk/news/5303140.South_Park_is_not_suitable_for_youngsters_says_Mum/ (accessed 22 January 2018).

Todorov, T. (1981), *Introduction to Poetics*, Brighton: Harvester.

Wells, P. (1998), *Understanding Animation*, London: Routledge.

Wells, P. (2002), *Animation: Genre and Authorship*, London: Wallflower Press.

Williams, R. (1975), *Television: Technology and Cultural Form*, London: Fontana.

15

Animation and/as Children's Entertainment

Amy Ratelle

On a broad scale, animation has been historically devalued and dismissed as 'kids' stuff' – loud, often obnoxious, poorly written and frivolous (Wells 2002: 61). Yet, animated programming forms a substantial portion of broadcasting for children in general and has been both incredibly lucrative for advertisers and a battleground on which culture wars have been fought in the name of educational content and the protection of 'childhood innocence'. However, animation studies has, paradoxically, continued to marginalize the study of animation for children. This chapter will address the oversight of children's animation by situating it in the larger historical, cultural and theoretical framework of children's media, and will explore the history of audience formation, the role of parents, educators and advertisers, and the effects of consumer culture on the form.

Children's animation is a global multi-million-dollar industry and has become as synonymous with childhood experiences as the nursery rhyme. Yet, scholarly attention to date has largely been characterized by nostalgia for the early television animation of the 1960s (Wells 2002; Mittell 2003), or focuses on the effects of cartoon violence on young viewers (Kirsch 2006; Blumberg et al. 2008). Yet, as Stephen Kline has noted, 'what might be taken for children's culture has always been primarily a matter of culture produced for and urged upon children' (1998: 95). This top-down approach, so to speak, can reinforce perceptions of children as passive consumers of media in need of protection and education, and works to conceal the role that films and television play in enculturing children to become (adult) humans in culturally specific ways. By examining American animation in the historical context of childhood as a particularly Western and middle-class concept, this chapter contends that animation as a medium for children has become prey to the oppositional discourses of education and entertainment on the battleground of consumer culture and that these discourses have contributed to its marginalization as a medium and as a scholarly topic.

A tale of two audiences

Our current conception of childhood as a unique state of innocence to be continually safeguarded, as separate and different from adulthood, is rooted in the Romantic period's idealization of nature and the emergence of a distinct middle class invested in education and self-improvement (O'Malley 2003).[1] During this time period, children were cultivated as a separate audience, to whom literature could be marketed. While religious texts and reading primers had, since the Middle Ages, been written for the education of children, it was not until the mid-eighteenth century that literature generated specifically for this burgeoning middle-class audience became a 'clear but subordinate branch of English literature' (Darton 1982: 1). How then, did children become a separate audience?

The answer lies largely in the enduring popularity of Enlightenment philosopher John Locke (1632–1704). Locke famously posited that children are predisposed to need educational instruction, as they were a 'yet Empty Cabinet' (1690: 23), or 'white paper, or wax, to be moulded and fashioned as one pleases' (1693: 179). The role of education was perceived as crucial because children could not be relied upon to process their own experiences and sensations to acquire the proper moral character (Ratelle 2015). The middle class, with its emphasis on productivity, pedagogy and purchasing, positioned itself against the privileged entitlement and perceived vices of the upper and aristocratic classes as well as against the poverty and grinding day-to-day existence of the lower classes. As Henry Jenkins argues, the 'bourgeois classes placed particular importance on the education and rearing of their sons as preparation for participation in the market economy. Out of the future-orientation of capitalism came a new focus on child-rearing and pedagogy' (1998: 16).

In this lucrative economic climate, John Newbery (after whom the prestigious American children's literature award is named) began in 1744 to publish illustrated books that not only provided a roadmap to a life of virtue and financial success, but were also entertaining to read. Newbery changed the face of publishing and solidified children as an audience separate from adult readers by capitalizing on their middle-class parent's disposable income, 'which they were more than willing to invest in shaping and securing their children's future' (Ratelle 2015: 6). Although the origins of capitalism date back to the Middle Ages, the eighteenth-century emergence of children's literature as a vehicle for cultural values tied household economic advancement to Locke's ideals of social advancement though education. Moral instruction adhering to these ideals was made palatable to the child audience with entertaining storylines, popular characters and anthropomorphized animals. This delicate balance between education and entertainment that made its appearance in early forms of children's literature still underpins much of children's media, including animation, to the present day.

From *Snow White and the Seven Dwarfs* (1937) to the Saturday morning cartoon

While Disney – the man and the company – can be considered problematic in many respects (see Schickel 1968; Giroux 1999; Eliot 1994; Davis 2006), he was among the first to prioritize animation as a prestige medium, focusing on 'believable characters who behaved in believable ways in believable manners in believable environments' (Stabile and Harrison 2003: 5). He also prioritized animation as a medium primarily for children. In contrast, animation by other studios during the Golden Age, such as Warner Brothers, was targeted more at adults.

Prior to Disney's dominance, the animation in the early 1920s made by smaller studios and animators had also been aimed at a broad audience. Cartoons such as Pat Sullivan and Otto Messmer's *Felix the Cat* (1919–28), the Fleischer's *Out of the Inkwell* (1918–29) series and the work of animators including Walter Lantz, who would later go on to create Woody Woodpecker in 1940, often featured characters engaged in adult activities such as visiting jazz clubs, consuming alcohol and flirting with women. Felix the Cat was notorious for such behaviour, which made him enormously popular with adult audiences (Furniss 2016: 52–55). As Karl Cohen (1997: 5) points out, however, there was also extensive insistence from 'pressure groups' that such conduct from animated characters was not acceptable to the moral majority, on the grounds of protecting children in the general audience from inappropriate material in which characters acted without moral consequence. As such, characters like Felix were considered poor role models for impressionable young viewers. In 1934 regulations were enacted to curb the depictions of such risqué on-screen behaviour until their repeal in 1968, when they were replaced with a more detailed rating system based on the content of the film (1997).

While the late 1920s to mid-1940s can be considered a Golden Age of cinematic animation (Wells 2002: 62), by the late 1950s and early 1960s, the animated cartoon underwent a drastic transformation that had lasting effects on the medium (Mittell 2003: 33). Animated shorts had been an integral part of the studio system, in that their exhibition was guaranteed as part of the practice of 'block-booking'. In this system, animated shorts were packaged along with features and other shorts as part of a programme of films shown in cinemas (Mittell 2003: 38). Block-booking, however, was declining as a practice, and was brought to an end by the 1948 Paramount anti-trust case, which destroyed the vertical integration stranglehold that major studios had over production, distribution and exhibition. Following the Paramount decree many of the smaller animation studios found themselves in decline and the theatrical short cartoon ultimately ceased production altogether (see Holliday in this volume). The decline of the cinematic short, however, coincided with the rise in popularity of a new household appliance – the television. Mothers in particular found television to be an ideal child-minder while they completed their daily household tasks without interruption (Seiter 1993: 15), positioning children as a significant audience for television programming, which became increasingly centred around animation.

One of the few remaining avenues of profit for animation studios, such as MGM, UPA, Harveytoons and even Warner Bros., was through selling back-catalogue former theatrical release cartoons to broadcasters, simultaneously generating revenue for the studios and solving broadcasters' dilemma of getting programming quickly and cheaply on the air.[2] The television programme *Disneyland* (1954–61), for example, incorporated the studio's own animated back catalogue of cinematic shorts introduced by a live-action host. Other studios followed suit, and by the mid-1950s, cheaper back-catalogue cartoons from various studios were thus scattered throughout the daily viewing schedule. However, as I argue above, other than Disney, these cartoons had been produced for a general audience and prioritized entertainment over moral instruction. Two streams of television animation were thus emerging at this time – one comprised of child-friendly material from Disney that was largely in alignment with Locke's principles of proper moral instruction; the other as a form of mass amusement.

Despite the popularity of the repackaged programmes such as *Disneyland*, the desire for original animated programming remained, as there were only so many ways to reformat the pre-existing material. Studios began experimenting with a new technique called 'limited animation', which minimized and/or repeated the same character action, significantly reducing the number of required drawings and drastically reducing production costs. This technique at its most extreme reduced movements down to an average of one movement per four seconds of animation, and could be produced for as little as $2500 per episode (Kanfer 1997: 180–181). Networks such as CBS began to capitalize on the potential of limited animation, and in 1956 contracted UPA to produce *The Boing-Boing Show* (1956–7). Hanna-Barbera subsequently produced *Ruff and Reddy* (1957–64) for NBC, exemplifying 'a shift in the animated form that would become typical for television productions: minimal visual variety, emphasis on dialogue and verbal humor, and repetitive situations and narratives' (Mittell 2003: 38).

Hanna-Barbera went on to change the landscape of television animation with such classic characters as Yogi Bear, Scooby Doo and Fred Flintstone by reducing the amount of animation to save on labour costs while emphasizing the dialogue to enhance the comedy. *The Flintstones* (1960–66) in particular was a runaway hit with the primetime family audience as a satirical take on the sitcom format, and the studio followed this success with *The Jetsons* (1962–3) (see Dobson on genre, this volume). A boom in animation followed, but came to an end when the market was glutted with *Flintstones* imitations seeking the prime-time adult/child crossover audience (see Wells 2002). After reaching market saturation, the 'anicom' (Dobson 2003, 2009) format was abandoned, leaving largely gimmicky offerings such as *The Secret Squirrel Show* (1965–8) and *The Space Kidettes* (1966–7).

While the original programming of the late 1950s and 1960s was initially intended for a prime-time audience which included both adults and children (see Dobson on genre, this volume), animation in general was gradually becoming targeted to the child audience, increasingly focused on mass entertainment, and broadcast on networks that were increasingly in need of advertising revenue to cover their production costs. Although the new medium of television was still broadly subject to the same kinds of regulations that had constrained the antics of Felix the Cat and his peers, there were no formal regulations in place to specifically govern children's programming, particularly in terms of how much advertising children could be exposed to. As a result of this lack of oversight, children's animation throughout the late 1950s and early 1960s continued to move away from the broader framework of education, virtue and self-improvement that prevailed in other forms of children's media, such as literature or radio, and was subsumed into a rapidly expanding consumer culture.

This rise in consumer culture also saw a considerable expansion in the toy market, a market that was increasingly tied to television and advertising. Disney's *The Mickey Mouse Club* (1955–9) was at the forefront of programmes marketing directly to children with a recognizable brand, seeing no conflict between providing child-friendly programming and advertising aimed at children (Kapur 1999: 126). Following in Disney's footsteps other companies, such as Topper Toys, Amsco and the newly formed Mattel, began to sponsor children's programmes in the hope of becoming household names (Seiter 1993: 78–80). In this period food companies also sought to generate brand loyalty by capitalizing on animation's reach to children with, for example, Kellogg's forming a long-lasting relationship with Hanna-

Barbera which would see characters featured on cereal boxes and Kellogg's advertising between shows.[3]

Consumer culture and broadcast regulations

By the late 1960s, television animation had lost any cachet it might once have had, through its subsequent association with the child audience, who were perceived to be 'uncritical' and accepting of any programmes, regardless of quality (Mittell 2003: 48). At this time, advertisers began to more aggressively market to children via television animation, with the crucial difference being that instead of creating toys based on pre-existing characters, the show was created to market pre-existing toys.

This shift in marketing strategy reached its heyday in the mid-1980s (see Engelhardt 1987) and was catalysed by the animated television special *Strawberry Shortcake* (1980), which featured a sweetly scented doll with an oversized head living in idyllic 'Strawberryland' with her 'berry friends'. The massive financial success of this one-off programme turned previous toy-marketing strategies on their heads. The new strategy of toy preceding programme was heavily reliant on corporate market research designed to synergize all levels of marketing, including the initial doll or figure, and the animated programme as well as other sources of revenue such as additional themed licensed products (e.g. lunchboxes, T-shirts), the live appearances of costumed characters in shopping malls and other performances, such as ice shows or musical concerts. The widespread presence of the characters in a wider marketing ecosystem generated a 'sense of ubiquitous stardom and desirability' for the young audience (Englehardt 1987: 73).

Reverse-engineered programmes of this nature were seen by concerned parents and educators as exemplary of particularly cynical and predatory marketing (Seiter 1993; Minow and Lemay 1995). In an overall climate of increasing concern for children and their exploitation by advertisers, Newton Minow, Chair of the Federal Communications Commission (FCC) from 1961 to 1963, famously characterized television as a 'vast wasteland' (Minow and Lamay 1995: 3). Minow's evocative declaration became a catalyst for parents, social reformers, and other media scholars and critics to galvanize their efforts in order to regulate children's broadcasting and protect children from advertisers. During Minow's tenure as Chair of the FCC, his reform plans centred around an increase in educational programming for children, hearkening back to the ideals of moral guidance and instruction that had been discarded when children's animation became increasingly treated as a vehicle to deliver advertising to children under the guise of mere entertainment.

As Minow notes, the 1970s were 'the first decade in which special note was taken of children and television' (Minow and Lamay 1995: 99), as part of an overall shift to return to the educational roots of children's media. Broadcaster Joan Ganz Cooney played a significant role in this shift and in 1968 she approached Minow and other non-profits and lobbyists to fund *Sesame Street* (1969–present) for network National Educational Television (NET) that would 'help and nurture all children' (Minow and Lamay 1995: 10). Ganz Cooney adapted the language of advertising to create a series of 'commercials' for letters and numbers animated by both established and emerging artists (Gikow 2009: 238–239). Many of these short films became iconic, such as *The Ladybugs' Picnic* (Bud Luckley 1975), *Pinball Number Count* (Jeff Hale 1976), and *I Want to Be Me* (Christopher Cerf 1989). By merging education with entertainment in much the same fashion as Newbery had 200 years before, *Sesame Street* opened the doors for additional innovative and educational children's animation from America's Public Broadcasting System (PBS).

Concurrent with the emergence of *Sesame Street* as a cultural force in children's media, PBS launched an initiative to resituate general programming in the public interest by fostering innovative and educational animation for the child audience, for example *The Magic School Bus* (1994–7) – one of the highest-rated PBS shows for school-age children (Green 1997: 48). Nickelodeon, who launched the first television channel specifically for children's programming in 1979, similarly capitalized on the demand for pedagogically sound animation, with *Blue's Clues* (1996–2002), which mixed live-action and simple animation, and *Dora the Explorer* (2000–2014), which remains particularly notable for its representation of a female character of Latina heritage.

Based in large part on the success of *Sesame Street* and PBS's overall efforts to foreground the need for educational and instructional television (Minow and Lamay 1995: 10), the Center for Media Education, an American non-profit organization dedicated to media literacy and broadcast standards, effectively lobbied US Congress into passing the Children's Television Act (CTA) in 1990. This act legislated children as a separate audience with special considerations, restored time limits to commercials aired during children's programmes and required broadcasters to air at least some educational and informative children's programming (Minow and Lamay 1995: 21–22).

However well intentioned the Act was, savvy marketers were still able to work within the letter of the CTA, if not necessarily its spirit, with prosocial messages added in to the programme to demonstrate a nominal compliance with the new legislation. One of the most infamous of these 'tacked-on' additions to pre-existing programmes was the animated series *GI Joe* (1985; 1990–91; 1995–7; 2008; 2010), which was based on Hasbro's line of action figures. At the end of each twenty-minute episode, the characters reappear in a short sequence in which they assist a child grappling with some kind of problem, such as bullying. After the issue has been resolved, the sequence ends with the catchphrase, 'Now you know! And knowing is half the battle'. Other prosocial programming was less action-oriented, focusing instead on the realm of human emotions and social engagement. Series such as *The Care Bears* (1983; 1984; 1986–7; 1991; 2002; 2007; 2008; 2015–16) emphasize sharing, caring, cooperation and communication. However, such programmes often reduce each character to limited personality traits and conflate emotional states with marketable products.

Complicating the complex negotiations between moral and educational instruction, entertainment and marketing is the reliance of programmes such as *Sesame Street* on their own toy licensing to subsidize their production costs. *Sesame Street* is able to mitigate some of the conflict that parents may experience, however, by foregrounding their child-centric reputation. Muddling education and marketing in this fashion does serve to undermine straightforward arguments that marketing-based programming is always bad and educational programming is always good. In this instance, *Sesame Street* relied on income from commercial activities to maintain their mandate of nurturing and protecting the child audience.

Recent animated programmes have also been able to find a middle ground between education and commercialism. For example, *My Little Pony: Friendship Is Magic* (2010–present), a reboot of the original *My Little Pony 'n Friends* (1986–7) based on Hasbro's line of toy horses marked on the flank with a glyph representing their dominant character trait, takes a more nuanced approach to emotional development and interpersonal relationships than its predecessor. While the original series has been dismissed by critics such as Englehardt as trite and unimaginative with passive characters, the new programme favours complex storylines that blend adventure and magic into a problem-solving framework (Kirkland 2017: 99–100). By working to flesh out the stereotyping common to children's programming, and of which Englehardt is so critical (see Dobson on representation in this volume), *MLP: Friendship Is Magic* negotiates the competing expectations to be both entertaining and instructional, as well as remaining marketable in terms of toy sales.

Other rebooted programmes, including *Teen Titans Go!* (2013–present), a comedic take on DC Comics' fictional superhero team, ironically reference the overt prosocial messages of both marketing-based animated programmes and the more pedagogically oriented ones from public broadcasters, while simultaneously providing actual instructional value. In both 'Pyramid Scheme' (2015) and 'And Finally a Lesson' (2016), for example, the team learns about the value of money, and how to build home equity. Similarly, in 'Think about Your Future' (2016), the team is visited by their future selves, who travel back in time to impart valuable lessons on the impact of their poor eating and spending habits. Entertainment and education are thus reconfigured for a contemporary audience of the children of parents well versed in the animation tropes of their own childhood, yet who still might want to engender good viewing habits in their own children.

Conclusion

As this chapter has demonstrated, attitudes towards children's animation are often deeply ambivalent. On the one hand, it bears the significant burden of striking a balance between entertainment and education. On the other, it has been devalued in the United States in particular for its association with consumer culture. As Donald Crafton notes, '"fun" is not ideologically neutral turf' (1998: 101), nor is the business of children's media. Shifts in thinking about children's animation reflect larger cultural tensions around children in terms of pedagogical value, emotional development and entertainment, as situated in capitalist culture. An unchecked marketing-led approach to children's animation in America resulted in the enactment of legislation to protect the child audience from the excesses of consumerism as the form drifted further away from the pedagogical-focus of earlier children's literature. And yet, even programmes such as *Sesame Street* are reliant on toy and product licensing in order to fund additional seasons, presenting a challenge in balancing the programme's needs against its mandate for nurturing and protecting the child audience. As their success indicates, it is indeed possible to negotiate this slippery terrain, combining education and prosocial messaging with innovative, entertaining and oftentimes experimental animation within a US media landscape largely occupied by networks and marketers.

Demand for and consumption of animated programming resulted in a major expansion of the children's animation universe in the United States, from the three major networks in the 1960s (ABC, CBS and NBC) to four separate commercial cable networks for children – Nickelodeon, Cartoon Network, The Disney Channel and PBS Kids. This universe is one in which quality educational programmes exist alongside toy-based programmes, which coexist with the same back-catalogue cartoons that were mainstays of the original Saturday morning timeslot. Recent additions to the viewing landscape include on-demand streaming services such as Netflix and Hulu, which license existing programmes in addition to their own original productions.

The ubiquity of children's animation across multiple viewing formats requires ever-more productions, bringing with them evermore licensing opportunities. In this sense, discourse around children's animation would benefit from a more overt acknowledgement that what we think we should do (e.g. educate and nurture children) is not always in alignment with what actually happens; despite what might be best intentions, programmes and broadcasters still exist in a capitalist framework and are thus reliant on product tie-ins. In this sense, we can read children's animation as a site of conflict, subject to a series of ongoing negotiations between competing interests that – however well intentioned – are nevertheless situated in a capitalist context from which it is nearly impossible to be extricated.

Notes

1   Although the Romantic period reached its peak from 1800 to 1850, its roots stretch back to the 1700s. This period is largely characterized by 'feeling and imagination', as a reaction to Enlightenment's emphasis on reason (Morrow 2011: 39).

2   Creating original cel animation for television at this point was prohibitively laborious, slow and expensive, as an average seven-minute MGM short, for example, cost between $40,000 and $60,000 to produce (Mittell 2003: 38). This cost was not feasible for networks, particularly given the amount of new short films they would need to fill the broadcasting schedule.

3   For more discussion on the connection between Hanna-Barbera and Kellogg's see *Cartoon Research*. Available online: http://cartoonresearch.com/index.php/a-kelloggs-cereal-cartoon-concert/

References

Blumberg, F. C., K. Bierwirth and A. J. Schwartz (2008), 'Does Cartoon Violence Beget Aggressive Behaviour in Real Life? An Opposing View', *Early Childhood Education Journal*, 36: 101–104.

Cohen, K. F. (1997), *Forbidden Animation: Censored Cartoons and Blacklisted Animators in America*, Jefferson, NC: McFarland & Company, Inc.

Crafton, D. (1998), 'The View from Termite Terrace: Caricature and Parody in Warner Bros. Animation', in K. Sandler (ed.), *Reading the Rabbit: Explorations in Warner Bros. Animation*, 101–120, New Brunswick, NJ: Rutgers University Press.

Darton, H. (1982 [1932]), *Children's Books in England: Five Centuries of Social Life*, Cambridge: Cambridge University Press.

Davis, A. (2006), *Good Girls and Wicked Witches: Women in Disney's Feature Animation*, Eastleigh: John Libbey.

Dobson, N. (2003), 'Nitpicking the Simpsons: Critique and Continuity in Constructed Realities', *Animation Journal*, 11: 84–93.

Dobson, N. (2009), *Historical Dictionary of Animation and Cartoons*, Lanham, MD: Scarecrow Press.

Eliot, M. (1994) *Walt Disney: Hollywood's Dark Prince*, New York: HarperCollins.

Engelhardt, T. (1987), 'The Strawberry Shortcake Strategy', in T. Gitlin (ed.), *Watching Television*, 66–110, New York: Pantheon.

Furniss, M. (2016), *A New History of Animation*, London: Thames & Hudson.

Gikow, L. (2009), *Sesame Street: A Celebration – 40 Years of Life on the Street*, New York: Black Dog & Leventhal Publishers Inc.

Giroux, H. (1999), *The Mouse That Roared: Disney and the End of Innocence*, Lanham, MA: Rowman & Littlefield Publishers Inc.

Green, M. (1997), 'Scholastic Productions Banks on Best-Sellers', *Broadcasting & Cable*, July 28, 127(31): 48.

Jenkins, H. (1998) 'Introduction: Childhood Innocence and Other Myths', in H. Jenkins (ed.), *The Children's Culture Reader*, 1–38, New York: New York University Press.

Kanfer, S. (1997), *Serious Business: The Art and Commerce of Animation in America from Betty Boop to Toy Story*, New York: Da Capo Press.

Kapur, J. (1999), 'Out of Control: Television and the Transformation of Childhood in Late Capitalism', in M. Kinder (ed.), *Kids' Media Culture*, 122–138, Durham, NC: Duke University Press.

Kirkland, E. (2017) '"Little Girls and the Things That They Love": *My Little Pony: Friendship Is Magic*, Audience, Identity, and the Privilege of Contemporary Fan Culture', *Camera Obscura*, 32 (2): 88–115.

Kirsch, S. J. (2006), 'Cartoon Violence and Aggression in Youth', *Aggression and Violent Behavior*, 11 (6): 547–557.

Kline, S. (1998), 'The Making of Children's Culture', in H. Jenkins (ed.), *The Children's Culture Reader*, 95–109, New York: New York University Press.

Locke, J. (2008 [1690]), *An Essay concerning Human Understanding*, Oxford: Oxford University Press.

Locke, J. (2007 [1693]), *Some Thoughts concerning Education*, New York: Dover Publications, Inc.

Minow, N. and C. Lamay (1995), *Abandoned in the Wasteland: Children, Television and the First Amendment*, New York: Hill and Wang.

Mittell, J. (2003), 'The Great Saturday Morning Exile: Scheduling Cartoons on Television's Periphery in the 1960s', in C. Stabile and M. Harrison (eds), *Prime Time Animation: Television Animation and American Culture*, 33–54, New York: Routledge.

Morrow, J. (2011), 'Romanticism and Political Thought in the Early Nineteenth Century', in G. Stedman Jones and Gareth G. Claeys (eds), *The Cambridge History of Nineteenth-Century Political Thought*, 39–76, Cambridge: Cambridge University Press.

O'Malley, A. (2003), *The Making of the Modern Child: Children's Literature in the Late Eighteenth Century*, London: Taylor & Francis.

Ratelle, A. (2015), *Animality in Children's Literature and Culture*, London: Palgrave Macmillan.

Schickel, R. (1968), *The Disney Version: The Life, Times, Art and Commerce of Walt Disney*, New York: Simon & Schuster.

Seiter, E. (1993), *Sold Separately: Parents and Children in Consumer Culture*, New Brunswick, NJ: Rutgers University Press.

Stabile, C. and M. Harrison (2003), 'Introduction', in C. Stabile and M. Harrison
    (eds), *Prime Time Animation: Television Animation and American Culture*,
    1–12, New York: Routledge.
Wells, P. (2002), '"Tell Me about Your Id, When You Was a Kid, Yah!" Animation
    and Children's Television Culture', in D. Buckingham (ed.), *Small Screens:
    Television for Children*, 61–95, London: Leicester University Press.

16

Video Games and Animation

Chris Pallant

At the time of writing (summer 2017), there is considerable excitement in animation and video game circles about the upcoming release of *Cuphead* (2017).[1] After debuting on YouTube in October 2013 and launching at E3 (the Entertainment Software Association's annual Electronic Entertainment Expo) in 2014, *Cuphead* has endured a protracted development, yet enthusiasm for the title has remained high. A quick review of Twitter posts between 1 January 2014 and 1 January 2016 containing the hashtag #Cuphead reveals a common interest in the game's 'unique aesthetic' inspired by 'vintage cartoons'. Video game and animation journalists have been equally enthusiastic about the numerous trailers and gameplay demos that have preceded the game's launch, with CartoonBrew's Amid Amidi noting how the developer had 'the classic animation look pegged, from lush watercolor backgrounds to authentic pie-cut eyed, rubbery characters who look straight out of a Fleischer/Iwerks short' (2013), while Chris Kohler writes as part of a feature for *Wired* previewing the most anticipated games of 2016 (the year in which many expected the game to debut): 'I've spent a lot of time playing *Cuphead* at various game expos last year, and the way it so faithfully replicates the look and feel of classic early-20th-century animation is absolutely jaw-dropping. Couple that with difficult (but fair) action gameplay reminiscent of *Gunstar Heroes* and you have a game we're just dying to play' (2016). These responses indicate the interest generated by the combination of animation aesthetics and the video game platform.

Fundamentally, all video games are animated texts. However, the way that interactivity serves as *the* key identifying marker of the video game, results in the (always) animated nature of video games being frequently ignored. This could be explained by the relative infancy of video games, video game culture, and the scholarly field of (Video) Game Studies. To establish the video game as an art form in its own right, the games industry, as well as games commentators, has promoted interactivity above all else as the form's distinguishing feature, thereby setting it apart from live-action cinema, with which games often share common elements, such as visual language, narrative and animated materiality.[2] Given the hesitancy that characterizes the extant scholarly engagement with the intersection of animation and video games, this chapter will seek to establish some of the key debates from game studies that might best guide readers wishing to consider the relationship between animation and video games. To that end, this chapter moves beyond the subject of interactivity, to consider more broadly how animation underpins and intervenes into three key issues in games studies: ludology, narrative and representation.[3]

The ludology perspective

The first two sections of this chapter focus on ludology and narrative, two themes that defined the early course of game studies. In the spirit of seeking to establish game studies on its own terms, scholars such as Espen Aarseth (1997, 2004), Gonzalo Frasca (1999, 2003), Markku Eskelinen (2001, 2004), Jesper Juul (2001, 2005) and Ian Bogost (2010, 2015) argued that the study of games should be centred around considerations of play, rules and experience. Furthermore, the likes of Juul, Aarseth, Frasca, Eskelinen and Bogost intentionally promoted this focus on ludological qualities as a means of critiquing what they perceived to be the incompatibility of narrative methods of interpretation of video games. At the core of this rejection of narratological approaches was a frustration regarding the seemingly straightforward mapping of an interpretational framework developed around less interactive and more linear texts (such as those found within the arts of sculpture, theatre, literature and cinema) on to the study of games. As Eskelinen notes in the first issue of the journal *Game Studies*:

> Outside academic theory people are usually excellent at making distinctions between narrative, drama and games. If I throw a ball at you I don't expect you to drop it and wait until it starts telling stories. On the other hand, if and when games and especially computer games are studied and theorized they are almost without exception colonised from the fields of literary, theatre, drama and film studies. (2001)

Consequently, for ludologists notions such as the 'magic circle' (Huizinga 1949) and 'flow' (Csíkszentmihályi 1975), which are explored in more detail below, held great appeal due to their non-narrative emphasis. Another important characteristic that notions of the 'magic circle' and 'flow' both share is animation.

Writing broadly about play and ritual in his book *Homo Ludens*, Johan Huizinga argues:

> All play moves and has its being within a playground marked off beforehand either materially or ideally, deliberately or as a matter of course. Just as there is no formal difference between play and ritual, so the 'consecrated spot' cannot be formally distinguished from the play-ground. The arena, the card-table, the magic circle, the temple, the stage, the screen, the tennis court, the court of justice, etc., are all in form and function play-grounds, i.e. forbidden spots, isolated, hedged round, hallowed, within which special rules obtain. All are temporary worlds within the ordinary world, dedicated to the performance of an act apart. (1949: 10)

In many ways, Huizinga's words – penned several decades before the advent of video games – offer an early sense of how deeply entwined the worlds of animation and video games are. The opening sentence could just as easily describe the process of animation: all *animation* moves and has its being within a *frame defined* beforehand either materially or ideally, *pose-to-pose* or *straight ahead*. This is wordplay, of course, but nonetheless it highlights an important tension between the potential freedoms afforded by play/animation and the regulation imposed by the playground/frame (perhaps a narrative framework, or principles of verisimilitude, or the physical limits of space itself if projection mapping is the type of animation employed). This tension remains at the heart of the video game experience, with animation being crucial to the player's negotiation of it. From entry into the game via home and submenu screens, through to the playable world itself, animation provides a perfectly malleable – or, to favour the language of animation studies, metamorphic – material with which to construct the 'temporary world' into which the player willingly enters.[4]

The bringing to life of the inanimate, digitally coded virtual world, relies upon the metamorphic power of the animated form to transport the gamer from the disengaged self-awareness experienced during (often lengthy) game loading screens to the deeply immersed psychological state enjoyed during gameplay. Although not always achievable, perhaps due to real-world interruptions or limited proficiency with the game's mechanics, when achieved, the complete involvement of the video gamer during play resembles what Mihály Csíkszentmihályi has termed 'flow'. For Csíkszentmihályi, games are good examples of flow activity, 'and play is the flow experience *par excellence*' (1975: 36–37). He writes:

> In the flow state, action follows upon action according to an internal logic that seems to need no conscious intervention by the actor. He experiences

it as a unified flowing from one moment to the next, in which he is in control of his actions, and in which there is little distinction between self and environment, between stimulus and response, or between past, present, and future. (1975: 36)

However, without animation there could be no flow state within the video game realm. Our sense of immersion, as video gamers, is established as we are gradually enveloped in the animated structures of the video game: from menu screens, to the avatar, to the graphical user interface (containing, for example, health bars, targeting cursors and location maps) and the scalable, scrollable, synthetic landscape of the level itself.

Games such as *Tetris* (1984), *Minesweeper* (1990) and the aptly named *flOw* (2006), which reject narrative entirely and feature game worlds not orientated around storytelling, highlight the appeal of attaining a state of flow – the feeling of complete immersion – above all else. However, games which foreground story also appeal due to their cultivation of the flow state. Consider, for example, how much of the longevity and commercial success of the *Tomb Raider* franchise is rooted in the Lara Croft narrative, and how much of that success stems from the grippingly immersive challenge of manoeuvring the twitchy Croft avatar across unforgiving cliff edges, high ravines and monumental ziggurats – every wrong move resulting in certain death and a painful reload from some now distant location. Having played several instalments of the franchise, it was the gameplay more than the narrative that prompted my return. Without doubt, a crucial appeal of the video game is player immersion within the interactive world, a feature made possible by procedurally generated animation (whereby the underlying code enables computer animation to be generated in real time). Yet, regardless of the obvious importance of these ludological characteristics to the video game experience, and despite what the ludologists claimed, narrative – and the narratological perspective – remains of similar importance.

The narratology perspective

The debate within game studies over the competing merits of ludological versus narratological interpretational frameworks has largely subsided now, and there is a broad recognition that both frameworks are valuable and can be used in combination. This section will consider how animation has proven instrumental in supporting a range of narrative ambitions within video gaming.

The clearest way that video games diverge from earlier storytelling forms, such as theatre, literature, radio, cinema and television, is through their ability to provide the experience of exploring an individualized, nonlinear story world. Of course, video games do not allow players *complete* freedom; all inputs made by the player result in either intended/anticipated pre-coded actions/animations or glitches (whereby something beyond the scope of the planned game world, or something 'transgressive', occurs). This highlights the digital cage in which all gamers operate – albeit a cage that often feels more like an open world. This is all made possible by the animated/animating nature of the code, which perpetually provides the gamer with choices: jump/double jump/don't jump; talk/don't talk; shoot/don't shoot/change weapon; beg/bribe/borrow/steal. These coded choices animate the gamer, and in return the gamer animates the game through their actions.[5]

To date, game development has sought to maximize these aspects of the video game experience, resulting in narrative frameworks that can be characterized as either 'branching' or 'foldback', which rely upon 'embedded' and 'emergent' narrative experiences (Adams 2013: 227–228). In simple terms, a branching game narrative will see all players start the game in broadly the same way (with some potential variance in avatar choice, difficulty setting and user interface configuration), and then progress down increasingly divergent narrative paths as a consequence of the choices made during a moment of narrative division. An example of a game that employs this embedded narrative framework is *Heavy Rain* (2010), which, according to Guillaume de Fondaumière, co-CEO of the game's developer Quantic Dream, featured more than twenty different endings (Johnson 2009). Each playthrough of *Heavy Rain* yields just one of these many endings, and it is up to the player to plot their own course through the many available narrative paths. In comparison, *Red Dead Redemption* (2010) also relies on embedded narrative, but offers enormous scope for players to blaze their own trail, yet only in-between key narrative checkpoints. Once such a checkpoint is triggered, the player, who might have been fully immersed in several side-missions at that point, is folded back into the core narrative experience.

In both *Heavy Rain* and *Red Dead Redemption* the game engine is harnessed to procedurally generate those embedded sequences that stitch the core narrative experience together. Historically, pre-rendered approaches were necessary to deliver embedded sequences, given the lower computational power of earlier PCs and consoles. Perhaps the most popular – if not infamous – approach taken was to rely on 'FMV' sequences, or 'full motion video', whereby filmed footage of actors portraying in-game characters temporarily invaded the game world, as seen throughout the *Command and Conquer* franchise (1995–2013), for example. A more time-consuming, but aesthetically complimentary approach was favoured by Square Enix for their *Final Fantasy* (1987–) franchise, whereby pre-rendered computer-generated animation was used to convey important narrative information.

Contrastingly, the experience of emergent narrative is unique to each gamer, and is rooted in the combination of play, experimentation, action and animation. For example, Bogost's satirical *Cow Clicker* (2010), which was intended as a critique of the exploitative micropayment mechanics of many of the most popular Facebook games at that time (such as *FarmVille* [2009–present], *Mafia Wars* [2011–16] and *ChefVille* [2012–15]), inadvertently ended up becoming a popular browser game in its own right. The popularity of *Cow Clicker* owed much to the social narratives of collaborative play that were constructed *around* the game by the players, rather than *by* the game for the players. In a game such as *Cow Clicker* – or *FarmVille, Mafia Wars and ChefVille* for that matter – while animation self-evidently provides the textual interface, there is a danger of overstating the significance of this animated materiality in claiming that it is central to the experience of emergent narrative. Simply put, in terms of the ambition and delivery of narrative, animation can be more significant in some games than others. Yet, on a fundamental level, all game narratives are essentially facilitated by animation.

Representation

Both narratological and ludological perspectives yield useful insights when considering the relationship between video games and animation; however, as Yussef Cole's (2017) article, 'Cuphead and the Racist Spectre of Fleischer Animation' highlights, all games rely on animated characters, and with this characterization comes the politics of animated representation. When asked about the implications of paying aesthetic homage to the 1930s animation of the Fleischer Studio, made in an era where racial stereotypes prevailed in US animation, *Cuphead* Lead Inking Artist and Producer Maja Moldenhauer noted: 'It's visuals and that's about it …. Anything else happening in that era we're not versed in it. Blame it on being Canadian' (Kleinman 2017). While Moldenhauer's sentiment might come from a position of naivety, it is also emblematic of a wider unwillingness on the part of the games industry to engage with the politics of representation in any meaningful way. The subject of representation takes on even greater significance given the unbounded scope of animation to represent whatever the mind can imagine. It is therefore disappointing to recognize, for example, an unhealthily one-dimensional approach to female character design, with heteronormative sexual appeal being the guiding principle that still shapes many video games. While male game protagonists are similarly straightjacketed in terms of sexuality, the physical representation of male characters draws upon a much wider spectrum of possibility than can be said of female characters. For example, whereas female characters are often small-waisted, big-busted and dressed in impractical clothes, there is more diversity in the physicality and appearance of male characters. Compare, for example, the rotund Mario, the ageing and partially sighted Solid Snake featured in *Metal Gear Solid V* (2015), the visually malleable CJ from *Grand Theft Auto: San Andreas* (2004), and the world-weary everyman Joel from *The Last of Us* (2013), with the uniformly limited physical characterization of Lara Croft, Princess Peach, Jill Valentine, Rayne, Mai Shiranui or any of the female characters from the *Virtua Fighter* (1993–2012), *Tekken* (1994–) and *Dead or Alive* (1996–2016) franchises.

Numerous scholars have sought to unpack this representational imbalance (see Kennedy 2002; Guins 2004; Nooney 2013), with Justine Cassell and Henry Jenkins making an important early contribution with their edited collection *From Barbie to Mortal Kombat: Gender and Computer Games* (1998). This book brings together a range of perspectives, with the intention of jumpstarting a more nuanced and progressive conversation about gender and computer games. While much attention has been paid to issues of representation by game studies, there has been little change in the games themselves, which can be seen to stem partly from the overwhelmingly male composition of the industry itself, as well as the narrow popular discourse surrounding it.[6] Cassell and Jenkins, writing in 2008, recall how responses to their 1998 book ranged from total rejection by the closed ranks of men who populated the games industry, reviews in popular publications (such as *Ms.* and *Playboy*) that sought to ridicule, and fan commentary that prioritized factual detail over the larger arguments about gender inequality (Cassell and Jenkins 2008: 10–11). Cassell and Jenkins write: 'So many of the young males who responded to the book seemed worried that some maternal presence might force them to tuck in their shirttails or that the companies would stop making games to their tastes once women became gamers' (Cassell and Jenkins 2008: 10–11). These are not simply observations about how imbalanced representations of gender are received by gamers, games journalists and games scholars, but this is also a commentary about how video game production remains wedded, in many quarters, to an uneven vision of gender politics.[7]

As Cassell and Jenkins observe, 'designers and critics alike have continued to find it difficult to avoid essentialising gender as designers seek to identify what types of games girls want to play and reformers seek to promote the kinds of games they think girls should be playing' (2008: 10). Furthermore, they assert that 'both sides have lost track of the fact that gender is a continuum rather than a set of binary oppositions: one is never going to design games that adequately reflect the tastes, interests, and needs of all girls' (2008: 10).

In her blog *Feminist Frequency*, Anita Sarkeesian tackles this subject through a series of posts called 'Tropes vs Women in Video Games', noting that when 'fictional female characters in games are dressed in impractical armor or clothing, it encourages players to view them as sex objects, and reinforces the already pervasive and harmful notion in our culture that sexualization is the most viable or only real route to power for women' (2016a). It is especially depressing to see this tactic of hypersexualization repeated given the unbounded representational potential of the animated form. Sarkeesian comments:

> Out of all the arguments that are tossed out to defend the impractical and objectifying clothing that women are made to wear in games, there is one in particular that I hear the most often and that is perhaps the most pernicious. That argument is: 'Maybe that's what she wants to wear!' Which is ridiculous. These women are fictional constructs. That means that they don't dress themselves or pick out their own clothing. [...] All these visual designs are deliberate choices made by the developers, and they serve a specific purpose: they communicate to straight male players that these characters exist primarily as sex objects to be consumed. In doing so, they also reinforce the larger notion in our culture that the value of real human women is determined largely by their sexual desirability to men. (2016a)

Beyond this demarcation of the female form as sexual site, Sarkeesian also turns her attention to the representational politics enacted in the workplace; in doing, Sarkeesian picks up, nearly two decades later, the mantle of Cassell and Jenkins, who in their 1998 edited collection placed a significant emphasis on providing a space for female voices from industry to be heard.

Sarkeesian also captured the fallout of the #womenaretoohardtoanimate hashtag that emerged following Ubisoft's 2014 E3 debut of *Assassin's Creed Unity*, at which Alexander Amancio (Creative Director) said that 'although there were originally plans to allow for female assassins, the development team couldn't add them because it would require "double the animations, double the voices, and double the visual assets"' (Sarkeesian 2016b). Here, it is the act of animation itself that is offered up as a gender-biased process, with the claim that one gender is easier to animate than another serving as a smokescreen for the wider failures of the industry and Ubisoft as a studio. This claim was roundly dismissed, with Jonathan Cooper, who had worked as an animator on *Assassin's Creed III* (2012) tweeting 'in my educated opinion, I would estimate this to be a day or two's work' (Cooper 2014), while Manveer Heir in characteristically provocative fashion paraphrased Amancio's sentiment as 'we don't really care to put the effort in to make a woman assassin' (Heir 2014). This is not an isolated example: Sarkeesian rightly highlights in her article 'Are Women Too Hard to Animate? Female Combatants' that it took EA twenty years to introduce female footballers in their hugely lucrative *FIFA* franchise, and it took Activision ten years to introduce female playable characters in their *Call of Duty* series. Clearly, significant work remains to be done, especially given the representational scope of the animated form.

Conclusion

Throughout this chapter we have considered how the study of animation provides new ways of intervening into the key issues of games studies. As a final remark, I would like to return to *Cuphead*, which at the time of writing feels like a genuinely significant moment in the shared history of animation and video games. Arguably, there is equal pleasure to be gained from experiencing *Cuphead* ludologically, as a gamer, as there is narratively, as a viewer. From a production perspective, *Cuphead* also serves as a reminder of the need to remain vigilant to the – intended/unintended – representational power of video game texts. Ultimately, by overtly calling attention to its animated surface *Cuphead* reminds gamers and viewers alike that without animation there could be no video game.

Notes

1 The historic distinction that has been made between video games (typically console based) and computer games (typically PC based) is becoming increasingly redundant, given the proliferation of electronic gaming platforms and the newfound multifunctionality of once dedicated devices (consoles such as the PS4 and Xbox One offer much more than just gaming). With this in mind, the more popular term 'video game' will be used as the shorthand to refer to both types of electronic games throughout this chapter.

2 For more on the subject of interactivity and distinctions between 'old'/analogue and 'new'/digital media see Manovich (2001 and 2013). For a discussion of the intersection of interactivity and mimesis within animated environments see Pallant (2015).

3 There is not the space to consider other salient subjects such as glitching, machinima, or recent alternate and virtual reality gaming developments, but hopefully this chapter will provide some solid foundations so that curious readers can continue to explore this topic. For more on glitching see Meades (2015), and for more on machinima see Ng (2013).

4 For an extensive discussion of the representational capabilities of animation see Wells (1998).

5 For a collection of perspectives on player agency within video games see: Wysocki (2013).

6 A recent survey (Campbell 2016) of the US Games Industry revealed 75 per cent of respondents identified as male, while a similar survey of the UK Games

Industry (Ramanan 2017) states that only 14 per cent of respondents identified as female.

7   There is not space in this chapter to fully retrace the #GamerGate outpouring, which dominated online discussion forums for over a year following a misogynistic blog post by Eron Gjoni about his game developer ex-girlfriend Zoë Quinn. For a more detailed account of this saga see: Golding and van Deventer (2016) and Quinn (2017).

References

Aarseth, E. (1997), *Cybertext: Perspectives on Ergodic Literature*, Baltimore, MD: Johns Hopkins University Press.

Aarseth, E. (2004), 'Genre Trouble: Narrativism and the Art of Simulation', in N. Wardrip-Fruin and P. Harrigan (eds), *First Person: New Media as Story, Performance, and Game*, 45–55, Cambridge, MA: The MIT Press.

Adams, E. (2013), *Fundamentals of Game Design*, Berkeley, CA: New Riders.

Amidi, A. (2013), 'If the Fleischer Studios Made a Videogame in the 1930s, It Would Look Like Cuphead', *Cartoon Brew*, 30 December. Available online: http://www.cartoonbrew.com/games/if-the-fleischer-studios-made-a-videogame-in-the-1930s-it-would-look-like-cuphead-93559.html (accessed 1 August 2017).

Bogost, I. (2010), *Persuasive Games: The Expressive Power of Videogames*, Cambridge, MA: MIT Press.

Bogost, I. (2015), *How to Talk about Videogames*, Minneapolis, MN: University of Minnesota Press.

Campbell, C. (2016), 'Survey Shows Game Industry Men Three Times More Likely to Earn Top Dollars than Women', *Polygon*, 12 September. Available online: https://www.polygon.com/2016/9/12/12891628/videogame-industry-salary-survey (accessed 10 December 2017).

Cassell, J. and H. Jenkins (1998), *From Barbie to Mortal Kombat: Gender and Computer Games*, Cambridge, MA: MIT Press.

Cole, J. (2017), 'Cuphead and the Racist Spectre of Fleischer Animation', *Unwinnable*, 10 November. Available online: https://unwinnable.com/2017/11/10/cuphead-and-the-racist-spectre-of-fleischer-animation/ (accessed 15 November 2017).

Cooper, J. (2014), 'In my Educated Opinion, I would Estimate this to be a Day or Two's Work. Not a Replacement of 8000 Animations', [Twitter], 11 June. Available online: https://twitter.com/gameanim/status/476638349097058304?lang=en (accessed 1 August 2017).

Csíkszentmihályi, M. (1975), *Beyond Boredom and Anxiety*, San Francisco, CA, Washington, WA and London: Jossey-Bass Publishers.

Eskelinen, M. (2001), 'The Gaming Situation', *Game Studies*, 2(1). Available online: http://www.gamestudies.org/0101/eskelinen/ (accessed 1 August 2017).

Eskelinen, M. (2004), 'Towards Computer Game Studies', in N. Wardrip-Fruin and P. Harrigan (eds.) *First Person: New Media as Story, Performance, and Game*, 36–44, Cambridge, MA: MIT Press.

Frasca, G. (1999), 'Ludology Meets Narratology: Similitude and Differences between (Video)games and Narrative', *Ludology.org*. Available online: http://www.ludology.org/articles/ludology.htm (accessed 1 August 2017).

Frasca, G. (2003), 'Simulation versus Narrative', in M. Wolf and B. Perron (eds) *The Video Game Theory Reader*, New York and London: Routledge.

Golding, D., and Van Deventer, L. (2016), *Game Changers: From Minecraft to Misogyny*, Melbourne: Affirm Press.

Guins, R. (2004), '"Intruder Alert! Intruder Alert!" Video Games *in* Space', *Journal of Visual Culture*, 3(2): 195–210.

Heir, M. (2014), 'We Don't Really Care to Put the Effort in to Make a Woman Assassin', #realrealityofgamedevelopment [Twitter], 11 June. Available online: https://twitter.com/manveerheir/status/476711390594752512 (accessed 1 August 2017).

Huizinga, J. (1949), *Homo Ludens: A Study of the Play-Element in Culture*, London, Boston and Henley: Routledge and Kegan Paul.

Jenkins, H. and J. Cassell (2008), 'From Quake Girls to Desperate Housewives: A Decade of Gender and Computer Games', in Y. Kafai, C. Heeter, J. Denner, and J. Sun (eds), *Beyond Barbie and Mortal Kombat: New Perspectives on Gender and Gaming*, 5–20, Cambridge, MA: MIT Press.

Juul, J. (2001), 'Games Telling Stories? – A Brief Note on Games and Narratives', *Game Studies*, 1(1). Available online: http://www.gamestudies.org/0101/juul-gts/ (accessed 1 August 2017).

Juul, J. (2005), *Half-Real: Video Games between Real Rules and Fictional Worlds – A Theory of Video Games*, Cambridge, MA: MIT Press.

Johnson, M. (2009), 'Interview: Inside Heavy Rain', *Spong*, 8 July. Available online: http://spong.com/feature/10109943/Interview-Inside-Heavy-Rain (accessed 1 August 2017).

Kennedy, H. (2002), 'Lara Croft: Feminist Icon or Cyberbimbo? On the Limits of Textual Analysis', *Game Studies*. 2(2). Available online: http://www.gamestudies.org/0202/kennedy/ (accessed 1 August 2017).

Kleinman, J. (2017), '"Cuphead": Why 1930s Animation Continues to Grip Contemporary Culture', *Rolling Stone*, 25 September. Available online: http://www.rollingstone.com/glixel/features/cuphead-and-the-surreal-influence-of-1930s-animation-on-modern-culture-w504847 (accessed 11 November 2017).

Kohler, C. (2016), 'Wired's Most Anticipated Videogames of 2016', *Wired*, 1 January. Available online: https://www.wired.com/2016/01/most-anticipated-games-2016/#slide-2 (accessed 1 August 2017).

Manovich, L. (2001), *The Language of New Media*, Cambridge, MA: MIT Press.

Manovich, L. (2013), *Software Takes Command*, London: Bloomsbury.

Meades, A. (2015), *Understanding Counterplay in Video Games*, New York: Routledge.

Ng, J. (2013), *Understanding Machinima: Essays on Filmmaking in Virtual Worlds*, New York: Bloomsbury.

Nooney, L. (2013), 'A Pedestal, A Table, A Love Letter: Archaeologies of Gender in Videogame History', *Game Studies*, 13(2). Available online: http://gamestudies.org/1302/articles/nooney (accessed 1 August 2017).

Pallant, C. (2015), *Animated Landscapes: History, Form and Function*, New York: Bloomsbury.

Quinn, Z. (2017), *Crash Override: How Gamergate (Nearly) Destroyed My Life, and How We Can Win the Fight against Online Hate*, New York: PublicAffairs.

Ramanan, C. (2017), 'The Video Game Industry Has a Diversity Problem – But It Can Be Fixed', *Guardian*, 15 March. Available online: https://www.theguardian.com/technology/2017/mar/15/video-game-industry-diversity-problem-women-non-white-people (accessed 10 December 2017).

Sarkeesian, A. (2016a), 'Lingerie Is Not Armor', *Feminist Frequency*, 6 June. Available online: https://feministfrequency.com/video/lingerie-is-not-armor/ (accessed 1 August 2017).

Sarkeesian, A. (2016b), 'Are Women Too Hard to Animate? Female Combatants', *Feminist Frequency*, 27 July. Available online: https://feministfrequency.com/video/are-women-too-hard-to-animate-female-combatants/ (accessed 1 August 2017).

Wells, P. (1998), *Understanding Animation*, London: Routledge.

Wysocki, M. (2013), *Ctrl-Alt-Play: Essays on Control in Video Gaming*, Jefferson, NC: McFarland.

PART THREE

Representation: Frames and Contexts

Introduction

As with all forms of visual media, animation raises questions of representation. Who is being represented, how and by whom? Animation's history is marked by problematically and pejoratively stereotypical representations along familiar lines including race, gender and sexuality. The questions raised about animation's (in)ability to represent diverse identities are explored in the chapters in this part across a range of historical, geographic and generic contexts, including race in early animation (Sammond) and contemporary TV animation (Loader), gender and sexuality (Dobson, Denison and Davis) and disability (Norris).

17

Race, Resistance and Violence in Cartoons

Nicholas Sammond

This is an abridged and edited excerpt from a chapter of Sammond's book, Birth of an Industry: Blackface Minstrelsy and the Rise of American Animation *(Durham, NC: Duke University Press 2015). The original chapter also covers additional key concepts and historical processes such as how a chattel slave (the imagined basis for blackface minstrels) has been considered an object, not a subject with agency. Another is the dynamic interplay between minstrel performers and their audiences, and how that dynamic carried into vaudeville and then early American animation. In minstrelsy, vaudeville and animation, audience members share a common experience of the performance instead of identifying with the star onscreen. This contributes to a sense of the cartoon character as both living and made, occupying a boundary between object and subject.*

The earliest days of American animation were relatively equal opportunity in their stereotyping of race, gender and ethnicity – caricaturing with gusto Africans, African Americans, the Chinese, Mexicans, Scots, Jews, the Irish, Germans and so on – parodies of Africans and African Americans, tied as they were to the vicious histories of slavery and segregation, offered a

This is an excerpt of Chapter 4 of *Birth of an Industry: Blackface Minstrelsy and the Rise of American Animation* (Durham, NC: Duke University Press, 2015). An online companion that features every piece of media discussed in the book from which this chapter is excerpted, and which discusses key concepts such as blackface minstrelsy, vaudeville and animation, may be found at http://scalar.usc.edu/works/birthofanindustry/index.

particularly virulent insult to human dignity and to the human bodies with which they were associated. In theory, European immigrants could expect to eventually assimilate into a generic American whiteness, while immigrants of Asian descent were sometimes afforded an uneasy accommodation as hardworking, clever and inscrutable – therefore nearly on a par with whites – in the eugenic hierarchies of the day (which has sadly continued to be the case in more recent quasi-scientific racial fantasies).[1] Other ethnic and racial stereotypes were subsumed slowly, in a process of grudging inclusion, and this only added further insult to the ongoing injury of white-black racism.[2] This is a difference not of degree but of kind, and cartoons have continued to be a place where the cruelty of the unredeemable stereotypes of blackness has found fertile ground for the ongoing expression of that distinction in animation.[3] Fantastic African American 'toons, whether minstrels or more direct racist caricatures, have performed a repetitive dream about the libidinous power of black bodies, and the desires and anxieties that attend that dream make those characters the targets of anxious violence – even as their very morphology constitutes an expression of the inherent violence of stereotyping itself.

To understand the transit and transformation of stereotypes, of racist caricatures and to appreciate them at a feeling level, one must attempt to situate one's self, and them, in the same historical frame. Performances of race and racial stereotype in American commercial animation have a distinct genealogy. Commercial animation at the beginning of the twentieth century turned to the minstrel stage to produce enduring continuing characters such as Felix, Krazy and Mickey. During the swing era, American cartooning looked to blackface's founding conceits, imagining the blackness of the minstrel as one link in an associative chain that stretched backward from the urban ghetto, through minstrelsy's fantastic plantation and on to an originary African jungle. When cartoons took up jazz they rendered an invisible world of (imagined) black culture visible, depicting jazz not just as a musical form but as a force able to produce an amalgamated embodiment of those three locations – the jungle, the plantation and the ghetto – a force that animated everyone and everything that dwelt there. For ostensibly white audiences, then, cartoons offered access to a forbidden territory of fear and desire, and the laughter they were meant to invoke is better understood, though not absolved, through a careful survey of that landscape.

The problem of understanding racism in American commercial animation is like that of discussing violence in cartoons more broadly. Generally, criticism of cartoon violence attempts to bracket it from the form itself, as if cartoons could simply be less violent and still be vital and interesting. This attitude ignores something that children and adults alike know and celebrate: animation, with its stretching, squashing and metamorphosis of bodies, relies on a certain abstract violence as an essential demonstration of its distinct formal properties, of what it does best and differently from live cinema, if not life itself. Likewise, the idea that cartoons could easily be evacuated of their racial overtones fails to attend to how fundamental those overtones have been to the social and cultural circumstances within which animation took form, to its understanding of the metaphysics of everyday life. And, finally, the blending of such racial and racist fantasies with animation's propensity for staging physically violent interactions with the human (or anthropomorphic) form itself isn't merely additive: racial stereotyping is a form of social violence that was often made literal through the visual iconography of animation. Cartoons have a conventional history of featuring misbehaving characters that beg to be disciplined by someone then to perform their unpleasure in the face of that discipline. In short, the (troubling) vibrancy associated with the cartoons of this period depends on a sadomasochistic racial fantasy that foregrounds the metamorphic qualities of the form, one that is played out again and again.

[...]Whether in the antics of *Bosko the Talk-Ink Kid* (1929–38) or in the swamp-bound parody of Harlem nightlife *Swing Wedding* (1937), again and again brutality is visited on ostensibly black bodies, whether they are physically assaulted or merely suffer the symbolic violence of grotesque caricature. And yet this racialized violence is performed in the service of a laugh, and in their manic pacing, jokes and visual ingenuity these cartoons may evoke laughter. The racist stereotypes that inform these sorts of cartoons emerged from a specific iconographic lexicon and have circulated in animation as commonplace expressions of contempt that dismiss the harm they express as ultimately harmless: in cartoons no one bleeds and no one dies. It's all good fun, and it's not really real. The intense affect of racism, instead of evincing either vicious malice or utter horror, is reduced to a joke, a double take, a gag and a disavowal.

[...]These early cartoons become a useful correlate for how black bodies were imagined by American popular and legal discourse at the beginning of the last century. The jokes that form the basis for racist cartoons are injurious because they participate in practices designed to inflict real injury and insult on specific people and to implicate others in inflicting that injury. They may be funny when we view them, not in the sadistic model that Freud elaborated in his earlier work on humour but from the vantage of his later work on empathy and shared affect.[4] In this view, the racist cartoons of the early to mid-twentieth century continue to be funny, not because today's audiences necessarily choose to continue to practice or suffer the active, overt racism that informed their making (though that may sometimes be true), but because the social and material struggles that underpin that racism are still very much alive. When approaching early American animation and its necessary involvement in contemporary racial formations, as well as its participation in overt racism – whether in the subtler racial codings that shaped enduring minstrel characters such as Krazy Kat or Mickey Mouse or in broader racist caricatures – delineating animation's varied uses of stereotype becomes a useful way to productively engage with this tension. This requires revisiting the performative and visual traditions of blackface minstrelsy popular at the birth of American animation, this time from the perspective of violence and humour.

Gentlemen please be seated:
Blackface and early animation

While a variety of racial and ethnic stereotypes facilitated the efficient shorthand of the gag in the early studio animation era, the metaphysics of the form favoured rather particular stereotypes of blackness in the form of the white gloves, wide eyes, voracious mouth and tricksterish resistance of the blackface minstrel. The fantastic and resistant form of the blackface minstrel was an embodied corollary to the plasmatic substance, the metamorphic form of the cartoon character, a being that could alter itself or its environment seemingly at will (and certainly at the will of its creator). Live minstrels lacked this total transformative power, but their transgressive nature and wilful resistance to the conditions of their making resonated with the metamorphic and disruptive qualities of the cartoon. The same racial formations that, in blackface minstrelsy, had positioned black bodies as in transit from the object status of slavery to (near) personhood – or as occupying both of those contradictory positions simultaneously – informed a logic of animation that saw in fantastic blackness a means to express the permeable boundary between the real and the ideal. The live blackface minstrel and the trademark cartoon character were cognates: both had the ability to cross boundaries – whether social or physical – if not to rewrite them altogether.

Yet animated minstrels did not simply replace their live counterparts. Blackface continued in vaudeville well into the 1920s, fading as vaudeville gave way to radio and the movies, but it experienced a brief renaissance in the late 1920s and early 1930s with the rise of popular two-man minstrel acts such as Miller and Lyles or Moran and Mack. Yet none of blackface's mediated forms – the minstrel show, vaudeville act, cartoon, live film, radio programme – simply replaced its predecessor. Their years of popularity overlapped, and one or more of these attractions could occupy the same stage in the same week – if not the same night.

Like the live minstrels before them, animated minstrel characters – Felix, Mickey, Bugs – were tricksters and interlopers at the boundary between the screen and the real, arising from a tradition of interplay with their creators and expressing a desire to escape two dimensions for the 3D world of their animators.[5] This was more than a matter of homology: the white gloves, big smile, and wide eyes that sat on a cartoon body (usually that of an animal) were the markers of minstrelsy. Likewise, the animated minstrels' *behaviours* – their resistance to both the animator-interlocutor who created them and to the physical strictures of animated space – underpinned both the fundamental gag structure of many an early animated short and the basic template of the trademarked continuing character. And like their live counterparts, animated minstrels performed a desirable and humorous irrationality that begged both admiration and punishment.

Eric Lott has described the minstrel's performance of imagined fantastic black characteristics as an act of 'love and theft', similar to what Stuart Hall calls the 'ambivalence of stereotype'.[6] This performance expressed (and expresses) a desire for an imagined liberation from social norms, one perversely located in subjugated bodies, a desire alloyed with a fear of the raw sensual power of those same bodies. Based as it was on a notion of the indolent and shifty slave, minstrelsy replicated a white fantasy of plantation life, of lazy African Americans wallowing in a sensual torpor, almost devoid of higher mental and moral functions, yet possessing an innate natural intelligence that made them crafty and sly. Torture, rape and forced labour – and all the institutions they supported and that supported them – were occluded in minstrelsy, leaving the rustic domesticity of the slave cabin. Saidiya Hartman has suggested that minstrelsy's playful show of resistance titillated precisely because of the threat of recriminatory violence at which it hinted.[7] On the minstrel stage blackness was not only abject but was also resistant, and these qualities were inextricably linked. The slave represented the nadir of labour's enthrallment to capital in an era when contract labour was called 'wage slavery' to signify its subordinate status. The minstrel, once removed from the slave, stood in for labour unchained: she/he was the slave who talked back, who resisted work in favour of carnal pleasure, whose very laziness was work wasted, a passive revolt[8]. (Likewise, the rakish yet absurd figure of the black urban dandy, such as Zip Coon or Jim Dandy, spoke both to a desire for fashion and style and for the incommensurate possibility of black cultural equality.)

In cartoons, that resistance was created for the purpose of its regulation. Christopher Lehman argues that following a revision to the Production Code, in animation 'slave figures receive[d] a more humane depiction ... and no cartoon produced after 1934 showed the whipping of slaves'.[9] This generous gesture, of course, did not apply to the violence inflicted on or by vestigial minstrel characters or to the implicit violence of the stereotypes themselves. The whip may have been removed, but the convention of animated characters violently disciplined for their rebelliousness had not. And, whether vestigial minstrel or racist caricature, cartoon characters in the 1930s encountered and engaged in increasing levels of violence – enthusiastic, exuberant violence – suffering incredible torments yet remaining, in the end, unscathed. [...]

Trader Mickey: The minstrel in the heart of darkness

The 1932 Disney short *Trader Mickey* performs this cyclical fantasy of resistance and violence explicitly. The cartoon follows a fairly standard format for early sound efforts: a minimal plot and a centrepiece musical production number highlight the wonders of the still relatively new technology of sync sound, and popular melodies and dance numbers play on the trends of the day. The story here is that Mickey Mouse and his dog, Pluto, are captured by cannibals and dance their way to freedom by playing on the natives' innate susceptibility to jazz rhythms. The film is significant not only for its inflection of the popular swing-era trope of jazz as 'jungle music' but also because Mickey's capture at the hands of these animated cannibals offers an instance of cultural contact between a blackface minstrel (Mickey) and the less oblique racist stereotypes that historically had informed the minstrel's libidinous, animalistic and uncivilized appeal. Reading a seemingly innocuous cartoon short, then, offers a shorthand look at the complex of race, violence and desire that charged fantasies of blackness in the early twentieth-century United States. It also provides an avenue for understanding how the figure of the minstrel became so embedded in animation during its silent era that by the time of Mickey's arrival in 1928, a direct association between trademark cartoon characters and blackface minstrels was fading into a set of conventions that maintained a less direct relationship to (an imagined) blackness. Trademark cartoon characters such as Mickey were becoming vestigial minstrels, carrying all (or many) of the markers of minstrelsy while rarely referring directly to the tradition itself.[10]

[...] Reinscribing Mickey and his fellow cartoon tricksters as minstrels, however, is not a mere act of (empty and symbolic) reparation; it is an effort to place the often marginalized but always extremely popular form of the animated cartoon short more firmly into a historically specific racial matrix that included the vaudeville stage, the minstrel show, the world's fair midway native village and the black-and-tan review – all of which, within a complex, varied and sometimes contradictory fabric of discourse, produced, contested and regulated race relations on the ground.[11] Beyond revealing the racial (and racist) foundations of beloved animated characters, the point of understanding those characters as minstrels is, first, to witness how stereotypical ideas that were considered increasingly unacceptable in one forum could pass relatively unnoticed in another. Yet beyond that, seeing Mickey, Bugs and Daffy as minstrels permits a more nuanced and detailed picture of animation as a fantastic, violent and excessive popular art form.

Framed by that history, *Trader Mickey* is an interstitial object that brings the conventions of blackface minstrelsy undergirding American animation into conversation with the violent and excessive racist caricatures that crowded the jazz-inflected cartoons of early sound cinema. So, witnessing the difference between the minstrel and the racist caricature in this cartoon may serve to alienate a few of the practices we have come to see as natural in animation – particularly its tendency towards excessive yet seemingly inconsequential violence. *Trader Mickey* describes the difference between the animate minstrel and racist caricature, and the cartoon illustrates how the minstrel's intimate associations with voice, silence and violence made it an appropriate avatar for the artisan animator increasingly constrained within an industrializing art form. [...]

Trader Mickey opens on Mickey and Pluto cruising upriver in a ramshackle paddle-wheel steamer loaded with cargo, passing hippos and crocodiles, their mouths agape. Mickey is perched atop his cargo, merrily plucking away at a banjo. Within a few shots, this seemingly harmless cartoon confection has presented us with a wealth of information. Making his way into the heart of darkness a year after *Trader Horn* (1931), in the same year as *Frank Buck's Bring 'Em back Alive* (1932), and several years before the onset of the tropical kitsch of Trader Vic, Mickey plays a trader in Africa like a vaudevillian donning a loosely fitting costume.[12] A trader of what? His makeshift boat is loaded with some sort of goods, but we are not sure for what (or whom) he expects to trade them before he heads home on his return voyage. The paddle wheel on his boat could just as easily signal the old South as a colonial adventure in an African rain forest. To be blunt: at best Mickey plays a dry-goods merchant working the byways of some colonial interzone; at worst he is slave-trader Mickey, and his trade is in the savage bodies he is soon to encounter. As a minstrel he is neither fully white nor fully black; as an anthropomorphic mouse, neither fully animal nor human: he is a liminal figure in a liminal zone.

In *Trader Mickey*, Africa, the originary locus of the black slave body collapses into the putative site of its eventual forced labour, the South. This is not so much an act of pentimento as the generation of a continuous alternative space of subjugation: one of a number of representations that imagined the Old South as symbolically contiguous with Africa (and in the jazz age, with Harlem), the film posits (or accepts) a fantastic geography based on race. Blackness simultaneously signifies the plantation and the jungle. This repeats one of the foundational conceits of minstrelsy. Early minstrel performers often framed their shows as anthropological reports: visiting the plantation they had witnessed the primitive dances of enslaved Africans (barely removed from the jungle) and were pleased and privileged to reproduce them for audiences distanced by geographical location and/or cosmopolitanism from their meanings.[13] Black or white, but always in blackface, minstrel performers were sometimes called 'delineators', as if what they performed were less a representation and more a re-presentation. The woolly wigs, burnt cork and greasepaint that delineated the head, eyes and mouth of the minstrel were only the beginning, as were the gloves that increasingly became a trademark of the form as the nineteenth century progressed.

What were delineated as well were dances, songs, speech patterns and the jumbled and confused thoughts of a primitive savage attempting to communicate in the tongue of his master – the mangling of which revealed both the limited intellect of the minstrel and the social and political contradictions inhabiting the common sense of the day. Lampooning the pretentions of the 'civilized' set, the banter between interlocutor and end men and the stump speech revelled in contradiction, performing through playful inversions a coded ressentiment.[14] [...]

The blackface minstrel, as stand-in for the chattel slave (or for his northern counterpart, the free but not fully assimilated black man), embodies the outside: as an object he is outside the flow of history; paradoxically his containment on the plantation places him outside free society. He exists on the margins of cognition, speech and action, yet that seems to be a privileged vantage point from which he converts institutional and immediate violence on his body into violence against common sense. Likewise, Mickey Mouse, as a made object granted a sentience and agency constantly in danger of being limited, doubles that liminal condition as a minstrel: he is doubly dislocated. In its verbal form, blackface minstrelsy performed the deformation and metamorphosis of language that cartoons would render visually in silent, 'plasmatic' form for their first fifteen years; with the coming of sound they would also admit the fast-paced patter of Bugs Bunny or Daffy Duck.

But more than just (dis)location connects *Trader Mickey* to minstrelsy. As he chugs upriver, Mickey is happily strumming a raggedy tune on his banjo, and this isn't the first time he has played music specifically associated with the minstrel stage. In his first outing in sync sound, *Steamboat Willie* (1928), Mickey played the minstrel standard 'Old Zip Coon' (also known as 'Turkey in the Straw') on the bodies of various farm animals as *that* steamboat made its way upriver.[15] Although *Steamboat Willie* is often erroneously celebrated as the first sound cartoon, rarely do those accolades mention its indebtedness to the minstrel stage for its sonic performance.[16] So in *Trader Mickey* the mouse is, quite simply and quite reasonably, a minstrel travelling steadily towards the headwaters of the tradition that spawned him. It is not just the happy strumming that signals him as such, though: Mickey sports the uniform of white gloves, black face, exaggerated mouth and wide eyes that marked both the popular animated characters of the day and their progenitor, the blackface minstrel. But beyond those obvious physical markers, he also performs the minstrel's traditional role of the trickster, the imp who operates on the margins of social and material convention and who embodies significant destructive and productive powers. He is a force of disruption – albeit one somewhat tamed by an emerging Disney aesthetic that increasingly eschewed extremes in favour of a performed moderate wholesomeness. Yet as that force he exists in a world of hurt, an animated cosmos in which incredible violence circulates through seemingly indestructible bodies, visiting itself on hero and villain alike.

Here and elsewhere, Mickey is more than just a trickster, a lord of misrule. As a minstrel, he is an indexical marker, a gesture towards the Old South, the plantation and slavery. Epitomized by minstrelsy's end men, Tambo and Bones, the minstrel did more than signify a generic African American body; she/he even invoked more than an enslaved African American. The body to which the minstrel referred and which informed the trickster figure of the trademark cartoon character – Mickey, Felix, Ko-Ko, Oswald and so on – was one that recalled the recalcitrant slave who, through an artful combination of stereotyped laziness, cunning and the performance of a studied ignorance, attempted to avoid the forced labour and regimes of punishment that were the lot of chattel slavery. For the central tropes of minstrelsy – the singing and dancing, the stump speech, good-naturedly misdirecting the interlocutor – all derived from the necessary fantasy of the slave as a creature closer in the natural chain of being to the (equally stubborn) mule or the cunning Br'er Rabbit.[17] This figure purportedly felt less pain than her/his white counterpart and was naturally inclined to hard physical labour in the open air. [...]

It was not just the capering of Tambo, Bones or Mickey that afforded audiences pleasure, but the very association of those characters, however attenuated, with the enslaved body, the system of chattel slavery and the larger racial hierarchy it embodied. This pleasure could be described as sadistic, deriving from the forced subjection of others. At the same time, though, according to Hartman, it was in witnessing minstrelsy's systematic and distanced performance of the institution of slavery that the black body became sensible as fixed in a natural order, an order through which one's own humanity might be affirmed if one were (able) to identify as white.[18] Blackface minstrelsy celebrated the black body as outside of and resistant to (white) civilization. Through that body's very necessary subjugation and its subsequent defiance of that civilization the minstrel delineated polite society's very humorous foibles and failings.

That in blackface minstrelsy this performance was often offered by a white man in blackface only added to its frisson. One could, watching this performance, participate in the subjugation and exchange of another person at a distance, visiting that economic and social control on a body simultaneously white and black. Like a sadomasochistic act, this pleasure combined the performance of subjection with the fantasy that its objects willingly entered into it, that the subjection was as pleasurable in its own right to the masochist as it was to the sadist. In those not infrequent cases of black performers blacking up in order to gain access to the stage (and a livelihood), the pleasure of witnessing subjection and an engagement in that system of domination was asserted even over ostensibly free black bodies. The black performer seemed to willingly yield to a system of signification that made reference to his or her own (potential) enslavement, in order to perform that enslavement as the positive condition of the happy darky. 'In this regard', Hartman argues, 'the donning of blackface restaged the seizure and possession of the black body for the other's use and enjoyment. The culture of cross-racial identification facilitated in minstrelsy cannot be extricated from the relations of chattel slavery.'[19]

In *Trader Mickey*, the mouse is inextricably entangled in those relations. When Trader Mickey sets foot on the riverbank and slaps his feet on the mud of the Mississippi/Congo, he is met by a tribe of ravening cannibals, led by a buffoonish king who can't stop laughing.[20] Mouse and dog are seized, and Mickey is thrown into a pot and prepped for cooking, while the king and his tribesmen sort through the items he has brought to trade with them.

Oddly, they find that much of Mickey's stock consists of trumpets, trombones, tubas and the like – the instruments for a jazz band. Mystified, the grotesquely caricatured cannibals try to play them and end up only injuring the instruments, themselves and others. But from this moment on the cartoon performs a continuum of animate being. Although the instruments are inanimate, they still strike back at the cannibals when abused. Similarly, in later scenes the natives will play not only the instruments but each other. In other words, both cannibals and trombones are relatively animate instruments. Plastic beyond the usual bounds of their being, their interaction reveals a mutual instrumentality, a common primitive bond. More tool than human, they share a certain happy deformability, and while each is instrument to the other, all are instruments to those above them.

Eventually, Mickey grabs an alto saxophone and begins playing, and of course the natives can't help but dance. That dance will bond the trader and cannibals under the sign of rhythm, which the fantastic black body, true to stereotype, cannot possibly resist. The tune Mickey belts out sets off a medley of standards that signify both the Harlem demimonde and the Old South, including 'St. James Infirmary Blues' and 'Darktown Strutters Ball'. Suddenly, even though the cannibals continue to play their instruments incorrectly, the tune is clear, and the audience witnesses a full-blown production number with Mickey and the savage king as its costars. This production number, which is the centrepiece of the cartoon, literalizes the fantasy of jazz as 'jungle music', replete with the thrills of cannibalism, upriver crossed with uptown. But Africa, Harlem and the South are not the only realms invoked in this number. Mickey and his captors blithely make use of the copious human bones that litter the village, playing them like percussion instruments, using them to adorn costumes, dancing atop piles of skulls: mass death is everywhere even as everyone happily rollicks their way through the Black Bottom and the Charleston. This visual iconography also placed African American social and cultural life in an underworld teeming with death and violence, fusing the seemingly innate joyousness of the natives to their ever-present chthonic threat.

[...]

Yet *Trader Mickey* goes further. As the natives dance and play, small details flit across the screen. Many of the cannibals wear bracelets and anklets with an odd extra ring as if they are shackles. It is a fleeting and random image, equally suggestive of an escape from bondage as of being ready for chains linking the ostensibly black body with slavery, of being both subject and chattel. As if this offhand gesture weren't enough some of the natives dance and play their instruments on all fours as if they were prehuman missing links. Here the anthropomorphism of the classic cartoon takes on a more subtle gradation: while somehow Mickey, an oversized mouse, is the most civilized creature present, the apparently African natives, who are meant to read as human, gambol apelike, playing their instruments with equal ease with either their hands or feet.

Yet even within the social order of the cannibals there are necessary gradations of humanity. At the high end of the spectrum, both the king and the chef, like Mickey, wear the white gloves of the minstrel. A chain of being presents itself in the dance number, which, like a minstrel show, is performed face-forward, and in many of the shots the characters clearly acknowledge their audience. This performance describes a developmental timeline that begins at the protohuman – the cannibals not yet upright – continues to natives on two legs and then on to those who have donned the minstrel gloves but are still savage, and ends at Mickey, an anthropomorphic minstrel mouse who dances for his life – and towards a civilization he will never fully occupy.

It would be enough to point out that this voracious dance of life, death and dirty blues produces a sadomasochistic fantasy in which ostensibly black bodies are so steeped in their own physicality, their own animal nature, that they revel in a world in which pain is an unremarkable part of a celebration of a sensual yet inherently incoherent life. It would be enough to point out that this particular cartoon hints at that primal fantasy about which Hartman speaks, one that traces the minstrel body back to the quasi-animal realm of the African native, and that it further implicates that minstrel figure in the slave trade. (For, again, what do the natives have that Mickey would want?) It isn't hard to read the cartoon as another in a long line of cinematic and performative fantasies in which the very nature of blackness masochistically invites its own torment.

But noting one more node in a matrix of fantasies about the African or African American body as a missing link between a white modern humanity and its roots among the apes does not tell the whole tale; nor does it fully account for the anxious violence that attends the cartoon minstrel. In addition to recapitulating a fantastic primate taxonomy, *Trader Mickey* also illustrates the minstrel's relationship to the slave as chattel, object and tool. What the landscape of the cannibal village reveals (and this is also true of animation in general) is that no body, no thing, is completely human or completely an autonomous subject. Because they are animated, and because they are located on a taxonomic continuum from the ape to the minstrel, every thing and person in the cartoon, up to and including Mickey, has the potential to be a useful object for anyone else in the cartoon. Of course, Mickey, being more civilized, is more likely to use than to be used, but this becomes assured only after he has deployed jazz to sublimate the brute force of the cannibals into song and dance. [...]

This is the fetishistic magic of animation: any object in an animated world has the potential to come to life, and any living thing or even one of its body parts may be reduced to an object. Subjectivity is ephemeral and uncertain, granted by external circumstances and revocable. Thus, while *Trader Mickey* allows for the neat turn of providing a primer on the fantastic relationship between the savage and the minstrel, a compressed history of minstrelsy's anthropological conceit, Mickey would still be a minstrel, his subject status still contingent, regardless of whether he were threatened by cannibals. He was a minstrel before and after this particular cartoon. What this scenario permits is a study in contrasts: the cannibals are classic racist caricatures, but they are not minstrels. They do not obtain the status of pretenders to civilization because they have not yet bought into (or, more accurately, been sold into) relations of exchange. Mickey on the other hand, as a trader in goods (and perhaps people), has. As a minstrel, Mickey embodies the animator's alienated labour: like the blackface minstrel who enacts the imperfect resistance of the recalcitrant slave, he may take pleasure in his rebellion, but he will never fully realize its fruits.[21] As a commodity that lives and works, Mickey enacts the fantastic relationship between property and labour, and in this, of never being fully the owner of his own self or his labour power. Minstrelsy is instrumentalism illustrated: the end men Tambo and Bones are both characters put on by their performers and the personification of the instruments they play, the tambourine and the bones: they are essentially instruments playing instruments.[22] All are subject to the whims of the animator, who in turn is subject to those of the producer ... in this case, Walt Disney. A chain of being is also a chain of abuse, stretching from the real to the fantastic, from Burbank to 'deepest Africa'. [...]

Conclusion

Is such a historical and instrumental explanation of the genealogy of the racist practices in animation that led from the minstrel to the more racist caricatures of the sound era exculpatory? No, and that's not the point. The point might be the specific historical relationship between racist stereotypes and the humour that some people found or find in them. According to Dave

Fleischer, Cab Calloway fell to his knees and rolled on the ground in hysterics when he saw the Fleischers' rotoscoped rendition of him singing 'Minnie the Moocher' as a ghostly walrus.[23] But Calloway's purported willingness to laugh at himself being reproduced as a 'spook' is not an absolution, any more than the widespread. African American acceptance of *Amos 'n Andy* in the late 1920s and 1930s is an indication of the accuracy or goodwill of the programme's depiction of African American life.[24] [...]

In such unresolved contradictions lurks the intense affect that charges racist laughter – an affect that policing does not undo. Veteran Disney animator Dick Huemer, was shocked by the suggestion that the crows he animated for *Dumbo* (1941), one of which was actually named Jim Crow, were racist caricatures and responded that the 'colored' choir that had voiced most of them 'liked it very much and enjoyed doing it hugely [...] I don't think the crow sequence is derogatory ... when someone mentioned the possibility to me, I was quite taken aback'.[25] Yet the impulse to situate this work in relation to race, and sometimes to rationalize it, has been no less true in animation than elsewhere. In conversation, some animation collectors and historians have readily agreed that the white gloves, broad mouths and overly large eyes that are standard for many animated characters derive from blackface minstrelsy.[26] Yet, a breath later, they have insisted that early animators' adoption of minstrelsy became sedimented in famous continuing characters for purely practical reasons: First, there was an issue of contrast: in the early days of animation, when the quality of film stock, cels and lighting was uneven, black bodies were easier to register than white ones. (To fully accept this answer, we have to overlook all of the early 'white' continuing characters, such as Hecza Liar, Bobby Bumps and Dreamy Dud, who are somehow less well remembered today than their minstrel counterparts.) Second, economy: white gloves on a four-fingered hand meant less repetitive detail to draw, since hands were hard to render well. (This, of course, contradicts the argument for contrast, even as it appeals to efficiency.) Third, clarity: the large eyes and mouths and broad gestures were more emotionally expressive, which was important in the short form. Somehow, these technical limitations required recourse to blackface minstrelsy.

So, yes, indeed and yes, but: one explanation does not contradict another. Exploring a forbidden terrain where images and gags might be racist and funny, it becomes possible to understand that these sorts of practical explanations are all at least historically valid, and that the practices they explain (away) were still grounded in racist institutions and discourses. They are historically reasonable in that they may have served as rational explanations given by animators at the time their cartoons were made, but that would not exempt them from the racial formations in which they lived and worked. That animators from the early twentieth century may have lacked the critical discourses available to animators today (i.e. that 'they didn't think of what they were doing as racist') does not immediately mean that the choices they made were not of a piece with racial and racist discourses of the time.

But it is sometimes difficult to raise this point, that racist attitudes were the coin of the realm for ostensibly white artists and audiences of the day, because it seems to suggest a maliciously racist intentionality (or duplicity) on the part of the discursive founders of animation and their patrons. And if that were so, it would require good people to disavow those cartoons as wrong, and not at all entertaining. It would certainly be enough to argue that broad racist caricatures and the use of the vestigial elements of minstrelsy point to black stereotyping as underpinning early animation practices. Accepting this, it becomes more valuable to read the presence of racial and racist formations in the emergence of American animation in discursive, institutional or structural terms rather than in personal ones. Whether any specific animator was or was not intentionally racist, the practices that animators by necessity entered into were, and that is worth noting. But it becomes a more significant exercise to explore how racial animus in animation was important to the joke itself, how the 'ambivalence of stereotype', the imbrication of intense fear and desire in the same derisive image, alloyed fear of racial difference with desire for that difference.[27] [...]

In his study of American animation, 7 Minutes, Norman Klein suggests: 'Blacks in musical comedy had so powerful a meaning in American entertainment, and they were so often played by whites themselves, they almost transcended the issue of race itself. Almost, but certainly never entirely. To say "almost" merely captures the sense of how important "blackface" was to the cartoon form'.[28] Klein admits to the centrality of African American music and dance, and of blackface minstrelsy, in the development of cartoons in the United States, but he does not explore exactly why race and minstrelsy so deeply informed the art and craft of animation. Nor does he quite explain the incredible tension in his surprising use of the word 'almost'. Perhaps we can understand it by considering the ambiguity hiding in the use of 'they' in the same passage. At first, it seems that Klein is speaking of the incredible influence of actual African Americans on the development of an (implicitly white) American entertainment. Yet as his thought unwinds, we discover that some of these influential blacks were actually whites in blackface and that being authentically black seems to be not about race but about performance, a performance rooted in the material world but leading inexorably away from it. The cartoon minstrel was almost real, almost uncontainable in its contradiction. The white hand of the animator created in that animated minstrel a compulsion to rebel against the conditions of its making, and destined it to fail in that rebellion. And if that makes for laughter, then that laughter is complicated; it is sometimes nervous and hesitant. Other times, it is raucous with guilty pleasure. As with its audiences, it is many and various. But it always begs the question of who is laughing, and how. The cartoon minstrel depended (and depends) for its vitality on the constant collapse of that distinction between figure and fantasy over which many a critic has stumbled over the years and it argues for a gentle reminder that behind each and every subject lurks a howling object much like ourselves, one that we might laugh *with*, rather than *at*.

Notes

1   For discussions of the relationship between immigration, assimilation and fantasies of blackness, see, for instance, Michael Rogin, *Blackface, White Noise: Jewish Immigrants in the Hollywood Melting Pot* (Berkeley, CA: University of California Press, 1996); David Roediger, *The Wages of Whiteness: Race and the Making of the American Working Class* (New York: Verso, 1991), and *Towards the Abolition of Whiteness: Essays on Race, Politics, and Working Class History* (New York: Verso, 1994); Eric Lott, *Love and Theft: Blackface Minstrelsy and the American Working Class* (New York: Oxford University Press, 1993); Daphne Brooks, *Bodies in Dissent: Spectacular Performances of Race and Freedom, 1850–1910* (Durham, NC: Duke University Press, 2006). For discussions of stereotype and fantasy, see, for instance, Stuart Hall, 'Racist Ideologies and the Media', in Paul Marris and Sue Thornham (eds), *Media Studies: A Reader* (New York: New York University Press, 2000), and 'Stereotyping as a Signifying Practice', in Hall (ed.), *Representation: Cultural Representations and Signifying Practices* (London: Sage, 1997); Richard Iton, *In Search of the Black Fantastic: Politics and Popular Culture in the Post–Civil Rights Era* (London: Oxford University Press, 2010); or James C. Davis, *Commerce in Color: Race, Consumer Culture and American Literature, 1893–1933* (Ann Arbor, MI: University of Michigan Press, 2007).

2   For an overview of eugenics in the United States, see Wendy Kline, *Building a Better Race: Gender, Sexuality, and Eugenics from the Turn of the Century to the Baby Boom* (Berkeley, CA: University of California Press, 2001); or Laura L. Lovett, *Conceiving the Future: Pronatalism, Reproduction, and the Family in the United States, 1890–1938* (Durham, NC: University of North Carolina Press, 2007). For a relatively recent example of a eugenic argument, see Richard J. Herrnstein and Charles Murray, *The Bell Curve: Intelligence and Class Structure in American Life* (New York: Free Press, 1994). For the ongoing potency of this discourse, see Sam Roberts, 'A Nation of None and All of the Above', *New York Times,* 16 August 2008.

3   See Jacqueline Najuma Stewart, *Migrating to the Movies: Cinema and Black Urban Modernity* (Berkeley, CA: University of California Press, 2005), 23–90; and Alice Maurice, *The Cinema and Its Shadow: Race and Technology in Early Cinema* (Minneapolis, MN: University of Minnesota Press, 2013), ch. 1. For an intelligent discussion of racism in early cartoons, see Jeet Heer, 'Racism as a Stylistic Choice and Other Notes', *Comics Journal* 301 Online (Web. Posted 14 March 2011).

4   Compare Sigmund Freud, 'The Relation of Jokes to Dreams and to the
     Unconscious', in *Freud, Jokes and Their Relation to the Unconscious*, trans.
     and ed. James Strachey (New York: Penguin Books, 1991 [1905]), with
     Sigmund Freud, 'Humor', in *Freud, Art and Literature*, ed. James Strachey,
     trans. Joan Riviere (New York: Penguin Books, 1990 [1928]), discussed here.
     For a discussion of this comparison, to which space does not permit a detailed
     reply, see Simon Critchley, *On Humor* (London: Routledge, 2002). For the
     sake of argument, Freud's 1928 essay collapses humour and joking somewhat,
     considering the similarities more important to the topic than the differences.
     It is important to note that in the earlier work, Freud does discuss empathy
     (see *Jokes and Their Relation to the Unconscious*, 239–59). However, that
     discussion centres more on naïve utterances, especially by children, and on
     jokes in which a lack of ill intent on the part of the teller is assumed.

5   The association between minstrels and trademark animated characters is
     long standing. Even in the sound era, as Lehman points out, that relationship
     continued: 'Iwerks also adapted Sambo and company to the animation trends
     of the mid-1930s. Sambo looks and acts just like Mickey Mouse – hardly a
     surprise, given that Iwerks helped to create the mouse. The boy is dressed in
     short pants and huge oval shoes just like Mickey's'; Christopher Lehmann,
     *The Colored Cartoon: Black Presentation in American Animated Short Films,
     1907–1954* (Amherst, MA: University of Massachusetts Press, 2007), 54.

6   Lott, *Love and Theft*, 38–63; Hall, 'Racist Ideologies'.

7   Saidiya Hartman, *Scenes of Subjection: Terror, Slavery, and Self-Making in
     Nineteenth-Century America* (New York: Oxford University Press, 1997), 29.

8   For a discussion of torture and humour in relation to the American conquest
     of Iraq, see Schuyler Henderson, 'Disregarding the Suffering of Others:
     Narrative, Comedy, and Torture', *Literature and Medicine*, vol. 24 no. 2, Fall
     2005, pp. 181–208.

9   Lehman, *Colored Cartoon*, 47.

10   One example of a Mickey Mouse short that makes direct reference to
     minstrelsy is *Mickey's Mellerdrammer* (1933). One can also read the early
     Warner Bros. Bosko shorts as intentional minstrel performances.

11   See Brooks, *Bodies in Dissent*; Wesley Brown, *Darktown Strutters* (Amherst,
     MA: University of Massachusetts Press, 2000); Knight, *Disintegrating the
     Musical*; Karen Sotiriopoulos, *Staging Race: Black Performers in Turn of
     the Century America* (Cambridge, MA: Harvard University Press, 2006);
     and Louis Chude-Sokei, *The Last 'Darky': Bert Williams, Black-on-Black
     Minstrelsy, and the African Diaspora* (Durham, NC: Duke University Press,
     2006).

12   Coincidentally, the Frank Buck films were produced by animation studio head
     Amedee Van Beuren.

13   This broad-stroke history admits many variations and contradictions. T. D.
     Rice claimed to have learned to 'jump Jim Crow' from an old, perhaps
     disabled, stable hand who may or may not have been a former slave; likewise,
     Zip Coon was a fantasy of the northern black dandy whose pretensions

ostensibly revealed the overreaching and uncivilizable nature of some African Americans. See, for example, Dale Cockrell, *Demons of Disorder: Early Blackface Minstrels and Their World* (New York: Cambridge University Press, 1997), 62–138. For discussion of the anthropological conceit, see Lott, *Love and Theft*, 38–62. See also Hans Nathan, 'The Performance of the Virginia Minstrels', in Annemarie Bean, James Hatch and Brooks McNamara (eds), *Inside the Minstrel Mask: Readings in Nineteenth-Century Blackface Minstrelsy* (Middletown, CT: Wesleyan University Press, 1996); or W. T. Lhamon, *Jump Jim Crow: Lost Plays, Lyrics, and Street Prose of the First Atlantic Popular Culture* (Cambridge, MA: Harvard University Press, 2003), 31.

14 Fredric Jameson, *The Political Unconscious* (London: Routledge, 1983), 172–193. See also Peter Stallybrass and Elon Whyte, *The Politics and Poetics of Transgression* (London: Methuen, 1986), for a discussion of the carnivalesque and coded resistance.

15 Mickey also makes use of the tune in *The Shindig* (1930). By 1935, it is Donald Duck who plays it as he disrupts Mickey's rendition of the *William Tell* Overture in *The Band Concert*.

16 As has often been noted, the film was not the first sound cartoon, merely the first cartoon to successfully demonstrate the potential of synchronized sound (and to link that performance to an effective public relations campaign). Of particular note were experiments by the Fleischer brothers in sound animation that predated Disney's work by several years. Yet in efforts such as their Song Car-Tunes and Screen Songs, the Fleischers also relied on standards from the vaudeville and minstrel stages, encouraging audiences to sing along by following the bouncing ball to songs such as 'Dixie', 'My Old Kentucky Home', 'Sleepy Time Down South' and 'Old Black Joe'.

17 For a contemporary example that makes a visual analogy between mules and African Americans, see *I Am a Fugitive from a Chain Gang* (LeRoy 1932). For Br'er Rabbit, see Joel Chandler Harris, *Uncle Remus and His Legends of the Old Plantation* (London: David Bogue, 1881).

18 Hartman, *Scenes of Subjection*, 31.

19 Hartman, *Scenes of Subjection*, 31–32. For discussion of the intersection of this racial dynamic with the emerging class politics of the nineteenth and early twentieth centuries, see Lott, *Love and Theft;* or Roediger, *Wages of Whiteness.*

20 The figure of the 'laughing coon' was extremely popular with white audiences in the early days of the twentieth century. See Laura Wexler, '"Laughing Ben" on "The Old Plantation"', in Elizabeth Abel and Leigh Raiford, eds, 'Photography and Race Forum', in *English Language Notes*, vol. 44 no. 2, fall/winter 2006. See also O'Meally, 'Checking Our Balances', 282. For a fictional interpretation of laughter as violence and violence averted, see Brown, *Darktown Strutters.*

21 The same may be said for 'free' or 'northern' minstrel characters such as Zip Coon or Jim Dandy. They may pretend to civilization, but the joke is premised on their falling short of the mark.

22 In this light, Ko-Ko's efforts to draw himself independent of Max's hand or Felix's use of his tail to reinscribe his landscape speak of (failed) attempts to claim possession of their selves as useful and independent objects/agents.

23 Joe Adamson, '"Where Can I Get a Good Corned Beef Sandwich?"': An Oral History of Dave Fleischer', 1969, 78, American Film Institute Oral History Project (now housed in the University of California, Los Angeles, Oral History Project).

24 See Ely, *Adventures of Amos 'n' Andy*; or Knight, *Disintegrating the Musical*.

25 Jim Crow was voiced by Cliff Edwards, a vaudeville performer who sometimes did a blackface minstrel act. Huemer, quoted in Joe Adamson, 'With Disney on Olympus: An Interview with Dick Huemer', *Funnyworld*, vol. 17, 1978, pp. 37–43.

26 Conversation with Ray Pointer, July 2006; conversation with Jerry Beck, August 2007. See also Klein, *7 Minutes*, 192–99.

27 Hall, 'Racist Ideologies'.

28 Klein, *7 Minutes*, 192.

18

We're Asian. More Expected of Us: The Model Minority and Whiteness in *King of the Hill*

Alison Reiko Loader

Focusing on the TV animated series King of the Hill, *Loader considers how the show represents Asian American identities as well as whiteness and masculinity in an article first published in 2006. Arguing that the series both reifies and challenges stereotypes, Loader here also considers the function of comedy and satire, ultimately arguing that animation can offer unique ways of representing difference.*

Representation, the model minority and whiteness in *King of the Hill*

During its thirteen-season run from 1997 to 2009, *King of the Hill* was the second longest running animated series in US television history (after *The Simpsons*). Co-created by Mike Judge of MTV's *Beavis and Butthead* and *Simpson*'s writer Greg Daniels, the now-syndicated Emmy Award-winning show features white, suburban, lower-middle-class life in small-town Texas. Central to the show are nuanced explorations of class, gender, sexuality and race, and most specifically 'whiteness' in its southwestern rural form. Glenn

Berger explains, 'For most of the country, it's a really cool, smart show about people they know. For New York and L.A., it's like an anthropological study' (Werts 2001).

In an article written for the *New York Times Magazine*, Matt Bai (2005) urges 'politicians and pundits' to watch *King of the Hill* as a way to 'understand the values of conservative America', noting that the 'subtle and complex portrayal of small-town voters' has consistently drawn support from Middle America. Ethan Thompson (2009: 3) describes the series as one that 'engages cultural change as narrative content' and contends that the programme focuses on character consistency and a 'greater attention to regional detail as a route to realism' (2009: 7). The programme operates without what Jonathan Gray (2006: 50) terms 'the amnesia of sitcom memory' with storylines (and injuries) often spanning multiple episodes. Furthermore, *King of the Hill* generally refrains from the deconstructive surrealism typical of *The Simpsons, Family Guy* or *South Park*. For example, there are no aliens, no talking dogs and no singing excrement. Although characters are crudely drawn and barely age, they are based on realistic human proportions and they often look more like 'real' people than many of the styl(iz)ed, sculpted and surgically enhanced actors from live-action television.

The series' central character is Hank Hill, a well-meaning but uptight propane salesman. He lives with his wife Peggy, a somewhat conceited substitute Spanish teacher and Boggle champion, and their son Bobby, an overweight pubescent who dreams of being a prop comic. Central to the series' overarching narrative is Hank's struggle to accept his son's unabashed and often gleeful resistance to normative masculine interests. Perhaps reflecting the concerns of its producers and 'mainstream' target audience, *King of the Hill* is primarily about the challenges of being a straight, middle-aged white guy.

Next door to Hank, Peggy and Bobby, live the Souphanousinphones – Kahn, Minh and Kahn Jr. (also known as Connie), a Laotian American family who mirror and often rival the Hills. Note that 'Kahn' is an anagram for 'Hank', thus being to him, like Edward Said (1979: 3) said of the Orient to Europe, 'a sort of surrogate and even underground self'. Yet several episodes foreground the challenges that the Souphanousinphones face as Asian Americans – issues of cultural isolation, racial prejudice, identity formation and assimilation. In its depiction of race and class, *King of the Hill* both deconstructs and perpetuates stereotypes. Comedy and satire play a complex role in racialized representation. *King of the Hill* demonstrates that animation can offer a unique strategy for addressing the politics of difference head on. It is precisely the presence of this Asian American family that prompted my interest in the series.

Asian American representation
on US primetime

As members of a group consistently under-represented in mainstream media, the Souphanousinphones are one of the few Asian American families who have appeared regularly on US primetime. When *King of the Hill* began in the late 1990s, people of Asian descent comprised 3.6 per cent of the American population, yet only 1.3 per cent of the television world (Larson 2005: 68). Characters of Southeast Asian descent, like the Laotian American Souphanousinphones, were almost never represented. Because of the relative paucity of televised Asian representation, Darrell Hamamoto (1994: xiii) might never have written *Monitored Peril, Asian Americans and the Politics of Representations* (tellingly almost titled *You'll Wonder Where the Yellow Went*). Instead Hamamoto sifted through decades of television history, including guest appearances and made for TV movies, in search of Asian and Asian American representation. For the most part, the portrayals he found were 'peripheral and one-dimensional', but he proceeded, asserting 'that racialized discourse of subordinate social identity must be accounted for historically and politically if they are ever to be subverted' (1994: ix). Conversely, Herman Gray, for his 1995 text *Watching Race Television and the Struggle for Blackness,* a decidedly more optimistic analysis, was able to narrow his focus to 1980s network series featuring blackness. He excluded from his analysis shows with primarily white casts that had only one or two black actors, as well as black shows that failed to explicitly showcase blackness. Had Hamamoto applied similar criteria, he might have had nothing to watch. (*All-American Girl*, the short-lived sitcom about a Korean American family starring Margaret Cho ran from 1994 to 1995, too late for an appearance in *Monitored Peril*.) Still, to this day, depictions of Asian Americans on television remain relatively scarce. The Souphanousinphones on *King of the Hill* are rare exceptions.

Unlike visible minorities that have more successfully crossed colour lines into American sitcom television with shows such as *The Cosby Show* (1984–8) and *George Lopez* (2002–07), most recurring Asian American characters on prime time appear in ensemble-cast one-hour dramas where they are the only Asian cast members on their shows – suggesting tokenism and the absence of Asian family life. However, the studies I found on televised Asian representation (Mok 1998; Shim 1998; Mastro and Greenberg 2000; Deo et al. 2008; Harwood and Anderson 2002; Shah 2003; Chin et al. 2006; Larson 2005) ignored animated sitcoms. They overlook *The Simpsons'* South Asian Nahasapeemapetilons and the aforementioned Souphanousinphones and neglect this genre's penchant for embracing difficult topics such as race and racism.

Operating on an iconic rather than indexical level, animation makes an excellent medium for social satire, parody and intertextual critiques of popular culture. Shilpa Davé (2005: 321) explains, because of 'the audience's suspension of disbelief, animated series can tackle issues and situations that would be unbelievable or inappropriate on live action sitcoms'. Its representations of race, gender, class and sexuality often traverse the boundaries of what is deemed politically correct. Animation's essential distance from reality makes its subversion not only possible but also more acceptable.

Thus, this examination of *King of the Hill* attempts to address two areas of underrepresentation – Asian Americans on prime time and animation in Asian American studies.

'Westie Side Story' and assimilationalist discourse

The Souphanousinphones were introduced as the Hills' new neighbours in season one's 'Westie Side Story'. The episode opens with Hank and his friends drinking beer and hanging out on their lawn tractors. A moving truck arrives at the house next door and the men immediately mistake the white movers for their new neighbours. After musing about the teenage son's athleticism and wondering if the father bowls, they decide that the new family will fit perfectly into their community. As soon as they learn that their neighbours are in fact Asian, their mood shifts from excitement to unease. Emerging from a blue minivan, the new arrivals are the picture of suburban banality. Yet, to the four white men, they are completely unexpected and exotic.

The friends debate their neighbours' origins, with Dale insisting that they must be Chinese since Japanese men wear glasses, suits and ties. Bill wonders if they speak English while Boomhauer, whose rapid mumblings are almost completely incomprehensible, mutters something about Chinese accents being impossible to understand. After introductions are made, Kahn Souphanousinphone explains that while they lived in California for twenty years, they were originally from Laos. In fact he repeats no less than five times that they are Laotian, getting increasingly more impatient. 'We are Laotian. From Laos, stupid! It's a landlocked country in Southeast Asia. It's between Vietnam and Thailand, okay? Population 4.7 million'. Still puzzled, Hank asks, 'so are you Chinese or Japanese?'

Portrayed as ignorant rather than malicious, the white characters regard the Asian Americans as exotic, foreign and inferior. Peggy Hill is delighted with the newcomers because, 'it's like we get to travel to the Orient without having to worry about getting diarrhoea or being jailed for our pro-democracy beliefs'. Calling them 'by nature, shy and reserved', she invites the Souphanousinphones to dinner where she greets them with halting English and welcomes them to the country. Scenes throughout the episode undermine the Hills' unwitting prejudices by demonstrating how like them (and therefore 'American'), their neighbours really are. Like Hank, Kahn uses a riding lawn mower, dotes on his dog and barbecues hamburgers. Peggy and Minh compete over baking and their children bond over not being the sons that their fathers desire. After hostilities escalate over missing (and perhaps eaten) dogs, conflict is resolved (albeit temporarily) with the realization that they are not that different after all.

Borrowing again from Herman Gray (1995: 85–87), I would describe 'Westie Side Story' as 'assimilationalist television discourse', marginalizing 'social and cultural differences in the interest of shared and universal similarity'; locating racial prejudice in readily resolved individual misunderstandings rather than systemic racism and unequal power relations; and placing the privileged subject position as that of the white middle class, in this case Hank Hill.

With this first appearance of Asian America in small-town Texas, a stage is set for shifted subjectivities and reinforcements to white hegemony.

'Man without a Country Club' and the myth of the model minority

The rule of white subjectivity plays out in the season six episode 'Man without a Country Club', when Hank is recruited by the all-Asian Nine Rivers Country Club in order to placate the Professional Golfers Association and take part in an upcoming PGA Tour. Nine Rivers is presented as an exclusive but well-known place of beauty and privilege, coveted by even white golfers. Through the audience's identification with Hank Hill and his role-reversed status as an outsider, the episode explores concepts of segregation, exclusion and tokenism.

In a sense, *King of the Hill* admonishes historic practices of segregation and contemporary all-white private golf clubs. In the episode, club recruiter Ted Wassanasong attempts to assuage Hank's concern that Nine Rivers is all Asian. He explains: 'This club was founded by an immigrant Vietnamese hot sauce tycoon after he was excluded from all the other clubs in Heimlich County. The first members were his friends, who also happened to be Asian. And then their friends joined, also Asian, and so on.'

Thus the segregated nature of Nine Rivers is, and is not, a product of intentional discrimination. While not necessarily condoning exclusivity or ghettoization, *King of the Hill* certainly naturalizes it. In the end, Hank declines his membership opting instead to invite Kahn into The Rainey

Street Country Club (essentially neighbours playing in their back alley). In lieu of opening or dismantling inaccessible institutions, the episode proposes the creation of alternate spaces – the very strategy that produced the problematic Nine Rivers to begin with.

Yet this episode is more than a critique of tokenism, exclusivity and a white man's lesson in becoming Other. Rather what interests me is how replete (as are frankly most storylines featuring the Souphanousinphones) it is with the myth of the model minority. Convinced by the notion that all Asian Americans are successful, Kahn complains to Minh about not being part of the elite club. 'Nine Rivers is the only all-Asian country club in Heimlich County. We're all Asian, we should be there.' To Hank, Kahn says, 'everyone at Nine Rivers comes from different places: Laos, China, Vietnam, Cambodia, Singapore, Malaysia, Thailand, South Korea ... but we all have one thing in common, our *love* ... of golf'. While Keith Booker (2006: 73) may describe Kahn and Minh as 'grasping, competitive and materialistic', their unwavering belief in Asian American success is not unfounded.

The myth of the model minority has been propagated through mainstream American media for decades (and *King of the Hill* to a large extent perpetuates it). This hegemonic discourse evincing attainment and assimilation is founded on the political silence and adaptability of Asian Americans and has circulated since the mid-1960s Civil Rights movement. Conservatism, lack of political activism, low (perhaps unreported) crime rates and reluctance to participate in social welfare programmes were celebrated as symptoms of lawfulness and self-sufficiency, rather than effects of government distrust. These narratives of acquiescence and productivity were useful in the face of growing racial unrest. In the post-Fordist 1980s, the myth expanded to focus on economic and academic success and encompass all Asians – conflating them regardless of individual immigration histories. It ignores the over-education of Asian Americans for comparable wages and that recent immigrants and refugees from China and Southeast Asia (including Laos) often struggle with poverty and integration (Thrupkaew 2008). The myth of the model minority continues to function as a justification for the status quo and a way to chastise less successful Americans, adding pressure to individuals like the Souphanousinphones to meet high expectations. Success is attributed to race rather than ability and effort.

In popular media, the myth of the model minority is propagated by 'positive stereotypes', which present Asian Americans as work-oriented overachievers. Thus on American prime time, Asian characters primarily appear in series featuring the workplace, frequently portraying high achievers such as doctors *(ER, Grey's Anatomy, Law and Order SVU)* and scientists *(Big Bang Theory, CSI, Dexter)*. Yet unlike most TV Asians (including their overachieving daughter Connie), Kahn and Minh are not part of the model minority. If they were, they would be a lot more successful or at least, not so loud.

Assimilation, authenticity and yellow voice

The Souphanousinphones are very vocal about their desire to be like fellow Laotian Americans Ted and Cindy Wassanasong, an elitist couple who are considerably more affluent and seemingly more 'white'. Yet Ted's acculturation appears dubious. He has a conspicuously robotic 'American' accent, his compliments seem practised and his delayed responses suggest a processing of information. When trying to convince Hank, who he has apparently researched, to join Nine Rivers, Ted says, 'think about it, Hank. Talk it over with your wife Peggy and son Bobby, age 13'. In season eight's 'Redneck on Rainey Street', when Kahn and Minh find the Wassanasongs at the Episcopalian church, Ted explains his family's conversion from Buddhism as 'just good business'. Thus storylines suggest that Ted's assimilation into North American culture is calculated and therefore inauthentic, thereby subscribing to the myth of the model minority discourse that at once promotes integration while deeming Asian Americans perpetually foreign.

In the 1971 *Newsweek* article 'Success Story: Outwhiting the Whites', an interviewee explained that Japanese Americans responded to their wartime internment by the US Government by saying 'I'll become an even better American', adding proudly, 'scratch a Japanese American and you'll find a WASP'. Robert G. Lee (1999: 190–191) compares the assimilation and therefore invisibility of the model minority to the supposed invisibility of the Viet Cong. He describes cinematic depictions of Asian Americans 'as an alien threat in [these] narratives of multicultural dystopia and besieged nationhood, at once ubiquitous and invisible, ersatz and inauthentic'. Likening Asian Americans to the hunted down 'replicants' in *Blade Runner*, Lee (1999: 196) writes, 'both the android "new friend" and the model minority are people without history; both are simulacra whom a programmed historical memory simultaneously renders functional and inauthentic'.

Of course, one might argue that Ted Wassanasong's voice is not fake, but is simply the way the actor who portrays him speaks (for example, like Shakespearean-trained actor, George Takei). However, Toby Huss who plays Ted is a white actor from Iowa who also portrays Hank's father Cotton and of course Kahn himself. In this instance Huss is not unlike actor Hank Azaria, who portrays *The Simpsons'* South Asian character Apu as well as a number of other characters from the show.

Is this the cartoon equivalent of yellowface? In that much maligned practice, actors (usually, although not always, white) wear makeup to conform to visual stereotypes of Asianness. Rob Schneider in *I Now Pronounce You Chuck and Larry* (2005) channelling Mickey Rooney in *Breakfast at Tiffany's* (1961), Christopher Walken's *Fu Manchu*-like turn in *Ball's of Fury* (2007) and Robert Downey Jr's performance in *Tropic Thunder* (2008) demonstrate that yellowface and blackface have not been completely banished. Nevertheless, such casting rarely goes unquestioned.

In examining the case of Apu, Shilpa Davé (2005) calls Azaria's vocal performance 'brown voice'. She explains that this is accepted because the actor remains largely anonymous and hidden during the performance. However, Davé contends, this is not a neutral act. Accented vocal performances construct fixed and ahistoric notions of identity, race and ethnicity. Huss, as Kahn, speaks with what I would call 'yellow voice' – an accent not specific to any linguistic origin but one that fulfils audience expectations of what Asians sound like, thus racializing them as foreign and all the same. Asian American actors routinely perform this 'Asian accent [that] isn't really an Asian accent' to conform to Hollywood conventions (Nancy Yuen Wang 2004: 260). Thus, Asian American actress Lauren Tom's performance as Minh features this 'yellow voice'. However, Tom does not use it to perform the assimilated Asian American characters – Connie Souphanousinphone and Cindy Wassanasong, whose accents are rather neutral. Yet, like Asian American guest actors on *King of the Hill* such as Lucy Liu and Amy Hill, Tom – 'yellow voice' not withstanding – has never voiced a non-Asian character on the programme.

While Asians are cast as all the same regardless of ethnicity and often expected to perform with this 'yellow voice', casting across colour lines even for a non-visual vocal performance remains a privilege reserved for white actors. Still, in season eight of *King of the Hill*, Kahn and Minh do get a chance to impersonate whiteness (of a kind).

'Redneck on Rainey Street' and white trash

In 'Redneck on Rainey Street', a prestigious summer school rejects Connie Souphanousinphone because as an overachieving Asian American, she does not fulfil their diversity policy (in other words they have an excess of the so-called model minority.) Kahn, frustrated with this latest setback, trades his sensible sedan for an El Camino and persuades Minh that they should stop working so hard. He pleads: 'Don't you see? This is for Connie. So she don't spend half her life losing at their rigged game. What do you say, Minh? Will you be my redneck bride?' The two joyously decide to 'give up' and instead, spend their days and nights drinking and partying with their new friends from Belcher's Grove (the 'wrong' side of town). Khan stops working and shaving and Minh starts sporting tube tops. Connie's classmate Stuart Dooley observes insultingly, 'your dad is white trash'.

Matt Wray (2006: 16) explains that poor whites are almost always described in terms of 'moral unworthiness'. He recounts colonialist William Byrd's creation of a foundational narrative of marginalized whiteness in America: 'The entire region had long had a reputation as a haven for runaway servants and slaves, criminals, and ne'er-do-wells of all sorts. In his travel writing and diaries, Byrd, borrowing a term from English culture, dubbed these backcountry dwellers "lubbers"' (2006: 25). Although Byrd was describing a way of eighteenth-century life around the disputed boundary between Virginia and North Carolina, he might as well have been talking about *King of the Hill*'s Belcher's Grove and the Souphanousinphones' new friends.

Byrd uses the term 'lubber' to evoke laziness and immorality. Lubberland was a well-known fiction of peasant utopia, similar to the Land of Cockaigne and the hobo paradise described by Depression-Era song *Big Rock Candy Mountain*. Characterized by freedom from labour, bountiful supplies of food and plenty of sex, it is a fantasy that resonates most powerfully with the disenfranchised, downtrodden, dispossessed and hungry, and is epitomized in the carnivalesque atmosphere of Kahn and Minh's descent.

Thus in their impersonations of marginalized whites Kahn and Minh, once again, personify the Other. Here they doubly reinforce the privileged whiteness of Hank Hill and the rest of the regular cast, through both race and class-based differences. Furthermore, the appearance of 'authentic' rednecks in 'Redneck on Rainey Street' complicates an overarching series premise that, as Michael Chaney explains, the 'underdog heroes in *King of the Hill* ... represent stigmatized subjects of white culture' (Chaney and Gallagher 2004: 170).

As potential rednecks, the primary white characters of *King of the Hill* shore up the 'normal and unmarked' whiteness of a more privileged America (its northern, urban and more affluent viewers). Throughout the series, Kahn and Minh reinforce this (as well as their own racialized status) by referring to Hank and his friends as 'rednecks' and 'hillbillies', with Hank, in particular, bristling against these labels. Yet the Hills' supposed marginalization is a masquerade of white otherness. They are neither poor nor disempowered. The denizens of Belcher's Grove (where Kahn and Minh find acceptance) are the true white Others. Rather Hank Hill embodies the 'honourable' and 'square-dealing' whiteness described so vividly by Richard Dyer (1997: 65) in his seminal text *White*. Dyer (1997: 35–37) contends that the American West has been crucial to 'the construction of a white (male) identity' based on the conquest of land and the establishment of order. While Hank and his friends are neither cowboys nor frontiersmen; their obsession with lawn care is a contemporary suburban form of conquering territory. Chaney and Gallagher (2004: 170) remark, 'the cartoon carves out a space for a white class consciousness that is initially marked as Other. But this marking is only tenuous'. Here we can understand *King of the Hill*'s popularity with those it purports to satirize. Hank's triumph at the end of every episode as the apparent voice of reason solidifies his place, and therefore that of small-town America, well within the boundaries of white privilege.

In 'Redneck on Rainey Street,' Hank restores order once again. Having discovered that the bank is about to foreclose on the Souphanousinphone house, Hank finds Kahn at the stick fights behind the lumberyard and convinces him to straighten up, reminding him, 'even when you and Minh went off the deep end, Connie never complained and never stopped trying, you couldn't drag that little girl into the muck with you'. By invoking the myth of the model minority, our privileged white hero suppresses both racial and economic unrest.

Concluding thoughts: Racial grief and alternate representations

My examination of Asian American representation on *King of the Hill* reveals an assimilationist discourse that, perpetuated by the myth of the model minority, privileges white male hegemony. According to bell hooks (1992: 120), 'grown black women' 'claim' the Sapphire of *Amos 'n' Andy* in opposition, because despite her character's loathsome disposition, they relate to her anger, adopting her as one of their own. Thus, I claim fellow Asian Kahn Souphanousinphone for loudly and persistently voicing his frustrations with discrimination and unwitting prejudice.

There is an implicit rule (or stereotype) that as the model minority, Asian Americans do not speak out against racial injustice. Remember, as Peggy Hill says, we are 'by nature, shy and reserved'. Furthermore, Hank Hill, whose morality rules the show, embodies whiteness with his 'obsessive self-control, rationality, order and repression of emotions' (Dyer cited in Garner 2007: 49). Thus the most satisfying moments of *King of the Hill* occur when Kahn breaks these two rules and expresses his frustration.

When, in 'Westie Side Story' Hank tells Kahn that his dog Ladybird 'can only love another purebred Georgia bloodhound', Hill's unwitting reference to the American South's antimiscegenation past provokes Kahn into shouting, 'you know what I think, Hank Hill? I think you're a narrow-minded redneck!' In 'Man without a Country Club,' when Hank laments having felt like an outsider, Kahn responds sarcastically, 'oh, yeah, you right. I always feel comfortable everywhere I go. You know, my original name is Smith. I just change it to Souphanousinphone when I move to Texas!' While in 'Redneck on Rainey Street,' Kahn wails to Hank, 'we flee horrible dictatorship, learn a new language, work hard and study hard. And our reward for doing everything right is to be told "Go to hell. You work too hard. You study too hard"'.

Expressions such as these, of Asian American grief in mainstream popular culture, are almost non-existent. Yet anger is a powerful political force and racial grief and grievance has performed a vital role in implementing change. As Anne Anlin Cheng (2001: 3) asserts, 'it is precisely at moments when racial injury is most publicly pronounced that its substance and tangibility come most stridently into question'.

Furthermore, it is refreshing to see representations of Asians that don't always conform to stereotypes. Stephanie Larson (2005: 67–70) lists the following Asian stereotypes prevalent in mainstream film and television: 'inscrutable foreigners, China dolls, dragon ladies, de-sexed sidekicks, criminals, nerds and mystics'. In *King of the Hill*, we are presented with two creatures rare to US prime time – a virile Asian American man (instead of an asexual nerd) and an Asian American woman who happens to not be a doctor in an interracial romance.

In the Souphanousinphones, and their struggle to join the mythical model minority, we find alternate representations and ones that do acknowledge a history of racialization. Although Kahn especially is portrayed as a marginalized and intolerant bigot (perhaps to demonstrate that protagonist Hank Hill is not), I can't help but enjoy (and almost admire) this Laotian American as he breaks the model minority rule of Asian silence, and the white rule of self-control, to complain about the unfairness that surrounds him. It is gratifying to see everyday prejudice towards Asian Americans acknowledged in popular culture. Mike Judge's Hank clearly is the 'King of the Hill', but there is room for other subjectivities. Thus we can enjoy Kahn's anger as a rare spectacle of Asian American racial grief and see that televised representations need not always be two-dimensional, even in cartoons.

References

Bai, M. (2005), 'King of the Hill' Democrats? *New York Times Magazine*, 26 June. Available online: http://www.nytimes.com/2005/06/26/magazine/26WWL.

Booker, M. K. (2006), *Drawn to Television: Prime-Time Animation from The Flintstones to Family Guy*, Westport, CT: Praeger Publishers.

Chaney, M. A. and M. Gallagher (2004), 'Representations of Race and Place in *Static Shock*, *King of the Hill*, and *South Park*', *Journal of Popular Film and Television*, 31(4): 167–175.

Cheng, A. A. (2001), *The Melancholy of Race*, New York: Oxford University Press.

Chin, C. B., Deo, M. E., Lee, J. J, Milman, N., and N. W. Yuen (2006), *Asian Pacific Americans in Prime Time: Setting the Stage*, Washington, DC: Asian American Justice Center.

Davé, S. (2005), 'Apu's Brown Voice: Cultural Inflection and South Asian Accents', in S. Davé, L. Nishime and T. G. Oren (eds), *East Main Street, Asian America Popular Culture*, 313–336, New York: New York University Press.

Deo, M. E., Lee, J. J, Chin, C. B., Milman, N., and N. W. Yuen (2008), 'Missing in Action: "Framing" Race in Prime-Time Television', *Social Justice*, 35(2): 145–162.

Dyer, R. (1997), *White*, New York: Routledge.

Garner, S. (2007), *Whiteness: An Introduction*, New York: Routledge.

Gray, H. (1995), *Watching Race: Television and the Struggle for Blackness*, Minneapolis, MN: University of Minnesota Press.

Gray, J. (2006), *Watching with the Simpsons: Television, Parody, and Intertextuality (Comedia)*, New York: Routledge.

Hamamoto, D. Y. (1994), *Monitored Peril: Asian Americans and the Politics of TV Representation*, Minneapolis, MN: University of Minnesota Press.

Harwood, J. and K. Anderson (2002), 'The Presence and Portrayal of Social Groups on Prime-Time Television', *Communication Reports*, 15(2): 81–97.

Hooks, B. (1992), The Oppositional Gaze: Female Black Spectators, in *Black Looks: Race and Representation*, Toronto: Between the Lines.

Larson, S. (2005), *Media & Minorities: The Politics of Race in News and Entertainment*, Lanham, MD: Rowman & Littlefield Publishers.

Lee, R. G. (1999), *Orientals: Asian Americans in Popular Culture*, Philadelphia, PA: Temple University Press.

Mastro, D. E. and B. S. Greenberg (2000), 'The Portrayal of Racial Minorities on Prime Time Television', *Journal of Broadcasting and Electronic Media*, 44(4): 690–703.

Mok, T. A. (1998), 'Getting the Message Media Images and Stereotypes and Their Effect on Asian Americans', *Cultural Diversity and Mental Health*, 4(3): 185–202.

Newsweek (1971), 'Success Story: Outwhiting the Whites', 21 June, pp. 24–25.

Said, E. (1979), *Orientalism*, New York: Vintage Books.

Shah, H. (2003), '"Asian Culture" and Asian American Identities in the Television and Film Industries of the United States', *Studies in Media & Information Literacy Education*, 3(3). Available at http://www.utpress.utoronto.ca/journal/ejournals/simile (accessed 7 June 2010).

Shim, D. (1998), 'From Yellow Peril through Model Minority to Renewed Yellow Peril', *Journal of Communication Inquiry*, 22(4): 385–409.

Thompson, E. (2009), '"I Am Not Down with That": *King of the Hill* and Sitcom Satire', *Journal of Film and Video*, 61(2): 38–51.

Thrupkaew, N. (2008), 'The Myth of the Model Minority: Southeast Asians Were Stereotyped as Bolstered by Strong Values. But When Immigrants Face Grim Economic and Social Conditions, Values Are Not Enough', *The American Prospect* (Cover Story), 2 April. Available online: http://www.prospect.org/cs/articles?article=the_myth_of_the_model_minority (accessed 27 July 2009).

Werts, D. (2001), 'Mimicking Real Life, "Hill" Takes Comedic High Ground', *Los Angeles Times*, 23 February. Available online: http://articles.latimes.com/2001/feb/23/entertainment/ca-28994/2 (accessed 30 August 2010).

Wray, M. (2006), *Not Quite White: White Trash and the Boundaries of Whiteness*, Durham, NC: Duke University Press.

Yuen, N. W. (2004), 'Performing Race, Negotiating Identity: Asian American Professional Actors in Hollywood', in J. Lee and M. Zhou (eds), *Asian American Youth*, 251–267, New York: Routledge.

19

Transformers: Rescue Bots: Representation in Disguise

Nichola Dobson

TV animation series aimed at children and teens often feature subtle (and not so subtle) content aimed at an adult audience. There are multiple layers of meaning which can be in the form of subversion for political purposes, simple pop culture references and/or more sophisticated humour to placate the adult viewing along with the child. According to Wells (2002), animation has a long tradition of multilayered and self-reflexive approaches, particularly seen in comedy from the Warner Bros.' *Looney Tunes* (1930–69) series to Matt Groening's *The Simpsons* (1990–). These animations thus appeal to a mixed range of audience members and can cater to different ages within one text. Over the last ten years, there has been a rise in TV animation created for children and pre-teen audiences with increasingly progressive political themes, appealing to adult fans and educating younger ones.

Recent programmes such as *Steven Universe* (2013–), *Adventure Time* (2010–18) and *My Little Pony: Friendship Is Magic* (2010–) include positive representations of a wide diversity of race and sexuality.[1] This tendency is also seen in the preschool variation of the *Transformers* series, *Rescue Bots* (Hasbro 2011–16). The series' main themes are of co-operation, teamwork and acceptance of difference and these are presented via smartly written self-reflexive, often intertextual, comedy. There is a great deal for adults to enjoy along with the children with parodies and spoofs of films and TV, as well as of their own franchise and toy sales. This chapter considers the extent to which *Rescue Bots* can be seen as a model of progressive representation of gender and sexuality, and whether an increasingly diverse voice cast gets reflected in terms of the way the characters are drawn in the show, both literally and metaphorically. However, it will also examine whether in an attempt to challenge stereotypes, *Rescue Bots* reinforces them.

The chapter will adopt a production studies approach using interview material, combined with textual analysis, to develop a discussion of the casting within the series and to consider how diversity is represented through the characters and cast. With a plethora of toy tie-in series available in a multi-channel, multi-platform televisual landscape, *Rescue Bots* stands out as an indicative example of children's television animation that struggles to negotiate the use of stereotypes while at the same time attempting a degree of diversity and inclusivity.

'Optimus Prime gave them this mission'[2]

Transformers: Rescue Bots, produced by Hasbro and animated by several studios over its four-year run, is a Daytime Emmy Award-winning show. The franchise has been incredibly popular with several elements, including books, live-action movies, video games, different animated series and the toys. While *Rescue Bots* is not overtly tasked with presenting progressive diversity or educating its audience, it diverges from simply being a toy commercial,[3] and interviews I conducted with personnel involved in the show's production revealed that the writers were keen to develop the narratives with a well-rounded, contemporary and thoughtful approach to help young children learn about the world. They did this by featuring a cast and character grouping which, as writer Brian Hohlfeld explained, would present 'a group of characters "that looked like America," as they say, so that any kid watching could have someone they recognize' (2017). That said, the series still leans on stereotypes of gendered identities and sexualities that potentially disrupt an overtly progressive reading of the series.

Transformers: Rescue Bots takes a different approach to the battle between good and evil (and consumerism) seen in the other *Transformers* series, instead featuring a side mission for four lost Autobots. They have ended up on Earth, in the small, fictitious island community of Griffin Rock, Maine, and instead of fighting their enemies, the Decepticons, they are charged with helping the humans in rescue work, while disguising their true forms. The four bots, in different vehicle guises of police car, fire engine, helicopter and bulldozer, are teamed with the Burns family – Griffin Rock's rescue team (human counterparts: police chief, fire fighter, EMT and civil engineer). The youngest Burns son, Cody, helps guide the bots as they learn about their new home planet and provides cover for the bots 'robot' identities from the town.

The show's overall message of helping, cooperation and teamwork, is appropriately pitched at a younger fan base in the preschool years, and the toys on which the series is based are also designed for smaller hands. As with many of the most successful preschool series produced in the 2010s (such as *Go Jetters* [2015–] and *Octonauts* [2010–]) the series uses diverse character types and voices to demonstrate acceptance of difference.[4] For *Rescue Bots*, as this chapter will argue, this acceptance comes late in the series, in its fourth season.

As previously suggested, it was important for the writers to include what Hohlfeld described as, 'a variety of diverse characters (in age, profession, ethnicity, philosophy, gender, etc.) [which] makes for better storytelling'. This was also important to the overall plot and the Rescue Bots' mission on Earth:

> Since the Bots' mission from Optimus was to learn the ways of humans, the more diverse humans there were, the more realistic and relatable the Bots' mission would be. So it wouldn't just be learning to fight bad guys or make rescues, it would also be them tacitly accepting a society that encompasses lots of different-looking people (as we hope our audience would be doing at the same time). (Hohlfeld 2017)

As such, both the characters and the actors who voice them were diverse in terms of race and gender, although with more male than female characters, but what is of particular interest in this chapter is *how* gender was represented.

'Learn from the humans, serve and protect'

The representation of female characters in the show has varied since its first year of airing; they were less visible in the early episodes with fewer female characters on screen and this was in part due to the presumed male demographic, despite the fact that there was already a keen female fanbase.[5] The show lacks significant female parental roles and both Cody and his best friend Francine (Frankie) Green are raised by very capable single fathers; as Hohlfeld admits, having no mother in the series is a well-used narrative trope. The two key female characters in the series, Dani Burns (Cody's older sister) and Frankie Green are very accomplished. As such they provide good role models for the audience while also reinforcing that females play equally strong roles to the male characters (interestingly both with the 'masculine' version of their names). However, the other female characters in the early episodes had few if any speaking roles and reinforced the notion of the smiling, pretty damsel in distress (Hayley in episode 14 'Small Blessings'), the cranky old cat woman (Mrs Neederlander, episode 5 'Alien Invasion of Griffin Rock'), or the silent trophy wife (Mrs Luskey, married to the Mayor). The range of speaking female characters increased over the years – and female bot Quickshadow was introduced in season 4 – arguably in response to fans' demand for female bots and reflecting the increasingly mixed gender production and writing team (as well as a female Network lead). This exemplifies David Gauntlett's observation that the inclusion of women in key creative production roles positively influences the number of women in television shows (2008: 64–65).

One of the key elements of interest in the show is its range of characters of different gender (albeit weighted towards the male in the early series), age and race to represent a diverse society, or 'all of America' in Hohlfeld's terms. This includes a range of stereotypical masculinities, from strong and muscular, non-emotive and boorish, to what might be termed as a sensitive 'new man',[6] which fulfil different functions for the audience. The stereotypes presented within the main character grouping demonstrate different possible masculinities but also challenge them by questioning their function within society via the bots' attempts to understand humanity. This allows for an interesting and arguably progressive discourse around masculinity for a children's TV show and develops the range of comedy within the series.[7]

Clatterbaugh (2004) suggests that many of the terms and meanings in the discussion of 'masculinities' are problematic, in that they either conflate masculinity with men, and thus adulthood, or confuse biological behaviours with socially constructed traits which are accepted as norms. He argues that there is a confusion in some respects between gender roles, roles we assume, and perceptions of gender, how we view these roles, and that this perception problematizes the very notion of what masculinity is. We could of course apply this to femininity as well or any discussion of gender or broader stereotypes but as the main characters in the series are coded as male, it is appropriate to consider these traits in the way that they are used as 'differentiating characteristics' (Clatterbaugh 2004: 204).

The pairing of bot and human counterpart becomes a way for the show to question certain notions of masculinity. For example, Police bot Chase is partnered with Police Chief Charlie Burns. Chase is strong, patient and considerate, but always follows the letter of the law and is fascinated by earth regulations. His extreme and unquestioning zeal for law enforcement can be problematic as he lacks understanding of human social cues and the subtleties of grey areas, such as white lies and protecting people's feelings. This is balanced by Charlie, perhaps the ultimate 'new man', who is thoughtful, patient, kind and a responsible father. He is also tough when needed but guides Chase (and the rest of the bots and his family) through the challenges of living in a modern society. Physically he is designed as a traditional 'masculine' body type with broad shoulders and a strong physique, and a very prominent, bushy moustache. Brownlee highlights the alignment of moustaches with masculinity in her discussion of *Spongebob Squarepants*, '"Patrick, you see I'm growing a moustache/and though I know I must ask you/does it really make me look like a man?" Faintly ludicrous and smacking of uncertainty, these lines typify how the film characterizes a kid's (or boy's?) preoccupation with manhood' (2011).

A fascination with what 'adult manhood' might entail, particularly in relation to body image, can be seen in 'One for the Ages' in season 2 when Cody is transformed into a grown up (in a *Vice Versa* [1988]/*Big* [1988] parody) complete with bushy moustache and again in season 3's 'Rescue Bots Academy' when Blur enquires about the different 'types' (sexes) of the humans:

Salvage: but only the males can have the thing above their lip?
Chase: Ah yes, the moustache, it appears to be a point of pride with some
   people ...
Blades: We don't know how it works but somehow it makes him more
   huggable ...

The notion of facial hair equalling male adulthood seen in 'One for the Ages', as previously mentioned, is a well-used trope. Brownlee again on Spongebob's yearning to be an adult, cites Hendershot, 'the icing on the maturity cake ... [is] sideburns' (2011). So, this discussion of facial hair is reasonably commonplace in notions of adult maleness and how children may view this. Arguably this then also reinforces how Charlie is designed to be viewed – as a proud, strong man – but as Blades suggests, still sensitive enough to be hugged. Charlie is the most fully rounded of all of the adult characters and is described by Hohlfeld as having, 'sensitivity and empathy, yet [...] still "masculine" in [...] physical capabilities, sense of honor, and gallantry ... modeling emotional intelligence paired with traditional male traits was very important for our audience' (2017).

Modelling emotional intelligence in this way through Charlie and main protagonist Cody shows that the writers were mindful of the potential role models they were creating for a young audience (albeit with a very traditional male body type in Charlie, his broad shoulders alone suggesting a dependable strength). The show tries to mitigate stereotypes with a balance of traits, what Hohlfeld referred to as a 'continuum of "masculinity" that our characters fall on ... all our characters, like real people, contain both masculine and feminine traits (in traditional societal and Freudian terms). Even Kade, who sees himself as a real "he-man," (and he-men are usually the only ones who see themselves that way), also exhibits sensitivity and empathy' (2017).

We see this in the other pairings where there is a stereotype which is often reinforced in the storyline but then challenged either by the bot or resolved in the plot. In the case of Fire bot Heatwave, he is presented as the very gruff and reluctant leader of the Rescue Bots; reluctant in that he is unhappy with the mission to hide their true identity – he feels that his skills would be better suited in the fight against a greater foe – but follows Optimus Prime's directive loyally. His friendship with the Burns family and respect for the town develops over the four seasons. He is fairly reactionary and although the show does not include any violence as such, he is quick to temper and could be termed as the most aggressive of the bots (or perhaps the most 'traditionally masculine' and an authority figure). He is partnered with the eldest Burns son, Kade – an arrogant, oafish, self styled 'he-man' with an ego the size of his appetite. However, he puts the job as rescuer first and is also fiercely loyal to his team/family. Kade and Heatwave share personality traits and gradually see this as a positive strength and work together. They challenge each other's authority, each wishing to be the alpha male or bot, but they always need each other to successfully and safely complete their mission. This teaches the importance of cooperation as well as showing that physical strength or a bad temper isn't the way to overcome adversity. Over the years of the series, this has further developed into a respectful friendship.

Another friendship, and one which is forged very quickly, is between the Bulldozer bot, Boulder, and his partner Graham. They are both engineers and scientists. Bulldozer is passionate about nature and is fascinated to learn about Earth. He is thoughtful, patient and very strong. These traits are complimented, rather than challenged, by Graham. He is a high-achieving academic but their combined force of brains and brawn (through Boulder's physicality) often resolves the crisis. Together these characters demonstrate that it is ok to be male and be clever and interested in learning, something Bulldozer reinforces as a stronger and more confident version of Graham. In season 3, episode 7 'Bugs in the System' Graham develops a special cologne to gain confidence to speak to a girl he likes but after things go wrong it is revealed that he always had confidence. This is a well-used trope in film and TV and here tries to teach the young audience that you have to believe in your own ability. Each of these pairings demonstrates different masculinities, sometimes challenging the stereotypes of traditional masculinity and occasionally reinforcing them (often for comedic effect). However, if we consider the fourth Bot, Blades, we see yet another challenge to stereotypical gender norms.

Blades was a 'ground-based EMT' in his previous Cybertronian life, but as the last to choose his bot mode, is left with no choice but to be a helicopter, despite a fear of heights. He is opposite to Heatwave in terms of masculinity; both care about the mission but where Heatwave is gruff, serious and 'masculine', Blades is often perceived as cowardly, silly and could be read as effeminate. There is a suggestion on one of the many Transformers wikis that Blades is a 'young' robot and as such we could surmise that his fear and curiosity about the human condition, as well as his love of pop culture, is a childish naivety, or represents the curious voice of the audience.[8] There is also something interesting in his pairing with the only female Burns sibling, Dani, as his 'gal pal' with whom he gossips and consumes all forms of pop culture, especially musicals.[9] All of these camp stereotypes are heightened in an early episode when he asks, 'does this make my hips look big?' after the addition of a new scoop claw attachment to aid in a rescue changes his physical appearance.

This combination of traits could encourage a queer reading of Blades, which would be an interesting addition to the types of masculinity in the series, however it is a rather broadly stereotypical representation of homosexuality and the opposition of his so-called cowardly, or less masculine traits, to those of Kade or Heatwave could be seen as problematic, giving negative connotations to his queerness. Alternatively, we could read this as an opportunity for the children watching to understand that there are different ways to be, especially as ultimately the bots all form an effective team (and Blades is often heroic).

This is further complicated by the fact that Blades is voiced by Parvesh Cheena, an openly gay actor who brought to the character his 'own ebullient personality' (Hohlfeld 2017). Cheena also willingly performs the character in a way that plays on existing vocal stereotypes of gayness, such as pitch and speech pattern (see Davis and Needham 2009). For example, Cheena's voice is higher in the show than in interviews or other acting performances. Later the writers used his performance to influence the script and character development, and Hohlfeld (2017) acknowledges that they embraced Cheena's vocal 'qualities that might be stereotyped as "gay" – his flamboyant side and his diva-like qualities'. However, Hohlfeld attests that:

> I know that as a child, I would have just thought Blades is silly and funny and nice. I'd like to think that straight kids watching our show will grow up and meet gay people and be accepting of them. If it's because they happen to recognize them as someone they know and like from TV, then we've done a good thing. And I'd also like to think that kids who are struggling with their sexuality will recognize themselves in Blades and see that the character is accepted and loved for who he is. (Hohlfeld 2017)

As the series progressed, the creators continued to emphasize Blade's camp traits, but they also challenged the earlier characterization of Blades as a young and inexperienced bot by allowing him to demonstrate his pop culture credentials, and giving him the role of wise conduit between the humans and the bots. This means that the later version of Blades can be simultaneously read as fun and funny as well as camp and reassuringly positive.

Blades's pairing with the only Burns female, Dani might be read as reinforcing his difference from the other bots and thus his queerness. However, while he could be seen as feminized via this pairing, Dani is not presented as 'girly' or soft, but strong, accomplished, with what may be termed as traditional masculine qualities (including being a terrible cook – a simplistic challenge to male and female stereotypes). Dani is an accomplished woman who is driven by career goals and cares for her family, but not to the extent that she is a surrogate mother for younger brother Cody and she displays few stereotypical female traits, besides the aforementioned gossiping. Her friendship with Blades develops over the series and although initially she has to adopt a maternal role in encouraging him to fly, their relationship is more of siblings as the series goes on. What this pairing does then is to present another type of masculinity and also show the similarities between the genders in what Hohlfeld previously referred to as a 'continuum' in which all characters display male and female characteristics.

The notion of the bots being 'in disguise' and, in particular, the revelation of the bots' true 'alien' selves in series 4, offers a potential queer reading of the series overall. There is much made in the first few episodes of the sense of panic and fear which the townspeople may have if the bots 'come out' to them and of fearing that which is different or we don't understand. The bots reveal their true selves and the town decides to accept them and allow them to live as bots without their disguises on the Island. The message of acceptance of difference is again reinforced and the initial worry is unfounded; with only a couple of exceptions (who are mocked and made out to be 'cranks'), the townsfolk are accepting of their true nature.

This brief overview of the main characters of the show demonstrates that the show uses stereotypes throughout in an attempt to create humour by challenging and addressing them, not always successfully. The bots are used to question the absurdity of life and human society through their lack of prior knowledge and attempt to fit in to their adopted home. By asking about the differences between male and female, for example, the show addresses, and implicitly challenges, current gender norms. The show also tries to educate the young audience on issues such as lying to protect your family, team work, trusting friends and accepting difference. Overall the series features a white, male protagonist with a largely male support network, however by representing different ways to be 'male' and 'female' as well as different races and sexualities, all voiced authentically by the cast (who at least in the case of the humans, look like their characters),[10] the series attempts to promote progressive diversity. By learning from the humans, the bots can complete their mission and by challenging some of the rules of society, they no longer need to remain 'robots in disguise'.

Notes

1   See Claire Burdfield (2014) and Kodi Maier (2015) which deal with masculinity in *My Little Pony* and *Steven Universe*, respectively.

2   The show's opening song has very specific lyrics which explain the premise of the series and the mission for the bots: 'Learn from the humans, Serve and

protect, Live in their world, earn their respect. A family of heroes will be your allies, To others remain robots in disguise' this signals to the audience that the bots and the Burns family are important but they need to remain 'in disguise'.

3　See Burke and Burke (1998) and Ratelle (this volume) on the increase in TV animation designed to sell toys to children in the 1980s.

4　In *Octonauts*, the characters are all voiced with different regional UK accents to diversify from the traditional received pronunciation commonly used in early British television. That the characters are all different types of anthropomorphized ocean creatures also helps to show diverse forms and appearance and foster an understanding of what we may not be familiar with.

5　In an interview with *USA Today* on the introduction of new female bots in the Transformers universe, *Rescue Bots* writer, Nicole Dubuc discussed the addition of female characters in the preschool version, 'that comes from little girls coming up to me saying, "I'm a Rescue Bot, I'd like to be on the team"' (Truitt 2015).

6　The term 'new man' was said to emerge in the 1980s and described men who were 'generally characterised as sensitive, emotionally aware, respectful of women and egalitarian in outlook' (Gill 2003: 37).

7　This area has received little study in animation but in cinema has seen an increasing amount of work since Steve Neale in 1983. His main thesis was about the way men's bodies are presented on screen and how we relate to this as spectators, building on Mulvey's (1975) seminal work on the 'male gaze' in cinema. This was argued to be centred around 'narcissistic identification' of the male as the 'image of authority' (Neale 1983: 7–8) which is arguably still prevalent on contemporary screens.

8　One of the most comprehensive is *Transformers Wiki* available online at http://tfwiki.net/wiki/Transformers:_Rescue_Bots_(cartoon) (accessed 21 February 2018).

9　Like many live-action shows, *Rescue Bots* had its own 'musical' episode, 'I Have Heard the Robots Singing', Season 3, episode 26.

10　The series uses black actors to portray black characters, unlike in the past (see Sammond in this volume), or even in some contemporary animation series such as *The Simpsons*. In the long-running series, the Asian character (and other ethnic minorities) Apu Nahasapeemapetilon is voiced by a white actor and has been the subject of a recent documentary, *The Problem with Apu* (Michael Melamedoff 2017).

References

Brownlee, S. (2011), 'Masculinity between Animation and Live Action, or SpongeBob v. Hasselhoff', *Animation Studies*, 6. Available online: https://journal.animationstudies.org/shannon-brownlee-masculinity-between-animation-and-live-action-or-spongebob-v-hasselhoff/ (accessed 21 February 2018).

Burdfield, C. (2014), 'Effeminate Ponies', *Animation Studies 2.0*. Available online: https://blog.animationstudies.org/?p=851 (accessed 21 February 2018).

Burke, K. and T. Burke (1998), *Saturday Morning Fever: Growing up with Cartoon Culture*, New York: St Martin's Press.

Clatterbaugh, K. (2004), 'What Is Problematic about Masculinities?', in P. Murphy (ed.), *Feminism and Masculinities*, Oxford: Oxford University Press.

Davis, G. and G. Needham (2009), *Queer TV: Theories, Histories, Politics*, London: Routledge.

Gauntlett, D. (2008), *Media, Gender and Identity: An Introduction*, 2nd edn, London: Routledge.

Gill, R. (2003), 'Power and the Production of Subjects: A Genealogy of the New Man and the New Lad', in B. Benwell (ed.), *Masculinities and Men's Lifestyle Magazines*, Oxford: Blackwell.

Hohlfeld, B. (2017), Email to author.

Maier, K. (2015), 'The Adult Appeal of "Steven Universe"', *Animation Studies 2.0*. Available online: https://blog.animationstudies.org/?p=1325 (accessed 21 February 2018).

Mulvey, L. (1975), 'Visual Pleasure and Narrative Cinema', *Screen*, 16(3): 6–18.

Neale, S. (1983), 'Masculinity as Spectacle', *Screen*, 24(6): 2–17.

Truitt, B. (2015), 'Female "Transformers" Come to the Fore', *USA Today*, 2 April. Available online: https://www.usatoday.com/story/life/2015/04/23/transformers-female-characters/26236633/ (accessed 21 February 2018).

20

Anime's Bodies

Rayna Denison

In this chapter from her book Anime: A Critical Introduction *(Bloomsbury 2015), Denison contextualizes how women's bodies in anime are read and understood by both Japanese and Western audiences. She examines their mutable and transformative properties, arguing that these properties are crucial to understanding the genres in which they appear, from horror, to science fiction, and even hentai (pornography).*

If any aspect of anime has drawn attention for its mutability, it is anime's depictions of human and humanoid bodies. Body debates in anime range across its genres, and from the industrial remediation of anime characters as toys to the ways female anime bodies are admired and even performed by fans. In all of these ways, discourses about anime have long centred on concepts of the body, which is all the more surprising in a type of media production that contains very few 'real' bodies. Christian McCrea suggests that the appeal of anime bodies lies in their 'discursive, disruptive and incredibly excessive' natures. He claims that the anime body 'is resolutely physical, but never truly available for us to interpret in the way … action films can be interpreted' (2008: 19). The fascination with bodies in anime is at least in part, therefore, a result of anime's ability to depict constantly mutating, metamorphosing and transforming bodies that exceed the possibilities of the real world, even going beyond live-action cinema. These transformations create impossible bodies that cross between genres from romance to horror, sometimes in the same text. Anime's bodies are therefore the subject of this chapter, in which I argue that discussions of anime's bodies play crucial roles in making sense of the genres in which they appear.

Gender studies-inflected debates are crucial here, with discussions of gendered power and dominance in anime frequently compared to Japanese culture's more rigid gender ideologies. Therefore, I begin with an overview of the analyses produced by academics and popular commentators about bodies within anime's varied genres, before focusing on a single example, canonized for its extreme representations of such gender and body issues.

Anime's powerful women have long fascinated commentators on anime, often framing debates about anime's cultural and aesthetic difference to other kinds of animation. These discussions of anime's bodies have, for this reason, normally focused on women's representations across the spectrum of anime's genres. While, as I intend to show, these debates about women range from the *shōjo* (adolescent girls) to horror, one particular industrial category has been key to these debates: pornography. While other genres play important roles in discussions of the anime body, pornography's place within anime culture has been perhaps the most emphatically contested beyond academic discussions, becoming a crucial part of anime's difference from other kinds of animation. During critical attempts to account for anime pornography, certain texts have come to define the discourse more than others. In this chapter, therefore, I examine the range of anime bodies discussed by academics before analysing how one particular medium, the original video anime (OVA), and one film series of that type, *Urotsukidōji* (Hideki Takayama, 1987–94), have shaped our understanding of anime's bodies, and with them, anime's body genres.

Anime bodies in Japan: From Disneyfication to toyetics

Before examining how anime's bodies have been understood transculturally, however, it is important to note that the anime body is also important in Japan. Not all of the body discussions in Japan are focused on the kinds of extreme anime bodies that have come to dominate English criticism, however. Manga and anime pioneer Osamu Tezuka has himself discussed the importance of transnational influences on the look of his characters. In his autobiography *My Life in Manga* (*Boku no Manga Jinsei*), for example, Tezuka talks at length about how he modelled Astro Boy after Mickey Mouse, mimicking Mickey Mouse's shape and Disney's method of keeping both of a character's ears on screen (1997: 111–113). Tezuka also reportedly borrowed his large character eyes from those of the Fleischer brothers' character Betty Boop (Ladd and Deneroff 2009). This transnational influence is significant for the way it commingles genres and styles, making even early anime part of global animation body debates.

The design and depiction of characters in anime is also frequently the subject of books on manga authors and animators in Japan. Usually titled *irasuto*, from the English 'illustrations', these image archives focus primarily on anime and manga characters (for a representative example, see Harada 2008). Images of anime characters also routinely grace the front covers of specialist magazines like *Animage (Animēju)*, *Animedia* and *Newtype* in Japan in the manner of the film stars and idols of other Japanese media industries. This kind of character representation is a product of anime's reliance on popular characters that can be exploited across a wide range of media formats. In Japan, this reliance on character has been recognized in the growth of a *kyara bijinesu*, or character business, in which characters are used as concepts around which entire franchises can be created. Such was famously the case, for example, when Takashi Okazaki had a figurine made of his *dōjinshi* character, Afro Samurai, which later became the central protagonist for a transnational anime co-production involving US star Samuel L. Jackson (Condry 2013: 80–82).

In many cases, the character business in Japan reimagines anime's heroes and heroines (and villains) to a wide range of new ends in order to extend the reach or fandom for a set of characters. Often, this involves more exploitative scenarios than those usually seen in their anime narratives. For example, Kyoto Animation's *nichijōkei* (everyday, or slice of life) anime *K'On!* (2009 and 2010) heroines are frequently depicted in more sexualized and provocative poses on the covers of popular anime magazines in Japan than those featured in the show's *moe*-style content, which is designed to produce protective feelings in fans (for example, see http://animage.jp/back_number/am_201403.html). For my purposes, the interest generated in this kind of character exploitation, a form of 'fan service' (LaMarre 2006), comes from the way it can create dramatic shifts in genre between an anime text and its promotional surround in Japanese magazine culture. As a result, these kinds of images acknowledge the importance of particular adult (usually male) fans while also indicating how central characters and their bodies are within anime's domestic culture.

As this suggests, there is a highly pornographic end of the Japanese anime market, but it remains the case that not all of the bodies of anime characters are understood or discussed in terms of exploitation. Japanese psychologist Tamaji Saitō, for example, has discussed the birth of a new kind of character in anime, the 'phallic girl' or beautiful fighting girl of whom he claims that:

> The icon of the beautiful fighting girl is an extraordinary invention capable of encapsulating polymorphous perversity in a stable form. She radiates the potential for an omnidirectional sexuality latent with pedophilia, homosexuality, fetishism, sadism, masochism, and other perversions, yet she behaves as if she were completely unaware of it all. (trans. J Keith Vincent and Dawn Lawson, [2000] 2011, loc.2189)

In Saitō's reading of anime's women, therefore, ambiguity rules. His most important intervention is in reading this 'thoroughly fictional construct' as one which 'nonetheless attains a paradoxical reality in the process of being desired and consumed' by otaku fans (loc. 287). Saitō's observation about the 'paradoxical reality' of Japanese anime women is thus bound up in their real-world consumption and in the ways fans interpret them psychologically.

Other Japanese scholars are more tentative in their claims, noting not the 'polymorphous perversity' of anime's characters, but their connections to indexical realism. For example, Misao Minamida argues for a reading of anime characters' closeness to real people in an analysis of Isao Takahata's anime adaptation of *Anne of Green Gables* (*Akage no An* literally, *Red-haired Anne*, 1979) and within a popular anime series with a racoon protagonist, titled *Rascal* (Hiroshi et al. 1977). Minamida wishes to evaluate this relationship 'because I think it [*Rascal*] is a work that masters the potential of anime on the point of drawing characters as "real people"' (2000: 34). This link to the 'real' is one Minamida goes on to trace through the faithful adaptation work undertaken by Takahata for his contribution to To-ei Do-ga's *Masterpiece Theater* series, but also through the ways these anime depict the everyday activities of their characters (34–36). In this variety of anime bodies, it is not the extremity or instability or exploitation of the body that shapes discourse, but the closeness of even anthropomorphized animal characters to lived human experiences and everyday events that gains significance.

Marc Steinberg's *Anime's Media Mix* offers a third, this time more industrial, interpretation of the anime body's significance (2012). In his detailed historical account, Steinberg quotes from a wide range of Japanese sources detailing the importance of characters to anime's economic success. He argues that as toys and other merchandise, anime's bodies are literalized and extended into new worlds. With the business of anime built around characters, Steinberg argues that 'the character is a particular combination of name and visual design that is in some sense independent from any particular medium' (2012: 83). In this respect, at least, Steinberg's industrial observations accord with Saito's psychological understanding of anime characters' meanings for Japanese fans. Crucially, it is the ability of characters to appeal to audiences as affective bodies within and beyond film and television that acts as a marker of their potential for success.

From big eyes to big breasts: Anime's bodies in critical commentary outside Japan

As this range of appreciations shows, there is no single approach to anime bodies, nor a single genre or issue around which anime body debates coalesce.

However, there are noticeable groupings of discourse that attend to anime's genres. Early in English-language commentary on anime, divisions between *shōjo* and *shōnen* manga and anime were grounded in aesthetic analyses of the body. For example, in one of the earlier books on anime in English, Antonia Levi compares the two categories, arguing that:

> Girls' and women's *manga* (*shōjo* manga) were precisely the opposite [of *shōnen*]. They focused on emotions and personal relationships. Plots were weak. Eyes, however, were enormous. Almost nothing happened, but you knew exactly how everyone felt about whatever it was that wasn't happening. (1996: 9)

The link between affect and physicality is presented as a core theme in *shojo* texts. The focus here on eyes in female character bodies in anime also helps to differentiate these texts from other, more masculine-oriented ones.

The idea that anime contained characters with 'enormous' eyes became something of a theme within English-language criticism. This seems to have begun with Frederik L. Schodt's *Manga! Manga! The World of Japanese Comics*, in which he asserts manga's role as an aesthetic origin point for *shōjo* styles, especially the aesthetics of the eye. Schodt writes that:

> By far the most striking visual aspect of girls' comics is the orblike eyes of the characters ... In contrast to men's and boys' comics, where the male characters have thick, arched Kabuki-style eyebrows and glaring eyes, heroines in girls' comics are generally drawn with pencil thin eyebrows, long, full eyelashes, and eyes the size of window panes that emote gentleness and femininity. Over the years artists have also come to draw a star next to the pupil that perhaps represents dreams, yearning, and romance – and beneath the star to then place one or more highlights. (1983: 91)

Romantic, gentle and overtly feminine in these interpretations, the large eyes of anime and manga have gone on to influence many aspects of the wider subcultures around Japanese media.

For example, fans have long emulated these *shōjo* eyes in everyday and 'cosplay' situations (Winge 2006). As early as 1995, Rick Marin and others were interviewing anime fans in New York who were wearing contact lenses to 'simulate little "toon twinkles in the corners of his eyes"'. Moreover, this aesthetic has become part of critical understandings of anime, even used in reviews of live-action films based on anime. For example, one reviewer of the Wachowski's failed blockbuster version of anime *Speed Racer* (Andy and Lana Wachowski 2008) said, 'this frenetic adaptation of the beloved 1960s Japanese cartoon bears little resemblance to that anime classic of yore, unless you count Christina Ricci's saucerlike brown eyes' (Hornaday

2008, for more, see Denison 2014). Satirical though this reading may be, it confirms the status of big eyes as one of anime's core aesthetic tropes.

However, to think that the *shōjo* and their bodies can be defined solely through these 'window pane' eyes would belittle the varied modes through which anime's female characters have been understood. Annalee Newitz began a conversation in the mid-1990s about the magical abilities of *shōjo* characters, particularly their powers of transformation. In what Newitz terms the 'romantic comedy genre' of anime, presumably a translation of the Japanese *rabu kome* or 'love comedy' genre, she names the 'chief subgenre: "magical girls"'. Among these magical girls, Newitz notes a penchant for traditional gender roles and 'slapstick-style encounters which are sexy but innocent' (1995: 4). Into these encounters, Newitz reads a regressive set of patriarchal pleasures available to Japanese and US fans alike.

Susan J. Napier, by contrast, reads the magical girls of anime in slightly different ways. Her analysis reveals a range of *shōjo* characters who 'all possess some form of psychic or occult power' while 'at the same time as they can be seen as intimately related with a young girl's normal femininity' (1998: 93). Napier argues that these versions of the *shōjo* were especially important for appearing during a period of significant change for Japanese women, dubbing them '*shōjo* fantasies' (105) that allow women's power to be explored through the liminal status of the teenaged girl protagonist.

In one particularly notable (and commented upon) example of the *shōjo* category, Rumiko Takahashi's *Ranma ½* (anime TV series produced in 1989 and 1989–92 engendering a multimedia franchise), Newitz examines gender trouble at the heart of the anime's narrative about bodily transformations. When the protagonist, Ranma, is splashed with water of varying temperatures he shifts back and forth between being a *shōnen* and a *shōjo* character, the latter signalled as his enchanted form through the use of red hair and an ample bosom. For audiences, Newitz argues that 'quite simply, *Ranma ½* demonstrates to the young man who enjoys romantic comedy *anime* that he is constantly in danger of becoming a girl' (6). Transformations from male into female bodies are figured here as a site of disquieting Otherness, with Ranma's female form equating to 'male fears at the heart of the comedy romance genre' (1998: 93). Napier's considerations of transformation and magic build on this early work and lead her to conclude that 'although references to genitalia are conspicuous by their virtual absence in *Ranma ½*, the sexual signifier of breasts is constantly evoked throughout the series to denote that something is "wrong"' (2005: 54). She goes on to link Ranma's gender swapping with Japanese transsexual *bishōjo*-nen (beautiful boy) narratives as another potential subgenre with which it might be possible to associate *Ranma ½* (60). Within these discussions, Ranma's female form becomes a problem for both gender and genre, shifting between the *shōnen* and *shōjo* in ways that these authors argue gives greater credence to the former category over the latter, thereby suggesting a bias against women in anime.

Transformations of other kinds are picked up on by Anne Allison and Frenchy Lunning. Lunning argues that the *shōjo* body is abject, that there is nothing 'under the ruffles':

> To the extent that gender becomes a fictive notion in favor of a magical state of shape-shifting, they swivel and switch dangerously, as if announcing the absence of an original gender state. For the creators of manga and anime, the shōjo body offers a substrate upon which is inscribed the tension between a desire to do away with gender and the inability to express gender conflict without gender. As a representation of the abject, the shōjo character becomes a thing of phantasm. (2011: 7)

To argue that these often active, powerful and complicated protagonists lack a 'core' denies the subjectivity of women in anime (for countercommentaries to this view, see Saito – 2000; 2011 or Sugawa Shimada 2011). Allison, by contrast, links transformative powers of anime's women to an altogether more materialist requisite: the need to create merchandising-led anime shows.

Allison argues that in many series, but especially those aimed at children:

> The fascination with bodies and their reconstruction into fusions of insect/machine, human/tool, nature/technology proceeds along two axes ... The first is transformation (*henshin*), and the second is union (*gattai*): assembling the individual bodies, robots and weapons ... into superconglomerates. (2006: 106–107)

Even though Allison is primarily writing about live-action series like *Power Rangers* (1975 – in Japan; 1993 – in the United States) in this analysis, her observations hold for many team-oriented anime television series. Allison's analysis also suggests good reason for the appearance of 'super-deformed' or *chibi* characters in anime – cute, truncated versions of characters that can be easily transformed into merchandising objects.

Allison, like Steinberg, thereby asserts that commodification is a crucial part of anime culture. She describes *Sailor Moon* (*Bishōjo Senshi Se-ra- Mu-n*, 1992–7) in these terms:

> The star of the show is a 14-year-old girl, Usagi Tsukino (Serena in English), who, guided by her talking cat, Luna, transforms into the superhero Sailor Moon by activating various sources of moon power, such as a penlike device called 'moon prism' and the tiara she wears when 'morphed'. (2000: 269)

Allison explains how important the shift from *shōjo* to an adult female body becomes within *Sailor Moon*, stating that 'her body becomes first naked and then reclothed, starting with a sailor bodysuit and followed by a miniskirted sailor outfit with a plunging neckline that shows off her newly developed breasts' (272). *Sailor Moon*'s transformation sequences thereby invert the logic of *Ranma ½*'s comedy with the adult female body, and specifically breasts, used to imply capability, power and self-confidence. It is also, however, a commodified body, reliant on objects of power (that were turned into merchandising in Japan) for the ability to transform from child to adult. It is here that her work accords with Lunning's claims about the 'fantasy of endless diversion' (2011: 8) at work at the heart of *shōjo* texts. In this way, both Lunning and Allison position anime's representations of women as liminal: as occupying an uncertain space that relies on replicability (through merchandise) while revolving around an empty centre.

If the *shōjo* category of anime is invested in the liminal status of women's bodies, held in tension between male and female or young girl and adulthood, the women represented in other genres of anime cleave closer to the kinds of debates usually limned for 'body genres' in US cinema, particularly horror and science fiction's cyborg narratives. Elsewhere, the idea of the cyborg was introduced as a post-human anime body, but it is worth noting that these debates about anime's cyborgs extend far beyond the discussions of *Ghost in the Shell* (Denison 2015: chapter 2). For example, the *mecha* genre is a key part of these debates. It is usually defined in the following terms: '*Mecha* films and shows place an emphasis on mechanical elements, especially robots and giant mechanical suits' (Ruh 2005: 73). Borrowing heavily from live-action *tokusatsu* (special effects) genre predecessors like the *Ultraman* (*Urotoraman*) and *Masked Rider* (*Kamen Raidā*) franchises (Allison 2006; Onoue et al. 2012), these anime present different sorts of transformation from what Allison calls *gattai*, offering more physical interminglings of the body and technology.

Nor is this discourse about intermingling restricted to discussions of women's bodies in anime. Brian Ruh reads the robots that grow from protagonist, Naota's, forehead in *FLCL* (OVAs 2000–2001) as symbolic of his sexual awakening process, and Naota's merger with robot, Canti, at times of strife as a sign of the protagonist's maturation process (2005). In Ruh's estimation, therefore, the male cyborg is relatively normative and combines with robots in ways that enable a discussion of the *shōnen's* liminal cultural status. By contrast, the transformations of Tetsuo at the end of *Akira* are understood by Napier as an example of the 'monstrous adolescent' whose 'frenzy of metamorphosis' allows the audience to be overwhelmed by the on-screen catastrophe (2005: 46). Napier extends this frenzy to cyborg characters like Sho, who merges with 'bio-booster armour' in the *Guyver* franchise (OVAs 1989–91) to become 'a recognizable version of the universal fantasy of a weakling's transformation into a superhero'

(2005: 92). However, this transformation is anything but pleasant for Sho, leading Napier to conclude that men's bodies are not as accepting of metamorphosis as women's in anime narratives.

This may help to explain the preponderance for investigating cyborg women in academic accounts of anime. For example, in an unusual discussion of a romantically framed cyborg, Thomas LaMarre's analysis of Chi from *Chobits* (2002) takes Silvio's argument about form and content further, arguing that the series formulates its cyborg woman as 'a metaphysical problem'. LaMarre contends that 'the woman-ness of Chi is an effect or symptom of something else, something beyond Chi as a physical being (a computer)' (2006: 54). In *Chobits*, the resolution to the problem of the cyborg woman is a platonic, yet sexualized, relationship. LaMarre calls this platonic love, which "implies a love of ideal forms over and above the crass material intercourse of bodies, even while soft-porn images of bodies remain desirable and even necessary. For *Chobits* is not simply about love over lust, or about ideal forms over matter. *Chobits* also includes a great deal of sex, or something like it" (57–58).

LaMarre's distinction between sexed and sexless relationships in science fiction anime is particularly significant for the way it can be mapped onto the romantic comedies and 'sexless' *shōjo* texts discussed earlier to explain fan service and many of the other generically incongruous moments instantiated by anime's magical girls.

Original Video Animation (OVA): Bringing anime's bodies into disrepute?

From discussions of cyborgs' metamorphoses and platonic sex, it is a short step to the discourses about anime's darker fringes and more explicit and extreme bodies. One category of industrial production has been continually invoked as a source for the disreputable anime body: Original Video Animation (OVA). Jonathan Clements, rehearsing a long-standing debate about whether the correct term for anime on VHS is OVA or OAV, quotes Yoshiharu Tokugi. Tokugi argues that OVA is as an industrial term used to denote 'straight to video' releases, whereas Original Animation Video (OAV) is a marketing term created to denote a new VHS text and not 'a repurposed work' (1999: 307, quoted in Clements 2013: 167). Clements's frustration about this lingering debate emerges when he declares that 'such quibbles seem pointless – the acronyms have persisted interchangeably in English, one suspects, because monoglot pundits wish to brag that they can understand one element on a page of Japanese text' (2013: 167). While Clements's assessment is devastatingly dismissive of the debate, he raises an important issue by quoting Tokugi. While the name of the category may not matter, there seems to be lingering confusion about what it contains and when to deploy it.

Something as simple as the production of 'straight to video' anime would seem straightforward enough. However, as Tokugi asserts, these home video releases comprise virtually every kind of anime text: from feature-length anime films, through to single television-length episodes of serialized anime, to collections of repurposed anime episodes or shorts. As this variety suggests, anime producers have been canny about the ways home video can be made to support new kinds of productions. Famously, director Mamoru Oshii was one of the founding members of Headgear, a company set up specifically so that the creators of the *Patlabor* (1988–9) OVA series would remain beneficiaries of any subsequent remakes and extensions of their work (Ruh 2004: 75). This kind of OVA series acts like a 'calling card' to industry, and if they 'acquired enough of a following to justify their upgrade into TV serials and movies' (Clements 2013: 168), then they could become the origin points for an entire franchise of anime texts.

However, this does not mean the relationship between 'traditional' media and OVAs has been straightforward. High-profile OVA series will often receive short theatrical releases, as in the case of *Garden of Sinners* (*Kara no Kyo* - kai, Ufotable, 2007–), a long-running OVA series of films, usually about an hour in length, that have enjoyed theatrical releases in Tokyo before being more widely released on VHS, DVD and Blu-ray (Joo et al. 2013). Advertising also plays an important role in the repackaging of anime texts on OVA. Take, for example, Katsuhiro Ōtomo's *Freedom* (2006), a series of anime advertisements for Cup Noodles that were later collected and repackaged across several Blu-ray and DVD releases.

Or, alternatively, there are oddities like Studio Ghibli's *Short Short* (2005), which collated the studio's advertising and music video works. In a bundling of perhaps even more obscure works, the *Fullmetal Alchemist Premium OVA Collection* (released by Aniplex in Japan in 2006 and by Funimation in the United States in 2009, see Figure 20.1) offered up animation created for a special theme park ride at Universal Studios Japan along with short promotional videos for the film *Conqueror of Shamballa* (Seiji Mizushima 2005), including one done as live-action in which a statue of one of the main characters, Alphonse, takes a journey to *Fullmetal Alchemist*'s production studio, Bones. This in addition to the reproduction of television shows and films on sell-through video and digital formats, as well as the kinds of 'midquels' described by Clements (2013: 168) and sequels described by Tsugata. The contradictory, highly commercialized content of home video anime releases in Japan might go some way to explaining why there has been such contestation about what to call it. In addition, though, this new set of home viewing technologies fostered a new set of markets.

In *Anime Gaku* (*Anime Studies*), Nobuyuki Tsugata argues that the first OVA was *Dallos* (Mamoru Oshii), released in 1983 (2011). Clements notes

FIGURE 20.1 Chibi wrap party from the *Fullmetal Alchemist Premium* OVA *Collection*.

that in fact 'Dallos was not initially intended as the first "original video anime." To many of its makers, it was regarded instead as a "failed" television project' (2013: 167–168). Tsugata claims that by the height of the boom in home video in 1989, there were over 400 OVA releases per year (2011: 32) and elsewhere, he explains this popularity by arguing that the success of OVAs was in part down to the appearance of young adult and adult anime (using the imported English term 'adult anime' to describe these films, 2011: 32 and 2005: 160). About the latter, Tsugata writes that the serialization of these adult-oriented OVA anime led to some enormously popular series including *Cream Lemon* (1984–) with nearly 40 OVAs, while science fiction fantasy *Legend of the Galactic Heroes* (*Ginga Eiyu–Densetsu*, 1988–97) achieved an extraordinary 110 OVA volumes (Tsugata 2005: 160).

Cream Lemon is an overtly pornographic work that shifts story worlds and protagonists across the series. McCarthy and Clements accord it importance, arguing that the 'erotic OAV opened up the possibility of showing erotica without such artifices [as seen in television anime]; the intended audience would know what they were getting. On video, with no possibility of offending the uninterested, erotica could thrive, and in this new market audiences got their first taste of *Cream Lemon* from Fairy Dust' (1998: 42).

In this, *Cream Lemon* and other erotic anime arose alongside a broader market for violence and pornographic live-action works, known as V-Cinema. Alexander Zahlten has done groundbreaking work on To-ei's V-Cinema in his PhD thesis and explains that To-ei's V-Cinema market seems to have grown up independent of its earlier work in OVAs, which began in 1986 (2007: 340). But the markets are parallel, with adult-oriented pornographic and violent films generally feeding a niche for adult-viewing materials without the need to pander to younger viewers.

These adult home cinema texts have been translated from industrial categories like OVAs and V-Cinema into new generic categories as they have moved abroad. However, McCarthy and Clements argue erotic anime take many forms and that despite the notoriety of some of them, there 'is no indication that they "took over the market" in any sense' (1998: 43). These *ero* (from 'erotic') texts, as they term them, were also differently generic inside and outside Japan. For example, McCarthy and Clements argue that the long-running *Cream Lemon* series was popular enough in Japan to create a new subgenre of texts with 'lemon' references in their titles (47). Outside Japan, this new industrial category of OVAs became just another set of anime texts being distributed on video, which was fast becoming the dominant means for consuming anime.

As a consequence, when violent pornographic anime like *Urotsukidōji Dirty Pair* (1985–90) or *Vampire Hunter Yōko* (*Mamono Hantā Yōko*, 1990–95) arrived in the United States and the United Kingdom, they were recontextualized by their distributors to form a very different understanding of 'anime' or 'Japanimation' to that perceived in Japan. Abroad, where the terms *ero* and 'adult anime' were less used, numerous Japanese terms came to be deployed to describe the subgenres of pornography making their ways to the United States and the United Kingdom, in particular *hentai*. Susan J. Napier explains that the term means 'pornography' (2005: x), but elsewhere, Philip Brophy proclaims that it means 'perverse' (2005: 130), whereas Mark McLelland explains that the use of the term *hentai* to refer to erotic or sexual manga and anime in general is not a Japanese but an English innovation. In Japanese *hentai* can reference sexual material but only of an extreme, 'abnormal' or 'perverse' kind; it is not a general category (2006: 3).

Susan Pointon's early article on Japanese animated pornography has been influential in painting all of anime pornography as *hentai*. However, Pointon was referring specifically to a single anime OVA series: *Urotsukidōji*. She notes *Urotsukidōji*'s generic hybridity, arguing that 'when viewed in isolation, this sex/magic/horror/romance synthesis may seem as alien to a Western audience as the exaggerated genital dimensions' of one of the main demonic characters, but that 'it follows the conventions of fantasy horror texts which were laid down in the late Edo period' (1997: 50). Nevertheless, Pointon also declares that 'these examples of *hentai*, a sub-genre of Japanese animation that literally translates as perverted, have managed through word of mouth to achieve a cult status among young adolescent males' (43) outside Japan. This recognition of *hentai* as a subgenre is important, and McCarthy and Clements attempted to address the slippage around anime pornography in their book on *ero* anime. In that book, McCarthy and

Clements present an holistic view of sex in anime showing just how diverse anime's engagements with this body genre have been. However, to do this regenrification work, they named a subgenre that now often replaces the idea of *hentai* in English: what they term 'tits and tentacle' pornographic anime, many of which, they argue, are the product of the new OVA culture in Japan (1998).

Urotsukidōji: Legend of a controversy

Worst of all, because most lovingly crafted, were the Japanese cartoons known as anime ... [that] often feature scenes of women being gang-raped by lascivious, leering monsters, aliens with tentacles that entwine and bind the victims before multiply penetrating them through various orifices. Heavily cut by the Board was a scene in which a monster with a huge metal phallus rapes a victim orally, exploding in her mouth into spikes which penetrate the cheeks .... In many of these cartoons, there seems to be an underlying hatred (or is it fear?) of women, which can only be slaked by the destruction of the female principle ... It is frightening to view the exorcising of such violent fantasies in cartoon of such technical brilliance. (British Board of Film Classification Report 1994–1995: 20, quoted in McCarthy and Clements 1998: 92)

This is a truncated quotation from a report by the British Board of Film Classification (BBFC), the UK's official film censor, which recounts in detail the offence given by a variety of scenes in the *Urotsukidōji* OVA series. The language used in the report is as explicit as the cut scenes from the series, and the report tars all of anime with the *Overfiend*'s phallic brush: anime 'hate' women, they delight in killing them and these 'violent fantasies' are all the worse for being technically accomplished (see Figure 20.2). Anime's problem, this report suggests, is its treatment of the female body and its representation of that body in extremis.

McCarthy and Clements quote this BBFC report in greater detail than I have done, by way of explaining the furore that arose around the (censored) releases of the *Urotsukidōji* OVA series. They argue that:

The two titles that did the most to create the modern-day anime business in the West have also arguably damaged it, by encouraging false expectations from the foreign audience. 'Everyone' has seen *Akira*. 'Everyone' has heard of the *Overfiend* .... within the journalistic community, it is the *Overfiend* that is most likely to get column-inches, and all anime, not just the erotic subgenres, are damned by association. (1998: 82)

Both authors were working in the UK's anime industries, reporting on and translating texts for distribution. Their assessment arises from a privileged position of knowledge and reflects the real fears of a fanbase that worried that *hentai*, or violent 'perverse' anime pornography, would become all that anime was ever known for abroad.

However, returning to this debate now, and examining wider review and newspaper coverage of anime texts from the period of the mid-1990s when the *Urotsukidōji* OVA series was released, reveals some slightly different patterns of discourse than might be expected. I have focused on UK news coverage as this is where the most overt debates were recorded (between the BBFC and fans, and by critics like McCarthy and Clements). However, as a useful point of comparison, I begin by examining the US coverage of Central Park Media's release of this series.

In *Video Week*, the kinds of promotion undertaken for the *Urotsukidōji* series start to be made clear. On the release of the *Urotsukidōji Perfect Collection* (Central Park Media 1993), for example, press notes are quoted that court controversy: 'Company touts Collection as entire story with 40 min. of outtakes deemed "so sexually violent that it could not be included in the theatrical features"' (*Video Week* 1993). Far from shying away from possible conflicts, the distributors were seeking even greater controversy for the films as the series went on. It is interesting to note, therefore, that US reviewers did not always respond to these shock tactics. Richard Harrington's 1993 review of the first in the series, *Urotsukidōji: Legend of the Overfiend* in the *Washington Post*, commented that it 'could just as well have been subtitled "Legend of the Oversexedfiends." This Japanese

FIGURE 20.2 Demonic imagery from Urotsukidōji: *Legend of the Overfiend.*

animation feature is so relentlessly drenched in graphic scenes of perverse sex and ultra-violence that no one's likely to challenge its "NC-17" rating. Iron-cast stomachs only!' His take on the film is humorous and his response to its content is to critique, not damn, its insistence on 'perverse sex and ultra-violence'. He finishes his review by commenting that 'the 108-minute film has been dubbed "erotic grotesque," but only the second term seems deserved'. This is a direct reference to the Japanese genre of erotic-grotesque-nonsense media production, implying either a press kit for the film that tried to situate it beyond pornography for US audiences or a deep knowledge on Harrington's part about Japanese media culture. The fact that the term recurs in the same newspaper when Desson Howe offers a shorter review of the same film is perhaps suggestive of the former (1993).

So if the US distributors attempted to place the *Urotsukidōji* series in relation to both existing Japanese genres of media and notions of extremis, how did the UK respond to the Overfiend? McCarthy and Clements quote an article by David Lister of the *Independent* as an example of the kinds of histrionic responses *Urotsukidōji* engendered (1998: 91). Lister writes with concern about the 'rape and abuse scenes' whose victims are 'usually under-age and often doe-eyed schoolgirls – a popular theme in Japanese films' (1993). However, despite all of the concerns he ends his response by quoting Kanjee Bates, a fanzine editor, who blames the UK's positioning of anime alongside Disney texts in shops for the controversy, and not the films themselves. Bates says, just before worrying about the ease with which children can buy adult VHS tapes in the UK, that 'it is regrettable that the only Manga films shown over here were the sex and violence ones, as there were many art films in the genre'. By giving Bates the last word, Lister confirms that there are problems with anime sex and violence in the UK, but the fanzine editor deflects the controversy onto UK retail chains and away from the content of the anime itself.

This kind of worried but not histrionic critique can be found in many other reviews and commentaries on the *Urotsukidōji* series. For example, when the first in the series was shown at a special screening at the London ICA, Derek Malcolm related that 'there are special late-night performances of Hideki Takayama's controversial *Urotsukidōji: Legend of the Overfiend*, praised for its brilliant technique, but accused of sexism, sadism and amorality' (1992). In this, Malcom could be quoting from the BBFC's later report on the series despite pre-dating it, so close is the language used. Once more, it is a pre-existing sense of controversy that shapes the response, but the tone of the review is balanced nevertheless.

Jonathan Romney's review of this same film for a National Film Theatre (NFT) anime festival in 1995 accords it a 'cult' status two years later, describing the film as an appeal to the Lolita complex which 'seems to go way overboard'. Romney states that 'it starts off as a raunchy college-kids romp, then turns into a horrendous feast of entrail-spurting and nightmare sexuality' (1995). The genre mixing is where Romney seems to have problems with *Urotsukidōji*, and its shift in gears between sex comedy and body horror is his central point of contention.

Rather than wholeheartedly condemning the *Urotsukidōji* series, therefore, critical responses show an acknowledgement of its extreme content working in concert with understandings of its genre film status and even its technical accomplishment. However, it is also worth noting that by 1995, mainstream UK newspapers were making New Year Resolution lists that included items like: 'Watch some manga films, read a graphic novel and be generally more aware of the cartoon renaissance' (*Observer* 1995). So, while McCarthy and Clements are right in arguing that *Urotsukidōji* and its ilk shaped discourses about the sexualized violence inherent in many of the anime being brought to the UK by major distributors like Manga Entertainment, not all of the responses were straightforward dismissals of the potential of anime as popular culture or art. While many journalists found the content of the *Urotsukidōji* series bemusing and at times grotesque, they were able nonetheless to see value, too.

Conclusions

As an extreme form of pornography, the 'tits and tentacle' or *hentai* genre of anime pornography was neither the main form of anime being produced in Japan in the 1980s, nor even necessarily representative of the wider *ero* genres of pornography that would have been available to distributors at the time. Moreover, in Japan, the genre itself is usually named as either *ero* or adult anime, without the histrionic labels invented outside Japan. The regenrification of these pornographic anime thereby reveals more about the media markets for animation outside Japan, and about distributor attempts to broaden the scope of those markets, than they do about animated Japanese pornography.

Titles like the *Urotsukidōji* series allowed Western distributors to create a new and controversial kind of anime that could augment the success of *Akira* by emphasizing that film's violence and metamorphic passages as key pleasures for the newly emerging foreign adult audiences for anime. This attempt to create a new market was met by gatekeeper fans with trepidation if not outright concern, as shown by Bates's comments about the laxness of the UK's VHS retailers that comes hot on the heels of the UK firestorm over video nasties (Egan 2007, for more, see Saito – [2000] 2011, loc. 2142). In these respects, opinions about anime were as reliant on the technology of video in the UK as they were back in Japan, though the debates shifted considerably.

In more general terms, it was the way the *Urotsukidōji* series treated bodies that seems to have generated disquiet. It became, therefore, one of the key texts around which popular and academic debates over anime and the body began to be formulated, as seen in Pointon's early article. These debates have been formulated around the aesthetics as well as the content of anime. It is not just the fact that bodies are transformed, exploded or mutated that concerned commentators, it was the fact that they did so *differently* to other kinds of animation. The newness of anime's bodies, from the big eyes of the *shōjo* to the *mecha*-clad *shōnen*, to the adults and children victimized in pornographic anime, was perhaps unsurprisingly challenging to critics and censors. It has been a difference that academics have leapt upon, producing wide-ranging assessments of anime bodies, often in conjunction with important zeitgeist-inflected theories of gender and genre. Such is certainly visible in the shifting discussions of the *shōjo*, who moves through discourse from active heroine to an abject, soulless, but well-dressed, character type.

The absence of a real referent for anime's bodies conjoins the two in discourse. The discussions of cyborg women in this chapter attest as much, envisioning the adaptive body of the cyborg woman as both object of investigation within narratives and a subject position that shifts across them. As Sharalyn Orbaugh argues in an article about cyborg affect and the limits of the human, 'given the nature of the medium, film requires a *visible* protagonist' (2008: 155). This, she argues, is why the narrative of the *Ghost in the Shell* sequel, *Innocence* (Mamoru Oshii 2004), shifts to Major Motoko Kusanagi's second-in-command, Batō, once the Major becomes incorporeal. As Orbaugh's argument suggests, one of the most compelling reasons for the scholarly and popular commentary on anime's bodies is this: anime bodies challenge our conceptualizations of what it means to be human. Anime contains so many anthropomorphized, mutating, transforming, displaced and exploding bodies because these bodies defamiliarize our concepts not just of animation's cultural purposes and potential, but of humanity itself.

References

Allison, A. (2000), 'Sailor Moon: Japanese Superheroes for Global Girls', in T.J. Craig (ed.), *Japan Pop!: Inside the World of Japanese Popular Culture*, 259–278, Armonk, NY: M.E. Sharp.

Allison, A. (2006), *Millennial Monsters: Japanese Toys and the Global Imagination*, Berkeley: University of California Press.

Brophy, P. (2005), *100 Anime*, London: BFI Publishing.

Clements, J. (2013), *Anime: A History*, London: BFI Publishing.

Condry, I. (2013), *The Soul of Anime: Collaborative Creativity and Japan's Media Success Story*, Durham: Duke University Press.

Denison, R. (2014), 'Franchising and Failure: Discourses of Failure within the Japanese-American *Speed Racer* Franchise', in *Mechademia 9: Origins*, 269–281, Minneapolis: University of Minnesota Press.

Denison, R. (2015), *Anime: A Critical Introduction*, London: Bloomsbury.

Egan, K. (2007), *Trash or Treasure?: Censorship and the Changing Meanings of the Video Nasties*, Manchester: Manchester University Press.

Harada, A. (2008), *Hell Girl Illustrations: Mirrored Flowers, Moonlight in Water [Jigoku Sho-jo Irasutore-shonzu: Kyo - ka Suigetsu]*, Tokyo: Ichijinsha.

Harrington, R. (1993), 'Movies; "Overfiend": Cyber Sadism', *Washington Post*, April 26: D7.

Hornaday, A. (2008), '"Speed Racer" Is Stuck on a Fast Track to Nowhere', *Washington Post*, May 9: C01.

Howe, D. (1993), 'Film Capsules', *Washington Post*, April 23: N33.

Joo, W., R. Denison and H. Furukawa (2013), *Manga Movies Project Report 1: Transmedia Japanese Franchising*. Available online: http://www.mangamoviesproject.com/publications.html (accessed 3 September 2014).

Ladd, F. with H. Deneroff (2009), *Astro Boy and Anime Come to the Americas*, Jefferson: McFarland.

LaMarre, T. (2006), 'Platonic Sex: Perversion and Sho- jo Anime (Part One)', *animation: an interdisciplinary journal*, 1(1): 45–59.

Levi, A. (1996), *Samurai from Outer Space: Understanding Japanese Animation*, Chicago, IL: Open Court.

Lister, D. (1993), 'Cartoon Cult with an Increasing Appetite for Sex and Violence', *Independent*, October 15: 10.

Lunning, F. (2011), 'Under the Ruffles: Sho-jo and the Morphology of Power', in F. Lunning (ed.), *Mechademia 6: User Enhanced*, 3–19, Minneapolis: University of Minnesota Press.

Malcolm, D. (1992), 'Film: Manga! Manga! Manga! Season of Japanese Animations', *Guardian*, October 22: 6.

McCarthy, H. and J. Clements (1998), *The Erotic Anime Movie Guide*, London: Titan Books.

McCrea, C. (2008), 'Explosive, Expulsive, Extraordinary: The Dimensional Excess of Animated Bodies', *animation: an interdisciplinary journal*, 3(1): 9–24.

McLelland, M. (2006), '*A Short History of "Hentai"*', Intersections: Gender, History and Culture in an Asian Context, no.12. Available online: http://intersections.anu.edu.au/issue12/mclelland.html (last accessed 20 July 2015).

Napier, S.J. (1998), 'Vampires, Psychic Girls, Flying Women and Sailor Scouts: Four Faces of the Young Female in Japanese Popular Culture', in D.P. Martinez (ed.), *The Worlds of Japanese Popular Culture: Gender, Shifting Boundaries and Global Cultures*, 91–109, Cambridge: Cambridge University Press.

Napier, S.J. (2005), *Anime from Akira to Howl's Moving Castle: Experiencing Contemporary Japanese Animation*, New York: Palgrave.

Newitz, A. (1995), 'Magical Girls and Atomic Bomb Sperm: Japanese Animation in America', *Film Quarterly*, 49(1) Autumn: 2–15.

Orbaugh, S. (2008), 'Emotional Infectivity: The Japanese Cyborg and the Limits of the Human', Mechademia 3, 150–172

Pointon, S. (1997), 'Transcultural Orgasm as Apocalypse: *Urotsukidoji; The Legend of the Overfiend*', *Wide Angle* 19(3) July: 41–63.

Romney, J. (1995), 'Manga for All Seasons', *Guardian*, May 4: T15.

Ruh, B. (2004), *Stray Dog of Anime: The Films of Mamoru Oshii*, New York: Palgrave Macmillan.

Ruh, B. (2005), 'The Robots from Takkun's Head: Cyborg Adolescence in *FLCL*', in S.T. Brown (ed.), *Cinema Anime*, 139–160, New York: Palgrave.

Saitō, T. ([2000] 2011), *Beautiful Fighting Girl*, trans. J.K. Vincent and D. Lawson, Minneapollis: University of Minnesota Press.

Schodt, F.L. (1983), *Manga! Manga! The World of Japanese Comics*, Tokyo: Kodansha International.

Steinberg, M. (2012), *Anime's Media Mix: Franchising Toys and Characters in Japan*, Minneapolis: University of Minnesota Press.

Tezuka, O. (1997), *My Manga Life [Boku no Manga Jinsei]*, Tokyo: Iwanami Publishing.

Tsugata, N. (2005), *Introduction to Animation Studies [Anime-shon Gaku Nyumon]*, Tokoyo: Heibonsha.

Tsugata, N. (2011), 'Animation History', *[Anime no Rekishi]*, in M. Takahashi and N. Tsugata (ed.), *Anime Studies [Anime Gaku]*, 24–44, Tokyo: NTT Publishing.

Winge, T. (2006), 'Costuming the Imagination: Origins of Anime and Manga Cosplay', in F. Lunning (ed.), *Mechademia 1: Emerging Worlds of Anime and Manga*, 65–76, Minneapolis: University of Minnesota Press.

Zahlten, A. (2007), *The Role of Genre in Film from Japan: Transformations 1960s–2000s*, PhD Thesis, Johannes Gutenberg University, Mainz.

21

Women in Disney's Animated Features 1989–2005

Amy M. Davis

Davis's chapter from her book Good Girls and Wicked Witches: Women in Disney's Feature Animation *(Indiana University Press 2007) considers Disney films between the years 1989 and 2005. By exploring changes in the industry, such as an increase in female personnel at Disney, Davis argues that this period evidences a change in Disney's thematic preoccupations and the representation of female characters; the films produced at this time are concerned with issues of equality and difference as well as featuring more active female characters. The chapter presented here is an abridged version of the original chapter 'Disney Films 1989–2005: The 'Eisner Era'.*

Throughout popular culture in America in the 1970s and 1980s, changes in the ways in which women were portrayed began to appear. The images of the happy home-maker and contented wife and mother did not disappear, but nor did they remain the only acceptable alternative shown to be available to 'respectable' women. Furthermore, the definition of a 'respectable' woman was beginning to broaden throughout this time, encompassing not just the housewife, but also the single career woman, the working wife and mother, the single mother and various permutations of these identities. Women's magazines expanded from covering only such topics as fashion, recipes and maintaining a youthful appearance, and began including articles about the ways a woman could 'have it all': being a wife, mother and career woman all at the same time, and finding equal fulfilment in her work both inside and outside her home.[1] Going also (though not completely gone) was the image of a woman whose goodness was exemplified by her being innocent and asexual, and beginning to emerge in this period was the woman who was kind, virtuous, good and aware of (as well as able to enjoy) her own sexuality.

During this time period, the overall make-up of the Disney studio itself shifted from one of male dominance to, if not full equality, at least a greater presence of women in leadership roles. A number of changes in the 1990s affected its animation department. Younger talent at Disney and an increase in the number of women in higher-ranking positions (such as writers Susannah Grant and Irene Mecchi, lead animators Nancy Beiman and Ellen Woodbury, clean-up artist Nancy Kniep, supervisors Janet Bruce, Karen Comella and Hortensia Casagran, and producer Alice Dewey) undoubtedly influenced not only the kinds of female characters the studio chose to portray, but also the ways these portrayals were shaped.

Animated films 1989 to 2005

A number of significant changes are to be found in the way such themes as love, independence, duty, goodness and evil were portrayed in the Disney Studio's animated films between 1989 and 2005, sometimes reflecting current trends in Hollywood, more often echoing ideas of arguably the most pervasive discursive influence of the 1990s – political correctness.[2] It is in the eighteen films produced by the Studio during this period, and particularly in the films covered in this study, that themes of multi-culturalism and tolerance of those who are different were depicted by Disney for the first time, and in which ideas about equality, integrity, honour and spirit take on a greater significance and depth. Unlike the earlier films, in which the heroines' honour was depicted and proven simply through her goodness and acquiescence, the heroines of Disney's animated films of this period show their integrity through their actions, rather than through their inaction. Furthermore, the level of action and independence demonstrated by these heroines grew exponentially with each film, and could still readily be seen even when the main character of the film was male and the leading female character was in a more supporting role.

The animated films made at Disney during this period most typically feature stories about humans, a change from the studio's earlier history. Why the Disney studio moved towards working more on stories about humans had many possible reasons, some of which may have been connected to the fact that technical and artistic advances in animation made it easier for animators to create more convincing and realistic human characters than was possible in the past. Another likelihood is that a relaxation of attitudes towards such topics as sexuality has allowed the animators to explore these issues more completely with human characters than was possible before.

In earlier films, stories about animal characters have a greater emphasis on the characters' sensuality and sexuality than do stories about humans. The idea of a fairy tale princess sauntering up to her intended, preening, hips swaying and flirting is impossible to imagine in the earlier Disney films. The only human characters who do such things are generally depicted as being not very nice, and in fact as being vain and oversexed (as is the case with the ugly step sisters, Anastasia and Drusela, in *Cinderella*). Yet in *Bambi*, a girl rabbit behaves in a manner which is exactly as described above, and, though the scene serves as a source of comedy, never is the rabbit's integrity or morality called into question.

By the 1990s the notion that a woman could be both good and sexy had ceased to be such an unimaginable concept in representations of femininity in much of America's popular culture. Within Hollywood cinema, women characters were beginning to exude a confident sexuality which in no way detracted from their portrayals as good, honourable individuals. Perhaps the ultimate example of this would be the character Vivian (played by Julia Roberts) in Touchstone's *Pretty Woman* (1990). Vivian is a prostitute in Los Angeles, and, as she reveals in the film, has ended up in that situation through what amounts to a series of bad choices and naïveté. She is shown to be unhappy in her current life, but is entirely unapologetic about what she does. And yet, despite her lifestyle and profession, Vivian is shown to be an extremely kind, thoughtful, loving person, and her goodness and integrity are never brought into question.

It is not just the ways the stories are told in films, such as *Pretty Woman*, however, but also that the stories themselves, containing as they all do strong, independent, intelligent female characters, are potentially indicative of just how much feminist ideology had entered into mainstream American middle-class values. By the 1990s, three basic categories had become apparent among the Disney animated heroines: Princess, which was of course the oldest but which, in the 1990s, underwent a fundamental shift in its nature; the Good Daughter, a new category for Disney but a fairly common theme in fairy tales; the 'Tough Gal', which was a particularly radical departure from more traditional characterizations of women at Disney. While further subdivisions and variations can be made in such categories, they are nonetheless the major divisions into which these characters fit, and are the headings to be used in defining and discussing them.

The princesses – Ariel, Jasmine and Pocahontas

There are four Disney films in this period in which the heroines are princesses: *The Little Mermaid*, *Aladdin*, *Pocahontas* and *Atlantis*. The category of 'princess' is fairly easy to define: a princess is a woman who is the daughter of a ruler or the wife of a prince. In all four examples in the period under discussion, the characters are princesses through birth, and all four are presented as having no mother, only a father (and it is the father who is the ruler; none of them have a mother who rules in her own right). Furthermore, all but Ariel in *The Little Mermaid* are shown as being only children (and indeed, Ariel's six sisters play such a minor role in the film that Ariel herself largely functions as an only child). In presenting them as having little or no parental guidance, the Studio continued the tradition within Disney films of 'orphaning' main characters.

Other than this, however, the Disney heroines of the latest period have little in common with their predecessors. Their independence, strength of will, determination to engineer their own fates and insistence on being true to themselves are unquestionably their strongest traits (both individually and as a group). With the progression of time, in fact, the choices made available to these four, as well as the decisions they make over the course of the films and the final solutions they reach, grow exponentially with each film. For Ariel the mermaid, her determination to live in the human world and to marry the human prince with whom she has fallen in love mean that she must overcome enormous obstacles, including growing legs, learning to walk, coming to understand and adjust to a whole new way of life, and living in a world in which she (literally) has no voice. For Jasmine in *Aladdin* (1992), as a princess who is trapped within her father's palace, she has no say in which princes come to court her (although in the beginning, it does appear that she has final say over whether or not she will marry them), and yet her determination to know a life outside of the palace leads her to disguise herself as a commoner. It is during the course of her adventure in the city that she first meets Aladdin, whom she will eventually help to overthrow the evil Jafar and save the life and the kingdom of her father, the kindly but bumbling Sultan. Pocahontas (in the 1995 film of the same name) takes this determination to overthrow evil and be true to herself even further when, behind her father's back, she meets John Smith and helps not only to stop a war between her people and Smith's, but even helps to establish communication and respect between the two groups by the film's end. Kida, who has been cut-off from the outside world within the remains of Atlantis, sees that her civilization is dying but is initially unable to prevent its decline because her father, the king, refuses to acknowledge it (and, in fact, is portrayed within the film as an elderly blind man). By joining forces with scholar and dead language expert Milo Thatch, the film's main character, she is able not only to save her civilization from the mercenaries who have come to steal its power source, but also is able to restore her world to prosperity and, because of her father's death, is able to assume the role of queen (in fact, Kida is the first Disney princess to succeed to the throne within the course of a film). In all four films, the heroines are initially shown to be adventurous, curious young women who are stuck within very definite boundaries which seem, at first, to be insurmountable; yet over the course of the film, through strength of will and hard work, all four go on to discover their rightful places in life.

Although from the start of this period of Disney animation, major changes in how women are portrayed were in evidence, it should nonetheless be emphasized that this transformation did not occur overnight. In the characterization of Eilonwy in *The Black Cauldron* (1985) the beginnings of this transformation may be discerned. Feisty and adventurous, Eilonwy's strength and spirit set a new benchmark for what comprised the personality of a Disney heroine. The fact that Eilonwy was still a pre-pubescent girl, however, allied her characterization with earlier Disney patterns of reserving such traits as wilfulness and determination either for the Studio's youngest heroines or for its villainesses.

By 1989, however, a definite shift had occurred at Disney when it came to handing out pluck to its leading ladies. At sixteen-years-old,[3] Ariel is assuredly old enough to be aware of herself as a sexual being, although her confidence in her maturity and her feeling it necessary to declare that she is 'not a child' demonstrate that, in many ways, she is still a girl. Nonetheless, from the first time we see her, Ariel is clearly differentiated from earlier Disney princesses.

Unlike Snow White, Cinderella, Sleeping Beauty and even Eilonwy, Ariel actively seeks adventure and works hard to achieve goals she has set for herself, rather than simply responding to the crises with which she is presented. Even the fact that the film's first shot of Ariel is on her own, away from home, in the midst of an adventure, serves as a marked contrast to the initial shots of earlier Disney princesses, who are first seen either within their homes or within the grounds of their homes (or, in Eilonwy's case, in the dungeon in which she is being held prisoner). More than simply reflecting a longing for excitement and adventure for their own sake, however, Ariel's true quest seems to be to discover a place where she can find enrichment. In what serves as one of the set-pieces of the film as a whole, Ariel, surrounded by all of the human 'treasures' she has collected in her explorations, sings of wanting more than a life filled with possessions, dreaming instead of living in a world where she is not just accepted, but valued. While the whole of the song is about her thirst for knowledge, it is this desire to be esteemed which comes through in such lines as:

Bet ya on land, they understand
Bet they don't reprimand their daughters.
Bright young women, sick of swimmin', ready to stand!

Furthermore, despite the urging she receives from other characters to see that her life is 'good enough' and to accept the world into which she was born (and in marked contrast to earlier Disney princesses, who accept far worse existences with cheerful smiles and infinite patience), Ariel cannot. Instead, she feels stifled and discontented, thwarted in her quest to fill what she considers to be an empty, meaningless life, and, defying her father's orders, continually goes to the surface of the sea to learn all she can about the forbidden, mysterious world of humans.

Yet all is not as positive in Ariel's portrayal as it initially seems. Unfortunately for her, she is (unknowingly) working with a heavy amount of misinformation and is depending primarily upon a well-meaning but nonetheless highly unreliable source (Scuttle, the seagull). The explanations which Scuttle gives Ariel of the various human artefacts she finds are so wrong as to serve as a source of comedy for the film (such as when he tells her that one item she has found, a fork, is called a 'dinglehopper' and is used by humans to straighten their hair). Of course, once Ariel is living as a human in the prince's castle and sees the humans' bewilderment at her using the 'dinglehopper' to comb her hair, it would seem that she must realize that perhaps other information Scuttle has given her might not have been accurate. In a later scene, however, as she is getting ready for bed, Ariel is shown again using the 'dinglehopper' to comb her hair, despite overwhelming evidence that her earlier information was very flawed.

Ariel's other source of information on how to live as a human – one which should have seemed to her to be even less trustworthy than the bumbling but good-hearted Scuttle – is Ursula, the sea-witch to whom Ariel trades her voice for a pair of legs. In a song she sings to Ariel while persuading her to make the trade, Ursula tells her that:

> The men up there don't like a lot of blather,
> They think a girl who gossips is a bore.
> Yes, on land it's much preferred for ladies not to say a word –
> And after all, dear, what is idle prattle for!
> Come on, they're not all that impressed with conversation –
> True gentleman avoid it when they can.
> But they don't as soon inform on a lady that's withdrawn –
> It's she who holds her tongue who gets a man.

Such a performance points out that there are elements in both the human and 'mer' worlds which trivialize the importance of a woman's voice, and that such attitudes can be used and played upon by the woman who is willing to make the temporary sacrifice of her voice (as, indeed, Ariel is). Nonetheless, what makes Ursula's advice particularly flawed is that it is Ariel's voice which Eric most clearly remembers from his encounter with her, and it is to her beautiful voice – a voice he clearly values very highly – that he makes repeated reference throughout the film. Indeed, it is not until Ariel regains her voice that Eric recognizes her as the 'woman' he loves.

Such a reading contradicts analysis such as that of Laura Sells, who sees the film as being a limited celebration of women's potential upward mobility and as a highly sanitized version of 'bourgeois feminism'.[4] For feminist interpretations of the film, such a comparison between the tale's older class associations and the film's gender-based interpretations are important. After all, in a society in which a number of gender distinctions take the form of economic and political discrimination, then the notion of moving from a position of female 'inferiority' to an alliance with 'male' power has a similar aspect to the kind of social mobility one thinks of in terms of moving to a higher class. In Ariel's undersea world, her voice has a very real power: it is praised by all for its beauty, and even takes on a kind of monetary power when she trades it to Ursula. Yet the undersea world is, in the Disney interpretation of the story, given many elements which link it with disenfranchised groups in American society: women, non-white ethnic groups[5] and third world nations.[6] The human world, by contrast, is shown as being thoroughly white, well-ordered and predominantly male. The only human woman featured is Carlotta, the housekeeper in Eric's castle, and the only other human women who speak in the film are washer women working behind the castle. Therefore, when Ariel enters this world, she is the only 'woman' shown on an equal footing with Eric and his advisor, Grimsby. Yet Ariel has no voice, and her attempts to communicate are not always understood. The trappings now surrounding her are strange to her, and she does not always know their proper uses. Furthermore, Ariel is only tentatively a part of the human world, and must accomplish a great task – win the prince's true love – or she will cease to be human and will have lost her soul to Ursula. In her reading of the film, Sells points out that, in contrast to the class themes found in Hans Christian Anderson's 1837 version of the tale, 'Disney's contemporary version has shifted colors from class to gender privilege', and argues that 'the Disney version, along with its ritual affirmation of women's coming of age, invites a reading of this film as a parable of bourgeois feminism'.[7] The fact that, ultimately, Ariel does both form an alliance with the human world *and* regain her voice is the hopeful stance of the film at its conclusion, but as the film ends at this point, with no allusion to what is to come, no more can be surmised as to either what the results of Ariel's triumph will mean to her – or the true extent of the film's promotion of late 1980s/early 1990s feminism.

However, while many aspects of Ariel's portrayal are ultimately positive, there are nonetheless a number of troubling elements. Her seeming inability to detect unreliable advice (even when there is substantial evidence that she should be wary), and her willingness to risk her life over the possibility that she *might* find true love show a tendency towards portraying Ariel as being the victimized innocent princess found in earlier Disney films. Yet her willingness to gamble, her determination to make her own choices and her tenacity in working towards what she wants out of life are all highly positive.

Although her ultimate wishes – to marry Price Eric and live as a human – are on the surface very traditional, symbolically this action can be seen as her ultimate assertion of herself thanks to the fact that it actualizes goals she set for herself. She has now achieved full status as a human, has learned how to function within that world and has even regained her voice, thereby giving her a say over what happens in her new environment. Therefore, while it cannot be denied that, as a 'feminist' film, *The Little Mermaid* has a number of flaws, nonetheless it does mark – at least within Disney animation – a move away from praising traditional solutions for women's unhappiness and hints at offering them choices beyond simple contentment with the role into which they were born.

As a Disney princess, the character of Pocahontas is one of the most interesting, unusual and, in a number of respects, one of the most positive. Like a number of other Disney heroines, Pocahontas is a princess, but, unlike most of them, she thinks for herself, controls her own destiny and is motivated in her actions not so much by romantic love as she is by the greater wisdom which she possesses. She is the only Disney princess (or, at least, the only grown-up Disney princess) who does not find romantic fulfilment by the film's end. Instead, although the choice is available to her, Pocahontas rejects love – which would mean leaving behind her people and her function as a leader – and chooses to devote herself to her people. No ceremonial princess, she is as much a leader of her people as her father, their chief, and in many ways her leadership is even more valuable for her tribe, since she has at her disposal the gift of female intuition. Indeed, it is this female intuition and wisdom which is credited by the film with preventing war and uniting peoples. This is shown as being more than simply an example of woman as nurturer and moral guide, however, through its portrayal of Pocahontas as a skilled diplomat and a careful decision-maker.

It is interesting to compare Pocahontas with the first of the Disney princesses, Snow White. In one sense, there is no comparing the two: Snow White's main goal is finding her prince. Even with her life constantly endangered by the evil Queen, self-protection is Snow White's secondary consideration. When given the chance (so she thinks) to make a wish for anything she wants in the world through the 'magic wishing apple' (really a poisoned apple) which the Queen, in disguise, gives to her, Snow White's wish is not that she be kept safe from harm, or that her kingdom be saved from the evil woman who controls it but that her prince find her and marry her. For Pocahontas, however, finding romantic love comes a distant second to her desire to find herself and identify her true path in life. Although she does find true love, in the end she chooses to stay behind with her people (rather than to journey to England with John Smith) and work to bridge the gap between the British and the Algonquins. Although it is made clear that Pocahontas truly loves John Smith and will miss him terribly, it is also made abundantly clear that she does not need him in order to be complete, or to fulfil her role with her people. In a more modern acceptance of feminine sexuality, and unlike Disney's earlier heroines, Disney's Pocahontas has more in common with Jasmine in 1993's *Aladdin* than she does with earlier Disney princesses in that she does not need a man either for identification or fulfilment, and it is, in fact, through association with her that her partner will gain both social and political status. Pocahontas will gain her power and authority totally through her own skill and determination, and not because she has married.

In another departure from earlier princesses, though again like Jasmine, Pocahontas has a mature, confident sexuality which she expresses comfortably. She does not act demure or shy about her feelings for John Smith or his feelings for her, but reacts confidently, and in some cases even takes the lead. This ability to express her romantic and sexual feelings, however, is never over-emphasized, but is shown as being part of her wisdom and self-awareness, just as with Jasmine it is part of her self-confidence and strength. Unlike any of their predecessors, this new breed of Disney heroine is able to express with confidence both love and attraction as a part of expressing her true self, but is not seeking love as the ultimate goal of her life. Instead, she is more interested in finding herself and her destiny, whatever that may include. For Jasmine, this includes love, but, more importantly, it includes respect. Jasmine must marry: it is the law of her land, and she must obey it no matter what. She puts off this marriage, however, saying that she wants to marry for love. In reality, what Jasmine clearly means by love – as can be judged in the way she speaks of and deals with suitors – is respect for her, and for her to be able to respect and trust her potential husband. Pocahontas does not have to marry, although her father encourages her to find a suitable husband. She has no intention of rejecting love, but her first and foremost concern is following her destiny. Within the story presented in the film, being able to hold onto love is not shown as being part of her destiny, and so, painful though it may be to her, she is nonetheless strong and confident enough to say goodbye to it and follow her destiny.

The idea that finding true love may or may not be part of a woman's destiny and that respect cannot be separated from love are fairly new themes in Disney films. The beginnings are to be seen in *Beauty and the Beast*, when Belle and Beast learn to respect and like one another first and love one another second, but their love for one another is not fully formed or romantically acted upon until fairly close to the film's end, when they have managed to overcome all of the emotional, psychological and physical barriers which have kept them apart. With Belle, and with Jasmine and Pocahontas – the other heroines with whom she shares the most in common – the paths to self-fulfilment, self-confidence and self-understanding may include finding love to some degree. But, in fact, it is finding out about themselves – and their own personal strengths and weaknesses – which are far more important in resolving the questions posed by the stories in which they find themselves.

What starts them onto their paths of self-discovery and potential romance, however, is not their own desire for adventure or their quests to find true love, but is instead their devotion to their fathers and their initial over-identification with themselves as being good daughters.

The good daughters – Belle and Mulan

The good daughter is, quite simply, a good daughter. A traditional motif and archetype within fairy tales the world over, the good daughter is (usually) a young woman who, out of loyalty to her good but naïve father, finds herself in a potentially threatening situation and must use all her personal resources to survive, an exercise which usually ends in personal triumph for the heroine. For Clarissa Pinkola Estés, tales of this nature hold a powerful archetypal significance as teaching tales for women:

> So many tales – 'Beauty and the Beast', 'Bluebeard', 'Reynard the Fox' – begin with the father endangering the daughter. But in a woman's psyche, even though the father bumbles into a lethal deal because he knows nothing of the dark side of the world or the unconscious, the horrible moment marks a dramatic beginning for her; a forthcoming consciousness and shrewdness.[8]

According to Estés, a psychologist and folklorist, stories which contain the archetype of the good daughter are a very old and traditional element in fairy tales which continue to resonate in Western culture as important tales with which audiences can easily identify and from which they can benefit.

There are two Disney animated films of this period which most clearly portray the theme of the good daughter – *Beauty and the Beast* (one which Estés cites as a typical example of this type of tale) and *Mulan*. Both feature heroines who, out of love and loyalty to their fathers, willingly put themselves in harm's way. Belle knowingly trades her own freedom to the Beast for her father's freedom, and Mulan disguises herself as a boy and runs away in the night in order to stop her elderly father from having to fight in a war by taking his place as a soldier.

Where there are differences in the characters of these two young women, they are usually more to do with the set of circumstances in which each must function, and particular aspects of their personalities are brought to the fore as befits their stories. They both have in common certain traits: neither fits in with the society surrounding her; none is initially interested in finding romantic love; none is initially interested in pursuing any particular goal; both, in some way, take care of their fathers and support their fathers' goals rather than having goals of their own; each, in her quest to serve her father's best interests, ends up both saving her father's life and finding a life of her own.

From the start, Belle is described as a scholar and a bookworm, and is described by the people of her village as being strange and not fitting in because she is more inclined towards intellectual pursuits. In fact, as the townspeople describe it in the song which opens the film, Belle's looks are more valued by them than her intellect, and it is because of her intelligence that she does not fit in with the others in the town.

The only person in the village who does not consider her strange is her father, Maurice, an eccentric inventor who is himself thought of by the townspeople as being slightly insane. Although they are quickly shown to be close and loving, her father, however, shows that he, too, shares the misconception of the others that it is upon someone's looks that they can be judged, replying to Belle's comment that she has no one in the village with whom she can talk, 'what about that Gaston? He's a handsome fellow', even though Gaston is boorish, self-centred, sexist and egotistical, as Belle is obviously well aware. Indeed, throughout the film, the personality traits which are emphasized most about Belle are her intelligence, her ability to judge character, and her curiosity and intellectualism. Indeed, of all the characters in the film, it would seem that Belle is the only one whose beautiful looks reflect a beautiful soul. Yet even Belle changes over the course of the film and grows from being an extension of her father to being a fully formed individual in her own right.

From the start of the film, Belle is characterized as being of an intellectual bent, yet this portrayal is not wholly born out by the film. First of all, the main proof that is given as to Belle's identification with intellectualism is that she is an avid reader. She always has a book in her hand, is often shown reading while she walks, and is shown in the book shop (where the owner is kind enough to let her borrow rather than buy books), looking for something new to read although she has read every book in the shop, some more than once. What seems to be overlooked, however, is that the only book Belle is ever shown reading – the book which she herself describes as being her favourite – is what seems to be a romantic fairy story. Otherwise, her portrayal as an intellectual is supported by the fact that she feels stifled in her life, describing her home as being 'this poor provincial town' and her experience of life there as always being the same. Furthermore, the provincial nature of the town is emphasized when its 'leading citizen', Gaston, says to Belle that 'it's not right for a woman to read! Soon she starts getting ideas, and thinking'. The provincialism of the inhabitants is also emphasized by the fact that other young women of the town are totally in love with Gaston and chorus, 'What's wrong with her!' 'She's crazy!' 'He's gorgeous!' when they see Belle reject Gaston's insulting, patronising, egotistical advances.

When she first meets the Beast, Belle is horrified both by his hideous appearance and by the fact that he is refusing to free her father. It is at this point that Belle earns her title of 'good daughter': when the Beast will not free her father, Belle asks that she be allowed to take her father's place as the Beast's prisoner. Of course, as soon as he is freed, Belle's father works non-stop to free Belle, but never succeeds in doing this. Instead, the Beast eventually frees Belle because they learn that her father is lost and sick, and the first thing Belle does with her freedom is to immediately find and rescue her father once more. Her loyalty to her father is even turned against her by Gaston, who creates a plan to force Belle to marry him in order to save her father from being committed to an asylum. Ironically, it is thanks to her first sacrifice for her father – allowing herself to be held prisoner by the Beast – that Belle is able to save her father a second time, by proving that Maurice's story about a beast in a castle is true. It is also by the chain of events she inadvertently sets in motion by revealing the Beast's existence that her story is brought full-circle: when she saves the Beast from Gaston's attack on him, she realizes that she is in love with the Beast and says so, thus freeing the Beast and his household from the spell and returning them all to human form. In each and every instance in the film, Belle is trying to help or take care of someone, considering her own needs to be secondary to those of her father and the Beast.

It is at the end, when she thinks first of herself – praying for the Beast not to die because she loves him – that Belle's good works are able to set the world to rights. This idea, however, is somewhat underplayed in the film. Her one 'selfish' act – to think of her own sorrow if the Beast died rather than thinking about the impact of his death on his servants and the tragedy of his losing his life – is rewarded by the Beast's transformation from beast to human and his being returned to life. However, when she utters her prayer, 'please don't leave me! I love you!' she does so in a whisper, and is only heard by the audience (and the force which can break the spell). The transformation of the Beast, which immediately follows her prayer, is done so dramatically as to overshadow the event which caused it, and the fact that Belle said what she said is not referred to again. The Beast/ prince does not explain to Belle what transformed him back into a human (this is explained, as voice-over narration, at the start of the film), and so (presumably) not only does she not learn that it was she who brought about the Beast's transformation, it is also not even emphasized for the audience.

This film's portrayal of Belle effectively shows that the woman who is selfless, giving and uses her wisdom only to support others is the good woman deserving a reward, rather than showing that it is okay for women to think first of themselves and secondly of others, at least sometimes. Of the characters in the film, Belle, in her constant selflessness and care-taking, has more in common with the Beast's servants than she does with the other major characters of the film. Belle's father, an inventor, puts his work first and allows Belle to take care of him and assist him rather than recognizing that, as her father, it is his duty to put her first. Gaston, the town 'macho man' who seeks to marry Belle because 'no one else in town but she/is as beautiful as me', always acts in his own interest, and it is not his selfishness, but his vanity, which is ridiculed by the film and which brings about his downfall. Even the Beast thinks of his own wants and needs first: it was this attitude which caused him to be cursed in the first place. Although in the end, he does learn to love Belle and place her needs ahead of his own (which he shows when he releases Belle so that she can rescue her father), it is not this which transforms him. Rather, it is Belle's learning to love him, in spite of his appearance and her initial impressions of him, which finally returns him to human form. In other words, the film's final message seems to be that an unselfish act by a man improves nothing, but an unselfish act by a woman can transform the world. As the film closes, with Belle dancing in the arms of the prince, the film tries hard to make sure that we are left in no doubt that Belle's selflessness is what brought about this happy ending.

However, by the time *Mulan* was released in 1998, seven years after *Beauty and the Beast*, a number of changes had occurred in the studio's characterizations of women. Stronger, tougher women had begun to appear, both within Disney films and in the larger arena of Hollywood cinema, as more women began to move into such key movie-making roles as producer and director. Certainly, at Disney, women's names have begun to appear next to various production credits, although thus far no women have directed one of Disney's animated films.[9] Elsewhere in Hollywood, however, the influence of women writers, directors, producers and actors, among others, over the kinds of female characters being portrayed on-screen, had begun to make some definite changes in the overall image of women as depicted by Hollywood. It is interesting to note that *Beauty and the Beast* was released in the same year as *Thelma and Louise* (1991), and that the two films were both nominees for Academy Awards during the same year.

While there are those commentators, feminist film historians and members of the industry itself who have (rightly) pointed out that Hollywood cinema has a long way to go in terms of the types/roles of women it portrays,[10] nonetheless there are numerous examples of positive portrayals not only of female strength and independence, but also of female friendships, relationships and opportunities. Films such as *Fried Green Tomatoes* (1991), *What's Love Got to Do with It* (1993), *The First Wives Club* (1996), *Practical Magic* (1998) and *There's Something about Mary* (1998) are all examples of films made during the 1990s which contain characters who are trying to carve out lives for themselves in which, although may not live (either through choice or through circumstances) 'normal' lives, nonetheless they have found ways in which they can be themselves.

Enter *Mulan*, which was released in 1998. *Mulan* is about a young girl in (what appears to be) medieval China who, from her first scene until well into the second half of the film, is shown studying and memorizing the rules by which she is expected to live. The only child of her parents (at least in the film version), she is shown in her first few scenes preparing to meet the local match-maker, and is worried that she will not be able to fulfil her role as a bride properly. The girl we are shown initially is a good, honest, forthright, intelligent, lively person with a kind heart and a strong sense of justice. Yet, in Mulan's world, none of these qualities are shown as having much value, especially in a woman. 'Quiet, and demure, graceful, and polite, delicate, refined, poised – punctual!' These are (supposedly) the qualities which a 'proper' young woman should possess and which Mulan is trying to memorize, writing them on her arm so that she will remember. Her very writing down of these qualities, not to mention her behaviour in the rest of the scene, shows that she has none of them, and yet the girl we are presented with is an entirely likeable one.

The day we first see Mulan is the day she is to be presented to the match-maker, and a great deal of time and attention in the first phase of the film is devoted to her experience of preparing for, going to and returning from her interview with the match-maker, all of which is an unqualified disaster. Try though she might, everything that is expected of Mulan as a good daughter and potential bride is at odds with who Mulan is. Much emphasis is placed on just how much artifice is involved in being the 'perfect bride', and the scene in which Mulan is dressed, made-up and sent off to join the other future brides is an interesting one. She is shown working hard to copy the behaviour the other four brides are exhibiting, but she is slightly behind, out of step and not nearly as good at being a 'proper woman' as they. She is enthusiastic and tries hard, yet it is these very qualities which, ironically, make her fulfilment of this role so impossible. During her interview with the match-maker, she is told to recite 'The final admonition', which she does by sneaking quick looks at the notes she has written on her arm. This 'final admonition', which Mulan finds so difficult to live by as well as to recite, is 'fulfil your duties calmly and respectfully. Reflect before you act. This shall bring you honour and glory'. Yet, as her interview goes completely haywire (ending with her accidentally setting fire to the match-maker's backside and being screamed at by the match-maker that 'you may look like a bride, but you will never bring your family honour!'), Mulan goes home with her mother and grandmother, feeling disgraced. It is at this point that Mulan sings of her desire to be true to herself.

As it turns out, the moment which Mulan wishes for in the song – that her reflection be an accurate one – will not come until the final fifteen minutes of the film. It is as this earlier scene is ending that news reaches Mulan's village that the Hun have invaded China and that her father has been called up to fight. Because her father is elderly and crippled – and because there is no one else to go to fight in his place – Mulan decides, rather than see her father go to what will certainly be his death, that she will disguise herself as a boy and take his place in the army.

The majority of the film is concerned with Mulan's experiences in the army (where she claims to be her father's son and calls herself Ping), during which she has to learn not only how to act like a man, but how to fight like a soldier (assisted, as part of the film's comic relief, by a dragon spirit voiced by Eddie Murphy). Her initial attempts at both these roles are so poor as to be comical, but eventually, having been told she can go home, Mulan becomes so determined to succeed that she very quickly begins to prove herself, both as a man and as a soldier. In particular during the scene in which her regiment fights the Hun, Mulan/Ping fights so bravely – and so intelligently – that she single-handedly wins the battle and saves her regiment from almost certain annihilation. In the process, however, she is badly wounded, and it is when the doctor is tending to her wound that her true sex is discovered. The penalty for a woman impersonating a man, as we learned early on in the film, is death, but because Mulan saved the life of Shang, her commanding officer, he decides not to execute her for impersonating a man, and instead leaves her behind, expecting her to return home once the army has moved on.

It is at this point in the film that Mulan is finally able to be successful as herself, and not as Ping. She is sitting alone and dejected when she sees that the Hun army, which had been assumed to be dead, has in fact survived the battle and are about to reach the Imperial city and attack the emperor. Realizing that her regiment is unaware of the danger, Mulan quickly rides to the Imperial city to catch up with them and warn them. However, now that she is a woman again, and furthermore because she had lied to them about who she was, no one will believe her warnings until it is too late and the Hun have managed to capture the emperor. Mulan, however, leads several of her regiment, including Shang, in a daring and successful rescue, only this time she is dressed as herself, and all those with her but Shang are dressed as women. In the end, the emperor rewards Mulan with a sword, a crest and an offer of a position in his cabinet, but Mulan refuses, saying that it is time for her to go home. In a dramatic moment, the emperor, as part of his thanks to her, bows, and all of the thousands around the palace kowtow to her. Mulan returns home to give her father the sword and the crest that the emperor gave her, but he drops them on the ground, hugging Mulan tightly and telling her that 'the greatest gift and honour is having you for a daughter'. According to the film, it was Mulan's allowing her true character to shine through – once she had the courage to be herself – which made it possible for her to be truly happy. Though, unusually for a Disney film, *Mulan* is largely without romance, it becomes clear that Mulan is attracted to Shang but, as Ping, of course, cannot tell him this. As Mulan, however, is fighting (as a woman) alongside Shang to protect the emperor, the idea that Shang is both impressed with – and attracted to – Mulan begins to become apparent. In the final scene of the film, back at Mulan's home, Shang comes to find her, on the pretext of returning her helmet, and the implication is that Mulan and Shang will be married at some point in the future. The implication is also that their relationship will be very untraditional, but will also be a very happy one possessing mutual respect and understanding.

Ironically, this probable marriage to Shang, a celebrated war hero from a powerful and influential family, will also mean that Mulan will 'strike a catch' which will be guaranteed to bring her family honour, and which will bring Mulan honour through her fulfilment as 'a perfect bride' and 'a perfect daughter', at least in the eyes of her society. The fact that this marriage will be of Mulan's choice and on her own terms, however, is important to the theme of the film. Mulan was not happy as 'just' Mulan, the tomboy who could not act like a woman, nor was she happy as Ping, the soldier living in constant fear of discovery by his/her fellow soldiers. As Mulan the soldier, however, the combination of both roles in which Mulan could act out both sides of herself, Mulan finally achieves true success. Although in her song Mulan sang that 'Now I see that if I were truly to be myself/I would break my family's heart' and 'Somehow I cannot hide who I am though I've tried', the film's end shows that such sentiments are completely incorrect, and that it is by truly being herself that Mulan is able to win both honour and love.

Mulan is a special case as a Disney film for the issues it considers and, more importantly, the way, it chooses to examine these issues. Yet its predominant issues – self-identity and the notion of gender as performance – are a part of a small but significant Hollywood cinematic tradition in which women who dress as men find for themselves advancement, success and the fulfilment of their dreams. Yvonne Tasker, in her book *Working Girls: Gender and Sexuality in Popular Cinema*, discusses the theme of female transvestism at some length, citing such films as *Victor/Victoria* (1982), *Yentl* (1983) and *The Ballad of Little Jo* (1993) as leading films in this off-beat sub-genre of the 'coming of age' film. According to Tasker, there are two basic kinds of female cross-dressers: cross-gender and cross-class. As an example of class cross-dressing, Tasker points to *Working Girl* (1988), which stars Melanie Griffith as a lower-class secretary who, during her boss' absence, masquerades as a middle-class, middle-management yuppie, and is able to transform herself from lower to middle class by dressing in middle-class fashion. Cross-class dressing is similar in intention to cross-gender dressing, according to Tasker, because both are about social advancement: men have more power than women, and middle/upper-class women have more power than lower-class women. As Lauren Bacall, Marilyn Monroe and Betty Grable attempted to show in *How to Marry a Millionaire* (1953), the idea seems to be that in order to become a member of a higher class, you have to at least look, if not live, the part.

In cross-gender dressing, however, the issues involved tend to be different. In films in which women dress and live as men, there is almost always a sense of desperation behind their transformation: their existence is threatened (as in *Victor/Victoria* and *The Ballad of Little Jo*), or their personalities do not allow them to function successfully as women within the strictures of their society (as in *Yentl* and *Mulan*). As men, such women are able to obtain a success and freedom which eluded them as young women within the societies in which they function. As Tasker writes:

> If anarchic men dress as women to learn about self-control whilst enjoying the evident pleasures of transformation, narratives and images of women cross-dressing relate to opportunity and achievement in different, though related ways. Both gendered and class cross-dressing is explicitly presented as allowing female protagonists an opportunity and a *freedom* (of both physical movement and behaviour) that they would not otherwise achieve.[11]

Mulan's success – defeating the Hun army and saving China from invasion, would seem to support Tasker's later statement that 'in the cinema, viewers are offered an explanation of female-to-male cross-dressing that can be understood as seeking to naturalize the transition, cast in terms of the desire for the privileges and freedom available to men. At the basic level of plot, the cinema offers us women who achieve freedom and/or success as male or masculine personas, their achievements typically presented as unique'.[12] After all, a single-handed defeat of an entire army is a fairly rare achievement for anyone – male, female or transvestite. Yet *Mulan* goes beyond this basic assumption – which is a more hardened twist on the idea of 'if you can't beat 'em, join 'em' – by having Mulan achieve her greatest success not as Ping, but as a Mulan who has been transformed by her experiences as Ping. When, as Ping, she achieves the defeat of the Hun army by causing an avalanche to fall on them and bury them, it would seem that she has achieved an ultimate victory. This is short-lived, however, when the key members of the Hun army manage to claw their way out of the snow and launch a briefly successful attempt to capture the Chinese emperor. Her final defeat of the Hun comes only when Mulan is truly herself and relies upon her own ways to defeat them.

In the first scene Mulan is in, she demonstrates her natural – albeit unorthodox – talent for problem-solving, such as tricking her rather unintelligent dog into chasing a bone tied to a rod on his collar, tying a sack of seed to his tail and then sending him running all over the farm, thereby scattering the seed for the chickens and giving Mulan extra free time to memorize what she needs to say to the match-maker. Her problem-solving is funny and successful, but simultaneously chaotic, causing momentary havoc on the farm. But, while living as Ping, Mulan acquires the discipline and tactical training necessary in a soldier, and is able, by aiming a single rocket at a huge snowdrift just behind and above the attacking Hun army, to set off the avalanche which seems to defeat them. Mulan's success, though more substantial this time, falls apart when the wound she suffers during the battle brings about her discovery. It is when she is once more Mulan, but is openly using the training she received as Ping and combining the 'masculine' traits of a soldier with female postures, dress and accessories, that Mulan achieves her greatest and most lasting success. In a comical but still telling part of this final battle scene, Mulan persuades her fellow soldiers to dress as women so that all of them can – and do – walk right into the palace (under the gaze of the Hun guards) because, as women, they are not assumed to be a threat. They then pull out the fruits they are using as false breasts and use them to stun the guards before defeating them in hand-to-hand combat. Later, when the Hun leader is about to kill Shang in revenge, saying 'you took away my victory', Mulan, standing nearby, says 'no, I did', and pulls back her hair into the way she wore it as Ping. In that instant, she has the body and dress of a woman but the head of a man, and it is in this instant that the tide turns for her, allowing her to achieve her victory moments later when, in a wonderful combination of her masculine and feminine skills, Mulan uses a folding paper fan to grab – and take – a sword away from the Hun leader, using the sword to pin him to the roof of the palace in time for him to be hit and blown up by a rocket.

In the end, however, Mulan willingly gives up all the power she has gained, rejecting the offer of a seat on the emperor's council, and returns home, where her first act is to bow to her father and present him with the sword and crest, saying that they are 'gifts to honour the Fa family'. It is also implied, shortly thereafter, that Mulan and Shang will be married, which means that Mulan will, in the end, follow the traditionally prescribed right of passage for a woman of her society, moving from her father's house to her husband's. The assumption is that, now that she is able to be herself, at least within the private sphere, she will be happier. Yet, as was shown in the initial scenes where Mulan was shown as a likeable but unruly tomboy, she was always able to be herself within her parents' house and that, although they worried about her ability to fit in with society, they nonetheless loved her and put up no barriers to her freedom. Nothing has changed about Mulan – or her parents' views of her – during her absence or as a result of her achievements, mainly thanks to the fact that they always allowed her to be herself. The only change is her having (probably) found a man to be her husband who would be equally tolerant of her ways. In other words, the successful blending of her masculine and feminine sides, while a personal achievement for Mulan, has not necessarily changed anything for her in the world in which she lives.

Although the 'good daughter' is a traditional folk/fairy tale theme, its appearance in the Disney canon is fairly recent. As ideas such as political correctness and the mainstreaming of feminism made it increasingly difficult for film studios (among other purveyors of mass culture) to show women giving up anything for marriage, old elements of male authority were resurrected as a way around this recent taboo. While it may have no longer been acceptable to a large segment of the American public to feature stories of women putting their needs as secondary to the needs of their husbands, the notion that a woman is willingly sublimating her needs to those of a kindly, loving father remained slightly more acceptable. When, like Belle and Mulan, she finally trades in the role of the good daughter for that of the good wife, the move is not portrayed as the lateral move which it in fact is (since the character is only trading one male authority figure for another), but as a liberation for the young woman, and a chance to finally 'be herself'. Belle has moved from life on the edge of her boring, provincial village to a castle where she has a library filled with books and a charming, intelligent, loving man to talk with and read to. Mulan has given up the life of a soldier, it is implied, to become the wife of a soldier whose skills are similar to her own, and who both understands and respects her. Yet the fact remains that, in both cases, the woman has moved (or will do someday, as is implied with Mulan) from life in her father's care to life in the care of her husband. However, each one's overall quality of life has improved, and through the more equal partnership they have established with a man, the situations they are moving into will be an improvement over the more subordinate one they had with their fathers.

The 'tough gals' – Esmeralda, Meg, Audrey and Captain Amelia

Of all of the Disney women and girls, there are four whose portrayals are starkly different from those of their 'sister' characters at Disney. They are Esmeralda from *The Hunchback of Notre Dame*, Megara (Meg) from *Hercules*, Audrey from *Atlantis* and Captain Amelia from *Treasure Planet*. From their first moments on screen until the very end of each's film, these characters exhibit a kind of strength, brashness and confidence not to be found elsewhere among most of Disney's animated heroines. Although their portrayals have strong links with the character of Slue-foot Sue from 'The Legend of Pecos Bill' segment of *Melody Time* (1948), these more modern characters surpass Slue-foot Sue in that they each have a voice and can match their gutsy personas with strong words. Although each has to overcome a number of disadvantages, and though three of the four have found true love at the ends of their films, nonetheless these characters are feisty, no-nonsense women who leave audiences in no doubt that, far from needing (or even wanting) a man, these are women who can – and do – take care of themselves.

The first shots we see of Esmeralda are of her pan-handling, dancing on the street for money. Esmeralda is a gypsy living in medieval Paris, and, though the laws of Paris make it difficult for the gypsies to survive,

Esmeralda is nonetheless making a living for herself and her goat, and although her life is hard, she is happy, finding sources of freedom despite the oppression surrounding her. She makes this sense of independence and self-reliance clear when, having claimed sanctuary in Notre Dame cathedral from Frollo, the evil Minister of Justice, she sings a song of prayer to God, asking not for help for herself but to help those who are worse off than she.

Throughout the film, Esmeralda is notable for the strong sense of justice and highly moral stance she takes, and is frequently contrasted with Frollo, a sanctimonious, self-righteous man full of corruption who sees evil everywhere he looks. In an interesting twist for a Disney film, the evil villain who seeks to destroy the heroine is a man, and, also interestingly, he expresses the attitude that a strong sexuality such as Esmeralda possesses is a sign of her evil nature as well as proof (in his eyes) of her being a witch. This attitude towards sexuality is easily detected in early Disney films which show the villainesses as sexually mature, self-possessed and malevolent, while the heroine is young, naïve and innocent. In *The Hunchback of Notre Dame*, however, Esmeralda's self-confidence – which includes confidence in her beauty and sex-appeal – are also proof of her goodness and strength, whereas Frollo's characterization of her and her sexual confidence as evil is proof that he projects this evil onto her from his own twisted desires.

Eventually, Esmeralda finds an ally in Febus, the captain of the guard who is supposed to be in charge of Frollo's men but eventually rebels against him because of his cruelty. Together, as Esmeralda and Febus move from fighting against one another to fighting on the same side, they also realize that the attraction they feel for one another – present from their first encounter – is, in fact, love. In the book, Esmeralda dies at Frollo's hands, but in the film it is she who helps to defeat him. At the film's end, she emerges from the cathedral, hand-in-hand with Febus, to the triumphant cheers of the people of Paris. She and Febus are portrayed as being very much in love with each other and having a great deal of respect and admiration for one another. They are shown throughout the film as being equals in strength, sense of humour, and sense of justice and Right, yet it is Esmeralda who – repeatedly – saves Febus's life, and it is she who helps him to see that Frollo is not just corrupt, but evil. Far from being her protector or her mentor, Febus is shown as owing Esmeralda both his life and his having found his true path.

Likewise, it is Meg – the heroine of *Hercules* – who helps the hero find out who he is meant to be and where he most belongs. As the film is largely Hercules's story, Meg does not appear until a third of the way into the film. Yet her role from that point on is a pivotal one for Hercules, who quickly falls in love with her and spends much of the film winning her heart through his wholesomeness, honour and honesty, qualities which – as we learn shortly after she is introduced – life has taught Meg not to look for in men. Meg states her ideas about men early on: 'You know how men are – they think "no" means "yes" and "get lost" means "take me, I'm yours!"' Meg is portrayed as a wounded, cynical young woman who was hurt when she traded her soul to Hades to save her lover's life only to be abandoned by her lover for another woman. Her hurt and anger towards men runs so deeply that, in a quip to Hades (who now controls her and forces her to do his bidding) she responds to his order that she 'handle' ('take care of') Hercules, 'hey, I've sworn off man-handling'.[13] When we first see Meg, she is in the clutches of a menacing river guardian. Hercules, on his way to Thebes to try and become a hero, thinks that Meg is in danger and insists on trying to save her, despite her order to 'keep movin', Junior'. When he asks her 'aren't you a damsel in distress?' her reply, said with a combination of authority and sarcasm, is typical of Meg: 'I'm a damsel. I'm in distress. I can handle this. Have a nice day!' Hercules, however, insists that Meg has to be saved and, with some trouble (mainly owing to his lack of practical experience) defeats the river guardian, much to Meg's annoyance. As we learn later, Meg has been ordered by Hades to get the river guardian to assist him in his plans to conquer the universe, and Hercules's 'rescue' has interfered with her assignment.

Like Esmeralda, Meg is street-wise and tough. Unlike Esmeralda, Meg is bitter and hurt. Over the course of the film, while under orders to stop him, Meg finds herself first liking Hercules (once she sees that his manner is not some 'innocent farm-boy routine' but is in fact his true personality), then – much against her will – falling in love with him. Eventually, she refuses to help Hades in his attempts to defeat Hercules and saves Hercules's life at the cost of her own, thus inadvertently freeing herself from Hades's service. Hercules, in turn, rescues Meg from the River Styx and brings her back to life, an act so brave and selfless that it restores Hercules to the status of god (which, in the film, is what he was when he was born). Because of his love for Meg, however, and her love for him, Hercules is allowed by Zeus to remain a mortal so that he can marry Meg and stay with her, since he has come to realize that it is at her side that he belongs. Meg, in turn, has lost her bitterness and been restored to the kind, selfless, trusting nature which led her to give herself up for a lover's life in the first place, and she becomes a happier, more trusting person, perhaps not so naïve as Hercules, but nonetheless just as honest and selfless. Having found and saved each other, Meg and Hercules are able to live happily ever after, each one (no doubt) keeping the other's weaknesses in check. Or, as Vivian/Julia Roberts says at the end of Pretty Woman when asked what the princess does when saved by the handsome prince, 'she saves him right back!'

What both Esmeralda and Meg have in common is their street-wise personas and sexual confidence, coupled with their innate goodness and personal senses of justice. Furthermore, as Disney heroines who are not only saved but do an equal share of the saving themselves, they are an unusual pair among the other women portrayed in Disney animation. They are both possessed of many flaws (Esmeralda is distrustful and confrontational; Meg is bitter and unfeeling), yet the flaws which hamper them most – and which they have acquired because of their difficult lives – are the ones which they also learn to overcome during the course of each's film.

A slight departure from these tough girl characters – at least in terms of the total lack of romance in the character's life – is Audrey from *Atlantis*. Audrey's youth is emphasized several times in the film, but she is still old enough to have not only become an extremely capable mechanic, but also to have accompanied the explorers on a previous expedition as well as this one to Atlantis. She is a total tomboy, wearing overalls for all but the final scene of the film, and teases Milo's timidity several times. She's shown as brave, cocky, confident, no nonsense and – it is hinted – is even less squeamish than the doctor of the group. This is shown when Dr Sweet tells Milo that he should not ask what Molière's story is, saying, 'believe me, you don't wanna know. Audrey, don't tell him. You told me, and I didn't want to know, and believe me, you don't wanna know!' She explains herself by saying that her father had wanted sons (to be a mechanic and a prize fighter), but had ended up with her and her sister. When Milo asks what happened with her sister, Audrey replies (as if it were a mundane piece of information): 'She's two and "O" with a shot at the title next month.' When, as the expedition is about to leave Milo behind and take Kida, Milo makes a point of questioning their values; it is Audrey who is the first to take a stand against Rourke, the mercenary expedition leader, and stand with Milo against the destruction of Atlantis. It is her example, in fact, which persuades the other characters (except Rourke and Helga) to help Milo, and she is one of the principal fighters in the climactic battle scene to rescue Kida.

Although Audrey is not portrayed as 'the' heroine of her film, she is nonetheless an important supporting character. She is unusual for a Disney character of her sex and age in that, instead of displaying any traces of sexuality or romantic longing at any point, she shows a complete lack of interest in such matters. Yet despite her overalls, she is portrayed as a pretty, voluptuous young woman who is definitely old enough (according to standards set for other Disney women) for romance. What is emphasized about Audrey, however, are her capability, her intelligence and her strength of character. Like Mulan, she has combined masculine and feminine roles in such a way as suits her character. Unlike Mulan, she has (apparently) never had to struggle to achieve this identity. Whether, however, this type of young female character is pointing the way towards a new trend in Disney women, remains to be seen. It could be argued however, that, in terms of this confidence in herself, Audrey is one of the most pro-feminist of Disney's characters, as well as being one of the most balanced, 'ordinary' portrayals of a human woman to be found in any Disney film.

Wicked women – A dying breed

Whereas strong heroines are a growing trend in Disney animation of this later period, evil women become an increasingly rare phenomenon. In this era of Disney animated features, there are only three evil women: Ursula (of *The Little Mermaid*), Yzma (of *The Emperor's New Groove*) and Helga St. Claire (of *Atlantis*). This ratio of three villainesses to thirteen heroines is much lower when compared to the 'Classic' era, which had a ratio of five villainesses to eight heroines, and is lower even than the 'Middle Period', which had one villainess to four heroines.

These modern villainesses cannot be discussed entirely as a group, however, because each stands out from the other in very definite ways. Granted, Ursula and Yzma are the most traditional villainesses of the three, but Ursula is the only one who easily fits the traditional perimeters of 'Disney Villainess': she is very much a 'monstrous other' who opposes a young heroine. She possesses magical powers (and is referred to repeatedly as being a 'sea witch'), and her attempts to thwart the heroine she opposes are based primarily upon jealousy of some physical attribute (in this case, Ursula wants Ariel's voice). There is also, in Ursula's case, an attempt to disguise herself when her previous efforts to harm the heroine have failed: in this case, Ursula disguises herself as Vanessa, a beautiful young woman with Ariel's voice, so that she may marry Prince Eric and capture Ariel's soul. When even this fails, she swells in size in an effort to crush her opponents, but Eric stabs her with the prow of a ship and kills her. Everything about her is a caricature of some earlier Disney heroine, to include her tactics. Even her look borrows elements from classic villainesses: she tries to appear glamorous and sophisticated, but her monstrous form (she has the body of a somewhat humanized octopus) undercuts this attempt. Like them, she also works in 'black magic'. Also like them, she is stopped from permanently injuring the heroine through the efforts of a male character who serves as the heroine's champion.

Yzma, at least physically, is similar to past villainesses: she tries to look glamorous, but is so ugly (in fact, she is repeatedly described in the film as being 'scary beyond all reason') that she is anything but glamorous (despite her long black dress and pearls). What is more unusual – and therefore more interesting – about Yzma (voiced by Eartha Kitt), however is that she is the first female villain to oppose a main character who is male. In this case, Yzma is advisor to Emperor Kuzko (voiced by David Spade), but is fired early on in the film because of her constant attempts to take over his throne. Seeking revenge, she and her dim-witted assistant/sidekick Kronk (voiced by Patrick Warburton) attempt to poison Kuzko, but only succeed (thanks to Kronk's blunder) in transforming him into a llama. After Kronk again fails to kill Kuzko, the pair set off through the jungle to find Kuzko so that Yzma can retain her new role as the ruler of the kingdom.

Yzma's motivation, in other words, comes not so much from jealousy as it does from an overwhelming desire for power. Her initial method – poisoning – is not derived from black magic, however. Instead, Yzma has a 'secret' lab (which most of the characters seem to know about), and concocts the poison through her apparent knowledge of chemistry rather than a knowledge of witchcraft. In other words, Yzma may look like a witch, but she has no magical powers; in fact, she must rely heavily upon Kronk for help, but his ineptness and – surprisingly for an evil henchman – his generally good nature mean that Yzma's efforts are doomed before they begin, and even when she is defeated she is not destroyed, but instead transformed through her own poison into a kitten, in which form she remains at the film's conclusion. She may be physically described as 'scary beyond all reason', but in fact she – along with all the other characters in this silliest and most slapstick of Disney's animated features – is very much a comic character, and is not menacing to anyone, to include the other characters in the film.

The final villainess of this period – and perhaps the most complex villainess of all of Disney's films – is Helga St. Claire, the lieutenant of the expedition which seeks to find Atlantis in the film of the same name. First and foremost of the most obvious qualities which set her apart from past villainesses, she is a beautiful young woman who possesses no magical abilities whatsoever. She wears ordinary clothing, speaks in an ordinary voice and works within – rather than trying to subvert – the rules of the group in which she operates (which, in this case, is a group of mercenaries). Most unusually – and it is this which makes her complex – she is the only villainess who seems, even fleetingly, to possess a conscience. When the expedition discovers that there are people living in Atlantis, she is the first one to comment that 'this changes everything'. The response she receives to this comes from the menacing Rourke, who tells her that 'this changes nothing'; even though she goes along with the plans, there are moments when she seems to doubt that she is doing the right thing, and she is never the most extreme in terms of evil. In the end, when all of the others have sided with Milo and only she and Rourke are carrying out their plan to steal the Heart of Atlantis, she is betrayed by Rourke, who throws her out of the hot air balloon. She falls to the ground, but before she dies she fires up at the balloon, contributing greatly in stopping Rourke from succeeding. Throughout, her motivation is shown to be her desire for money, not a desire for power or control. She also does not directly oppose Milo and Kida; they are merely on the 'wrong' side, and therefore she is working against them. In the end, her revenge against Rourke's betrayal will be what saves Kida from being taken away, and ultimately what saves the existence of Atlantis.

These villainesses – but in particular Yzma and Helga – stand out from their predecessors. They have different motivations and serve different purposes in their films. That – and the fact that villainesses are rare in later Disney films – are the features which most distinguish them from earlier eras of Disney villainesses. It should be noted, of course, that they are not the only evil characters in this era of the Disney studio's features: there are in fact fourteen major villains in this period (as well as numerous henchmen), more than in any other era of the studio's film history.[14] In the 'politically correct' atmosphere of the 1990s in America, this focus on male villains may have been an attempt to steer away from sexist portrayals of evil, sexually frustrated women (except in the case of Yzma; she is portrayed in such comic terms, however, that she is at best a caricature of the early villainesses). Yzma's appearance, however, may demonstrate a 'lightening' of this attitude. The characterization of Helga, however, is complex enough – since she is more of a flawed, greedy woman rather than an evil witch – and is balanced enough in *Atlantis* by female characters with stronger morality that she could arguably be seen as not so much an anti-feminist figure as a misguided individual.

Conclusion

For all of the criticism directed at the Disney Corporation, the 1990s witnessed a more dynamic period of changing patterns than has any other decade in the company's history (except – arguably – the 1930s). Certainly the overall size of the company expanded by leaps and bounds, saving it not only financially but also literally from being broken up and sold off. Furthermore, the 1990s witnessed a rehabilitation in the Studio's reputation for film-making. As more money, time and creativity were lavished on the animation studio, in particular, than was the case in the period immediately after Disney's death, Disney feature animation remained a leader in its industry despite more serious competition than had ever before been the case. The Disney Corporation expanded in every area in which it was involved, and on a financial level now looks safe for years to come.

In terms of its recognition of changes in American attitudes towards the portrayals of women – particularly those which are likely to be seen by younger audiences – this period sees a noticeable shift in its characterizations of women. Certainly, the Studio recognized that its older portrayals – Snow White, Cinderella and the rest – were being seen more often by young people now than at any other period in film history thanks to the rise in home entertainment technology. Throughout the 1990s, the increasing normalization of feminist values within American culture was reflected in the Studio's attempts to create more interesting, dynamic female characters who could serve as more positive role models.

Overall, these efforts have attained varying levels of success. Mothers have fared little better in the Disney films of the 1990s than before. As with earlier heroines (and heroes), most characters have lost their mothers, though many have managed to hold onto their fathers. In terms of the overall portrayal of what it means to be feminine, and to be good, however, there have been significant changes. All of the heroines of the era covered by this chapter go on adventures, despite the fact that none of them are little girls. Age seems to have no effect either on the kinds of adventures they undergo or the degree of success they experience at their adventures' end. Although romance continued to be a major theme in Disney films, for almost all of the characters it ceased to be their major goal. Rather than sitting contentedly, waiting for their handsome princes to find them, the young women featured in the 1990s sought knowledge (Ariel, Belle, Jasmine, Jane and Kida) or justice (Pocahontas, Esmeralda, Meg, Mulan, Audrey, Amelia and Nani) in some form, and when romance came, it was less a goal and more a pleasant surprise – the icing on the cake. Darker themes also began to creep into these films – particularly in *The Hunchback of Notre Dame, Mulan, Tarzan* and *Atlantis*, which seem to have been perceived by audiences as being less intended for younger children and more for adolescents and adults. Yet the heroines of 1990s Disney films, although more in keeping with feminist attitudes, are not by any stretch of the imagination heroines to feminists, with the possible exceptions of Audrey and Captain Amelia (though it must be remembered, however, that both are supporting characters in their films). They are often devout care-takers of those around them, require the protection – or at least the affirmation – of a male authority figure (usually in the form of a father, which, owing to the ages of many of the characters, is perhaps more acceptable to modern audiences), and live out adventures which are at least sanctioned, if not rewarded, by the patriarchies in which all of the characters live.

Notes

1   On women's magazines and related issues of consumerism, see Kathy Peiss, 'Making up, making over: Cosmetics, consumer culture, and women's identity', in Victoria De Grazia with Ellen Furlough (eds), *The Sex of Things: Gender and Consumption in Historical Perspective* (Berkeley: University of California Press, 1996), pp. 311–36. In the same book, Rachel Bowlby's piece 'Soft Sell: Marketing Rhetoric in Feminist Criticism', pp. 381–87, also contributes to the discussion of marketing aimed at women.

2   'Politically correct (or incorrect)' is defined by *The Oxford English Reference Dictionary* as 'conforming (or not conforming) to a prevailing body of liberal opinion, esp. in avoiding (or not avoiding) language, behaviour, etc., which might conceivably be regarded as discriminatory or pejorative to racial or cultural minorities or as reflecting undesirable implicit assumptions' (Oxford: Oxford University Press, 1996), p. 1121.

3   Ariel very firmly reminds her father 'I'm sixteen! I'm not a child!', thereby allowing us (both as scholars and as members of the audience) to define her as being an adult, at least in a physical sense. Her very shapely, feminine figure serves to confirm this.

4   Laura Sells, '"Where Do the Mermaids Stand?": Voice and Body in *The Little Mermaid*', in Bell, Haas and Sells (eds), *From Mouse to Mermaid*, p. 177.

5   Patrick D. Murphy, '"The Whole Wide World Was Scrubbed Clean": The Androcentric Animation of Denatured Disney', in Bell, Haas and Sells, *From Mouse to Mermaid*, p. 132.

6   Murphy, 'The Whole Wide World Was Scrubbed Clean', 132, and Sells, 'Where Do the Mermaids Stand?', 178.

7   Sells, 'Where Do the Mermaids Stand?', 177.

8   Clarissa Pinkola Estés, *Women Who Run with the Wolves: Myths and Stories of the Wild Woman Archetype* (London: Rider, 1998), p. 396.

9   This was true at the time of the original publication of this chapter (2007). Jennifer Lee later became the first woman to (co-)direct a disney animated feature in 2013 with *Frozen*.

10   Yvonne Tasker discusses these issues at length in her book *Working Girls: Gender and Sexuality in Popular Cinema* (London: Routledge, 1998). Tasker, in her introduction, quotes Whoopi Goldberg's comments on the roles on offer to women, made while hosting the 1996 Academy Award ceremony. Karen Hollinger, in *In The Company of Women: Contemporary Female Friendship Films* (Minneapolis: University of Minnesota Press, 1998), also looks at the anti-feminist themes found in many films of the 1990s.

11   Tasker, *Working Girls*, 35.

12   Tasker, *Working Girls*, 37.

13   This remark is in response to Hades's directive that she needs to stop Hercules from attaining the status of hero, saying that his other 'assistants' were not able to handle Hercules as a boy, and that he needs someone who can handle him as a man.

14   There is only one pure villain in the 'Middle Period', the Horned King in *The Black Cauldron* (though Amos in *The Fox and the Hound* and Mr. Snoops in *The Rescuers* come close). In the 'Classic Era', there are the Headless Horseman (*The Adventures of Ichabod and Mr. Toad*) and Captain Hook (*Peter Pan*).

22

Taking an Appropriate Line: Exploring Representations of Disability within British Mainstream Animation

Van Norris

Norris's discussion of British animated series Creature Discomforts *(2007–8), in an article first published in 2008, examines the representation of disability in animation, an otherwise relatively neglected, but important, topic. He argues that Aardman's use of comedy allows for a particularly nuanced representation of disability. Using the concept of comic incongruity, Norris suggests that the comedy functions in a number of ways, but notably to challenge prevailing stereotyping and ignorance around disability.*

This article discusses how representations of disability operate within the mainstream animation narratives of the British *Creature Discomforts* (2007–8) series. These images are constructed as a response to concerns about broader social perceptions of the physically disabled and once scrutinized it is apparent that they are managed through established notions of comic incongruity. This is a framework that not only aids a less reductive insight into the lives of those restricted in mobility but it provides a comic contrast to the serious messages being imparted about ignorance, stereotyping and access. Through the application of incongruity there emerges a modification of representation here and one that builds upon and subverts extant depictions of physical impairment within previous animated discourses. This reframing refines our understandings around representation within contemporary media and constructs here a hybrid of several extant discourses that services an overall more nuanced conception of day to day life for those who are physically disabled.

Directed by Aardman Studio's in-house animator, Steve Harding-Hill, *Creature Discomforts* are a group of short animations that were released online and as print adverts in November 2007 and were shown on UK TV from January 2008. The first batch came with four shorts with a further four released online in July 2008. These were initiated by the Leonard Cheshire Disability Charity as part of their public re-launch but primarily were devised to be an open-ended ongoing series. Peter Dicken, the Leonard Cheshire Visibility Spokesman, stated in interview that the shorts came in response to extensive market research made by the organization which suggested that 'the public had lost contact with disability as an issue and a cause worthy of note in the same way the public views, say, the environment, cancer or animal welfare' (2008). Through humour and applications of personality animation the mission was to challenge moribund and reductive perceptions around disability and to highlight issues of discrimination, access and representation.

The organization, which was founded in 1948, works across the UK and some fifty-four other territories (including a number of developing countries) and it functions under the official mission statement of 'providing day care, skills training and rehabilitation, independent living and residential care ... to relieve the consequences of physical and/or mental well-being of disabled people' (N/A 2008: paras 4–8). And it was after consultations with their advertising agency, Freud, that the idea about using Aardman emerged in 2006 which led in turn to the adaptation of the *Creature Comforts* series and deploying the twist of incorporating disabled characters into the narratives. The results, promoted under the banner, 'Change the way you see disability,' resulted in the shorts garnering an award in the Disability Category at the Charity Awards in 2008.

Formally *Creature Discomforts* remain identical to the original 1989 template, directed by Nick Park as a one-off narrative and as part of five separate animations for Channel Four's *Lip Synch* series. Constructed as edited segments, this animation presented Claymation animals talking in monologue of their dissatisfactions with life, transposing their zoo-life experiences against the pre-recorded voices of humans bemoaning their own *real*-life environments. Here this is shifted to disabled characters expounding on their treatment from mainstream society. In each setting they express dismay at the misconceptions perpetuated by the general public within daily social life that contains and typecasts them. Since Park's film the concept has experienced a remarkable life-span in that it has spawned two series of twenty seven, ten minute episodes for ITV from 2002, a range of advertisements for British Gas and an American derivation of the format funded by CBS in 2007.

Indeed the concept of animating to extant dialogue was hardly new, even by that point. Other examples of this include Faith and John Hubley's *The Cruise* (1966) and *Windy Day* (1968) and, notably, Aardman's own Peter Lord and David Sproxton's, *Animated Conversations* (1978) all of which make use of 'grabbed' conversations, animated in cel and stop motion forms after the event. These operate within (as Kevin Macdonald observes when interviewing Park in 1996), Alan Bennett-style celebrations of not only a specific, parochial regional bias but also in the gentle tone and warmth found in the humour (1996: 66), and this is backed up by Paul Wells's assertion that the shorts, 'defers to a nostalgic belief in the common but unaddressed aspects of the ordinary' (1998: 60). The idea of small lives defined by observational details and rendered through direct monologue, which references British comic traditions, here gently burlesquing what Andy Medhurst refers to as, 'the performity of everyday life, the codes that demarcate conventions, the way that the English say things', the shorts are allied to a strain of humour that defines itself as a 'comedy of the overlooked and the unfashionable … comedy without sneers' (2007: 161).

Assessing the incongruous

In this instance we are presented with 'Peg the Hedgehog', 'Slim the Stick Insect', 'Flash the Sausage Dog', 'Tim the Tortoise', 'Spud the Slug' 'Sonny the Shrimp', 'Callum the Chameleon' 'Ozzy the Owl', 'Roxy the Rabbit', 'Cath the Cat' and 'Brian the Bull Terrier' who across both series conform to the models who have appeared in previous Aardman narratives and all are manipulated well within the formal boundaries expressed earlier. What is noticeable is that these individual sketches function in relation to familiar comic tropes of incongruity. Not only is this a mode located historically across many forms of comedy but, in the application here, incongruity complements and enhances the discussions of disability presented and deepens the understanding of each situation.

Key texts discussing the incongruous in comic contexts, by authors such as Michael Clark, Roger Scruton and Murray Davis, are built on the analytical platforms offered by Schopenhauer and Locke, which stresses this mode as being tied into assessments of 'wit'. Clark summated incongruity as being the point in perception within a text when 'the greater is the ludicrous effect which is produced by the contrast. All laughter is occasioned by a paradox, and therefore by unexpected subsumption, whether this is expressed in words or in actions' (1987: 146). Davis further reasons that the construction of a system of observations moving beyond the simple joke or 'a unit of analysis' into more imaginative, absurdist narrative realms was founded on the notion of 'two different ideas suddenly connected to comic effect' (1993: 21), placed in unexpected combinations. This was, he observed, seemingly demonstrative of creative thought and of an expansive knowledge in terms of subject/language/semantics and, described by Davis, as a comic phenomenon resting on the 'shock of agreeable comparison' (1993: 21).

Michael Billig refers, in turn, to The Third Earl of Shaftsbury's assessment that historically comic incongruity arises from an inherent desire, aesthetic or otherwise, for a 'sense of order ... and a preference for harmony and due proportion' (2005: 77). Admittedly implications of a problematic sense of superiority permeate that particular rationale but certainly a kernel of reason resides there, as satirist, Hogarth, shares the belief that incongruity was realized through the subversion of symmetry, which he saw as inspiring a sense of 'confidence' within a reader/viewer within art or narrative. True comic incongruity was, for him, all about the insertion of dissonances, gaps and contrasts (1955: 165). It is a mode assembled around destabilizations of expectation and subversions of a desired outcome. Excluding any shifting set of culturally or temporally defined moral imperatives, what emerges here is that incongruity in any number of settings can be used as a tool to rationalize that which does not conform to the current project of reason (2005: 63–64).

Bearing this in mind Davis opines that comic incongruity only really functions within an established experiential 'expectation system ... Incongruity is a relational concept: nothing can be incongruous in itself but only by standing out phenomenologically from an otherwise congruous system' (1993: 12–14). As all comedy conceits are, of course, dictated by judgement how funny we find a situation depends very much on the balance between the quantity and quality of the incongruities in tandem with our knowledge and connection to the expectation system under attack. Too many in one context will confuse the issue and provide no solid ground for the clashes to operate. The success of the project thus resides in how essential the experience system is to us and how much investment we attach to the system that is being detonated. What emerges from this is that assessing humorous incongruity is as much about determining boundaries and acceptability, which is a prime component in any comic enterprise and undoubtedly serves our purpose here in looking at how representations of disability have been organized within animation forms.

Breaking down system expectations within *Creature Discomforts*

Simply in the interests of remaining within the confines of this paper's word count I have highlighted just three of these 'breakdowns' at work in the context of *Creature Discomforts*. Other notable incongruities are undoubtedly tied to our unquestioning acceptance of this comic universe and they can be traced individually through with each gag or situation ad infinitum, thus incongruities build on incongruities. Each setting includes disparate subjects interacting in the same language, all acknowledging an interviewer that appears to have no issue, ideological, physical or otherwise, with interviewing talking animals, insects and the like and this in turn offers a breach that leads us into the concept that these fully articulate creatures lives all appear to co-exist alongside (unseen) humans. They all, also, adhere to aspects of human lifestyles, behaviour and use specially designed humanized props that are made to measure such as wheelchairs, cups and flasks. A multitude of further incongruities can be traced within the development and execution of each narrative's comic moments such as with the third short in the first series when Slim the Stick Insect's crutch reveals itself to be another, (child), stick insect, as a visual punchline to underscore and complement his message about adapting to new situations. The incongruous rub comes when the expectations offered around an immobile prop are subverted by the moment when the stick grows arms and a face, which not only subverts the expectations around fixed, inanimate objects but deftly and subtly shifts the register from one universal 'reality' of expected physical laws to another. This also acknowledges the trope of metamorphosis that stretches back to animation's earliest years. However these three observations provide an entry into this concept and demonstrate how this idea informs representation.

Subverting documentary form

Despite mainstream animation today dominated by slick, fast and affordable three-dimensional computer adhering to the stop-motion form, using clay figures has contributed to the *Creature Comforts* series retaining its unique position within the cultural landscape. Significations of tradition, whimsy, continuity, stability and craftsmanship are juxtaposed here with attendant suggestions of depth, texture and weight that benefit from using this particular mode of animation. This provides for the viewer a sense of believability and a verisimilitude that extends further than the abstracted (albeit generalized) 'cartoon-y' aesthetic offered by 'cel' animation. This particular universe works in an 'immersive' context. By this I mean that the objects/characters in the frame are articulated within their own totally animated setting, one that is compatible and corresponds to the physical laws laid out within its own stated schema.

If we accept that incongruities are intensified by undermining the documentary form, then Ann Pointon's observations on how narratives around disability within documentary, helps us frame this concept further.

Using BBC TV examples Pointon notes that representation tends to be primarily grouped around 'transformation, tragedy, normalisation and spectacle' (1997: 86). While no transformative journey is detailed in any linear fashion within *Creature Discomforts*, the shorts do project a 'hero' in one form but the only lessons imparted towards the audience is that of, arguably, a sense of enlightenment (1997: 87–88). The uncomfortable aspects of 'voyeuristic intrusion' into disability, deformity or disfigurement, that she identifies, are absent here (1997: 91). These narratives refute any emphasis on the surrounding network of support, this conforms to Pointon's fourth statement in that these shorts are actually about 'social skills, personality, powers of acceptance and adaptation of the disabled person themselves', and most importantly, the denial of victimhood (1997: 89). Everyday life is shown as something to be surmounted in a direct, non-sensationalistic fashion, all of which profoundly informs the intent of *Creature Discomforts*.

In terms of incongruity Park had already outlined a profound breakdown of system expectation back in 1989. The original short was inspired by Park's love of outtakes and blooper reels and the central conceit that develops from this is that the shorts are somehow recording within a given 'reality'. Thus each short retains the familiar fixed camera position, (or in the sole case of Slim the Stick Insect this is broken by a very slow left to right pan) and the insertion of background noises and sounds that suggest a basic directional recording technique to infer immediacy. Engagement with documentary form depends on a belief within the viewer that what they are watching is 'real' or at the very least constructed from recorded events. By shifting those imperatives into a format so rigorously constructed, premeditated and mediated as clay animation this of course creates an initial schism within our acceptance systems. The incongruity deepens further here through the implication that a journalist or reporter is not only physically able to interview a range of insects and animals but is then able to penetrate the boundaries of language, space and communication. Incongruities continue when in achieving this they then report that the animal's experience magically mirrors many of our own anxieties. The extension continues into yet another stage of subversion. In that the fashion by which the information is gathered from 'real' people giving testimonies to separate situations and then is placed beneath a constructed, 'unreal' animal to tell a different story or highlight a seemingly unrelated plight. The common understanding/expectation of how this information is managed within documentary situations is also shattered here, in a breakdown of trust where such formal devices have been historically used to suggest an unmediated truth or imply a direct, linear reportage.

Undermining expectations around the animated body

Of the characters within the concept, Brian the Bull Terrier from the fourth short of the first 2007 run, (voiced by forty-five-year old Spina bifida sufferer Kevin Gillespie), offers the most potent example and overt set of attacks on anticipation. In this case the subversions taking place are those based around preconceptions surrounding the animated body and indeed of physical disability itself.

Brian is rendered as a small, white talking dog and combines the expected anthropomorphic tensions such as human uses of language, gesture and posture along with animalistic attributes such as a dog collar, head and ear shapes. He is modelled with thin mobile arms, expressive features that helpfully correlate to human facial signals, offering openness and yet given eyes that sit wide apart and an overbite to create a more 'cuddly' 'Park-ian' look.[1] The legs are rendered as small, inconsequential, hanging down just below the seat of the wheelchair and tucked in underneath the comically rounded body. This tripartite gesture simultaneously deactivates *and* acknowledges the negative significations of tenacity and aggression normally attached to a dog of this breed and also maintains brand coherence.

Admittedly *Creature Comforts* have always built their pleasures around anthropomorphism. As Kevin Sandler notes, this has long been tool to foster identification within animation that also conveniently negotiates any experiential schism for audiences (1997: 49–50). This process of transference and recognition of human attributes upon animal models serves the narratives perfectly. But the already incongruous concept of animals conducting very human endeavours is here assigned a deeper layer by presenting a sentient model that refutes expectations around the physically challenged. The idea of a dog engaging in the pursuit of a dangerous sport, that is, bungee-jumping, functions as a deeper comic tier. The physical state of the animal itself leads us to more clashes that informs the narratives at a profound level and plays with our expectation. In Classical cel animation, where most of our cultural understandings around the body with mainstream animation have been forged, the body is fluid and malleable. Reconstitution and a sense of deathlessness is commonplace as in service to narrative requirements and/or comic effect. For example, when Tex Avery's wolf character in *Little Rural Riding Hood* (MGM 1949) splits himself into different body parts registering extreme shock he is soon reassembled on *and* off-screen to conveniently allow the next situation to play out. In stop motion this fluidity has been denied more often than continued. Especially when one considers this against the heritage of the rigorously attempted verisimilitudes conjured up by Willis O'Brien and Ray

Harryhausen and others or the rigid, staccato continuities offered within George Pal's 1930s/'40s 'Puppetoon' films. While Floriane Place-Verghnes notes that such elasticity provides a counterbalance to the sadism (certainly inherent in Avery's work) and acts as a way of diffusing trauma it also suggests in its rebelliousness a questioning of the boundaries of reality itself: 'The very fact that his cartoons are not bound by reality is indeed a mark of their not belonging to the realm of prosaic things' (2006: 174). A freeform plasticity has certainly informed physical models in the work of Douglass Smith (through his incarnation as Ivan Stang for the 1978, *Reproduction Cycles Among Unicellular Life Forms*), Will Vinton, (in the 'hell' sequence in the 1985 *Adventures of Mark Twain*, for example) and, (notably once more), Sproxton and Lord's rather self-explanatory, *Morph* (1977–95), which arguably shares that conceit. These (among many other examples too numerous to name here) provide a counter statement that are concerned with pushing the boundaries of the stop-motion body and rejecting any limiting 'realistic' index.

Within Harding-Hill's shorts expressive action and movement are not a part of the established grammar – stasis and economy are. Any such articulacy is relegated to facial movement and occasional accompanying hand/paw gestures to illustrate points made by the central speaker with any faster, more dynamic advancement banished to background gags and characters. Thus any distortion possibilities are contained. The conformity of physicality is dictated by the demands of the narrative itself. Although commenting on the un-dead qualities of Wile E. Coyote and the construction of the Anime body, Christian McCrea's comment about the 'dreaded anvil of physicality' bears transposition here (2008: 19). As in this context the body remains fixed, discrete, breakable, vulnerable and sealed to understand correlative physical movements – albeit those as much framed within human as any animal traits. Thus the body here resides well within Paul Wells's observations on Park's initial short as inhabiting a 'cartoon' and 'animation' anthropomorphic hinterland (1998: 59). Incongruity is thus located within a massive and inherent irony of an expressive form deployed to offer non-expressivity, a *lack* of transmutation.

Challenging notions of representation within animation

Representations of the physically impaired bear the weight of a grim past. Lennard J. Davis posits that physicality has been historically defined against the problematic term of the 'norm' – a culturally defined measurement that he observes emerged through modernist French and British medical and statistical discourses. Though never a universal given as such, this troublesome concept of 'the average' in time and became embroiled into debates around eugenics, with physical disability as a result being labelled as an 'undesirable trait' within a 'healthy' society (1997: 17). Those with disability often found themselves combined with criminality, heightened sexual activity and mental illness as societal 'others' with the end result being that the concept of the disabled body became 'formulated as a definition excluded from culture, society' (1997: 11–21). This is cemented by Paul Longmore's assertions that disability in cinematic and televisual contexts has been co-opted too often into depictions of monstrousness, villainy, criminality and revenge (2001: 1–17). Because of this history of negative stereotyping it is understandable why disability and humour have remained traditionally uneasy bedfellows.

Extending this away from live-action forms, certainly representations of disability within animation has been limited at best. In formulating approaches to disability the few examples available to us can be located within three distinct groups to date.

The first model of representation follows an earnest, educational stance. This is animation that can be seen, as Paul Wells summates, as a 'democratising' tool in offering up subjective views of a particular condition (1998: 123–126). In less mainstream examples, like Stephen Palmer's *Blindscape* (1994) and Tim Webb's 1987, *A Is for Autism*, issues of perception and subjective personal experience are discussed and the freedom of animation as a form can be utilized to illuminate an experience blocked off to mainstream audiences. Animation, in its formal flexibility, scores over film here through its ability to address areas of perception and to transcend boundaries. As Wells confirms, animation can access states of existence that supersedes any simple recording or transcribing process.

The second example is a more recent development fed through broader comedic trends that revolves less around any attempt to truly depict the direct experience of those who are physically challenged and is more about the policing of boundaries of taste. This ambivalent paradigm challenges the (problematic) concept of 'political correctness' and seeks to detonate taboo within comedy narratives.

Commercial animation has rarely engaged with disability directly apart from the occasional throwaway set-up for a gag, such as in Bugs Bunny's mock infirmities in Bob Clampett's *The Old Grey Hare* (1946). However several recent examples have materialized. In the controversial BBC/CHX/ Moi J'aime La Television production, *Popetown* (2005), disabled children are featured as comedy props to complement the central narrative. In the first episode of the single series, 'The Double', an under-explored sub-plot is detailed of a group of children in wheelchairs who have won a trip to meet the Pope. These figures appear to be comprised of the same pliable material as their wheelchairs which all conform to a tried and tested 'squash and stretch' articulation. The joke being here that the children are far from restricted in movement, (as expected), and in fact they exhibit a deliberately cartoon-y sense of speed and physicality which exists merely to render a range of background sight gags. Through such actions this reinforces a heroic, beatific and admittedly exclusionary depiction that contains them away from the story itself.

More challenging attempts at representation can be found within Canadian animator/cartoonist, John Callahan's Media World production *Quads!* (2001) and in Matt Parker and Trey Stone's Comedy Central programme, *South Park* (1997–to date). Through over twenty-six half-hour episodes and two syndicated series Callaghan offers up a whole range of disabled characters as a de facto family of minorities, that presents depictions of blindness and amputees, as headed up by quadriplegic Reilly O'Reilly. Each character appears as abusive, conflicted, flawed defiantly hard-drinking and confrontational in some fashion. Parker and Stone's provocative characters 'Timmy' and 'Jimmy Vulmer' too provide an equally potent example of the shifts in contemporary comedy and animation which has resulted in both becoming accepted mainstream figures. Wheelchair-bound, palsied, aphasia sufferer, 'Timmy' (who arrived in the episode, *Tooth Fairy Tats 2000*, April 2000) and crutch-wielding stand-up comedian, 'Jimmy Vulmer' (who first appeared in *Cripple Fight*, June 2001) are along with the constructs in *Quads* typical of this type. In that they are rendered as intelligent, wholly integrated models that admittedly nod towards normalization but often they are placed into their narratives solely to subvert expectations as much as confirm them.

To present a positivist reading of this the animation form's distance from direct representation and adherence to caricature could arguably be seen to be flattening out depiction into the kind of equal opportunity burlesquing coined by Terry Lindvall and Ben Fraser when discussing the troublesome depictions of race within Classical animation (1998: 121–136). In that the comprehensively unflattering character designs in each example suggests a comic animated universe where no-one is privileged and that the physically impaired fare no better or worse than the more able bodied. Indeed the highly self-conscious limited, flat, minimalist aesthetics displayed in both the Flash animated *Quads* and Parker and Stone's text in particular positively encourage this practice. The removal from a naturalistic design sense cushions the viewer and creates a buffer between representation and offence.

These constructs are emblematic of larger shifts within the mainstream initiated by writer/comedians in live-action comedy within cinema and television settings across America *and* Britain. The likes of The Farrelly Brothers, Larry David, Chris Morris, Ricky Gervais and Stephen Merchant have all foregrounded disabled characters and have used them as foils to discuss areas of social discomfort and of issues of reduction through alliance to a set of seemingly progressive but in fact often restrictive, loaded narratives of supposed equality. These types of representations are, in truth, more focused on the able-bodied people around them and their attitudes.

Social acceptability is the real agenda here, in tandem with an examination of what is deemed acceptable within the (perceived) post-PC landscape of appropriate interpretation and language. Certainly this is exemplified in series two of BBC TV's *The Office* (2003) which features a recurring wheelchair-bound character, Brenda, (as played by real-life disabled actress Julie Fernandez). She is posited to not only reveal central character, David Brent's (Gervais), own inadequacies in social interaction and self-awareness but also she highlights his innately reactionary nature through his misconceptions and misreading of the acceptable terminology and its subsequent applications surrounding the physically impaired.

These concur with Ann Pointon and Chris Davies's point on representation that these characters are, while well intentioned, in fact still retain the function of a cathartic device where we are permitted a glance into our innermost fears surrounding disability (1997: 8). In this case this could potentially mean social limitation, or at worst, exclusion. More generously this address here does use humour to re-conceptualize a laudable social space for the 'marginal'. It also supplies (an at times dubious) release valve aimed at alleviating tensions around addressing the 'unknown' quantity of minorities as well as nodding to a welcome process of normalization.

In the Aardman text we have here a third typology that offers a fresh depiction and that builds on incongruity. Murray Davis sees that jokes made at the expense of minorities have been continually popular due to this undermining of multi-incongruous systems and the play with social propriety that sits at the heart of egalitarian ideologies (1993: 12). Through this there is an inference that this particular comedic space follows similar aspects of the second model, in the demarcation of a processing space for audiences to adjust in approaching potentially difficult subject matter. As the animation medium's plasticity facilitates the negotiation of issues of discomfort and offence for the minority represented and it allows the smuggling in of serious issues under the shell of a form perennially typecast as being in service to the simplistic.

Similarly in line with the formal space that animation tenders, the deployment of anthropomorphism further aids the deactivation of anxiety. It is clear that in the models on offer in both runs all maintain behavioural and articulation in line more with humans than animals, they are active, personable and self-aware. Each sketch relies on placing the characters in 'real world' situations that imply a connection to society and refutes tired notions of disability as linked to isolation. From Flash the sausage dog's inference over a mastery of 'the right equipment' when referring to the bicycle wheels he has in place of back legs, Roxy's proclamation of a highly sexualized self, (in itself an animation 'first' arguably in terms of tone and maturity) to Tim the Tortoise's matter-of-fact description of his regular journey to the sweet shop for his children the characters are, as demonstrated by the careful placement of setting, located and functioning within a recognizable everyday environment. The narratives present them as self-aware, independent individuals who can express themselves intelligently and can make valid points about their frustration with issues of mobility and their perceived invisibility within society.

This third model also borrows from the two previous ones in that it presents subjective experience while still disputing expectation. In contrast to most narratives the subjects have been brought into the creative process via the charity's own research on the subject of access and they are placed at the very heart of the narratives. While authorship is still contained within the expected channels the shorts refutes positioning of this representation beyond that from acting merely as cipher, as a satellite feeders of lines to able-bodied performer and neither is there present here a patronizing dialogue of deification. From which approach troublesome dialogues of 'Noble-isation' can thus emerge.[2]

Thus we have in operation a more subtle gradation in depiction and one which, despite the minimalist setting, uses this framework to provide a more complex, multifaceted construct. This is one that combines both subjectivity, (through the expression of individual experience), objectivity (in the manner by which these messages are presented) and a sense of connection that comic animated forms fosters through the processes of identification facilitated by anthropomorphism. Roger Scruton offers a summative point for us here when he suggests that through the collusion of caricature and exaggeration, key determinants in animation, the contrasting of differing surface perceptions in effect can and should be used to present a deeper message: 'It is an incongruity that illustrates a deeper *congruity* between an object and itself' (1987: 160). The presentations of disability through comedy and using the medium of stop-motion work in the *Creature Discomforts* series leads us away from staid representations and through incongruous discourses allows an access to richer truths – surely the project of any animation?

Notes

1   Despite seen by Nick Park as one of his most 'personal films' the short has become the design lynchpin of much the post 1990s Aardman output (1996: 79). Park himself has noted that the 'wide-mouthed, eyes close together' character aesthetic has become dominant among a cadre of different animators and has created a sense of an entire studio being typecast by the success of one author's work. Regular Aardman animation character designer, Michael Salter, adds to this in interview with Lane when he states that 'My style had so many similarities to Nick Park's but so many jobs came in that wanted "the Nick Park look" that I started doing it even more and now I can't do anything else now: it's sort of ingrained' (2003: 103). Indeed the very concept of 'cuteness'

in terms of character design has been discussed at length across a range of literature and in animation contexts it has been discussed predominantly against Disney and Anime settings. Gary Genosko's survey across a range of animation media asserts that the deployment of ethological definitions of rounded features and body shapes within animation forms function through the presentation of infant-like movements, awkwardness and general demeanour to accent identification, reinforce stability and ultimately serve a commercial intent (2005).

2 As Laurie E. Harnick notes, this is a worthy but troublesome and unsatisfying process, which is highlighted within two recent animated releases featuring Victor Hugo's tortured Quasimodo figure (*The Hunchback of Notre Dame* from 1995 for Goodtime productions and from 1996 by Disney). Harnick sees that in both adaptations the darkness of the original text is discarded with the titular figure is ascribed a more heroic set of sympathetic, less ambiguous and saintly connotations (2001: 92). Though not physically impaired, as such the issues of reduction and stereotyping assigned to his deformity and the resultant societal rejection makes Quasimodo a relevant model here. And this is reinforced through the agenda present in the 1995 film which stresses the mistreatment of the disabled at the hands of the state. This process arguably includes (as Harvey Deneroff very kindly points out in his online column – July 2008), the likes of Long John Silver in *Treasure Planet* (2002).

References

Billig, M. (2005), *Laughter and Ridicule – Towards a Social Critique of Humour*, London: Sage.

Clark, M. (1987), 'Humor and Incongruity', in John Morreall (ed.), *The Philosophy of Laughter and Humor*, 139–155, New York: State University of New York Publishing.

Davis, L. J. (1997), 'Constructing Normalcy – The Bell Curve, the Novel and Invention of the Disabled Body in the Nineteenth Century', in *The Disability Studies Reader*, New York and London: Routledge.

Davis, M. (1993), *What's so Funny? – The Comic Conception of Culture and Society*, Chicago: University of Chicago Press.

Deneroff, H. (29th July 2008), *Animation Unlimited 2008 – harvey@deneroff. com – Comments and Thoughts on Animation and Film*. Retrieved 14th August 2008: http://deneroff.com/blog/.

Dickens, P. (26th June 2008), Email correspondence.

Fraser, B. and T. Linvall (1998), 'Darker Shades of Animation: African-American Images in the Warner Bros. Cartoon', in *Reading The Rabbit – Explorations in Warner Bros. Animation*, New Brunswick, NJ and London: Rutgers University Press.

Genosko, G. (2005), 'Natures and Cultures of Cuteness', *Invisible Culture – An Electronic Journal for Visual Culture*, 9. Retrieved 11th November 2008: http://www.rochester.edu/in_visible_culture/Issue_9/genosko.html.

Harnick, L. E. (2001), 'Lost and Found in Translation: The Changing Face of Disability in the Film Adaptations of Hugo's Notre Dame de Paris: 1842', in *Screening Disability – Essays on Cinema and Disability*, Boston: University Press of America.

Hogarth, W. (1955), *The Analysis of Beauty (1753)*, Oxford: Clarendon Press.

Lane, A. (2003), *Creating Creature Comforts – The Award Winning Animation Brought to Life from the Makers of Chicken Run and Wallace and Gromit*, Oxford: Boxtree Publishing.

Longmore, P. K. (2001), 'Screening Stereotypes: Images of Disabled People', in *Screening Disability-Essays on Cinema and Disability*, Boston: University Press of America.

Macdonald, K. (1996), 'A Lot Can Happen in a Second – Nick Park Interview by Kevin Macdonald', in *Projections 5 – Filmmakers on Filmmaking*, London: Faber Publishing.

McCrea, C. (July 2008), 'Explosive, Expulsive, Extraordinary: The Dimensional Excess of Animated Bodies', *animation: an interdisciplinary journal*, 3(1): 9–24.

Medhurst, A. (2007), *A National Joke – Popular Comedy and English Cultural Identities*, Oxford: Routledge.

Place-Verghnes, F. (2006), *Tex Avery: A Unique Legacy*, Malaysia: John Libbey Publishing.

Pointon, A. and C. Davies (1997), 'Introduction', in *Framed: Interrogating Disability in the Media*, London: BFI Publishing.

Pointon, A. (1997), 'Disability and Documentary', in *Framed: Interrogating Disability in the Media*, London: BFI Publishing.

Sandler, K. S. (Fall 1997), 'Pogs, Dogs or Ferrets: Anthropomorphism and Animaniacs', *Animation Journal*, 6(1): 44–53.

Scruton, R. (1987), 'Laughter', in *The Philosophy of Laughter and Humor*, New York: State University of New York Publishing.

Wells, P. (1998), *Understanding Animation*, London: Routledge.

N/A (2008), *Introducing Leonard Cheshire Disability*. Retrieved 2nd July 2008: http://www.lcdisability.org/?lid=32.

INDEX

Note: Locators with letter 'n' refer to notes.